HENRIK IBSEN

By the Same Author

Enigma: A Life of Knut Hamsun
Henry Miller: A Life

HENRIK IBSEN

A New Biography

ROBERT FERGUSON

RICHARD COHEN BOOKS · London

British Library Cataloguing in Publication Data:
A catalogue record for this book is available from the British Library

Copyright © 1996 by Robert Ferguson

ISBN 1 86066 078 9

First published in Great Britain in 1996 by
Richard Cohen Books
7 Manchester Square
London W1M 5RE

1 3 5 7 9 8 6 4 2

Designed by Margaret Fraser

Typeset in Linotype Postscript Baskerville by
Rowland Phototypesetting Ltd,
Bury St Edmunds, Suffolk

Printed in Great Britain by
Mackays of Chatham plc

Contents

Ibsen's Plays

Acknowledgements

My thanks to the following:

Erik Henning Edvardsen; Peter Normann Waage; Sidsel Marie Nilsen and Ladislav Reznicek; Kjell Rosenberg; Hubert and Paula von Bechtolsheim; Oliver Møystad; Peter Næss; Gjert Laading; Ingrid Nordhagen; Axel Bernhoft; Astrid Sæther, Turid Gustu Eriksen and Anne Cathrine Almaas at the Oslo University Centre for Ibsen Studies; Professor Otto Hageberg; the staff at the Circolo Scandinavo, Rome; the staff at the University Library, Oslo; the staff at the Austrian Embassy, Oslo; the staff at the Ibsen museums in Oslo, Skien and Grimstad; P. M. Braunworth; Jan Kjærstad; Helen Iggulden; P. K. Heggelund Dahl; Åse Ryvarden and Helen Eie at Cappelen; Richard Cohen; Tony Whittome; Gloria Ferris; Rivers Scott; Jørgen Winsnes; my wife Nina.

The author and publisher wish to thank the following for permission to reproduce illustrations:
Henrik Ibsen caricature by Olaf Gulbransson, © DACS 1996, title page.
J. W. Cappelens Archives, plates 2, 3, 10, 13, 14, 15, 19, 21, 35, 36, 37.
Mary Evans Picture Library, plate 26.
Fylkesmuseet for Telemark og Grenland, plate 1.
Popperfoto, plate 6.
Mrs Eva Reichmann, page 271.
Royal Library, Copenhagen, plates 5, 17, 18, 20, 23, 40, 41.
University of Oslo Library, Picture Department, plates 7, 8, 9, 11, 22, 23, 24, 25, 27, 28, 29, 30, 34, 39 and front and back cover.

Preface

With a writer as famous as Henrik Ibsen it is hard to recall a time when one did not know the name. I must have heard it first as a schoolboy in the 1960s, when I assumed, with an insularity typical of the period, that he was an Englishman with a funny name. My personal involvement with him began in a roundabout way, when my interest in another Norwegian writer, Knut Hamsun, led to my learning the language and eventually settling in the country with a Norwegian wife in 1983. Later I was asked by BBC Radio to translate and adapt some of his plays.

Later still, in the early 1990s, the National theatre in Oslo began its annual Ibsen Festival, offering an unrivalled opportunity to become familiar with the plays in performances from all over the world, from permanent features of the repertoire like *A Doll's House* and *Hedda Gabler* to such rarely performed plays of Ibsen's youth as *Catiline* and *Lady Inger of Østråt*. Among memorable highlights I have seen *Peer Gynt* played in French by a group from Burkina Faso; a Polish *The Lady from the Sea*; and a production of *Brand* in which Einar entered and left the stage on a motorbike. But what remains above all from that production of *Brand* is the memory of our laughing as an audience at some of the exchanges on stage. My perception of the play as wholly sombre was pleasantly shaken, and the experience brought home to me as rarely before the sheer plasticity of the medium. A second striking theatrical experience – I cannot quite remember if it was the same festival or a later one – was John Barton's production of *Peer Gynt* at the Oslo Amfiscenen. This was an enchanting, utterly magical evening. It reduced all of us watching to children again, seeing make-believe for the first time. I remember walking away from the theatre and wondering why a man who could create a cosmic circus like that should choose to devote the rest of his life to writing a series of dark analyses of unhappiness. It was on that evening that the spirit of curiosity necessary to write about Ibsen was fully born.

The discovery of North Sea oil in the 1960s changed Norway almost overnight from a poor nation into a rich one. Since that time much has happened. The country has established itself as an imaginative diplomatic partner at negotiating tables around the world. It voted against membership of the EU, asserting its independence from the rest of Europe and, perhaps just as importantly, from its former colonial overlords, Denmark and Sweden. In 1994 it qualified for the first time ever for a place in the Football World Cup Finals. A pop group from Norway has topped the American hit parade, and Norway has even won the Eurovision Song Contest. Yet the popular image abroad of a dark and brooding and unhappy people has scarcely kept pace with all this. With some help from Edvard Munch the image was almost entirely Ibsen's creation, and it is unnecessary to point out that it is not remotely accurate. Ibsen's art was infinitely more personal than this; but the nationalist concerns of the age in which he worked insistently put this cast on it, seeing his characters and their concerns as peculiarly representative of his countrymen.

Some knowledge of the state of affairs leading up to the creation of the modern state of Norway in 1905 is necessary for an understanding of Ibsen's early career, and for the fact that he chose voluntary exile for most of his writing life in order to avoid the intensities of the political debate at home. The Viking Age of expansion began about 800 and ended shortly after the unification and Christianisation of the country in the year 1000. For some three centuries, in the so-called saga age, Norway prospered as an independent nation under a series of kings. This came to an end in 1319, when Magnus Eriksson became king of both Norway and Sweden. This was a purely personal arrangement, with no common administration, and in due course the Norwegian earls invited his brother Håkon VI to wear the crown. With Håkon VI's death in 1380 the line of kings ceased and, after a period in union with Denmark and Sweden, Norway lost its status as a separate kingdom in 1536 and became part of Denmark.

In 1814 Sweden took over as the colonial power, but the Norway into which Ibsen was born had a cultural and bureaucratic heritage steeped in 400 years of Danish domination. Growing up, he and other young men like him took a vivid interest in the restoration of the country's former standing and pride, with the status of the native language one of the most fiercely fought issues. In the world of the theatre colonial fashion dictated that actors were Danes and spoke Danish from the stage. During both occasions in his early life when Ibsen worked as a theatre director in Bergen and Kristiania the aim of the theatres was to promote the right of people to act and experience plays in Norwegian, as it was also to foster a home-grown drama. The nationalist urge of the century that concluded in 1905 with the ascent to the throne of King Håkon VII explains many things, not least a golden age of Norwegian arts which saw Ibsen, Edvard Munch and Knut Hamsun all working in their different fields at the same time. Edvard Grieg's explorations of Norwegian folk music were a vital aspect of the same kind of cultural revivalism, and the nationalist background explains why the same impulse to collect and preserve came so late to England, where Butterworth, Vaughan Williams, Holst and Grainger, as citizens of an imposing empire, were able to set out on their song-collecting expeditions at a more leisurely pace. As will be clear from the biography, it is my view that Ibsen was never passionately nationalist, even in his younger days; but nationalism forms an influential background to the development of his early career and explains the exceptional encouragement he was given by his fellow-countrymen anxious to foster a great dramatist of their own.

One result of the campaign was that the Norwegian language was in an almost constant state of flux throughout Ibsen's life. The most striking example is in the spelling of the capital Kristiania/ Christiania, later renamed Oslo for the same sort of reasons as Leningrad was renamed St Petersburg. Save where the spelling has the authority of a proper name as in 'the Christiania theatre', I have preferred the more Norwegian 'Kristiania'. In all other cases I have tried to standardise the spellings to their most recent Norwegian form. All translations from Ibsen are my own, as are all others except where noted. In translating from Ibsen's letters I was faced with the choice of reproducing accurately the Latin-inspired 'businessman's prose' he favoured for almost all his correspondence; or putting it into a plainer English. Judging his prose style to be an important part of his personality I chose by and large to attempt the former; but where he was personal and urgent I have tried to reproduce this too. Where I quote from Ibsen's poems I make no claims for these translations other than to have conveyed the sense.

Ibsen is one of the great academic industries of the world; but remarkably few of the books written about him make the bald claim to be biographies. Undeniably, in his extreme discretion, he is a hard man to write about. The difficulty is perhaps symbolised by the fact that there is not a single photograph of him alone with his wife and son, or with either of them separately, and that after his death his wife Suzannah burned most of the letters that passed between them. Biographies by the Norwegians Halvdan Koht, Bergljot Ibsen and Hans Heiberg have all been translated into English over the last fifty years. The most recent biography to appear in English is Michael Meyer's in 1969–70. At the time of publication Arthur Koestler described it as a contribution of permanent value for students of European literature, and its continued and deserved popularity in the years since then has proved him right. However, recent researches have unearthed important material that casts new light on Ibsen's early years, including his letter admitting paternity of the illegitimate child Hans Jacob Henriksen, details of how he was sentenced to forced labour for failing to pay his child-support in 1851, and of his terrible financial troubles just prior to emigrating to Rome in 1864. Of less significance, but still illuminating, the diary kept by Emilie Bardach which Meyer believed to have been lost has re-surfaced in a Parisian library. The slight mystery surrounding her true age has also been cleared up.

Meyer's is a study of Ibsen's life and times, a biography of the spread of his reputation; in the present work I try to look more closely at the man behind the reputation, for it seems to me that the popular definition of Ibsen as a liberal humanist is misleading in its simplicity and obscures several paradoxes. A sometime republican, he was also what one can only term an abject monarchist; he was distinctly a feminist, yet strongly anti-democratic and an opponent of the party political system; and along with his profound religious doubt he expressed great admiration for the pan-Germanic dream of tribal unity, and claimed that it had influenced his writing. Without proper consideration of such apparent anomalies our picture of the man remains incomplete.

Any biography of the author of twenty-five full-length plays must devote a good deal of space to a study of these, and in the context of a biography it seems to me natural to adopt a predominantly biographical approach to them. This does not mean, of course, that I hold other approaches to be inferior. In discussing the plays I have considered them primarily as the texts Ibsen wrote and sent off to his publisher rather than in this or that isolated performance filtered through the understanding of a particular actor or director. Ronald Gray in *Ibsen – A Dissenting View* (1977) makes the point that 'there is still a large body of opinion that remains unconvinced by the reputation Ibsen has gained as the greatest dramatist of the last hundred years, as the modern Aeschylus, Shakespeare or Racine', and cites the dissent of W. B. Yeats, D. H. Lawrence, T. S. Eliot, Mary McCarthy and F. R. Leavis. In the case of some of the later plays I share a degree of this scepticism, for reasons which I try to explain. However, my love for *Brand* and *Peer Gynt* has only increased with study, as has my admiration for the two much-underrated plays preceding *Brand, Love's Comedy* and *The Pretenders*.

In offering this new book – and with the proviso that there is no such thing as a 'definitive biography', only as many different pictures as there are biographers – I do so in order to provide an alternative look at one of the world's most famous writers; and from a personal point of view to try to find even a partial solution to the mystery of what happened to the man who wrote *Peer Gynt*.

PART ONE

THE PAST

1

The Family

Towards the end of Ibsen's life, when he had returned to his native Norway after twenty-seven years of self-imposed exile, his son Sigurd received in the post a copy of his father's baptismal certificate. In the covering letter the sender, a man in Bergen, explained that he had called in at a watchmaker's shop to collect his watch and on taking it home found that the paper in which it had been wrapped was the enclosed certificate. It recorded the facts of Henrik Ibsen's birth in the small town of Skien, on the south-east coast of Norway, on 20 March 1828, to Knud Ibsen and Marichen Altenburg Ibsen; his baptism at home on the twenty-eighth, and in Skien church on 10 June. The only oddity about it was the circumstance of its discovery, and there was nothing to support a suspicion that this most secretive of men once divulged, when drunk, to two friends of his youth in Grimstad: that he was not the son of Knud Ibsen at all but of an old flame of his mother's, a politician and poet from the Telemark district named Thormod Knudsen.[1] Ibsen never broached the subject again. The likelihood is that he was only indulging a common fantasy of the gifted adolescent, that someone as disappointingly ordinary as his own father could never really have sired someone as unusual as himself. Yet the doubt was expressed, a fitting keynote to sound at the start of a life lived in the exploration of doubt.

Knud Ibsen was a merchant and shopkeeper. He acquired his licence to trade in 1825 and on 1 December the same year married Marichen Altenburg. Knud was twenty-eight, Marichen two years younger. Their first child, Johan Altenburg, was born in 1826 and died on 14 April 1828, three weeks after Henrik's birth. Fate thus made an eldest child of Henrik, in the same way as it had formerly made an eldest child of his father. Knud and Marichen had four more children – Johan Andreas in 1830, Hedvig Kathrine in 1832,

3

Nicolai Alexander in 1834 and Ole Paus in 1835. Hedvig and Ole Paus shared with Henrik a hereditary defect in one eye which accentuated the size of the other, something which in later life, when Ibsen's reputation for sphinx-like inscrutability was at its height, was commonly associated with the profundity of his psychological insight.

Marichen's father was one of Skien's wealthiest men and the owner of property to the value of between twenty and thirty thousand riksdaler,* including a large town house, a distillery at Lundetangen which was the second largest in the district, as well as a country farm at Århus and two ships engaged in timber trade. On his death his property passed to his widow, who passed it on to Marichen after her marriage. In accordance with the laws of the time it automatically became her husband's property. She was a small, slightly built woman, dark-haired, with deep-set, melancholy eyes. Hedvig Ibsen described her as a 'quiet, loving woman, the heart of our house, everything for her husband and children, always willing to sacrifice herself.'[2] According to a neighbour 'Henrik loved her very much'.[3] He used her as his model, 'with certain artistic liberties taken',[4] for Peer Gynt's mother Åse, and for Inga, the King's mother, in *The Pretenders*, confirming in both portraits the self-sacrificing and self-effacing woman of Hedvig's description.

Apart from these partial portrayals the only extant likeness of Marichen Ibsen is, appropriately enough, a silhouette. Of Knud Ibsen there are no surviving likenesses at all. In compensation there are Ibsen's fictional portraits of his father, notably as Peer's father Jon Gynt, Daniel Højre in *The League of Youth*, and Hjalmar's father Old Ekdal in *The Wild Duck*, and the recollections of the children next door of him as 'extremely amusing and lively, a very sociable man'. Once when he visited he did a solo dance for the little girls – 'that's what he was like'. He also left behind him a fair amount of legal paperwork which came into being in connection with his business enterprises and his fondness for litigation.

Knud Ibsen was a man whose social and professional ambitions bordered on the grandiose. As well as dairy products, groceries, glassware, cloth and hardware he sold wine and spirits from his shop on the groundfloor of the Altenburg house. From here he traded direct with merchants in London, Hamburg, Newcastle and

* Roughly £90,000

4

Flensburg and exported his grape-brandy to Norwegian cities like Egersund and Bergen. In partnership with others he also exported timber. His business dealings, supported by the accession of wealth from his wife, were immediately and superficially most successful, and by 1833 he was the sixteenth largest contributor among the town's 275 tax-payers.

With great rapidity, however, his rise was reversed. In December the distillery at Lundetangen was sold at auction to pay off a bank debt. Further auctions took place at regular intervals throughout the following year, at which the family's modest holding of livestock (six cows, four horses and four pigs) were sold. The Altenburg house followed, with its fixtures and fittings including the bed-linen and mirrors, some outhouses, a paddock, and various small parcels of land owned by the family. In August 1835 two boat-houses went under the hammer, and with that the Ibsens' ruin was complete.

The precise reasons for the extent and the rapidity of Knud Ibsen's economic collapse have never been firmly established. Some years later Johan Andreas emigrated to America, and in writing home expressed his surprise at the egalitarian atmosphere in the American workplace: 'A merchant here doesn't think himself too good to carry a sack of corn or coffee, see to his animals, sow potatoes, sow corn, in short share in every kind of manual labour which would at home be considered demeaning'.[5] The implication is clear enough: that Knud Ibsen was not a man to get his hands dirty, even in a crisis. It is possible he may have suffered catastrophic losses as an unnamed partner in a timber ship that sank without cargo insurance, such insurance being a rarity in those days.

He himself blamed the failure of the Lundetangen distillery. Knud had something of Hjalmar Ekdal's unreliable conviction concerning the nature of 'the coming thing' and invested heavily in new equipment and repairs for this plant. He was unfortunate in his contractors and his workmen, and was taken off-guard by a large increase in spirit-duty which he was unable to pay.

There is a mystifying coincidence of expansion and recession, wealth and poverty between 1833 and 1835 which suggests that he managed his affairs and his ambitions with the same fatal mixture of self-confidence and arrogance as John Gabriel Borkman. Indeed, as early as 1828 he was borrowing heavily from creditors in Hamburg. In an autobiographical fragment Ibsen refers with muted enthusiasm to the incessant hospitality offered by his father in the days before his fall, and the references to the feasting at the house of 'the rich Jon Gynt' in *Peer Gynt* are probably recollections of his father's prodigality:

> Spend it, waste it, let it go!
> Quiet, Mother – doesn't matter at all!
> Rich Jon Gynt is having a party –
> Hurrah for the family Gynt!

In 1833 Knud Ibsen had acquired a summer estate at Venstøp in Gjerpen, some four kilometres out of town, and it was here the family moved in something approaching disgrace around June 1835, although Knud's ploy of mortgaging everything he and Marichen owned staved off the ultimate social horror of bankruptcy and loss of political and social privileges. The house was large, set in thirty acres of farmland, so the family's poverty during their eight years there was genteel. For a long time afterwards Knud Ibsen continued to apply for 'respectable' jobs and posts; but in that small world his past always caught up with him and he was never successful. His main sources of income after 1835 were humble: growing potatoes, keeping chickens, selling corn and hay, a little office work now and then, some agenting for skippers when America fever began in the 1840s. He managed to keep some of his old friends, played host to the Gun Club at Venstøp and went on wolf-hunts in the Eikornrød woods. Later he began to drink.

Marichen Ibsen was martyred by the family's fall from grace. She withdrew from her husband and her housekeeping into a world of water-colour painting and wooden dolls.The children played, and teased Faster Ploug, a demented elderly relative who had become the family's charge and who slept upstairs in the loft with them. She wore a hat in bed and spoke in a strange, old-fashioned way that made her a figure of exotic, amused fear. Some fifty years later Ibsen made use of her and her strange stories of betrayal by a treacherous lover as the model for the Rat Wife in *Little Eyolf.* The loft itself, with its dark crannies and boxes of mysterious junk left behind by a former owner, also exerted a permanent hold over his imagination. Hedvig's enthusiastic account of such a place to Gregers Werle in *The Wild Duck*, which that man so wretchedly abuses for his own ends, is undoubtedly an echo of young Henrik's fascination with the place:

GREGERS: And in there, it's like its own little world, I suppose?

HEDVIG: All of its own. And then there are so many strange
things.
GREGERS: Really?
HEDVIG: Yes, big cupboards with books in; and lots of them have
pictures in.
GREGERS: Aha!
HEDVIG: And there's an old desk with drawers and struts, and
a big clock with figures in it that come out. But the clock
doesn't go anymore.
GREGERS: So time stands still there, where the wild duck lives?
HEDVIG: Yes. And then there's old colouring boxes and
things, and all the books.
GREGERS: You like to read them, I suppppose?
HEDVIG: Yes, if I can. But most of them are in English, and I
can't read English. But then I can look at the pictures. There's
this really huge book – *Harryson's History of London*, it's at least
a hundred years old, and there's an unbelievable number of
pictures in it. At the front there's a picture of death, with an
hour-glass, and a maiden. I think it's horrid. But then there's
all the other pictures with churches and castles and big ships
that sail on the sea.[6]

Henrik was not a playful child. Hedvig recalled him as an unsociable
boy who from an early age preferred to shut himself away in a small
room beside the kitchen which was his domain, and where he would
amuse himself painting, drawing and reading or playing with his
toy theatre. He also cut out cardboard figures and models and
earned himself pocket-money by selling them through a woman
who had a fruit stall in Skien market-place. These lonely pursuits
of his cut him off from his brothers and sisters and the other local
children, turning him into an introverted, bookish child who on
occasion was beaten up for being *viktig* – a big-head, self-important.
Inevitably he became a source of amusement himself, and the children would throw stones and snowballs against the walls of his den
until his patience snapped and he emerged in a fury to chase them
off. Thalie Kathrine Ording, whose family lived next door to the
Ibsens at Venstøp, must have been caught by him at least once. She
recalled him uncompromisingly as 'an unpleasant lad. Really nasty.
Spiteful and cruel. He used to beat us up as well. When he got older
he was very handsome, but nobody liked him because he was so

spiteful. Nobody wanted to be with him. He was always on his own'.[7]
He was also 'disgracefully vain'.

At the age of about twelve he turned a small annex at the side
of the house into a puppet theatre, using the window as a stage and
standing inside himself to operate the strings and provide the voices.
A member of the young audience at one of these early performances
recalled them:

> There was a wooden platform made of planks at the back, and
> behind them a corridor hidden by a curtain. The dolls were
> worked from this corridor by means of strings. Henrik himself
> did this, along with a trusted assistant, usually Theodor Eckstorm
> from the farm at Grini. The performance cost a half-skilling.
> Some were admitted free, and people came from a long way
> around to see the shows. But some of the boys came just to make
> fun.
>
> The great attraction for the female members of the audience
> was the large doll representing Isabella of Spain. Oh, she was
> wonderful! Jet black curls, crinoline of rose-red silk. They could
> make her move down from the edge of the stage and the little
> girls loved it then. Then Fernando the knight came on. Plumed
> hat, red tunic with gold braid. Slowly and with dignity he
> approached Isabella. Then – oh no! – a blackamoor rushes on,
> grabs her and makes to run off with her. But Fernando pushes
> him over so hard he can't get up again. After that Fernando and
> Isabella wave to the audience. And that was the end of the play.[8]

In this enterprise too Henrik's seriousness proved irresistible, and
two boys who had come just to make fun ruined one performance
by sneaking into the theatre beforehand and cutting the strings.
Henrik chased them off in a rage. On another occasion he became
furious with two little girls whom he had discovered playing with
the dolls. Clearly the toy world had become a psychic necessity to
him, one which he guarded with a fierce jealousy which must have
been baffling to other children. He also gave performances as a
conjuror and ventriloquist, performing in front of a large covered
trunk in which one of his younger brothers was secreted to assist
him. Johan Andreas or Nicolai played on their brother's fear of
ridicule to blackmail him into paying for their help with the threat
of exposing the tricks.

*　　*　　*

Theatre as an art form in the Norway of Ibsen's childhood was underdeveloped but growing rapidly in popularity. Developing from primitive and ritualistic forms of folk-entertainment, like the mystery plays and the syncretic *Julebukk* and *Gregoriusbrud*,* came nativity plays which, by deviating from the Bible to introduce Herod as the personification of Evil, marked the beginning of imaginative writing in drama. In Bergen the so-called 'star plays' developed, with exact stage-directions and strictly observed conventions dictating that the Virgin Mary always have yellow hair and Joseph be always a figure of fun, with his jacket on backwards, stiff-legged in his gait or hunchbacked and carrying an axe. Erik Pontoppidan, Bishop of Bergen in the 1750s, suppressed the theatres, claiming that they belonged in hell; but from the end of the eighteenth century onwards the union kings of Norway patronised the theatre, and the early years of the nineteenth century saw a rapid growth in the development of dramatic societies in the larger Norwegian towns, Trondheim, Bergen and Kristiania.† These were in the main the enthusiasm of the daughters of the new merchant class which was slowly replacing the old elite of civil servants and administrators established during the centuries of Danish colonial power. Though formally a thing of the past, the historical opposition of the Church to the theatre remained evident in the claims to edifying purpose these societies used as their mottoes: above the stage of the Kristiania society were the words *For vid og smag* ('For learning and discernment'). Trondheim offered *Gavnlig Moroe* ('Edifying Entertainment').

In the years after the Napoleonic wars, as a result of which, in 1814, Denmark ceded colonial power in Norway to Sweden, the dramatic societies fell into decline. Norway entered a period of economic growth, and in consequence of the new affluence there arose a desire to see others entertain on the stage rather than to provide the entertainment oneself. A number of touring theatrical companies entered the country to cater for this demand, almost excusively Danish and trading on the cultural authority of Copenhagen. The 1830s and 1840s were the heyday of these in southern

---

* In *Julebukk* boys paraded at Christmas with a goat mask on a pole covered with a cloak beneath which a boy danced while the others sang. In *Gregoriusbrud* young girls dressed in flowers and ribbons went collecting from door to door on 12 March, St Gregory's Day, as Brides of Gregory.

† Kristiania was renamed Oslo in 1925.

Norway, before their disappearance beneath the wave of puritanism that overtook the region in the 1850s, and it was through their activities that Henrik's early interest in the theatre was deepened. Their stage when in Skien was the Limie House, named for its owner Anders Pedersen Limie, who bought the mansion in 1832 and turned it into Skien's social centre, equipping its main floor with large springs so that dances could be held there.

Ibsen was a keen member of the audience at these performances, perhaps Marichen too. This was a liberal, worldly, relaxed era, and for a small entrance fee of twenty-four skillings they would have the pleasure of seeing comedies, romances and light entertainments with music. Plays by the Frenchmen Scribe and Dumas *fils* and the Danes J. L. Heiberg and Adam Oehlenschläger were in particular vogue at the time. Ludvig Holberg, the founder of Scandinavian drama, was always popular.

Of Henrik's earliest formal education there is no record. He may have attended a school attached to nearby ironworks at Fossum for the workers' children. Later he attended a primary school in Skien, walking the four kilometres there and back. His earliest mature ambition was to study medicine and become a doctor, for which he would need his *artium* if he were to go on to university. Yet when the time came he did not attend the local Latin school. Instead, in 1841, he was enrolled at Scheel House, a school run by two local theology students, Johan Hansen and W. F. Stockfleth. Knud Ibsen, by all accounts proud of his precociously intelligent son, yet wanted him out at work and independent as soon as possible.

Hansen and Stockfleth's middle school provided him with a good general education, including classes in German, Latin, history and religion. He was grateful for this, although he nurtured the memory of a misunderstanding which arose between himself and Stockfleth over one of his essays. The original essay has not survived, but it impressed a fellow pupil sufficiently for him to note down its essence, and in 1878 it appeared in the Kristiania newspaper *Faedrelandet* in a form that Ibsen was happy to acknowledge. *A Dream*, written when he was about fourteen, describes how he was visited by an angel who instructed him to accompany him – 'I'll show you a vision – human life as it really is'. The angel takes him down to the world of the dead – 'See here for yourself, all is vanity'.[9] A great storm arises, the dead awaken and reach out for the dreamer who escapes from his dream with a shout of fear.

In all its brevity this exercise displays the narrowness, profundity and consistency of some of the major concerns of Ibsen's life as an artist: the idea that there exists an absolute and attainable truth about human beings; the instinctive placing of himself at an advantageous position in the pursuit of this truth; the fear not so much of dying itself as of being claimed *from life* by the dead. So precociously gloomy a vision excited the suspicions of his teacher and Stockfleth accused him in front of the class of having plagiarised another's work, souring relations between them for a time.

In 1843, when Henrik was fifteen, the family moved back into Skien, to number 27 Snipetorpen, a house that was part of a property recently purchased by one of Knud Ibsen's affluent half-brothers. Shortly afterwards, on 1 October, he was confirmed at the local church. In his own youth Knud Ibsen had been first to be called up by the priest at his confirmation and it was a great disappointment to him that his son had only been allotted third place. Perhaps he had become oversensitive after his ruin, for he believed it to be a deliberate slight on his family and maintained afterwards that the fathers of the two boys first up had bribed the priest with gifts of fresh veal. It gave him a low opinion of priests, an attitude which he successfully passed on to his eldest son, but which brought relations with the rest of his family to breaking-point during the wave of religious fanaticism that swept over the town in the 1850s. Generally, however, the relationship between father and son was unsuccessful, and one of Henrik's enduring memories was of an occasion on which his father had promised to pay him for planting some potatoes, only to renege on the promise once the job was done.

By the time he left school he was privately determined to be an artist of some sort, probably a painter; but the ambition cannot have struck his father as realistic. Perhaps recalling his old friend and hunting companion, Heinrich Mülertz, who ran the Skien dispensary until his death in 1837, Knud despatched the boy to nearby Grimstad to take up a post as apothecary's assistant. Mülertz was a rich man and, until his death, the legal owner of the Venstøp property. It was through his generosity that the family had been allowed to live on there after Knud's ruin. It has been suggested, on no particular authority, that Henrik went along with the idea in the hope of using the training as a springboard to medical studies at the university in Kristiania, but it was without much enthusiasm that he left Skien on the coastal ferry *Lykkens Prøve* (the *Lucky Chance*), in late December 1843, three months short of his sixteenth birthday, for the four-day trip to Grimstad.

2

The Apothecary's Apprentice
Catiline

Ibsen's employer in Grimstad was a man named Jens Arup Reimann, proprietor of a newly established business in Storgaten. The pay was poor, the food merely sufficient and the living accommodation cramped. The ground floor consisted of two rooms – the Reimann family's sitting room, and the dispensary itself, which also functioned as a post office. Upstairs were three connecting bedrooms. The Reimanns and their youngest children slept in the outer one, Henrik in the next with the three older boys, and the two maids in the inner bedroom. The door between the two inner rooms was left open at nights in cold weather, as the maids had no stove of their own and had to share the heat from the stove in the boys' room.

Grimstad was in many ways similar to Skien, though with eight hundred inhabitants it was less than half the size. The streets were narrow, poorly lit, and without sewage. Water was drawn from wells. Most of its young men went to sea once they left school. The least wage-earner would invest some part of his savings in a trading ship, thus making capitalists of them all as well as protecting single investors against cargo loss. Ibsen used the general set-up of the town and the functioning of its economy as the framework for *The Pillars of Society*, in 1877.

Being a sea-faring town there were customers requiring attention night and day, and when the night-bell rang it was Ibsen's job to pull on his dressing-gown and, passing through the maids' room, climb the precipitous staircase down to the dispensary. For the next six years he had to live 'in the open' like this, never alone, always observed, powerless to control any aspect of his immediate environment. The effect on his personality was profound, and when success and money finally made it possible for him he would indulge his need for privacy until it bordered on the pathological.

His first days in this small, primitive town were lonely and uneventful, and he dealt with his loneliness by immersing himself in work, mastering the art of preparing adhesive tape and acquiring a basic knowledge of the medicinal properties of herbs. In this way he became familiar with the *doktorlatin* which he occasionally makes use of in his plays. When Norwegian Latinists complained of a usage in *Brand*, Ibsen responded: 'Well it was certainly good Latin in my day, though of course it was *doctor's Latin*. Any medical man will tell you this is the stock phrase used for prescriptions when a powder is sold not by weight but by requirement.'[1]

Gradually he settled in, and by 20 May he was writing to his friend Poul Lieungh in Skien that he was 'very well content and have never regretted coming here, because Reimann is very good to me, and does all he can to encourage my interest in apothecary work, which wasn't all that great in the beginning.'[2]

On Sunday, his one free day in the week, he would row out to nearby Maløya, or climb in the hills behind the town with his paint-box. At night he studied, hoping to pass the university matriculation exam which would allow him to take the so-called 'Norwegian' medical exam, a university degree without Latin. Often he would stay up reading and writing until two in the morning.

Between working for Reimann and pursuing his own studies young Henrik remained an unknown quantity for the youth of Grimstad. On the few occasions on which he did venture out into company he was obliged to participate in pastimes and amusements which can only have distressed him, such as wrist-wrestling and primitive weight-lifting contests with the boy next door and his companions. As they had done in Skien his solitary ways and introspective nature made him an object of suspicion among the local young, and it was surely a mistake for him to have arrived in town wearing his confirmation suit, and to continue to wear it at all times, even if, as seems to have been the case, it was his only suit. He appears to have been mildly bullied and was often ducked in the snow. The local girls nicknamed him *Spætus*, meaning 'Weedy'.

Not surprisingly, he found the company of older people more congenial. One companion of this early period was Mina Wahl, a Danish woman nine years his senior who worked as governess for the local parish priest and shared Henrik's hobby of landscape-painting. Svend Fjeldmand, another immigrant into the community, was a serious-minded man in his late forties who helped out in the shop, chopping ingredients and washing bottles. He and Henrik some-times walked over to the cemetery at Fjære on Sundays, where now stands a tourist-inspired monument to Terje Vigen, the eponymous sea-faring hero of Ibsen's long ballad written in 1862.

With the maids of the house there developed an enforced inti-macy. Marie Thomsen, the kitchen girl, was gossipy and sharp-tongued, and there were frequent clashes between the two in which she triumphed by banishing Henrik from the kitchen; but as quickly as his temper flared it would subside again. She remembered how in his unhappiest moments he would complain of his father's neg-lect of him, and lament that he was certain he would never find his rightful place in the world. The melancholic confidences aroused mothering instincts in the women, and the nanny Katrine made him a dressing-gown. Ibsen's capacity for study impressed them, as did the fact that he painted proficiently. The Reimanns too were impressed by his art works and hung them on the walls of the house.

The other maid, Else Sophie Birkedalen, Sophie as she was known, was twenty-eight, ten years older than Henrik, and by the standards of the time almost an old maid. Ibsen had reached puberty early and wore already a full brown beard, displaying and yet con-cealing what was within him. Like him, she was from a family that had come down in the world, and this may have established a bond between them. By the early new year of 1846 they had become lovers.

Else Sophie became pregnant and in the summer went home to her parents in Vestre Moland, east of Lillesand, where on 9 October, 1846 she gave birth to a son, christened Hans Jacob Henriksen. In his investigation into attitudes towards illegitimacy in Norway between 1831 and 1850, the sociologist Eilert Sundt found telling regional variations, from great tolerance in Trondheim in the coastal midlands, where almost half the recorded births were illegiti-mate, to strong disapproval in the south and west of the country. The lowest figures of all for illegitimate births per hundred were from the Grimstad area, so Else Sophie and Henrik could hardly have chosen a worse place for their fateful liaison. A detailed legal apparatus was in place to deal with illegitimate births, and a month after the christening a formal statement of Else Sophie's claim for financial support for the child was submitted, and Ibsen was asked to confirm or deny that he was the father. On 7 December he sent his reply via the local Justice of the Peace:

Hr Byfoged Preus,

In response to Your Grace's request for a statement confirming or denying that I am the father of a baby boy born to the maid Else Sophie Jensdatter Birkedalen, christened Hans Jacob on October 24, I hereby respectfully submit that, in spite of the maid's association with other persons of the male sex during the period in question, I cannot with any certainty deny the charge that I am the father, since I have unfortunately had intercourse with her, encouraged as I was by her flirtatious ways and by the fact that we both lived and worked at Reimann's dispensary.

I am now in my twentieth year, own absolutely nothing apart from a few articles of clothing, some shoes and bedlinen, and I shall shortly be leaving Grimstad apothecary, where I have been employed since the summer of 1843 as apprentice, with absolutely no other income apart from board and lodging. In the first instance I shall be compelled to turn to my father, still living, one of the smaller merchants in Skien and a man of extremely modest means.

Grimstad 7 December 1846.

Yours respectfully

Henr. Ibsen*

By a council resolution of 18 December Ibsen was then ordered to contribute to the child's upkeep to the tune of eight speciedaler annually for the first five years, seven for the next five, and six for the years between Hans Jacob's tenth and fifteenth birthdays, the money to be paid quarterly in January, April, July and October. After that his legal obligations would be over.[3]

Ibsen seems never to have spoken of this child of his, nor the mother, nor expressed any interest in their fate. No surviving letter makes mention of them, no interview with old friends, nor contemporaries from his Grimstad days like Marie Thomsen nor family members refer to them. It is not even possible to know whether his mother and father in Skien were told what had happened, although one must imagine they were. It is as though Elsie Sophie and her child never existed. The secret went inside him, intensifying his

* The letter contains two curious inaccuracies; he was eighteen, not nineteen years old, and all the documentary evidence indicates that he came to Grimstad in late December 1843, not in the summer.

already secretive nature, developing into that obsession with guilt, shame and Nemesis which is the chief characteristic of his art.

Much as he might have wanted to disappear, Ibsen must soon have realised that there was nothing to be gained by leaving Grimstad, and life continued as before. Reimann proved, after Knud Ibsen, a second unsatisfactory male role model for the youth. Already heavily in debt by the time Henrik joined him, he revealed a tendency to retreat from his problems into alcohol. Such early experiences of ineffective fathers can only have contributed to the low opinion of men in general that is such a feature of Ibsen's work. They illuminate his observation later in life to Henrik Jæger, his first biographer, that 'the men in his family had been on the whole weaker than the women'. Twice, in August and November 1845, Ibsen had acted as a witness to guarantees signed by Reimann for his creditors, and in August 1846 his employer gave up the unequal struggle and his business was sold at auction.

After an interim period in the hands of a new owner the business was sold again in March 1847 to a young man named Lars Nielsen, who had been Ibsen's predecessor as Reimann's apprentice in Storgaten. Nielsen at once moved the premises to Østregata in a better and more central part of town. Ibsen had by this time served out the first term of his apprenticeship. After presenting himself for examination in nearby Arendal he now had the right to call himself 'qualified assistant', a title which brought him a rise in pay.

The living quarters in Østregata were also an improvement on conditions at Reimann's, though Ibsen was still denied the luxury of a room of his own. For the next three years he shared, with Nielsen, a room behind the dispensary which was at once their duty-room, laboratory, dining-room and bedroom. It can still be seen in Grimstad, just as it was in Ibsen's time, preserved even down to the primitive trunk bed in which he slept.

Ibsen also began to acquire a circle of friends after the move to Østregata. One was Christopher Due, a youth who came to Grimstad in 1847 to work as a customs clerk. By the time of Due's arrival Ibsen had, possibly by reason of the affair with Else Sophie Birkedalen, become a local curiosity. Due recalled how a companion asked him if he had yet seen the apothecary's boy who had arrived in town some while ago. The youth said he had noticed that there was 'something odd about him'.[4] His curiosity aroused, Due presently paid an exploratory visit to the shop. There was no one there. He knocked on the wooden counter:

> and shortly after there emerged with some haste a rather small young man with an attractively lively face. I should say here that in his youth Ibsen wore a precociously full and handsome beard which gave his face an air at once energetic and harmonious, a fact which photographs taken later will confirm. The overall impression was of a comely, well-proportioned young man. On this occasion, however, his face was set in what was unmistakably and impatiently a question-mark that clearly implied that the potential customer was not at all welcome. I requested four skillings worth of plaster and this he expedited quickly. No words passed between us, but as I took the plaster our glances met, and I observed in his attractive eyes a glint that made an impression on me.[5]

The two young men presently became acquainted, and Due was soon spending his evenings regularly in Ibsen's company. He was particularly attracted to Ibsen's intelligence and sense of humour. A basically conventional youth, Due also enjoyed Ibsen's provocative views on religion and morality, and did his best to counter them.* This was no easy task, given Ibsen's talent for sarcasm. Due provides an example of it in the story of a friend who had suggested to Ibsen that he too might benefit from daily reading of a certain devotional book, since he himself could *never get enough of it.* Ibsen retorted that he doubted it, since there could not possibly be any real nutritional value in something of which one could *never get enough.* Voltaire was one of his heroes at this time, and he now openly denied the existence of a personal God. Another memorable outrage was the assertion that when he married he and his wife would occupy separate floors, meet only at mealtimes and address each other by the formal pronoun *De.*† Due took this to be an example of Ibsen's sense of humour at the time, not realising that it was in fact close to his idea of the perfect marriage.

As Ibsen's reputation for shocking spread, the dispensary became a meeting-place for the intellectually inclined youth of the town.

---

* In his memoir Due wrote, '*Der var forøvrigt i Grimstad særdeles gode moralske Forholde*' (Moral standards in Grimstad were particularly good).

† The informal pronoun, used between friends, intimates and young people, was *Du.*

These first admirers perceived an entertainer in Ibsen, 'with his lively humour and his sarcasms.'[6] The type of humour involved is apparent in Ibsen's earliest surviving verse, a mocking epitaph for 'Sigurd von Finkelbeck' whose fondness for drink led the poet to predict that even the flowers that would one day adorn his friend's grave would exude a faintly alcoholic aroma. In another poem which has not survived Ibsen improvised a long, rhyming sequence based on melodies from a Danish vaudeville popular at the time, *Gjenboerne*. In a series of cartoons he drew to accompany the verses Ibsen depicted the adventures of a young man whose horse ran out of patience during his master's gallant but too protracted farewell to his sweetheart, and bolted without him. Succeeding cartoons showed the young man's ludicrous misadventures as he strove to recapture the horse. Ibsen's purpose in composing the sequence was to ridicule a local youth who was considered pompous, and cunningly playing on his victim's fondness for the tunes from *Gjenboerne* he managed to trick him into singing the verses. Due wrote that 'Ibsen's pleasure at the amusement caused among the gang when we persuaded the victim of the ridicule to sing for us the comic verse of which he was himself the subject was indescribable.'[7] As an early instance of Ibsen's sense of humour it shows it to have been fuelled by more than a touch of cruelty.

Ibsen kept the fact that he also wrote 'serious' verse a secret from his friends except Due, who recognised from the start that Ibsen was the real thing. At the time Due was Grimstad correspondent for a new Kristiania newspaper, the *Christiania Posten*, and in this capacity was responsible for getting Ibsen published for the first time. One of these earliest works was 'The Skald in Valhalla', a valediction on the death in 1850 of Adam Oehlenschläger, the most famous Scandinavian poet and dramatist of his time, who had introduced into Scandinavia that self-conscious cultivation of national identity that became such a feature of nineteenth-century Europe. For Danes and Norwegians this meant the reviving of the idea of a nordic golden age of Viking expansion and Viking art in order to shame the flabby and featureless present into self-improvement. Oehlenschläger's plays and poems were of great cultural and literary significance for the young Ibsen, and a number of his earliest poems take up the theme of the golden past. A noticeable feature of them is Ibsen's consistent use of the word 'skald' as his word for 'poet', for it was in the figure of the skald of Old Norse poetry that he found his first satisfactory image of the writer. Though the skaldic art itself was elaborate, and demanded of its practitioners a thorough knowledge of its techniques and mythological and historical frames of reference, the spark itself was considered the divine gift of Odin. As Jatgeir in *The Pretenders* says, 'the skaldic art cannot be learnt, my lord'. And although the art was usually associated with young men of good families it was not necessarily so, as the career of the low-born Sneglu-Halli at the court of Harald Hardruler shows. Indeed, poetic talent, correctly handled, could be any young man's passport to status and wealth in tenth- and eleventh-century Iceland. The situation had parallels with nineteenth-century Norway, a society without a native aristocracy but in which the path of literature, successfully navigated, offered the writer the chance to achieve a status and an authority not far removed from that which, in other societies, was associated with the aristocracy. And Ibsen's concern for status was always great, perhaps greater than it might otherwise have been had it not been for his family's fall from grace.

A skald, being attached to a king, functioned as his conscience, and this was an aspect of the role which attracted Ibsen. A number of the poems of his Grimstad days were addressed to Oskar I, king of the Swedish-Norwegian union, or to the people of the union, for a poet was also the conscience and educator of his people. 'Scandinavians Awake!' was a call to Norwegians and Swedes to go to the aid of their Danish brothers against the German invaders in Slesvig in 1849. The poet appealed directly to the king:

> Why not summon your men, majesty?
> They'll heed your call at once,
> The ancient glories of the North still shine!

Ibsen's interest was in the role and status of the skald, less in the art itself, and this early verse makes little attempt to reproduce its complex metrical rules and its use of fantastic implied similes known as *kennings*.

His assertion that 'they' rather than 'we', still less 'I', will follow the king into battle marks a more revealing deviation from the original models. Naturally the verses of a twenty-year-old chemist's assistant from provincial Norway would hardly come to the notice of the king; even so Ibsen wants it clearly understood that he sees the role of poet as purely advisory. There will be no question of his personally attending at the field of battle, musket in hand, to fight for his king. This view of the writer as a highly vocal but passive spectator of life, essentially a passer-on of good advice, was one which he confirmed on many occasions later in life.This distinction between being brave on paper and brave in the street was problematic for Ibsen, though he remained unaware of the problem for many years.

Something else he gained from the image of the skald and his world was his first comparative perspective on Christian religion and morality. The Bible was among his earliest reading at Venstøp; but of the thirty poems which survive from his six years in Grimstad only one contains Christian references. Several, such as 'The Giant Oak', 'Scandinavians Awake', 'To Norway's Skalds', refer extensively to Old Norse mythology, while the poem on Oehlenschläger's death is an account of the reception given to dead poets in Valhalla which shows Ibsen's detailed knowledge of the procedure. The Christian exception among the poems is 'Doubt and Hope', a short, moving poem in rhyming couplets in which the poet recalls how often he has mocked the notion of doomsday. A wild lightning storm overhead one night reawakens his old fear of God and now he can't sleep. He finds himself addressing once again someone in whom he has 'long ago ceased to believe', and to this God he offers all earthly wisdom for the power to pray again one honest, childlike prayer, even as he realises that his offer is doomed:

> But look, I'm no child anymore,
> my mind is not a child's mind.
> The road faith shows the innocent eye
> is hidden from me.

In the end the poet decides to try to sleep again, certain that when he wakes up this time his child-like faith in God will have returned. But it is an unconvincing conclusion to the poem, and it leaves us in no doubt that for the twenty-year old Ibsen the Christian faith, with all its moral certainties, was already a vanished world, gone like his childhood and his innocence lost at eighteen in the arms of Else Sophie. All his life he retained a belief in at least the symbolic truth of the account of the Fall of Man; he once told the Danish literary critic Georg Brandes that Raphael's art had never attracted him because 'his characters belong before the Fall'.[8]

Heaven had become a moral impossibility for him. Entry to

Valhalla, on the other hand, set only one relevant condition: did he possess the required literary talent? Heathendom offered no coherent vision of an afterlife, but the huge premium it put on posthumous reputation elevated fame to the level of an afterlife. 'The Havamal' says

> Cattle die, kinsmen die,
>   one day you die yourself;
> I know one thing that never dies –
>   the dead man's reputation.

and it was on the heaven of lasting human fame that Ibsen now knew he must set his sights if his life were to have meaning. Yet as 'Doubt and Hope' shows, the abandonment of his Christian heritage was not easy, and from this simple poem a connecting thread of spiritual quest twists its way through all the plays and the finest poems of his early years.

Over the meal-table at Lars Nielsen's house Ibsen had many a spirited discussion with Nielsen's mother, an intelligent and religious woman who found it in her heart to forgive the young man's blasphemies in the belief that they were offered in a spirit of honest doubt and a desire to hear the views of others. Her friend Fru Crawfurd was another who found Ibsen's seriousness sympathetic. She had a large library, with works by Oehlenschläger, Kierkegaard, and the Norwegian poet and dramatist Henrik Wergeland. There was also a local reading circle, forerunner of the lending library. Ibsen is not listed as a subscriber, presumably because he could not afford it; but with Fru Crawfurd and Nielsen both members Ibsen doubtless had access to the collection, which included translations of Sir Walter Scott, Dickens, and Trollope as well as the collected works of Ludvig Holberg, whose satirical dramas of human folly and mordant, pessimistic essays Ibsen grew to love and admire. The collection also housed the short stories of Mauritz Hansen, a popular Norwegian writer of the period who is sometimes credited, in all his obscurity, with being the true inventor of the modern detective story. Ibsen knew Hansen's work well and admired his prose style; later in life he praised it as the only Norwegian prose which could not equally as well have been written in Danish.[9] Aspects of Hansen's narrative technique probably influenced the development of Ibsen's dramatic technique, notably his use of a late revelation in the plot to resolve a hitherto enigmatic situation and change the moral destinies of the characters involved.

Thirty poems have survived from Ibsen's time in Grimstad, twenty-six of which were collected in a homemade book which he entitled, in down-to-earth fashion, *Various Poems from the Years 1848, 1849 and 1850*, presumably for his own reference. The earliest, 'Resignation', was from 1847. Three were from 1848, thirteen from 1849 and nine from 1850. Taken as a whole, the selection shows that Ibsen was not, in his youth, a political animal. Nor were his political instincts notably radical. Of this collection only three show traces of the revolutionary spirit: 'The Giant Oak', with its depiction of the decay of the great world-tree Yggdrasil and its prophesy of the rise of a pan-Scandinavian political and social consciousness; 'To Hungary!', which identifies with the Hungarians' struggle for independence from Austria, and which Ibsen was able to recall at a reception in his honour in Budapest some fifty years later; and 'Scandinavians Awake!', where the political urging is again littered with references to heathen mythology and the obligations imposed on Scandinavians by their remote past.

Many of the remaining poems were inspired by his admiration for girls from prominent local families with whose brothers and cousins he had become friendly. 'Clear Star' ('Klare Stjerne') punning gently on her name, was one of several poems he wrote to Clara Ebbell. Clara was nineteen years old, of good family, in her love of music and poetry the sort of girl a sensitive young poet should have saved himself for. Ibsen inundated her with his feelings in these poems, but kept them clinically free of eroticism: 'Clear star, send down a twinkle from on high!' After Else Sophie sexuality seems to have been banished to a remote part of his mind, where it fused with his image of the muse of poetry to create the hybrid dream woman, part-symbol, part-flesh-and-blood, who remained the real love of his life:

> Others have theirs,
> and I too have a lover!
> but she's no earthly woman,
> the one whom I call mine;
> only a vision, spun from
> unattained longings,
> unattainable, perhaps!

Ibsen even painted this lover of his, depicting himself as a bearded, dreaming Joshua and his muse as a bare-legged blonde angel floating in white robes just above Joshua's left shoulder.

In 'Ballroom Memories – A Fragment in Poetry and Prose' the young narrator is concerned to defend his impulsive decision to enter a ballroom with the cry that was to become the motif of many of Ibsen's most notable creations – *I must!* – In the next paragraph he addresses the reader: 'Remember these words, unfeeling one, who so coolly condemns the storm of passion in a human soul! Remember them, and do not forget that in them you read the justification for so many lives, bewildering, and annihilating!' The contrast between the banality of the overt situation – a young man entering a ballroom – and the passion of the outburst suggests that the poet is actually referring to an experience of a quite different order.

The improvement in material circumstances while working for Nielsen gave Ibsen the chance to resume his ambition of a career in medicine. In his free time he began studying Latin texts with a local tutor and submitting essays, which were largely exercises in style, to another in the capital. These short prose efforts from 1848 show another side to the wan pierrot and rabble-rousing patriot of the Grimstad poems and one with more obvious links to the spartan realism of Ibsen's maturity. In 'On the Importance of Self-knowledge' he writes that self-knowledge matters because a person who wants to explore his less good sides 'will find himself forced, time and again, to confront his own humiliation; yet this cannot lead to a lessening in his self-respect, for it only shows the power of his will and his honest striving towards his goal in life – the development of his spiritual powers and the care of his earthly well-being'. Such precision is a clear reflection of his own inner struggle to remain on terms with himself despite his 'fall'. These same few lines, inscribed with his signature and the date 5 February 1848, appeared on the reverse of that wandering baptismal certificate that turned up in Bergen so many years later. Coincidence perhaps, but possibiliy an indication that they had become watchwords for him at that time.

A second essay, 'Work is its Own Reward' defends the premise with the same firm sense of involvement and certainty. Work is 'not merely a means but the only means whereby we can harness our powers to act for good'. Ibsen distinguishes clearly between the material gains of work and work's true reward, which is that 'the mind is cheered and ennobled' as it progresses towards the great goal, 'Perfection – in the degree to which it is granted the human race to reach this point'. A third title, 'Why Ought a Nation to Preserve the Language and History of its Forefathers?' evokes the same deep show of seriousness: language witnesses to a people's commonality of origin, and should be developed and ennobled without losing sight of these beginnings. It is a heritage which must be handled with respect and care '– the achievements of previous generations for those living now ought in turn to be handed on to the generations to come, for the present too belongs to the past'.

These were very much the sentiments of the intellectual leaders of Norway at the time, those who in Kristiania in 1851 formed the Society for the Promotion of the People's Education to 'promote the education of the people, particularly their spiritual development and ennoblement'. Such sentiments formed part of a large-scale cultural campaign that was conducted in Norway during the second half of the nineteenth century as the desire for national independence grew. Its aim was the civilising of the peasantry, so that peasant clothing, customs, dance music and folk tales could with less distaste be adopted by the bourgeoisie in the cities and advertised to the outside world as 'quintessentially Norwegian'. Ibsen's subscription to such values and aims shows the extent to which he was aware of what was going on in the capital, his instinctive identification with the aims of its leaders, and why it was so important to him to acquire an education.

Latin studies for his matriculation exam were carried out in the all-purpose duty-room in the apothecary, where he and a teacher named Emil Bie, with interruptions to attend to customers and deal with Ibsen's frequent nose-bleeds, made their way through the university's list of set books – Cornelius Nepos, chosen for his influence on La Fontaine and H. C. Andersen; Cæsar on the Gallic wars; Sallust's Catiline and Jugurthine conspiracies; Cicero's speeches; Phaedrus, two books of the *Aeneid*, three of Ovid's *Metamorphoses*, two books of Odes by Horace, extracts from Herodotus, Plato, Xenophon, Homer, Bion and Moschus.

The real fruit of his studies was *Catiline* (*Catilina*), a verse drama in three acts which he wrote in the winter and spring of 1849. Ben Jonson, Dumas *père* and the sixteenth-century French poet du Bartas had all previously written about this Roman rebel, though Ibsen could hardly have been aware of their efforts. *Catiline* was written at breakneck, almost expressionist speed, mostly at night, which Ibsen said accounted for the fact that so much of the action takes place in the dark. When he was finished Due made a fair copy of the play, faithfully reproducing even the numerous dashes the rushing writer had littered across the manuscript when temporarily stumped for the right word or phrase (though Ibsen was actually a believer in dashes – a rhetorical couplet in one early poem is followed by twenty-seven of them). Another friend, a law student named Ole Schulerud, took the play with him when he left Grimstad to resume his studies in Kristiania in the autumn of 1849, and submitted it to the city's only theatre, the Christiania theatre in Bank Pladsen. The three friends were optimistic about its chances and waited impatiently for a decision.

Catiline remains, under the circumstances, a remarkable literary debut. From the beginning Ibsen showed the sureness and boldness of his artistic instincts in the freedom with which he handled his source materials. He begins by conflating two details mentioned by Sallust: that two among Catiline's many sexual conquests were a young woman of aristocratic family, and a vestal virgin – the girls whose duty it was to guard the eternal flame in Vesta's temple. The penalty for losing their virginity was to be buried alive. Shortly after the play opens we learn of the hero's infatuation for one of the virgins, Furia. Desperate to win her favour he swears to carry out vengeance on the seducer of her sister, Tullia, who drowned herself in the Tiber. Directly he has made the vow he and Furia both realise that it was Catiline himself who was responsible for Tullia's dishonouring and death, so that in effect he has sworn to take his own life. This encounter with Nemesis is what provides Ibsen with his plot. Catiline's tormented and shifting attitude towards carrying out his promise develops parallel with his changing attitude towards the 'historical' plot, the proposed *coup d'état* and burning of Rome with the assistance of disaffected Allobroge tribesmen and sundry supporters up and down the peninsula. Sallust's account describes how the plotters were betrayed by Fulvia, the mistress of Catiline's fellow-conspirator Curius. Here Ibsen improvises for his own ends, changing Fulvia into Furia, leaving Curius and Catiline with an infatuation for the same woman that rationalises Curius's betrayal of the conspiracy at Furia's behest as a proof of his love for her.

To counter Furia's demonic influence Ibsen introduces Catiline's wife, Aurelia. Overruling Sallust, who dismissed her as 'a woman in whom no man ever found anything to praise except her beauty', Ibsen presents her as a paragon of womanly virtues, generous, long-suffering and all-forgiving. These two wrestle for possession of Catiline's soul. Aurelia urges him to leave Rome with her, abandoning public life for a life of personal happiness with her. Furia reminds him constantly that he has an obligation to keep his promise to her that transcends his desire for personal happiness. In the play's final scene Furia appears to have won the day. Catiline rejects Aurelia with the horrible words 'love will nevermore find its abode within this breast' and departs, intending to keep his word to Furia by soliciting his own death in battle. Failing to die he returns, chases Aurelia off-stage and stabs her, then hands the dagger to Furia, who stabs him. The mortally wounded Aurelia staggers back on and falls at Catiline's side, leaving Furia to return into darkness and husband and wife to enter the Elysian Fields together.

Ibsen never treated his play as juvenilia, and permitted its inclusion in the Norwegian and German editions of his collected works that appeared in 1898, although the version used was a revision of 1874. In a preface to the revision he wrote of how *Catiline* had anticipated so many of his later concerns as a playwright: 'the conflict between ability and longing, between what is willed and what is possible, the simultaneously tragic and comic in the individual and in mankind'. It contains other harbingers of what was to come, including the earliest manifestation of his lifelong obsession with the image of being *buried alive,* here where Furia is walled-up in an underground tomb for the crime of having neglected the sacred flame. Here, too, is the use of a contrasting pair of women to symbolise a man's inner struggle with himself. Furia and Aurelia are the first in a long line of such pairings that stretches through *The Vikings at Helgeland* (Hjørdis and Dagny, 1858), is a central aspect of *Hedda Gabler* (Thea and Hedda, 1890), and moves with undiminished strength through *John Gabriel Borkman* (Gunnhild and Ella, 1896) to *When We Dead Awaken* (Maja and Irene, 1899).

Catiline was conceived and composed in 1849, at a time when Europe was still reverberating to the revolutions of 1848 in Rome, Venice, Naples, Milan, Prague, Berlin, Vienna. In the Preface to his revision Ibsen recalled this atmosphere as an influential factor in the play, mentioning especially the February uprising of 1848 in

Paris and the revolt led by Kossuth in Hungary, 'which had a deep and maturing influence on my development, though it remained undigested for a long time afterwards'.[10] Norway was at the time intellectually and geographically remote from the rest of Europe, and political activity among the young directed more towards the search for a unique cultural identity in the remote saga-past than in the discovery and implementation of radically new political ideas. The revolutions of 1848 were only cursorily covered in newspaper reporting and apart from Ibsen's elliptical reference in the form of *Catiline* left no mark on the national art at all. As Ibsen ended his life European rather than national in outlook, his outward-looking in *Catiline* might seem an early hint of his later position, especially since Due described him at twenty as 'a full-blooded Republican' and recalled a Reform Banquet they held at which Ibsen delivered a fiery speech 'against all emperors and kings, these monsters of society, but *for* Republicanism, the only possible form of government'.[11]

And yet, as with the poems, the claims of a meaningful political radicalism seem almost wilfully misleading, for beneath the veneer of the revolutionary theme, and the lipservice paid to the historical Catiline's social conscience, *Catiline* is essentially a deeply private meditation on character. Peering through the mist of his schoolboy Latin at Sallust's tale of ancient times, it dawned on Ibsen at some point that he could suspend within it his own baffling encounter with sex, guilt and Else Sophie Birkedalen; and yet remain hidden – doubly hidden – as Catiline and as Brynjolf Bjarme, the pseudonym under which he wrote the play. He discovered the confessional and therapeutic possibilities of art, and that art might be strong enough to fill the gap left by the loss of his religious faith. Compared to the attractions of this, 1848 and its revolutions were irrelevancies. Exactly fifty years afterwards Ibsen described the play that turned out to be his last, *When We Dead Awaken*, as a 'dramatic epilogue' to his career. *Catiline* was, just as accurately, its dramatic prologue.

The Christiania theatre kept the friends waiting for a decision, and presently Ibsen's patience snapped. Blaming him for the delay he wrote an anxious and intemperate letter to Schulerud. Schulerud's reply must have been impressive, for Ibsen's reply to him of 15 October is a handsome apology:

I hope you can appreciate the mood of disappointed expectation with which I have had to greet each new post, it is most unpleasant, since I, not being there, cannot easily imagine the reasons for the delay, and the uncertainty raises a thousand doubts in me, all the more painful because deep down I can't say a single one of them was warranted. Your letter has cleared up any doubts I may have had about the wisdom of your way of doing things, and I would be a poor friend indeed if I did not readily take back anything I may have written in my letter that casts unseemly aspersions on your motives.

Ibsen, the track-coverer, was already sufficiently certain of posterity's interest in him to ask Schulerud to burn the letter – 'I don't like the thought of it being in your hands'.[12]

No doubt the need to make money was a factor in Ibsen's anxious outburst. He had now been paying maintenance for Hans Jacob for three years, and with the cost of his Latin tuition and his study books there was scarcely even money left over to clothe himself. Enclosing Due's thanks to Schulerud for a guitar which had been sent Ibsen added his own for the gift of a pair of trousers.

The waiting went on, and Ibsen put in the time working on a number of new plays, a poem and a short story:

Now a few lines about my literary activeties. As I probably mentioned before, I have almost finished the first act of *Olaf T.* The little one-acter *The Normans* has been revised, or, more accurately, will be revised, as I am in the process of revising it at the moment. In its new form it will serve as the vehicle for a more advanced idea than that for which it was originally intended. I have used a couple of tales and sketches from Telemark as the basis for some minor poems, set to well-known folk-tunes, so I have tried my hand at Nationalist writing. And I have half-finished a longish, perhaps slightly melodramatic poem entitled 'Ballroom Memories', inspired by my infatuation of last summer. But my main work since you left is a short story on a national-historical theme which I have called 'The Prisoner in Agershuus'. It's about Christian Lofthuus's sorry fate.*

* In a letter to Schulerud, Ibsen refers to his source for this Lofthuus story as 'an old document that has fortunately come into my possession'. The landed Lofthuus was Else Sophie Birkedalen's grandfather: was it she who supplied Ibsen with some treasured old newspaper article in melancholy proof of her family's former status? If so, it reinforces the idea that there was more to the relationship between them than just the one sexual encounter.

The Normans emerges later as Ibsen's second play under the title *The Warrior's Barrow*. *Olaf Tryggvason* ('*Olaf T.*') was never finished, and nothing of it has survived but the title, which is enough to confirm the nature of Ibsen's emerging preoccupations. Olaf Tryggvason was the king who in 995 brought Christianity to Norway in a brutal fashion, torturing and killing to impose his will. Evidently Ibsen's literary instincts were leading him to trawl the past in search of times and societies characterised by the same kind of moral tensions he was experiencing within himself. The object of the 'self-deluding summer love affair', Clara Ebbell, not long after became engaged to an uncle nearly twenty years older than herself, a small-town, incestuous liaison of the type that nourished Ibsen's growing horror of little worlds.

The Christian Lofthuus whose 'unhappy fate' he refers to was betrayed. Loftuus was an eighteenth century Norwegian landowner who farmed an estate in Lillesand, in southern Norway. Tiring of the bullying exploitation of local people by the resident Danish officials he travelled to Copenhagen, where he presented his case to the king. Back in Norway his enemies conspired against him, falsely accusing him of planning an alliance with Sweden to overthrow the Danish colonial rule. He was betrayed, captured and transported in chains to the dungeons at Akershus Castle in Kristiania, where he languished for ten long years without trial. In 1797 he was pardoned, but died before hearing the news.

The Agershuus Prisoner is one of the few attempts Ibsen made to write imaginative prose, and as an example of a path not taken it makes an interesting study. The story begins with a description of a mysterious woman who regularly visited a certain grave in a Kristiania graveyard until one day she stopped coming. The narrator calls himself 'Brynjolf'. But with the obvious intention of getting him to tell us the whole story about the mysterious woman and the occupant of the grave he soon introduces his uncle, Bjarme. Young Brynjolf quickly finds it preferable to interest his readers by ridiculing the old uncle and his literary pretensions than by letting him take the stage and get on with the tale. Old Uncle Bjarme manages to tell Brynjolf that the strange old woman once played a part in a story he refers to as his 'masterpiece', at which point young Ibsen's sarcasm takes over completely:

Uncle's masterpiece! I cried in some surprise, for which I had two reasons; one, that I had never heard tell of such; and two, that it had never occurred to me to connect my uncle's 'works' with the concept 'masterpiece'.

'Yes indeed, my masterpiece. Unfortunately it lies unfinished in a drawer in my desk, because I could not find a way to end it.'

'That's a terrible shame', I answered, for I remembered that when reading through uncle's work the end was always the bit I most looked forward to.

Not surprisingly, the tale survives for only one more page after this subversion of its teller. The destructively self-conscious narration, epitomised by the almost schizophrenic decision to divide his pseudonym in two, perhaps sheds light on why Ibsen never seriously considered a career as a writer of prose, for the blank spaces between the lines of a play give the dramatist far more space in which to hide than the novelist will ever find.

News of the theatre's rejection of *Catiline* reached Ibsen in December 1849. He took it well, merely urging Schulerud to try to sell the rights to publish it in book form to a Kristiania bookseller (there were no publishing houses in Norway at that time). In the end Schulerud offered to pay for the printing at his own expense. A first edition of 250 copies was in the bookshops on 12 April. Schulerud was not disheartened at this lack of commercial interest. He viewed it as an aberration of judgement which would soon be corrected, and even contemplated abandoning his studies altogether to devote himself full-time to publishing the 'two or three plays a year' he was sure Ibsen would 'easily' be able to write. With the profits of their literary enterprise, he suggested, they would soon have enough to take that trip through Europe and the Orient of which they had so often spoken with Due in the dispensary at Grimstad.

With a first play written and published and his name – albeit Brynjolf Bjarme – in the Kristiania newspapers, Ibsen's destiny was beginning to take shape. Now was the time to move to Kristiania, finish off his studies and submit himself for matriculation at the university. He wrote to Hedvig of his intentions, and she made him promise to visit Skien first on his way to the capital.

Hedvig wrote to her cousin Hanna Stenersen, 'You can bet I'm longing to see my bebearded brother again'. Knud Ibsen is said to have paraded his son off proudly to the neighbours, but most of Ibsen's time was probably spent with Hedvig. In old age she recalled the day they walked up the Bratsberg hill together and he told her his ambition, startling in its starkness, simplicity and scope. It was to achieve 'the greatest and most perfect of all possible forms of greatness and perfection'. And after that? After that he would die. The words recall the obsessed and ambitious Catiline as well as the deadly serious young essayist determined to achieve 'perfection – in the degree to which it is granted the human race to reach this point'. They signal the petrification of willpower around the splinter of shame lodged inside him, and announce his intention of transmuting it at whatever cost into a pearl.

This ten-day visit to Skien turned out to be the last time he saw any member of his immediate family, with the exception of Hedvig. She, Nicolai, and Ole Paus were still living at home. Johan had already emigrated to America in the late 1840s, during the early years of emigration fever. In a literate and informative letter home from Wisconsin he described life as a store-keeper's assistant at one hundred dollars a month and all found. This, his only surviving letter, offers no evidence of any break within the family: 'When any of you write to dear Henrik, say hello to him from me and ask him to write to me', he asks. But Ibsen never wrote home again after this last visit, and whether or not he would have made an exception for Johan must remain an academic question, for Johan disappeared shortly afterwards and was never heard from again; according to one rumour he died on his way to the California gold-fields. Ibsen, in search of a different kind of gold, likewise disappeared to his family, if not as dramatically then just as absolutely as Johan, when he said goodbye and boarded the steamer for Kristiania at the end of April 1850.

3

A National Romantic
The Warrior's Barrow

Ibsen arrived in Kristiania on 28 April 1850, some two weeks after the publication of *Catiline*. He had just turned twenty-two, was 'small and thin, though well-built, dark-complexioned, with a great mane of hair hanging down over his forehead, and an uncertain, averted gaze'.[1] He moved into Schulerud's attic-flat on the corner of Filosofgangen and Vinkelgate, in Vika. This was a working-class area of the centre of town, not far from the old Vestbanen railway station and just a couple of minutes' walk from the university. The landlady, Mor Sæther, was Schulerud's aunt. She had a reputation as a healer, and was something of a celebrity among her student lodgers for having ministered to the poet Henrik Wergeland in the last stages of his terminal illness.

Ibsen's immediate goal was matriculation at the university the following August, and to this end he enrolled at Heltberg's private crammer. He had arrived in the capital at a time of considerable social and political turbulence. Much of this was due to the activities of Marcus Thrane, the first socialist in modern Norway. One of Thrane's keenest followers was Theodor Abildgaard, a twenty-four-year-old law student from Arendal who lived downstairs from Ibsen at Mor Sæther's. Through Abildgaard, Ibsen became briefly and peripherally involved in this turbulence. Thrane's main call was for universal male suffrage. His larger aim was the abolition of poverty, and to this end he started the first Workers' Union in the country, along with a newspaper to support the new movement which, by the end of 1850, had 6,000 subscribers and many more readers. His success was all the more remarkable for the fact that Norway was at the time a largely agrarian society, without the urban, industrial work-force that communist theory presumed necessary for the establishment of socialism. He was unable to win the support of young intellectuals, however: of the ninety-six delegates at the first national congress held on 31 July 1850, only three were teachers and only one – Abildgaard – a student.

At his crammer Ibsen also met the Telemark poet and writer A. O. Vinje, at thirty-two a very mature student, and it was probably through Abildgaard that he met Paul Botten Hansen, twenty-six years old, a second-year student at the university, handsome, witty, apolitical. Along with Schulerud these were to be his closest and most influential friends over the next eighteen months. It was probably Abildgaard who persuaded Ibsen to attend a political meeting, for the first and only time in his life, at Klingenberg on 29 May 1850, to protest against the expulsion from Norway of a Danish revolutionary writer and newspaper editor named Harro Paul Harring. Harring's anti-monarchist play *American Testament*, liberally spiced with blasphemies, was the direct cause of his expulsion. At the meeting a resolution was passed deploring the government's decision. Ibsen was among the signatories, along with Vinje, the dramatist Bjørnstjerne Bjørnson, and A. B. Stabell, editor of *Morgenbladet*, the leading national newspaper. After a collection for Harro the crowd followed him down to the quayside and cheered him on board the *Nordkap* which was to take him out of the country.

But politics were no more than a diversion for Ibsen. His sights were still set on the *examen artium* in August. Given the lack of privacy and time at Grimstad and his own literary activities this was always going to be a struggle, and when the examination results came they were poor. On a scale where 1 represents the highest grade and 6 the lowest he managed a 2 in German, a 3 in Norwegian style, Latin translation, French, religion, history, geography and geometry. He was marked 4 in Latin style, 5 in Latin oral and 6, or 'Failed', in Greek and arithmetic. The only real surprise must be the unexceptional showing for style in his native language.

Though he now had the right to the title 'student', Ibsen did not qualify to matriculate at the university, and would have no chance of doing so unless he were prepared to resit his two failures in Greek and arithmetic. This he was not, for the very good reason that his career as a writer was already so well advanced by August 1850 that the point of a university education as the key to some orthodox career, in medicine or elsewhere, might have faded. Though *Catiline* had found neither theatre producer nor commercial publisher it had nevertheless been published, and noticed. The publication of a play was in itself an event in the tiny world of mid-nineteenth century Kristiania. Reading, unless it were religious, was not a widespread pastime. Of the less than 200 books published annually at this time the great majority were theological works. *Literature* meant foreign writing, European writing – Oehlenschläger, Ingemann, Blicher, Heiberg, Tegnér, Bellmann, Heine, Dumas, Sue, George Sand, Walter Scott, Dickens, Captain Marryat. *Technical literature* meant German writing. There had been a permanent theatre in the capital since 1827, but *drama* still meant Danish, German, or French drama. The remarkable fact is that *Catiline*, written during his spare time by a twenty-year-old apothecary's assistant from Grimstad, was the first new play by a Norwegian to be published in Norway since Henrik Wergeland's *The Venetians* in 1843. It received its first, welcoming review in *Samfundsbladet*, a handwritten student newspaper, some two weeks before Ibsen's arrival in the capital on 28 April, by Paul Botten Hansen, who could justly lay claim to be Ibsen's discoverer and who continued to be of great assistance to him all during the early years of his careeer.

Catiline was reviewed again on 16 May in the *Christiania Posten*, where the reviewer found that, in spite of its manifest failings, it 'reveals an unmistakable talent'. *Norwegian Periodical for Science and Literature*, the leading periodical of the time, was less kind, but its sarcasms were mitigated in a rider added by M.J. Monrad, professor of philosophy at the university, who stressed the importance of the presence of an *idea* (we would say an 'ideal') in the play.

And by the time this review was published, Ibsen had already written his second play, *The Warrior's Barrow* (*Kjæmpehøien*), a revision of *The Normans* that he worked on during his last days in Grimstad, while waiting for news of the fate of *Catiline*. Short and sketchy, its cast of Vikings was nevertheless more likely to appeal to the emerging public taste for national romantic works than *Catiline*'s remote Romans, and it was accepted for production within days of being submitted to the Christiania theatre. Ibsen was present at the première of his first stage play on 26 September 1850 and found it an agonising experience. 'It was dreadful,' he said later. 'I hid away in the darkest corner of the theatre.' His fee was a mere fifteen speciedaler,* and the play was performed only twice more that season.

* About £230.

The plot is a slight affair involving love and revenge, crudely dependent for its outcome on a central character – Bernhard – who perversely insists on hiding his real identity from the others. *The Warrior's Barrow*'s real interest lies in the fact that in it Ibsen discovered the *brytningstid* (struggle-time) of the tenth century as a crucible in which to examine the moral conflict between the Christian demand to forgive and the Viking imperative to seek revenge. Christianity wins a fairly easy victory. But from this rude little shack of a play, and invoking the same basic moral problem, Ibsen would eventually go on, by way of *The Vikings at Helgeland*, to create the palatial *Emperor and Galilean* in 1873.

Ibsen and Schulerud had moved from Vika by this time, and were living in a small apartment in Møllergata, apparently on Schulerud's monthly allowance. For a while they employed a somewhat unreliable old man as a servant, but when hard times came they had to manage by themselves. Abildgaard and Botten Hansen were regular visitors. The four would drink, play cards, talk, and from these discussions emerged the idea of launching a literary and satirical magazine, to be edited along the lines of the much-admired Danish *Corsaren*. Ibsen, as Brynjolf Bjarme, was to be its regular poet and theatre reviewer; Vinje would provide the political satire, and Botten Hansen, with ambitions to be a writer himself, the book reviews, original prose, drama, and articles about European literature.

The first issue appeared in January 1851. It had no title and became known by default as *Manden* (*The Man*), after the lanky figure who featured in its political cartoons. It was never much of a success, and in the nine months between January and the final issue in 28 September 1851 only picked up about a hundred regular readers. Ibsen was for the same period the elected editor of the student's magazine *Samfundsbladet* in succession to Botten Hansen, an office he neglected to such a degree that in the second quarter only one issue appeared, and in the third none at all. But as a drama critic he was entitled to a free pass to all performances at the Christiania theatre. His dozen or so reviews in *Manden*, some of them quite lengthy, involve discussions of long forgotten plays; but they provide interesting insight into his developing ideas about the nature and purpose of drama.

Though honing his taste for sarcasm and irony in the company of Vinje and Botten Hansen he did not see the reviewer as the enemy of the writer, and unless the writing and performance were beneath contempt he tried always to be constructive in his criticism. Later, when his own plays began attracting attention, he made the same demands of his own critics.

Over the months his regular exposure to the highest standards of theatre writing and acting available in Norway led him to question the quality of these: 'something new is needed; ... we produce nothing ourselves, neither do the Danes. Scribe is finished: what is left?'[2] But in spite of such insights, he was still too much in thrall to the prevailing theatrical conventions to provide this new direction himself. Theatres were still primitive places, and acting styles reflected this. Serious drama still meant submission to a set of rules from Corneille, Racine and the French classicists, filtered through Goethe and Schiller at the Weimar theatre. Stage directions rarely demanded more than one set, with no more than a table and a couple of chairs to represent the 'salon' or 'palais'. Actors, usually overdressed to compensate for the primitive setting, stood as close to the front of the stage as possible, and declaimed their lines facing the audience.Good diction was highly prized as an end in itself and often rewarded with prolonged applause. Tragedians were taught to move with a serpentine grace. The actors often kept to the extremities of the stage, the one on the right gesticulating always with his left arm and vice versa, a convention designed to avoid their faces falling into shadow or the need for them to turn their backs on the public. Actors even practised fencing left-handed to avoid appearing in profile. Displays of emotion were likewise subject to convention. 'Worry' was played with the right hand pressed to the forehead. A handkerchief held to the eye signified tears. Deep thought was enacted with the left foot forward and the body tilted backward to take the weight on the right leg. There was an immense distance between such institutionalised falsities and the credible impersonation of everyday reality on stage. Vaudevilles, light entertainments with simple plots and plenty of singing, provided relief from these pressures, but they were hardly demanding and had little to attract the serious young dramatist.* Yet the discipline of analysis benefited Ibsen greatly, and by the time of his last reviews for the magazine he was confident enough to produce a programmatic

* Vaudeville may be compared to the English ballad-opera, of which John Gay's *Beggar's Opera* is the most well-known example.

declaration that pointed not only to the plays of his own immediate future, but beyond them to the greatest creative period of his life:

> Our national dramatic literature is no more advanced now than it was before the performance of *Huldrens Hjem.*'* And it always will be so, as long as writers fail to distinguish between the challenges of reality and of art, as long as they lack the taste to smooth off the raw edges of reality before reproducing it in the framework of drama. And then too they will realise that the cause of the national in art is not promoted by narrowly reproducing scenes from everyday life; they will realise that the truly nationalist writer is the one who understands how to provide his work with that basic keynote that sounds to us from mountain and valley, from hillside and coast, but above all from within our own selves.[3]

It is as though, somewhere high in the mountains, Brand and Peer Gynt hear their names being called.

Ibsen continued to write poetry while in Kristiania. In the beginning this was in the same vein as the verse he had produced in Grimstad, naïvely stirring paeans to nationalism and pan-Scandinavianism alternating with romantic poems about love, loneliness and nature. Clara Ebbell, the object of his infatuation in Grimstad, visited Kristiania in 1850, and once she was safely back home again in Grimstad Ibsen sent her copies of six new poems. Though none could be described as love poems, he accompanied them with a hollow-eyed note apologising if anything he might have said had been misunderstood by her, indeed apologising for writing to her at all.

Of course, life in the city, and regular contact with scoffers and practitioners of irony like Botten Hansen and Vinje, introduced a new note into his poetry; but even at his most wilfully cynical Ibsen never really killed off the romantic in himself, and it would return to reassert itself in the plays of his old age, in Borkman's descents into melodrama with Ella Rentheim, in Professor Rubek's uneasy reminiscing about past happiness with Irene.

The best of the poems sent to Clara was untouched by either romanticism or self-irony. '*Bjergmanden*' ('The Miner', literally 'mountain man'), was a powerful poetic realisation of Ibsen's unglamorous psychological destiny that developed the nightmare image of being buried alive first used in *Catiline*. Here the buried man

* A nationalist play with songs by P. A. Jensen.

triumphs over his living death by continuing to function inside his tomb, crawling about inside it and mining its hidden riches:

> Rock, break with the crack
> of my hammer blows;
> I must forge my way down
> toward a goal I scarcely comprehend.
>
> Deep in the mountain's silent night
> its treasures twinkle,
> Diamond and jewel
> between the light veins of gold.
>
> Here in the deep is peace,
> the peace of eternal night.
> Soon in the chamber of earth's heart
> sounds the beating of my hammer.

Most of Ibsen's poems during this period in Kristiania were printed in *Manden*, most using the pseudonym Brynjolf Bjarme although some appeared under his own name. Over the next fifteen years, as he became a good poet, he put some of his most personal thoughts about himself into his poetry, and his abandonment of the form as a vehicle for serious expression after the publication of *Digte* (*Poems*) in 1871 reflects his recognition of just how much of himself he had revealed in them. It was in the five-year period that concluded with the publication of *Poems*, after the successes with *Brand* and *Peer Gynt*, that he carried through the transformation of himself into the impenetrable Henrik Ibsen of a thousand dour cabinet portraits, black-hatted and grim-lipped, who then, in the words of his biographer Gerhard Gran, disappeared into his work-room and locked the door behind him. Yet he remained aware that the poems were still 'out there' to betray him. Many years later, at a dinner party in the 1890s, he found himself arguing with a guest over how much of himself he had revealed in his writing. He stead-fastly maintained that the answer was nothing at all; but when his opponent suddenly raised the spectre of the poems Ibsen surren-dered, smiling slightly and murmuring that those 'little devils' should never have been published.

At about the same time as *Manden* was launched, Theodor Abildgaard was appointed editor of *Arbeider-Foreningernes Blad* (*The Worker's Post*), the paper started by Marcus Thrane. Abildgaard had by this time become a leading figure on the right-wing of Thrane's movement. His aim was to turn the workers' movement into a support organisation for the left wing of the parliamentary opposition, with the ultimate goal of introducing parliamentary government based on a majority in the *Storting*. A second right-wing faction, more class-conscious than Abildgaard's, advocated a form of ur-communism, with workers running their own shipyards, administering their own help funds and assuming responsibility for their own education. There was a centre, following Thrane in making tactical use of the authorities' fear of violent revolution by presenting themselves as responsible political beings who were doing what they could to hold the others in check. Abildgaard's rise to power within the movement was a middle-class radical coup, and the reason he was given the job of editing the paper was because he was the only person, besides Thrane himself, who was sufficiently literate to do so.

In discussing this brief period of Ibsen's life, formative of his attitude towards the notions of revolution and political parties, Henrik Jæger maintains that Abildgaard initiated both Ibsen and Schulerud into the movement's idealistic and practical ambitions, but that Ibsen found these plans 'altogether too fantastic, too childish, the whole thing so unclear, the whole setup too immature and silly for him to give himself wholeheartedly to it'. Jæger had the benefit of talking to Ibsen himself in the later stages of writing his biography, so his analysis here has a special authority. Ibsen did contribute unsigned articles to *Arbeider-Foreningernes Blad*, for which he probably got paid, but by his own account these were 'things of no importance'. The paper also reprinted articles from *Manden*. Ibsen's most definite gesture of support for the movement may have been to assist Abildgaard at the workers' own Sunday school, seven to ten a.m. and no wages.

In July the offices of the *Arbeider-Foreningernes Blad* were raided. Thrane, Abildgaard and four other leaders of the movement were arrested and for a time Ibsen was worried that some of his own articles might have been seized for use against him. A month later serious disturbances broke out at Hønefoss, north of Kristiania, as the authorities intensified their campaign to break up Thrane's movement. On two occasions mobs of working men prevented the arrest of Thraneite leaders, and the military was sent in. Ibsen reported on the goings-on for *Manden*'s readers, adopting an ironic tone that made it clear he was not associating himself with the rebels.

At the trials of the leaders the government tried to break the movement. Thrane was sentence to seven years, Abildgaard to four, having already spent four years in custody. Ibsen was not wholly indifferent to the fate of Abildgaard, neither was he greatly concerned. Twice, during the term of his imprisonment, he enquired about him in letters to Botten Hansen. But there wasn't much radical indignation at the price his idealistic friend had to pay for his idealism. If he ever felt such indignation his nature would be to swallow it. Jail and violent confrontation with authority were beyond the terms of his contract with socialism.

The lessons of his involvement with *Manden* and *Arbeider-Foreningernes Blad* and the workers' movement generally defined once and for all his attitude towards social change. It should be a matter of fine tuning and slight alteration rather than the kicking down of doors. He remained unchanging in this, and some thirty years later, just three years after the controversy over the morality of *Ghosts*, Ibsen would remain deafeningly silent as two younger writers, Hans Jæger and Christian Krohg, were given jail sentences for publishing 'immoral literature', the aims of which – increased personal freedom, greater sexual equality for women – were much the same as his own literary aims.

Ibsen had in any case a great deal to occupy his mind beside politics during these months in Kristiania, suffering further humiliating repercussions of his affair with Else Sophie Birkedalen. He was late paying her the two speciedaler for July 1850, and just before he was due to sit his matriculation exam received an official letter of warning from the Kristiania Justice of the Peace responsible for seeing that fathers met such obligations. He responded, but was again very late in paying the fourth quarter. The problems continued into 1851, with the payment for 9 January not being sent until early in May. The bailiffs, in the meantime, had been to his apartment in Møllergaten but found nothing there worth confiscating to meet the outstanding debt.

The authorities had just one option, and they took it: by a resolution of 17 June, taking account of the fact that Ibsen was 'without means, not in the military, has no legitimate children to support, and is about twenty-five years old and in good health',[4] he was sentenced to forced labour at Akershus Prison until the outstanding debt was paid. The commander of the watch at the prison was ordered to arrest him and escort him to jail. Two-thirds of the money earned there would be deducted for board and lodging, so that in all he would have to work for about thirty-four days before the two speciedaler were earned.

The law was handled with considerable flexibility, however, with periods of grace allowed to enable the debtor to earn the necessary money on his own initiative, and Ibsen seems to have benefited by this arrangement. But the respite was only temporary. He was simply unable to raise the money, and when another investigation by the bailiffs revealed nothing worth seizing in his rooms, a second resolution was passed on 20 August ordering his attendance at Akershus Prison. This time the sum to be earned was four speciedaler, requiring something like sixty-eight days' work.

Fortunately for Ibsen, before any of this nightmare could come true, his literary talent came to his rescue. In September the violinist Ole Bull arrived in the capital to raise money for a new theatre he had opened the previous year in Bergen, the second city of Norway. The original and important aspect of Bull's venture was that it would be the country's first wholly Norwegian theatre, with Norwegian directors and a company of Norwegian actors performing plays in their native language. This was a first assault on the continuing cultural hegemony of the Danish language in Norway, still, despite the transfer of colonial power from Denmark to Sweden at the end of the Napoleonic wars, the high-status written language of the country, and with the passage of time bearing an ever-diminishing resemblance to the language spoken by the people. This deliberate attempt to assert the prestige of Norwegian against Danish was an important aspect of the creation of a national identity which took place from about this time onwards, a process which would culminate in the creation of an independant Norwegian nation in 1905.

Ibsen, with something of the same slight mixture of attraction and contempt with which he regarded the workers' struggle, was initially disposed to find the call for Norwegian voices on stage a touch ridiculous. In one article from around this time he referred to the growing opposition to Danish actors on the Norwegian stage as 'a piece of trendiness'. But he allowed himself to be swept up in the popular enthusiasm for Bull's idea, and the refusal of the *Storting* to offer financial help to his venture, the cost of which Bull had so far borne entirely from his own pocket, galvanised the students. After a lively debate in the union on the matter they resolved to hold an 'Evening of Musical Entertainment' to raise funds for the new theatre, to take place on 15 October in the Freemasons' Great Hall in Bank Pladsen. Ole Bull was to play, three choirs would sing, and there would be an appearance by the opera singer Emma Dahl.

The event attracted a huge crowd, and hundreds had to be turned away at the door. Ibsen had written a prologue to get proceedings under way. Never happy on a stage himself, he left the reading of the verses to Laura Svendsen, the actress who the year before had played Blanca in *The Warrior's Barrow* at the Christiania theatre. Stirring, patriotic and personal at the same time, the prologue judged the occasion perfectly. In the closing lines Ibsen anthropo-morphised the theatre as the homeless, wandering art; but he also acclaimed it as the most popular of the arts, the highest of the arts:

> For life is there most truly interpreted
> sharp and clearly focused to our gaze.

At the benefit evening 300 speciedaler were raised, a sum not far off the annual figure of 500 that Bull had been seeking from the *Storting*. As well as the prologue Ibsen had written a song, 'The Power of Art', for which Bull provided the music. 'The Power of Art' was just the sort of simple, stirring, nationalist statement Ibsen knew would impress Bull, and along with the prologue and the two plays he had already written it earned him the offer of a job as dramatist-in-residence at the new theatre. On 16 October, his ticket paid for and his debts presumably settled by an advance from his new employer, he left Kristiania on the *Gyller* to take up his duties in Bergen.

This was real recognition for an inexperienced playwright still several months short of his twenty-fourth birthday. And yet along with the recognition there came a strengthening of that legacy of humiliation from the affair with Else Sophie Birkedalen and the subsequent role of the state in the matter. His brush with prison in the summer of 1851 can only further have socialised his morality, binding him yet closer to society in a relationship that mixed in equal parts fear, respect, and perhaps even hatred.

4

Writer in Residence
St John's Night · Lady Inger of Østråt · The Feast at Solhaug · Olaf Liljekrans

It was the job that brought Ibsen to Bergen in the winter of 1851; but he had family roots in the town. His earliest traceable ancestor was one Simen Ibsen-Holst, a sea-captain born there in the 1570s. He moved to Stege in Denmark, married and raised a family. His son Rasmus, also a sea-captain, had three sons who returned to Bergen when they grew up. One married Birgitte Holtermann, daughter of a local merchant, in 1721, and it was through her father that the name Henrik entered the family. Their son Henrich, Ibsen's great-grandfather, followed in the family tradition and became a sea-captain. He died in 1765, leaving a widow, Wenche Dishington, and small son, Henrich. She married a priest named Jacob von der Lippe, and it was with his posting to a small parish near Skien that the family became established in the south of the country. Henrich went to sea like his forefathers, until the *Caritas*, the ship he commanded, foundered with all hands off the Grimstad coast in late 1797. One of his two surviving sons was Knud Ibsen, Henrik Ibsen's father. It is a relatively simple matter to keep track of one's roots in a small society like Norway, and the Student Ibsen whose arrival was announced in the Arrivals and Departures column of the *Bergens Blade* (*Bergen Post*) for 26 October 1851 was aware of his connections with the town.

Until overtaken by Kristiania in the 1830s, Bergen had been the largest town in Norway. It was the ancient capital of the country, home of kings in that golden age to which young writers like Ibsen and Bjørnson, and artists like Tidemand and Gude, so insistently turned in their poetry and painting. In virtue of its former status as a Hanseatic port, and its steamship links with Hamburg, it was as cosmopolitan in its atmosphere and outlook as the capital, and there was a healthy sense of competition between the two. By 1850 it had

44

some 25,000 inhabitants and was recovering from a recent outbreak of cholera which had claimed 700 lives. Running water had been laid on, gas lighting had arrived, and there were newly opened banks, insurance offices and steamship companies as well as a telegraph office. But in private houses the atmosphere was still Rembrandtian. For indoor lighting the poor made do with a candle on the table; a little higher up the social scale came those who could afford cod-liver-oil lamps; only in the houses of the wealthy was it common to use several lamps on an everyday basis. This was still some time before the advent of the animal-fat lamp with glass funnel, and the first consignment of paraffin would not reach the country until 1862.

Culturally speaking the town had little to offer before Ole Bull's theatre initiative. The travelling Danish theatre troupes were regular visitors, but their quality was variable, and the frequent use of German actors fleeing an overstocked market at home and speaking an impenetrable form of heavily accented Danish was a discouragement to potential theatre-goers. Theodor Mügge, a German who visited Bergen in 1844, wrote that any form of public entertainment was unknown there – there were no concerts, no bandstand performances, no café life. He did attend one event, however, a concert by Ole Bull given in the theatre building, which he described as large but ugly, filled with an Egyptian darkness and an overpowering stench of fish. 'One must be well used to it if one is to tolerate it,' he wrote, attempting to account for the fact that most of the audience were women. Bull's performance was saluted by hefty stamping on the floorboards which raised up great clouds of dust.[1]

Ibsen arrived on 4 October 1851. Four weeks later he signed a contract in which he undertook to 'assist the theatre as dramatist'. He also agreed to attend all committee meetings at which decisions on the repertoire would be taken. 'Assisting the theatre' involved mainly producing prologues and occasional poems for performance; as part of the theatre's committment to foster the work of a living young native dramatist there was also an informal agreement that he would try to provide an original play each year, to be performed on 2 January, the anniversary of the founding of the theatre in 1849. There was a small but honourable tradition of Norwegian drama from the eighteenth century represented by Ludvig Holberg, Johan Hermann Wessel and Nordahl Brun; but apart from the efforts of Henrik Wergeland, who was essentially a poet, the recent

45

past offered little to build on beyond the populist efforts of writers like Riis and Henrik Bjerregaard. Bjørnson, later to become Ibsen's great rival, was still a student and had published nothing. Of Ibsen's exact Norwegian contemporaries only Andreas Munch showed signs of being able to write serious and successful drama.

It was a considerable challenge for such an inexperienced young man. Shortly after his arrival he met one of the company's actresses, Marie Midling, in the street one day. She accosted him cheerfully and wished him the best of luck in his efforts to teach them all the art of theatre, implying that it would not be an easy task. Ibsen replied that he heartily agreed with her, admitting that he was himself just a learner but urging her not to tell the others – 'maybe they won't notice'.

But everyone involved in the new venture, from the administration downwards, was inexperienced, and early in the new year, in recognition of the fact that this lack of experience was a genuine hindrance to Ibsen's artistic development, the committee awarded him a grant of 200 speciedaler to be spent on an educational trip to Denmark and Germany. His brief was explicit:

> to visit over a period of three months certain foreign theatres, to wit those in Copenhagen, Berlin, Dresden and Hamburg, for the purpose of acquiring the knowledge and experience that will enable him to carry out his job at the theatre as director, hereunder including the instruction of the company as well as everything connected with scenery, stage equipment, costumes etcetera.[2]

As he sailed from Bergen on 15 April 1852 his sense of anticipation must have been high at the prospect of breathing the intellectual and artistic air of Copenhagen. For the last half-century 'the Paris of the north' had been the centre of the Danes' own cultural golden age, whose outstanding figures such as Adam Oehlenschläger, the educational philosopher N. F. S. Grundtvig, B. S. Ingemann, Carsten Hauch and S. S. Blücher had exerted such an influence on Ibsen's own generation. An equally important contributor to this golden age was the dramatist, historian, philologist and astronomer Johan Ludvig Heiberg, who from about 1825 onwards gradually supplanted Oehlenschläger as the arbiter of taste and new ideas in Copenhagen. Heiberg was responsible, in the face of considerable aesthetic opposition, for introducing the vaudeville into Denmark and Norway, which went on to achieve great popular success. A cool, sharply critical and ironic essayist with a gift for self-publicity, he never managed to replace the more romantic Oehlenschläger in the public's affection, though his intellectual siredom was probably greater. Now little known and unperformed outside his native country, it was Heiberg who gave initial encouragement to the two other Danish writers who went on to achieve world stature, Søren Kierkegaard and Hans Christian Andersen.

Ibsen travelled with a husband and wife from the Bergen troupe, Johannes and Louise Brun, both just twenty years old. Ibsen had just turned twenty-four and was in charge of the party. In keeping with his newly acquired status as artistic director he now affected a flamboyant style of dress that seems sharply at odds with his shy personality. Someone who knew him in Bergen told the Danish novelist Herman Bang: 'He was elegant, almost pedantically so in his dress. He wore a shirt with a frilled front and large, frilly ruffles around his wrists. When walking he carried a little cane.'[3] Ibsen took a room not far from the Royal theatre, where J. L. Heiberg was the director, and where much of his studying was to be done. Heiberg was now sixty and enjoying great prestige both in his own right and as the husband of Johane Louise Heiberg, the most famous Danish actress of her time. He had ceased to write plays and already begun down the road of reaction, distrustful of new writing that did not resemble old writing. But Ibsen and company were warmly received at one of his bi-weekly audiences at the theatre office and issued with free passes to the theatre, but discouraged from attending rehearsals; it was late in the season, Heiberg explained, and little new or interesting was in preparation. The Bruns attended dancing classes run by a local solo dancer named Hoppe, and Ibsen studied theatre.

There was some unease on the part of the Norwegians about the goal of their mission, being so very openly the overthrow of the yolk of Danish culture in their own country; but so far from finding them protective of their own interests, Ibsen found the Danes only too willing to help. Indeed, they expressed surprise that such a move towards cultural independence had not been made long before. Thomas Overskou, a long-time director at the Royal theatre, showed Ibsen round the theatre and demonstrated to him the workings of the backstage and understage machinery for shifting scenery and lowering curtains. Overskou's brief reference to the occasion in a letter to his daughter referred to Ibsen as 'a small, dour Norwegian with alert eyes'.

Of his social life during this period Ibsen relates nothing. There are no wide-eyed letters of enthusiasm to Botten Hansen or Vinje on the thrills and discoveries of wandering in a big city, only dutiful reports back to the committee in Bergen, all of them written in the impersonal business style he adopted, with few but important exceptions, for all his correspondents. He had been sent to Copenhagen to learn about plays and playwriting and that is exactly what he did, noting along the way the performances of great actors like Phister, N. P. Nielsen, and Michael Wiehe, as well as appearances by Fru Heiberg so memorable that he recalled them with rare enthusiasm in a tributary poem some twenty years later.

Among the works performed during the six weeks of his stay in Copenhagen were *King Lear, Romeo and Juliet, A Midsummer Night's Dream* and *Hamlet*, the latter in a performance by Frederik Høedt which was noted by contemporaries for a realism which effected a break with the 'academic-idealistic' style favoured by Heiberg, an interesting item in the light of Ibsen's preoccupation with the portrayal of strong, thinking, self-doubting characters on stage. The scenic architecture used in a performance of *Kvindens Vaaben* (*A Woman's Weapon*) by Scribe, with the same Høedt as the comic lover Grignon, attracted his notice, and he saw top-class performances of plays by masters like Holberg, Oehlenschläger and Heiberg, as well as works by successful contemporaries such as Henrik Hertz, whose *King René's Daughter* had a long stage life in both Scandinavia and London, and J. C. Hostrup, whose best plays, mainly in a genre called 'student comedies', are still performed in Denmark.

While Ibsen was in Copenhagen Hostrup's musical *Mester og Lærling* (*Master and Pupil*) had its première at the Casino in Amaliegade, the second of the three main theatres in the capital (the third was the Royal Court). This play attracted much discussion at the time, being an unfamiliar mixture of romance and realism that used supernatural beings (*Ellefolket*) to set its plot in motion. Ibsen seems to have been especially attracted to it, and visited Hostrup at his house in Frederiksberg. Hostrup later recalled his 'quiet, withdrawn personality'. Deeply anxious to make a success of his new career Ibsen must have already been working in his spare time on the first of the original plays he hoped to provide for the Norwegian theatre, *Sancthansnatten* (*St John's Night*), and the Elves and Goblins who get the action under way in this play owe something to Hostrup.

Other notable events of the Copenhagen trip included a meeting with Hans Christian Andersen, who encouraged him to try to pay a visit to Vienna while he was in Dresden, to catch performances at the Burg theatre; an evening meal with the Heibergs, at which the sophisticated Heiberg spared his young guests literary talk and instead spoke to them of his favourite dishes; and a performance of Christian Richardt's vaudeville *Deklaration*, in aid of a new students' union building, graced by the presence of the popular King Frederik VII. Ibsen and the Bruns were invited too, and after the play heard the king address the audience. Seeing in the flesh a royal patron of the arts was just another part of the important complex of impressions Ibsen was picking up in his stealthy, observant way during this visit. It must have meant something to him too, to read in Copenhagen newspapers the numerous articles and letters calling for a statue of Oehlenschläger, his first great literary hero and the subject of one of his published poems. In Heiberg and H. C. Andersen he had met living famous men, an encouraging reminder to the aspirant that the famous, too, are only flesh and blood. From such indices Ibsen will have seen for himself the status and impact on a society it was possible for a successful artist to achieve, and the experiences can only have strengthened his commitment to continue along the road on which he had started out.

The season at the Royal theatre ended in May, and as previously arranged the Bruns returned to Bergen, taking with them copies of the plays Ibsen had bought to extend the repertoire. These included Sheridan's *The Rivals*, and works by Hertz and Scribe. The committee in Bergen had already worked out the packages of entertainment most likely to please their audiences: either a three-act play followed by a vaudeville; or a one-act light entertainment followed by a musical. With these requirements in mind Ibsen had also invested in a number of tried and proven light entertainments by Thomas Overskou, who had not forgotten to promote his own interests while showing Ibsen the workings of the backstage machinery at the Royal theatre.

Ibsen travelled on alone to Dresden, leaving Copenhagen on Sunday 6 June and arriving on the following Wednesday. Dresden was the home of the Norwegian painter J. C. Dahl, and some sort of informal arrangement had been made for Dahl to act as his guide and contact during his stay. Dahl, born in Bergen, was now an elderly man, a famous artist who counted the writer Ludvig Tieck and the painter Kaspar David Friedrich among his friends. He was an enthusiast for the values and aspirations of Norwegian national romanticism, and the first artist to draw attention to the beauties of Norwegian stave church architecture and foster the idea that Norway should be proud of it.

No doubt he would have been in sympathy with Ibsen's mission to assist in the creation of a national theatre in Bergen, but unfortunately for Ibsen, Dahl was away when he arrived, and Ibsen spent his first week in Dresden alone. When Dahl did return from his stay in the country he arranged for Ibsen to be shown round backstage at the Hofteatret, and was probably instrumental in getting a notice into the local paper announcing Student Ibsen's presence and purpose in the city. But he found the young visitor's extreme shyness a bore. He complained pointedly about the number of Scandinavian visitors who turned up on his doorstep expecting to be received, and treated Ibsen to coffee only once, in his studio, not at his home. Nor did his influence extend to getting Ibsen a free pass to performances at the Hofteatret, and Ibsen had to pay for any tickets out of his own pocket.

Short of money, with only a schoolboy's grasp of the language, and knowing no one, Ibsen probably spent most of his time alone, wandering the streets, visiting the castle, the cathedral and the city's other architectural wonders, thinking, reading, visiting the theatre and working on his new play. Not this, however, but the cycle of poems *I Billedgalleriet* (*In the Picture Gallery*) turned out to be the great literary fruit of his presence in Dresden. This was probably conceived during his wanderings in *Der Zwinger*, the city's famous complex of pavilions and galleries, though it was not written until later, and not published until 1859, with a note from Ibsen describing it as spiritual history, a work about his recent past. This accompanying note contained an early formulation of an idea Ibsen expressed many times, that his writing was the result not of something *opplevd* (experienced) but of something *gennomlevd* (lived through), in modern parlance, that his writing was therapeutic. *In the Picture Gallery* is a remarkable autobiographical document, another stage in the unfolding history of Ibsen's religious doubt first expressed in 'Doubt and Hope'. The self-doubt expressed in the poem about his own writing probably reflects the mood of the years closer to publication in 1859 than Dresden in 1852; but the references to an almost religious experience in his confrontation with the great art of the past undoubtedly refer to Dresden. The poem is a passionate rejection of the words of the black demon he conjures in the opening lines:

> Can't you see yourself, he whispers,
> how futile your whole journey is,
> you who have lost faith in God and the world?

Not in the churches but here in the art gallery, before the Rafaels, the Correggios and Murillos, is where he senses the presence of a God.

> Yes, here I feel God in me;
> I am spellbound, intoxicated
> by unfolding beauty.

> Clear and plastic I see the God-thought;
> and now the swelling of my soul,
> the crushing of the demon within me!

Other verses articulate the loss of faith, but the substance of the discovery remains unaltered: not only can art function as a substitute for orthodox religious faith, it may even prove stronger, and have the power to reverse the apparently irreversible effects of the Fall:

> My childhood Eden was closed and locked,
> I stood outside the gates;
> On the wall hung my confirmation suit–
> well, so that was the cherub with the sword.

> Cast out from my own world
> and an alien world before me;
> hollow and dead it seemed,
> and I longed to return home.

Back in Bergen Ibsen was offered a new contract with the theatre that set out in greater detail his obligations as director. The detailed direction of actors by non-participants was in itself a fairly new idea at this time. Bergen followed a system established in Denmark in which the work was split in two. The senior director was a man called Herman Laading, a native of the city fifteen years older than Ibsen. He was responsible for directing the actors, analysing the characters they played and providing them with essential historical background for their roles. Ibsen, whose salary was increased from 240 to 300 speciedaler by this second agreement, was his assistant, officially described as *Sceneinstruktøren* (the stage director), meaning that he was responsible for the entrances and exits, how the cast conducted themselves while on stage, where and how to stand, when to group, what to do with their hands while speaking, while listening. Poor lighting facilities, poor acoustics, primitive stage mechanics and limited rehearsal time meant actors routinely unfamiliar with their parts and so obliged to remain within hearing distance of the prompter's box at the front of the stage. These factors had saddled performances with a set of stylised rules that made such a post necessary. The unavoidable amateurishness of Norwegian theatre, during the years of its infancy in the 1850s and for many years to come, was to be one of Ibsen's greatest frustrations, increasing in proportion as his art became more sophisticated, more intimate and more concerned with the validity of the illusion. As he came to see it, one of his main tasks over the five years of his contract in Bergen was the professionalising of the theatre and the cultivation among the company of his own idea that acting, writing and directing were vocations to be approached with reverence, not jobs.

He approached his work methodically, keeping three separate notebooks, one to cover casting, one for props and one for the scenery. They were painstakingly detailed documents, none more so than that covering his first assignment as director for *Don Cæsar de Bazan*, a 'historical entertainment' in five acts by Dumanoir and D'Ennery, best remembered now as the basis for Vincent Wallace's opera *Maritana*. Here he noted down the comings and goings of the characters, dotting diagrams of their routes to and from the wings to form the conventional, audience-facing arc at the front, with a precision Samuel Beckett would not have improved upon. On the opposite page he provided literal descriptions of the moves.

Laading's was the ultimate authority, however, and despite an obscure clash which apparently led Ibsen to challenge Laading to a duel which, one can only imagine, Laading declined, they were well-teamed in their difference. Laading was the more natural director, warm, sympathetic and outgoing. Ibsen sat off on his own, remote, gruff, unsympathetic. The reminiscences of actors, actresses, committee members and functionaries who recall him from the Bergen days strike similar notes: Ibsen was 'quiet, didn't speak much'; his eyes had a 'a half-veiled gaze that seldom lit up, and then only in flashes'; he was 'extremely reserved and timid', and his footfalls 'quiet, almost soundless'. According to Peter Blytt, the chairman of the committee, there was an aura of helplessness about him, and he would become acutely embarrassed whenever it was necessary for him to step in and advise or correct a performer. If it were a woman his embarrassment would be all the greater. References to his pathological shyness abound, and to the way he would cringe back into himself whenever a moment's spontaneity had tricked him into saying something possibly revealing about himself. Summing up his reputation Blytt said that he was looked upon with 'a certain shy reverence', that he was 'respected, but not well-liked'.[4] The actress Lucie Wolf found him 'a silent, remarkably shy man, who kept himself apart from the rest of us, and whose nature absolutely did not inspire one to approach him in any spirit of intimacy'.[5] He was polite, but in a manner that led her to state her business and leave as quickly as possible.

The uniformity of these reminiscences tells its own story, of a young man crucified between shyness and arrogance, his great brown beard, dandified clothes, yellow gloves and cane giving off their tortuously double message: desperate to be looked at, terrified of being seen.

Ibsen wrote three original plays while employed by the Norwegian theatre, adapted two from earlier works and began work on a sixth, *Hærmændene på Helgeland* (*The Vikings at Helgeland*). Much has been made of the allegedly wretched fate of these plays, but their reception was merely unexceptional for the time.[6] Moreover throughout the six years of his residency Ibsen had the inestimable comfort of knowing that whatever he wrote would be performed.

The first, *St John's Night* (a Romantic Comedy in 3 Acts) had its premier, with specially painted scenery, on 2 January 1853.* Set in Telemark in the present, the plot is a conventional love story in which the young lovers Julian and Juliane eventually overcome all obstacles placed in their way. There is a mischievous troll in it, a magic potion, much dancing and singing, and the debt to *A Midsummer Night's Dream* is even more obvious than that to Hostrup. Less obvious is the influence of Holberg on the character of the

---

* Ibsen had originally begun it in collaboration with a student from Kristiania, Theodor Christian Bernhoft. But Bernhoft, a theology student, became caught up in a religious revivalist movement and dropped out.

would-be national romantic poet Julian Poulsen, whose pretensions to ethnic and primitive authenticity are lightly ridiculed throughout. A city man, part of the wave of enthusiasm for all things rural, he arrives from Kristiania wearing a sheath knive and affecting to speak *nynorsk*, the dialect of the peasants. But it soon emerges that he is even unaware of the well-known rural custom of celebrating midsummer night with a vigil round a bonfire. Out in this rugged, proud countryside, he tells his hosts, he has realised his heart's ambition. Here his wild, primitive self can be reborn. Someone interrupts to point out that they are merely sitting in a garden. Poulsen retorts that a little twist of the imagination is all that is required to fix that particular problem.

Poulsen has a story, and after drinking the magic potion he begins to tell it to Juliane. He describes his life's tragedy, how he came to Kristiania to study and there fell among aesthetes who corrupted him and led him astray from nationalism. A great conflict arose in him. He walked to Drammen to try to work it out. On the way he fell in love with the most nationalist creature imaginable. Who was she? asks Juliane. A milkmaid? No, says Poulsen, a troll. But on discovering her long tail he was filled with horror: 'Aesthetics and Nationalism fought in mortal combat within my breast; but I'll tell you straight out – this time discipline won over nature and I abandoned my love. What a price to pay – and yet it had to be.' After that he pursued nationalism with dedicated enthusiasm and adopted his habit of wearing a sheath knife and using phonetic spelling in his poetry.

Ibsen took a considerable risk with his audience in this play and it did not work out for him. In satirising Poulsen for his pompous insistence on knowing everything, for his peasant pretensions, for promoting an image of himself as an unpredictable, half-wild savage when he is so very plainly a harmless bookworm, he was making an early attempt to strike the collusive modernist bargain with them (allow my hero to have a striking personality and I will agree to destroy him); but Poulsen survived his creator's ridicule. His satire is too sharp, too true. Ibsen's personal journey from romanticism to self-irony had taken place too quickly for his audience to follow, and national romanticism was still too serious a subject for mockery. Not until *Peer Gynt*, fourteen years later, would a Norwegian public be self-confident enough to laugh at its own flirtation with the 'primitive'.

The first performance of *St John's Night* was sold out, but the second – and final – on 5 January was less well-attended. The reviewer in *Bergens Stiftstidende* praised the play's 'many fine touches', and compared it favourably with a play performed the previous year. But the overall judgement was that it was 'not a particularly successful piece of work'. Never performed now, it remains the closest thing to unadulterated self-portrait Ibsen produced during these early years, and the satirising of Poulsen's nationalism casts interesting light on Ibsen's own nationalist poetry and prose of the period, suggesting it was something he made professional use of, essentially a way of engaging his public in dialogue rather than an expression of deeply felt patriotism.

Ibsen's next offering was a rewritten version of his Kristiania play, *The Warrior's Barrow* (Verse Drama in 1 Act). Throughout the 1850s Ibsen continued to pursue his interest in comparing and contrasting the two ancient cultures he had recently become familiar with, Old Norse and Classical Antiquity, and in the spirit of the times these comparisons took the form of racial generalisations about Germanic and Romance peoples. To accommodate this interest the setting of *The Warrior's Barrow* was changed from Normandy to an island near Sicily, and the main male character's name from Bernhard to Roderick. An ancient temple ruin appears in the background, and Blanka meditates in a soliloquy on the obvious symbolic meaning of the ruin, that the glories of the southern people belong only to history; but her father has told her of another land in the far north, cold and vital, and it is of this land she dreams. The simple plot then runs its course, and once the confusions over identity have been cleared up Blanca and Gandalf set off for this Germanic northern dreamland of hers.

The Warrior's Barrow managed two performances. One reviewer felt the revision showed signs of the progress Ibsen had made since 1850, and though the public at large remained unimpressed Ibsen could console himself with an assurance in *Bergens Blade* that he was earning the respect of the town's *cognoscenti*, who had greeted *The Warrior's Barrow* with 'wholehearted approval'. The play was printed in the same newspaper's columns,[7] a unique tribute reflecting pride in the play's native origins and language rather than a sense of its right to a life in print as an outstanding piece of drama.

Ibsen followed this in 1855 with *Fru Inger til Østråt* (*Lady Inger of Østråt*) ('a historical drama in 5 acts'). Both previous plays had appeared under his own name, but for this one he carried out a curious deception. One day in the autumn of 1854 he approached Peter Blytt with the manuscript and asked Blytt for his opinion of it, telling him it was the work of a friend of his in Kristiania. Blytt read the play, was enthusiastic, and recommended it for immediate production.

As this was Ibsen's official 'annual offering' for the 2 January slot, Blytt soon guessed that Ibsen himself was the author, and an incident at rehearsals presently made this plain to the company at large. For productions of his own plays the usual system of working with two directors was abandoned to allow Ibsen full artistic control over his own work. On this occasion, however, the fiction was that this was not his own work and Laading was accordingly engaged in the detailed directing of the acting performances when, to general surprise, at a certain point in the proceedings Ibsen abandoned his customary silence, hurried to the stage, and taking the prompter's copy of the manuscript from his hands, gave a demonstration to Jakob Prom, the actor playing Nils Lykke, of how his speech should be read. The prompter noticed that though he held the script in his hands, Ibsen did not appear to consult it while giving the direction; and from the passion with which he read the lines – a description of Lady Inger's spiritual and aesthetic claustrophobia – it was obvious to everyone who the author was.

Lady Inger is set in Trondheim in 1528, at a time when Norway, Denmark and Sweden were joined together in a political union. Ibsen's historical aim was to describe Norway's last important gesture of independence before final submission to the colonial power of Denmark. Lady Inger feels herself called to lead Norway out of the union; but she has in the past given birth to an illegitimate son, and her concern for the boy's fate hinders her from acting decisively. Eventually she orders the death of a young pretender, unaware that it is, of course, her own son. The existence of this secret child is Ibsen's own invention, and though its dramatic function in the context of the play is obvious enough, it also invites speculation that Ibsen here was returning to his own secret, the nine-year-old boy in Grimstad. He had touched on this earlier, in Julian Poulsen's account of his meeting with the troll-woman, a reference that is also the prototype for Peer Gynt's involvement with the Green Clad Woman and the monstrous child she bears him. *St John's Night* also features a trivial financial intrigue involving 'papers' relating to the ownership of an estate called 'Birkedal', a name almost unnecessarily close to Else Sophie's family name Birkedalen.

Nineteenth-century Norway was a small world and in the Bergen theatre company there was an actor who was an exact contemporary of his from Grimstad. Another who 'pursued' Ibsen to Bergen was a man named Poul Stub, with whom he engaged in an acrimonious debate in the columns of the local newspaper on the quality of Stub's theatrical reviewing. Stub was one of the tutors to whom Ibsen had submitted matriculation essays in 1850 and the patronising title of his first polemic, 'Assessment of Ibsen's efforts to promote a Norwegian drama', indicated that Stub proposed to resume their relationship on its earlier footing. All things considered, Ibsen's concern for the correct expression of Lady Inger's claustrophobia suggests the speech in question had been written straight from the heart.

Lady Inger was received with encouraging words by a more sympathetic reviewer than Stub, who found that it 'contains bold and extremely interesting depictions of character which, in certain really quite well executed scenes, function very well together'[8] and that 'the dialogue is good, at certain points brilliant, and the work in general extremely promising'. After its première on 2 January 1855 it went on to become the first of Ibsen's plays to achieve extended theatrical life. Indeed, during the thirteen years of the existence of the Norwegian theatre in Bergen, only one serious historical drama achieved more performances. Yet it is a turgid play, and hard to follow without previous knowledge of the plot. Even in Norway, where it may count on a degree of historical interest, it has rarely been performed.

Despite some kind words from the critics Ibsen had still not had the 'hit' he needed for his self-esteem and the theatre needed to make its books balance. On the subject of success he would have been encouraged at his meeting with J. L. Heiberg in Copenhagen to find the great man so open about his commercial instincts, for Heiberg regarded writing as a profession like any other and made no secret of the fact that for him a literature without a public was an absurdity just as a shoemaker without customers was an absurdity. In his next play *Gildet på Solhaug* (*The Feast at Solhaug*), which had its première on 2 January 1856, Ibsen addressed himself properly to this challenge of acquiring an audience.

Like *Lady Inger* and all these early plays, *The Feast at Solhaug* turned out to be more interesting in its parts than as a whole, especially where those parts predict concerns dealt with more fully in the plays of Ibsen's maturity. Like *Catiline* it features the remarkable pairing of 'dark' and 'light' women who compete for the same man. The sisters Margit and Signe are both in love with the outlaw minstrel-poet Gudmund Alfson. Margit betrayed her love for him by marrying for security and position. Now she sits in her manor hall awaiting his return after an absence of seven years, and in soliloquies bemoaning the fate of being trapped in a loveless marriage she articulates Ibsen's obsessive fascination with the idea of being bound in a living death inside rock or stone: 'I must get out, out into the green valleys, here inside the mountain chambers I die!' Later, in a desperate attempt to regain her freedom, she tries to poison her husband. The attempt fails: 'For me it's all over, the mountain is closed! The sun shines no more and all the stars have gone out'. Ibsen also continues to explore his fascination with the possibilities of syncretism, notable in the combination of two faiths, Christianity and *alvetro* ('belief in trolls'), in the name *Gud*mund *Alfsøn*; and in the scene in which Alfsøn calls to Signe from outside the church. While others cross themselves in fear her heart goes out to him, 'As though some deep, mysterious summons reached me from beyond the church walls'. Finally, after various intrigues, Margit enters a convent to atone for the attempted murder of her husband and Gudmund and Signe win each other.

Formally the play shows Ibsen still in thrall to the French school of Scribe, and William Archer noted coincidences of plot that recall Scribe's *La Bataille de Dames*, which was among the plays Ibsen purchased while in Copenhagen and one of the first he directed in Bergen. Ibsen's contemporaries pointed to similarities with Henrik Hertz's hugely popular *Svend Dyrings Hus*, notably in the use of the heroic ballad as the model for those parts of the play in verse. The accusations irked Ibsen, as any impugning of his originality irked him. In a general sense he accepted that complete originality in literature was impossible, and in a lecture delivered at about this time, 'On the Heroic Ballad and its significance for literature', he pointed out that such ballads were not the work of any one individual but ' the sum of a whole people's combined literary powers'. But he disliked admitting to specific influences, and in a specially written Introduction to a second edition of the play published in 1883 he returned to the subject, claiming with solid pre-Freudian confidence that he had never much admired Hertz and therefore could not possibly have been influenced by him. Yet as the Danish critic Georg Brandes pointed out, 'There seems to me to be no depreciation whatever of Ibsen in the assertion of Hertz's right to rank as his model. Even the greatest must have learnt from someone.'[9]

The Feast at Solhaug did indeed give Ibsen the popular acclaim that had eluded him since his arrival in Bergen. It also enhanced his reputation in Kristiania, where it was performed at the Christiania theatre six times, and became the first of his plays to be commercially published. Thomas Cortes's travelling Danish troupe added it to their repertoire, and when Cortes added *Lady Inger of Østråt* he billed it as 'by the author of *The Feast at Solhaug*', as he did with Ibsen's next-but-one play, *The Vikings at Helgeland.* Cortes performed *The Feast at Solhaug* in Kristiansand and Kristiania, but success tastes sweetest at home and how Ibsen must have loved the curtain call at the Bergen, and the visit of the theatre orchestra later in the evening to serenade him outside the window of his rooms in the theatre annex. The play was later taken by the company on a trip to Trondheim in 1856, and a review of the performance there gives an intriguing hint that Ibsen's ideas on the presentation of realistic behaviour on stage were already evolving. Perhaps taking advantage of the presence of gas lighting on the Trondheim stage, he seems to have instructed his actors to address one another when speaking, rather than the audience, a mannerism so unusual that the reviewer commented on it.

The play's greatest moment came some months later when it was chosen for a command performance for the visiting Louis Napoleon, Emperor of France. The emperor wanted to see for himself the state of local theatre and announced his intention of being present for a performance the following night. Alas, no performance was scheduled, half the company was on holiday, and the orchestra was already booked to play for guests on board the steamship *Patriot* on its way up the fjord to Hardanger. Unwilling to disappoint the royal visitor Peter Blytt began, at ten o'clock that night, the difficult task of organising a performance. Ibsen was summoned from his bed, his irritation soothed by Blytt's suggestion that they perform *The Feast at Solhaug*, and together the two of them worked through the rest of the night and all the next day to get things organised. During the performance itself Blytt sat behind the prince and whispered a

German commentary on the action into his ear. Afterwards, at the reception, Ibsen was introduced and presented the guest of honour with a leather bound copy of *The Feast at Solhaug*. The prince drank with Ibsen, praised Louise Brun's performance as Margit, and requested a copy of Schediwy's incidental music. He also promised to have the play translated into French and performed at his private theatre at St Cloud, although he does not appear to have kept his word.

Olaf Liljekrans, a serious romantic drama, was Ibsen's last play written specially for the theatre in Bergen. It had its premier on 2 January 1857. Perhaps as a result of the success of *The Feast at Solhaug* he had been able to negotiate a fee of 100 speciedaler for it, the first time he had been rewarded for a play beyond the terms of his annual salary. *Olaf Liljekrans* was loosely based on a half-finished manuscript from 1850, *The Justedal Grouse*, itself based on a folktale from the plague days of the fourteenth century about a girl (the grouse) found living alone in the mountains. The eponymous hero of the play is due to marry the daughter of a wealthy neighbour. Olaf does not love Ingeborg and is marrying only to please his mother, who insists that without her dowry their family cannot survive. But Olaf has been bewitched by a supernatural girl, Alfhild, and as the hour of his wedding approaches the conflict between duty and love exercises him, with duty seemingly favoured to triumph. Conventionally, however, a second young man, Hemming, is then introduced who does love Ingeborg and whose love is reciprocated, so that after trials and misunderstandings Olaf can marry Alfhild, with his mother's blessings, and Hemming marry Ingeborg.

Olaf Liljekrans was not a success and was performed only twice. And despite an attempt in 1861 to use a version of it as an opera libretto Ibsen, who in later life showed remarkable loyalty to these plays of his early years, was not fond of it and did not permit its publication until 1902, as part of his collected works. Again its main interest now is where it serves to confirm or predict the development of some of his most characteristic themes and obsessions, perhaps most notably in its exploration of the betrayal of love, here Olaf's for his sweetheart Alfhild, in the name of duty. This was already a staple of Ibsen's drama. Margit of *The Feast at Solhaug* carried through the self-betrayal and became the first to take her seat in that particular hell which would later house both Hedda Gabler and John Gabriel Borkman. In *Olaf Liljekrans*, however, the great crime is avoided at the last gasp and true love triumphs over the obstacles. A background detail contains a first reference to Ibsen's lasting obsession with the image of a dead child: while Olaf meditates on the dirty and inglorious finality of death, wilfully rejecting Alfhild's vision of a pleasant afterlife as he tries to steel himself to reject her love, a funeral procession carrying a tiny coffin to burial passes across the stage behind him.

Alfhild's father is a ballad singer whose verses move the action along rather like the chorus in a Greek drama. Indeed the whole play was an attempt to cast a medieval ballad in dramatic form. Ibsen was a member of a debating group, the Society of 22 December, and it was before them, on 2 February 1857, that he delivered the lecture 'On the Heroic Ballad' which, though it came slightly after the première of the play, showed *Olaf Liljekrans*'s intellectual origins.* It was part of Ibsen's determined effort to find ways to make the past work for the present, and in his lecture he seemed almost to be apologising to his listeners for using historical settings for his plays when he explained that what is new can only appeal to people if it also, in certain important respects, seems old. It must have the benefits of familiarity and avoid seeming strange or peculiar, in much the same way as the makers of the first railways carriages designed them to resemble the familiar horse-drawn carriages. In *Peer Gynt* he would finally achieve this syncretic literary dream, using a simple folk-tale character to depict a complex, modern human being; but plays like *St John's Night* and *Olaf Liljekrans* could not succeed as long as the technical theory behind them lay so far in advance of Ibsen's ability (psychological or literary) to express something powerfully modern in them. The result is that in spite of the presence of interesting characters like Julian Poulsen, Margit and Olaf Liljekrans these Bergen plays of the 1850s remain essentially museum pieces.

Ibsen had only two addresses in Bergen. The second of these, from the spring of 1853 onwards, was the theatre annex. The first was Fru Helene Sontum's *pensjonat* in the Nordnes district of central Bergen. Among their neighbours were the Holsts who had a daughter, Rikke. One day as Ibsen sat smoking his pipe and drinking coffee on the hotel porch she came skipping by and called out to

---

* He also delivered a lost lecture on Shakespeare's influence on the Scandinavian stage.

him, 'Hello, Ibsen! Have you a piece of cake for me today?', a memory which caused Ibsen to note that she was always very fond of sweet things. Since the 'episode' with Else Sophie Birkedalen it seems as though his sexual appetite had gone into hibernation. He had obvious difficulty in relating normally to girls of his own age and finding this child spontaneous, natural and light-hearted, in the spring of 1853 he entered into a gentle parody of a romantic relationship with her. Arne Duve, a Norwegian psychiatrist who for years worked a cabbalistic trawl through Ibsen's life and work in pursuit of proof that he had already, before moving to Grimstad, fathered an illegitimate child in Skien, with an under-age girl as the mother, found significance in Rikke's extreme youth;* and yet the innocence of the relationship was, from Ibsen's point of view, its whole benefit. Their walks were chaperoned. They never held hands. Ibsen never even used the informal pronoun *Du* when addressing her. Some seventy years later Rikke Holst recalled the impression Ibsen made on her, 'a well-dressed, vain chap, who with his pleasant and modest manners gained entrée to all the best houses in Nordnes'.[10] He wrote love poems to her, 'Meadow Flowers and Potted Plants' (she is the flower, the other girls mere potted plants), 'To my Auricula', verses as swelling and romantic as any to Clara Ebbell and the Grimstad girls. They bound rings together and threw them into the sea as a sign of their undying love. Finally, in the beginning of June, he sent her a proposal in verse form: 'Now one word from your mouth/Shall decide my future'. Rikke, not yet confirmed, showed the letter to her father. Søren Holst, who had relatives in Grimstad, may well have known the secret that Ibsen kept hidden beneath his great brown beard, and forbade Rikke to see him again. She defied him, and one day when they were out walking together her father caught them. He challenged Ibsen, who, with heroic timidity, turned on his heels and ran away. End of the affair, save for a poem, 'A Bird Song', which edited away real life's undignified conclusion to the relationship and pencilled in lyricism:

> I painted word-pictures,
> played with colours:
> two brown eyes lit up,
> laughing, listening.

* In Duve's view the historically verifiable event with Else Sophie Birkedalen had no great effect on Ibsen.

> Above us we hear
> whispers and laughter;-
> but we, we parted sweetly,
> and never met again.

The affair with Rikke is perhaps best understood as an experiment in being alone with a woman. As such it forms a prelude to Ibsen's encounter with Suzannah Daae Thoresen, whom he met and fell in love with early in 1856. Born on 26 June 1836, she was the daughter of a priest who had been widowed twice and was by this time married to a third wife, the children's former governess Magdalene Thoresen. Suzannah was nineteen years old at the time she and Ibsen met. Her outstanding physical feature was her chestnut brown hair, which when she let it down reached to her feet. She had large, spiritual eyes, a clear complexion and full, sensual lips. Her voice was warm and strong, her tone declamatory. As a child she loved to read and play at 'theatres' for her family. She was a gifted mimic with a good sense of humour and was also something of a tomboy. At the age of nine, during an over-realistic performance of a play about pirates, a small boy began to cry when hit. 'Phooey, if you wear a moustache you mustn't cry, it isn't manly!' was her derisory response. She did not like to be seen crying, to admit to any weakness or need, a pride she took to such lengths that in later life she was often regarded as cold and unfeeling by those who knew her only casually. Some called her 'the Queen of Iceland', a reference to the fondness for saga literature which she shared with Ibsen.

Magdalene Thoresen was one of the moving spirits behind the Norwegian theatre in Bergen, so Suzannah and the house dramatist must have been at least on nodding terms before their first formal meeting. This apparently took place at a literary gathering at the Thoresens' house on 7 January 1856, just a few days after the triumph of *The Feast at Solhaug*. It is a remarkable index of the isolated life Ibsen led in Bergen that five years could pass before he breached Magdalene's socio-cultural citadel; or perhaps she contrived to exclude him, for he bore little resemblance to her idea of what an artist should look like and how he should behave. She later described him as:

> a timid little marmot of a man. There was something odd, not attractive, but rather clumsy and anxious about his manner of

being; he was terrified of being laughed at; he has not yet learnt contempt for his fellow human beings, and so lacks self-assurance; he has, moreover, a certain boundless admiration for the refined.[11]

The decisive encounter between Ibsen and Suzannah took place a few days later, at a ball at the philharmonic society at which neither of them danced but sat talking together the whole night. After they had parted Ibsen wrote and told her that if she would consent to be his, he was certain he could amount to something in the world.

Within a month of this first meeting he had sent her a proposal of marriage in the form of a lovely poem, 'To the Only One'. By prior arrangement he presented himself at the house for her reply. His unshakeable earnestness continued to invite teasing, and Suzannah could not resist playing a practical joke on him, hiding beneath the sofa while he paced the floor in impatient distress. By one account she made him wait for two hours before revealing herself: 'I just wanted to see how long you would wait for me. You've done well. Now come on and help me up.'

Ibsen wrote other poems to Suzannah during the period of their courtship and engagement. She destroyed these before she died, as she destroyed whatever letters they may have exchanged during the period of their courtship, believing that 'the relationship between us is nobody's business but our own'. It leaves us with only a sketchy idea of how their love developed. Even so, one other verse which survives in addition to the proposal, 'To Suzannah Thoresen', gives a compelling picture of Ibsen's lonely need for someone to shore him up in his haunting obsession with his own slow petrifaction and his fear of death in life:

> I dreamt that I was laid in my coffin
> and lowered down into the grave,
> earth was cast on to my final
> resting place.

He hears the prayers being said over his body, and finds himself alone, living dead. He prays in the dark, looks up and sees Suzannah, his salvation, with her 'rich, blooming child's soul'. Considering the true extent of Ibsen's emotional inhibition the chance he took in so openly placing his happiness in the hands of another becomes in restrospect a quite remarkable act of daring. Fortunately it was fully justified. Suzannah became everything to him. She was his helpmeet, his comforter, his best friend, his reference book, above all his muse. He was paying her the highest compliment he knew of when he likened her to his own dramatic creations: 'Now you are Eline',* he told her once, 'but one day you will be Lady Inger.' They confounded Bergen society with the formality of their inter-course, continuing to use the formal pronoun *De* to each other even after their engagement, and establishing the basis for a relationship in which, as one of their acquaintances later described it, 'they maintained, along with comradely intimacy, a discretion, an observa-tion of protocol, and a horror of revealing themselves in the spiritual equivalent of a negligée, which is rare in Norwegian marriages'.[12]

In April 1857 Ibsen's five-year contract with the theatre expired and was renewed for another year. But the success of the nationalist venture in Bergen had not gone unnoticed in the capital, and urged on by regional jealousy a Norwegian theatre had opened in Møller-gaten in 1852 which presently set its sights on acquiring Ibsen's services. From its opening until July 1857 the artistic director had been a Dane, Jens Cronberg; but in the middle of the month the theatre's governing body wrote both to Cronberg and to Ibsen in Bergen asking if they would be willing to compete for the post of artistic director. There was obviously going to be a strong element of positive discrimination in favour of the Norwegian candidate; and that Cronberg, after five years' service, was unwilling to submit to competition is understandable. The field was thus left open for Ibsen, who obtained his official release from Bergen on 4 August, signed his contract with the Møllergaten theatre on 11 August and assumed his responsibilities officially at the start of the winter season on 3 September 1857. Suzannah remained in Bergen for the time being.

The six years Ibsen had spent in Bergen as director and dramatist were, as he later wrote to Herman Laading, 'in truth the years of my apprenticeship'. They had been lonely years, perhaps; but in Suzannah he had met the salvation of his loneliness. He had written and seen performed five original plays, and directed dozens. His superior at the Bergen theatre, Peter Blytt, wrote of the 'the fruitful good fortune' of Ibsen's sojourn there. Perhaps surprisingly, Ibsen

---

* Eline is Fru Inger's daughter.

was already being described, in an article in the *Bergenseren*,[13] as 'by now unquestionably the greatest Norwegian dramatist', on the strength of a half-dozen plays not one of which has survived in the repertoire of modern Norwegian theatre on its own merits. He was moreover still not yet thirty years old. It hardly supports his frequent contention in later life that he had been badly treated by his own countrymen. Yet such a contention was in itself only a necessary part of the creative disharmony of his personality, with which he was still deeply dissatisfied and which he was still struggling to express effectively in the form of a work of art. Ibsen refers to this dissatisfaction in a letter to C. J. Anker, a military man with whom he went on a walking tour from Bergen to Hardanger and back again in the summer of 1856. From Kristiania he wrote to Anker of how much he had enjoyed their brief association:

> I have often wondered what you really thought of me, if you did not find me surrounded by a certain aura of repellent cold which makes me seem unapproachable. And yet I found you easier to get on with than anyone else, for there was a youthful spirituality about you, a joy in life, a generosity of spirit which did me good. Hang on to this: believe me, it is not pleasant to see the world from its dark side, and yet, ridiculous as it may seen, there was a time when that was all I wanted. I've longed for, almost prayed for some great sorrow which would really fill my life, give meaning to my existence. It was silly, I've fought my way out of it, but there is always the memory that remains.[14]

Anker was one of those, like Suzannah's stepmother Magdalene, like Suzannah herself, like Rikke Holst, whose clear, self-assured personalities both attracted Ibsen and set his own guilt-ridden, secretive and uneasy personality sharply in focus. But it was the refinement of his unease Ibsen sought, not release from it.

5

The Artistic Director
The Vikings at Helgeland

Professionally the post of artistic director of the Norwegian theatre in Møllergaten was an improvement on Ibsen's status in Bergen. Personally he already had a circle of friends and admirers in Kristiania from his previous stay in 1850–1, notably Paul Botten Hansen, who in the intervening years had come to prominence as editor of a literary and cultural magazine, *Illustreret Nyhedsblad* (*Illustrated News Magazine*). Another factor might have been Ibsen's desire to start married life with Suzannah away from her large and well-established family circle in Bergen, although financially the move was something of a gamble. By arrangement with the theatre he was to receive 7½ per cent of the gross box-office takings, with a guaranteed minimum annual income of 600 speciedaler; but this alone was twice what he had been earning in Bergen. Artistically the challenge was inspiring. The major difficulty, as his critics would never tire of reminding him in the years to come, was that he had been appointed to the post at Møllergaten not as the individual dramatist Henrik Ibsen but as a representative, literary Norwegian. This put him under intense pressure to produce a recognisably *national* drama.

There was competition to deal with too. In Bergen the Norwegian theatre had had the field to itself; in Kristiania the Christiania theatre had been operating successfully in Bank Pladsen since 1827. As Brynjolf Bjarme, Ibsen had seen his own *The Warrior's Barrow* performed there in the autumn of 1850; and as *Manden*'s reviewer of plays he had held a free pass there during his earlier sojourn in the city. The Christiania theatre's profile was Danish, its directors and actors Danish, and where its repertoire was Scandinavian and not French or German the plays were imported successes from Copenhagen. The locations of the two theatres reflected their relative status: Bank Pladsen was a handsome, open square close to the city centre; the Norwegian theatre was in Møllergaten, a dirty, working-class area of town, where its neighbour was a drinking shop favoured by horse-traders. Patrons would have to fend off whores, drunks and louts on their way to and from the theatre. A writer in the *Christiania Posten* characterised the two sets of patrons as, respectively, those who attended in *Selskabs kjole* (evening dress), and those who wore *Kontorfrakke* (office jackets). At Bank Pladsen the thing was to see and be seen, something which the provision of a new chandelier after a recent rebuilding facilitated: 'It is not quite so light in the Norwegian theatre, where the boxes do not separate so clearly the different classes and make so apparent the distinctions between rich and poor. Here the short jacket of the peasant may be seen side by side with a coat made by Nord the tailor.'[1] Ibsen's task was to educate this non-intellectual public in its cultural heritage; to entertain it; and to run the theatre profitably.

Ibsen's immediate concern was the completion of a half-finished play he had brought with him from Bergen, *The Vikings at Helgeland*, and while working on it he lived a peripatetic existence. He stayed first, briefly, with his old friend and supporter from the *Catiline* days, Ole Schulerud. It was one of Schulerud's last acts of generosity towards Ibsen, for he was to die in 1859, at the age of thirty-three. For a while Ibsen lived at the Hotel du Nord at Dronningens gate 13; then at Akersgaten 35, on the corner of Karl Johans gate and just five minutes' walk away from the theatre; and at Kristian Augusts gate 15.

He returned to Bergen in the summer of 1858 and he and Suzannah were married there on 18 June. Back in Kristiania they lived briefly in Kristian Augusts gate before moving to Maltheby, or *Skibet* (the ship), as they called it, a newly-built and fashionable residence on the corner of Akersgaten and Teatergaten. It was here that their only child was born, on 23 December 1859, christened Sigurd at his mother's request after a character in *The Vikings at Helgeland*. Bjørnson stood godfather to the boy. After two years in Bergen as Ibsen's successor at the theatre he had returned to Kristiania in 1859 with his wife, Karoline Reimers, a childhood friend of Suzannah's. The Bjørnsons lived briefly at Maltheby, and it was here that the enduring and troubled friendship between the two men got under way. Literary Kristiania of the period was a faction-ridden little world, and Ibsen and Bjørnson were already regarded as rival

candidates for the title of leading young Norwegian writer, each
with rival sets of supporters for their candidature. Born in 1832
the son of a priest from Kvikne, Bjørnson had in abundance the
self-assurance Ibsen so signally lacked. He was also handsome, charismatic, flamboyant and flirtatious. He made his name as a dramatist
at the age of twenty-five with the historical play *Mellom Slagene*
(*Between Battles*), performed at Bank Pladsen in 1857, and consolidated his position with three hugely successful short stories of peasant life, 'Synnøve Solbakken', 'Arne', and 'A Happy Boy' and a
number of nationalist poems like 'Det ligger et land' ('There is a
land') and 'Ja, vi elsker dette landet' ('Yes, we love this land'), which
later became the Norwegian national anthem. In a rivalry so firmly
predicated in nationalism his personality and literary instincts gave
him an enormous advantage over Ibsen in its early days. Yet there
was deep mutual respect between the two of them, and an attraction
of opposites, and in this honeymoon period of their relationship they co-founded a society, *Det norske Selskab* (The Norwegian
Society) devoted to the promotion of nationalism in the arts, before
in 1860 Bjørnson took off again on a lengthy *bildungsreise* through
Europe.

Not long after the birth of Sigurd, Suzannah shocked her immediate circle by announcing that she would have no more children.[2]
In 1860 the only way to avoid further pregnancy was to practice
abstinence, and it has been suggested by some that from this time
onwards the marriage was platonic. It had got off to the worst possible start anyway, with the death of Suzannah's father Prost Thoresen
on 15 June, just three days before the wedding. Ibsen, by nature
shy, also had to contend with his guilty memories of the episode
with Else Sophie Birkedalen. Several of her acquaintances described
Suzannah as a woman who had a tendency to idealise people she
admired: if, like Tolstoi, Ibsen made a point of confessing his sexual
past to his wife just before the marriage (if, indeed, he ever told her
about the incident at all) perhaps Suzannah found herself unable to
continue idealising her husband unless the sexual element were
absent from their relationship. *Love's Comedy*, a play Ibsen wrote in
the summer of 1862, has at its heart a rejection of physical in
favour of ideal love, with the lovers agreeing to part rather than
risk compromising their ideals in marriage. It is Svanhild, a character
modelled on Suzannah, who proposes this high-minded step, and
under her influence the Ibsen-figure, Falk, is converted from

cynicism to a similar high-mindedness. On the way to his self-discovery he remarks the fall of a certain Pastor Straamand, once Falk's hero for his dedication to his Call, now ridiculous to him above all for the fact of his twelve children and worn-out wife, so perhaps Ibsen was testing out in the play a rationalisation of the necessity for a man of principle to practise self-denial to the point of celibacy.

But even if the main motive for Suzannah's decision were simply that Sigurd's birth was so painful she never wished to repeat the experience, the effect on their married life would have been the same reduced level of sensuality which is a common feature of the sexual relationship in Ibsen's plays. In the marriages of the couples of his later plays – the Helmers, the Tesmans, the Solnesses, the Borkmans – there is a frenzied concentration on the mental or 'ideal' side of the relationship to the exclusion of the physical, and it is perhaps not merely coincidence that *Love's Comedy* was the first play Ibsen wrote around the notion of a man jousting with a challenge (here *Løgnen*, the Lie) which is entirely abstract in its focus, and not related to any physically attainable goal.

What characterises the marriage over the next forty years, what seems to hold it so firmly together, is that both parties shared the religious notion of a call in their lives. Suzannah's was to ensure that Ibsen became a great writer, and Ibsen's was the same.

Ibsen's friends now were a circle of young men gathered around Paul Botten Hansen at his house in Raadhusgaten 28, known as *Pipergaarden*. The shocking fate of his friend Abildgaard probably remained fresh in his mind and the break with the overtly political elements of his first stay seems deliberate. Other members of the group were Jakob Løkke, a schoolteacher; Michael Birkeland, a librarian who worked in the National Archives; and a young classical scholar, Ludvig Daae. This core of five made up *Det Lærde Holland* (the Learned Holland), as they styled themselves. The novelist Jonas Lie described them as 'a group of people with varying enthusiasms but all more or less bookish'.[3]

The name derived from a shared enthusiasm for the plays of Ludvig Holberg. Botten Hansen possessed the largest private library in Norway (after his death it formed the basis of what is now the Bergen Public Library). 'Devil take the Dutchman! He has his spies everywhere!' was Daae's admiring comment one day on his friend's bibliophile talents, quoting Jesper in *Jakob von Tyboe*. Elaborating on Daae they dubbed themselves the *Hollændere* (the Hollanders), Botten Hansen 'the Head Dutchman' and his library 'Holland'. Their informal nicknames derived from Holberg's plays too. Ibsen was often known as Gert, after Gert Westphaler, the eponymous hero of Holberg's play. Gert is a chatterbox of a barber, and Ibsen's later cultivation of a sphinx-like silence might lead one to suspect the name was ironically meant; but in the company of people he trusted there is no doubt that he liked to talk and once in full flow was hard to stop. Humorous paradoxes like the invention of a fish with a fear of the water, and unanswerable riddles – do two and two add up to four on Sirius? – were typical of his contributions, some of which were filed away for later use in *Peer Gynt*. One imagines too that Falk's cynical observations on life and love in *Love's Comedy* give something of the flavour of the persona Ibsen cultivated among friends. Jonas Lie was not a member of the group, but saw enough of them together to observe 'the degree to which Ibsen was liked and respected'. It seemed to him that 'he was actually the silent heart of the group'.

They usually met on Mondays, in Botten Hansen's library. If they went out, it would be to Nibbes kafé, Hotel d'Angleterre, L'Orsas, Peters Restauration ('St Peter's') or Engebret Christoffersens. Birkeland called this going *paa vidderne* (on the heights). They observed feast days on their own birthdays – Paul Botten Hansen on *Paalsmesse*, 18 November, Michael Birkeland on *Mikkelsmesse*, 16 December. In conventional terms this was perhaps the most sociable period of Ibsen's life. But, perhaps depressed at the difficulties of trying to write with a crying child in the house, he also spent a lot of time alone in cafés. Daae has described how Suzannah would direct visitors who came in search of her husband to try a round of the city's bars. Ibsen would typically be found alone in a favoured café, L'Orsas, 'all afternoon sipping at a single glass of beer'. When joined by others, heavily bearded and forbidding in his 'mormon's hat', he might suddenly become drunk: 'Then he was like a volcano; extremely brutal; attacked his best friends'.*

In the view of some the Holland were not good company for Ibsen. The sarcasm and self-protective irony they cultivated seemed

* In Hans Eitrem's notes of his interview with Daae the word used is *fuld*, meaning 'drunk'. *Beruset*, meaning merely 'intoxicated', is crossed out. Daae denied a rumour that Ibsen was ever *forfalden*, 'degenerate'.

only to reinforce his own misanthropic tendencies. In a letter to Ibsen, Bjørnson once characterised them as 'your so-called friends', describing them as 'absolutely appalling people to be with . . . Just a bunch of theoreticians and mockers. What they lack, all the lot of them, is the most important thing of all: ordinary, decent *humanity*.'[4]

But they were demonstrably much more than 'so-called' friends to Ibsen. Each in his own way proved very helpful to him. Botten Hansen, having discovered him back in 1849, when he gave *Catiline* its first enthusiastic review, now opened the columns of *Illustreret Nyhedsblad* to him. This, a more sophisticated successor to *Andhrimner*, was founded in the autumn of 1851 and continued to appear until the end of 1866. Botten Hansen was its editor for most of that time. Its brief was nationalistic, to spread an appreciation of Norway's history, people and nature among its Kristiania readers. Its circulation hovered around the one thousand mark for most of its life. Many of Ibsen's poems and articles appeared in it. *Lady Inger of Østråt* was first published there, in 1857, as was his lecture 'On the Heroic Ballad'. *The Vikings at Helgeland* appeared in its pages in 1858 and *Love's Comedy* was the magazine's New Year's gift to its subscribers in 1863.

Botten Hansen did more: when an article in *Aftenbladet* claimed that *Hærmændene*, with its Viking Age setting, had been influenced by Bjørnson's *Halte-Hulda*, a recent work set in the same period of Old Norse history, *Illustreret Nyhedsblad* took pains to point out that Ibsen's and Bjørnson's literary interest in the period had developed parallel with each other. Indeed, the magazine promoted Ibsen and his work so openly that a letter of complaint appeared in the *Christiania Posten*, alleging that under Botten Hansen *Illustreret Nyhedsblad* was conducting an almost military campaign aimed at securing Ibsen's success, and that his talent did not warrant such attention. In response Botten Hansen wrote that, on the contrary, 'in that respect we have remained as neutral as it is possible to be, indeed even more neutral than we are towards other writers'.[5]

Michael Birkeland was the author of a determined letter of support for Ibsen when he was applying for a government grant of annual support after leaving the country in 1866, supplementing the letter with a request to his friend Heffermehl to plead Ibsen's case personally with Frederik Stang, a leading member of the cabinet who also happened to be Heffermehl's father-in-law. At a later date, when Ibsen planned an edition of his selected poems, Jakob Løkke spent a great deal of time and energy collecting them from their many and often obscure places of first publication. And when Ibsen was researching for *Emperor and Galilean* it was Daae, the classicist, who read and summarised for him Eunapios's biography of one of the plays central characters, the mystic Maximos. Clearly these were more than just 'so-called friends'.

Marriages put an end to the Holland as a young man's club, with the marriage of the Head Dutchman Botten Hansen in November 1860 as its death-knell. Describing the occasion in a letter to Daae, Birkeland wrote that[6] 'Løkke, Ibsen and I represented Holland; but we were in quiet and melancholic mood on this ostensibly happy occasion'. The reason was that 'I am afraid Fru Hansen has sworn to put an end to the Holland and all *Hollændere*'. Ibsen at the meal-table 'was at his most incorrigible'. Perhaps he was playing the part of the cynical Falk at the wedding, to amuse his friends and distress their wives. There were jokes that Botten Hansen would soon 'be under the rule of the slipper', and one guest played a practical joke on the groom, raising his glass and offering a mumbled toast to Paul *Dotten*, meaning something like Paul *Fluff*, to which Botten Hansen's trusting acknowledgement was the signal for general merriment.

In later life Ibsen sometimes felt that the time spent in the company of the Holland had been time wasted, yet he retained vivid memories of them, particularly of Botten Hansen, who died in 1869, and in 1888 Ibsen wrote a note to Daae, thanking him for a biographical appreciation of their old friend: 'It was curiously and powerfully moving to feel myself once again returned to those surroundings which exercised such a decisive influence on my later development, and from which, at the deepest level of my being, I have never quite torn myself free, nor ever really wished to.'[7] By the end of his life Daae, perhaps unwilling to accept that for an obsessed man like Ibsen even friendship must yield to the demands of ambition, had come to a conclusion of his own, that in reality Ibsen had never liked any of them, 'not even Botten Hansen, who helped him so much'. 'He had no sense of humour', said Daae, 'his whole personality made real happiness impossible.'[8]

Ibsen was aware that his efforts at the Møllergaten theatre would mainly be judged by the criteria of nationalism: how Norwegian was the repertoire? How many new Norwegian plays had been performed? How genuinely Norwegian was the language employed by the company? The first performance for which he was personally responsible, Bjerregaard's *Fjeldeventyret*, with its companion piece, Wergeland's *Efterspil til Fjeldeventyret*, on 17 September 1857, augured well for his tenure. It ran for seventeen performances – a great success by contemporary standards. But the pool of original drama by Norwegian writers was small; and despite the presence of Johan Herman Wessel's *Love Without Stockings*, several plays by Ludvig Holberg and C. P. Riis's perennial favourite, *Til Sæters*, the repertoire was crowded out with vaudevilles and light entertainments, many of them the work of professional Danish crowd-pleasers like Erik Bøgh and Thomas Overskou. These entertainments attracted the public and made good economic sense, both for the theatre and for Ibsen personally with his percentage of the box-office takings; but they soon alienated the nationalists and cultural watchdogs on the capital's newspapers. Over and over again during his five years as director Ibsen would hear complaints of the lack of original Norwegian drama on the menu, and of the artistically worthless nature of what was performed. His response in the pages of *Illustreret Nyhedsblad* to such attacks illustrates one of the great strengths of his character: a pragmatic open-mindedness on the subject of writing that permitted him to learn aspects of the craft even from such ephemera as these. These recent French works, he wrote, 'are usually technically highly accomplished, something the public appreciates. Moreover they make no gestures at all in the direction of poetry, and the public appreciates that even more.'[9] It was, after all, Scribe, not Goethe, nor Molière, nor Racine, who taught him the value of the closed room with three doors.

Ibsen's first season in charge was not judged too harshly. It was generally accepted that his comparatively late arrival on the scene absolved him from responsibility for the repertoire and the performance of the company. A competition launched in November 1857 and offering a first prize of 1,000 speciedaler for the best new three-act play by a Norwegian showed that he had every intention of uncovering new native talent. But by season's end only three entries had been received, and all were rejected as unperformable. Despite good ticket sales the theatre remained in debt at the end of the season. But the committee were optimistic about their prospects and took out a new 600 speciedaler loan to cover the costs of the summer.

The 1858–9 season opened with new machinery in place to speed up changes of scenery. Six new plays in the early part of the season were welcomed by the critics, and it seemed that the Norwegian theatre was now able to offer serious competition to the theatre in Bank Pladsen. A season of subscription-only concerts on Wednesdays proved so popular that at the opening performance on 27 October some had to be turned away at the doors. But the major event of the early part of the season was the première of Ibsen's own *The Vikings at Helgeland* on 28 November.

The Vikings at Helgeland, set on the north-west coast of Norway in the late years of the tenth century, was the fruit of the saga reading Ibsen had been doing since the mid-1850s, in versions by N. M. Petersen. The problem of how to make their own cultural history accessible to contemporary audiences exercised writers of the national romantic schools in both Denmark and Norway. Ibsen had discussed it at some length in his lecture on the heroic ballad in 1857, and by his own account had been working on a version of the play since early 1855. The two women who later became Dagny and Hjørdis, and a large feast at which rioting broke out, were to be his starting point. Meeting and falling in love with Suzannah he found his mood too light for the sombre tragedy he was planning, and influenced by his enthusiasm for Landstad's recently published collection of Norwegian folk ballads he changed his mind and set to work on *The Feast at Solhaug*, adapting the basic pattern of two women in love with the same man to create Margit and Signe, and transforming his saga hero Sigurd into Gudmund Alfsøn. *Olaf Liljekrans* further delayed the tragedy; and by the time he returned to the idea in 1857 he had abandoned his original intention of writing it in verse.

The plot borrows from a number of sources, including *Njals saga*, where the friendship between Gunnar and Njal provided him with a model for the relationship between Sigurd and Gunnar, as well as Gunnar's wife Hallgerd, whose unforgiving nature has much in common with Ibsen's Hjørdis; and *Egils saga*, where he found the original for the old warrior poet Ørnulf who loses all his sons in battle, contemplates suicide by self-neglect but is reminded in time of the restorative power of poetry and composes the long, thera-peutic lament which is essentially a rewriting of Egil's *Sonnatorek*. The *Volsungs saga* and *Laxdæla saga* also provided Ibsen with back-ground for a play that is most interesting as an early meditation on

75

one of Ibsen's favourite themes, the destructive power of the *livsløgn*, (the life-lie). The marriage between Gunnar and Hjørdis is built on the lie that it was Gunnar, and not Sigurd, who won the right to her by slaying the white bear that guarded her at night. This deception is revealed as the cause of Hjørdis's unhappiness, and it leads in the end to a conventional mass slaughter of the main characters.

Adjudging the facilities of his own theatre inadequate Ibsen had first submitted the play for the consideration of the Royal theatre in Copenhagen, and when it was rejected there tried the Christiania theatre, which accepted it, then failed to perform it, finally forcing him to put it on at Møllergaten. He was very angry with the Christiania theatre's rejection, and in complaining of it in *Aftenbladet* on 10 March 1858, in an article 'On the behaviour of the Christiania theatre's Danish Board' ridiculed the reason given, that the theatre could not afford to put on new work by Norwegian playwrights because this would require them to pay royalties to the author*. The situation enabled him to plead simultaneously for one of his own works and to berate the main theatre for cultural treason in its standpoint. Characteristically he portrayed the situation in black and white, urging everyone to declare themselves either *for* a Norwegian language theatre attempting to promote Norwegian drama, or *for* the main theatre, with its Danish company and its mixed cultural identity.

A typically fiery Norwegian newspaper debate ensued. An article in *Christiania Posten* dismissed Ibsen's case out of hand, and Ibsen himself as a 'thoroughly unimportant writer about whom the nation cannot with any enthusiasm plant a protective hedge'. The writer claimed familiarity with both *The Feast at Solhaug* and *Lady Inger of Østrât*, and said that if these were anything to go by then Ibsen's new play deserved its rejection. The leading 'serious' living Norwegian playwright was Andreas Munch, whose new plays were regularly performed at the Christiania theatre. Had it been Munch on the receiving end of such treatment, the writer opined, it might be worth making a fuss about; but in his view Ibsen wasn't in the same class as Munch. Ibsen's replies over two issues of *Aftenbladet* show at an early stage his developing sense of being not only a Norwegian but also a European. He wrote that all attempts to develop a national

* Norway had no copyright arrangement with other countries, so that theatres were not obliged to pay royalties for plays by foreign dramatists.

culture would inevitably 'serve the cause of the greater European culture', and that a prerequisite for the successful development of pan-Scandinavianism was that each Scandinavian land must develop a distinct sense of national independence which was political, literary and cultural. The publicity generated by the debate did the play no harm. Botten Hansen published it in *Illustreret Nyhedsblad*, and told his readers that it had been well reviewed in *Svenska Tidningen*. This was the first time Ibsen's work had been noticed outside his own country, and the resultant prestige taught him a tactical lesson in how to manipulate public opinion which he was to put to good use in later life.

Having decided to do the play at Møllergaten Ibsen spared no expense. New costumes were made up, new scenery prepared. Madame Hundevadt, the company's leading lady and a darling of the public, played Hjørdis, and with the newspaper debate fresh in mind there was a full house on opening night. The reception was excellent, Ibsen took a curtain call and there was a small party in his honour afterwards. This was Ibsen's greatest triumph in his combined roles as dramatist and director, and it was his alone, for the 'Danish' division of directorial functions practised in Bergen was not used here. The play was performed eight times in all during the season 1858–9, and the first four performances alone brought in 2,300 speciedaler at the box-office, of which Ibsen's royalty fee as author was one quarter, about 580 speciedaler.

A striking feature of the repertoire that season was a performance of Holberg's *Jeppe paa Bjerget* (*Jeppe from the Hill*). An attempt was made to relocate the play to Kristiania, underlining for Norwegians the irony that their greatest and indeed only writer of European stature was more or less a naturalised Dane. Critics complained that the adaptation was haphazard, though one suspects even a thoroughgoing adaptation would have been rejected, for a code of stage conventions as rigid as any of those governing the tragedies of Racine and Corneille held that 'real life' in the sense of street-life, working-class life with working-class accents, had no place on the stage. Only idealised life was to be portrayed. It points up the impossibly contradictory nature of the demands made of Ibsen by his nationalist watchdogs, that he should in effect promote Norwegian culture on stage at the same time as idealising the culture to the point of unrecognisability.

In the spring of 1859 Ibsen put on a production of *Lady Inger of*

Østråt, after this too had been rejected by the Christiania theatre. Despite its modest history of success – performances in Bergen in 1855 and in Trondheim in 1857, and publication in *Illustreret Nyhedsblad* – and despite Madame Hundevadt in the title role and the popular Madame Døvle as young Eline, the play's unhappy ending did not appeal to the theatre's essentially vaudeville public. *Aftenbladet* complained that the actors were inadequate to the demands of the roles, but offered general praise for Ibsen the dramatist: 'If there is one thing his plays are above all they are dramatic, that is Ibsen's real strength. It is only right and proper that they should be performed.'[10] *Lady Inger*'s gloom was soon dispelled by the dancing Healey Sisters from England, Christine and Agnes, whose every performance drew a full house.

In his annual report to the committee at season's end Ibsen could boast of thirty-one new productions; but this prodigality in itself was one of the factors behind the large financial loss the theatre again sustained that year. Ibsen enumerated other factors: the new stage machinery, decor, and wardrobe; the cost of providing music, paying choristers and extras; the frequent rehearsals making for large gas bills; the royalties paid to translators and writers. The largest single outgoing was the rent. The Møllergaten theatre had been leased for an eight-year period from 1852. Now, with the period of lease about to expire, the owner offered it to the company at 15,000 speciedaler. A subscription appeal was launched in *Morgenbladet* and backed up by hundreds of letters to private individuals. By mid-June some 2,000 speciedaler had been raised.

By the time of Ibsen's third season, 1859–60, the competition between the two theatres had intensified and both continued on a resolutely downmarket course. The theatre in Bank Pladsen imported with great success from Copenhagen the phenomenon of *Pepitaraseriet*, a coinage to describe wild enthusiasm for the dancing of Pepita d'Oliva. Møllergaten took up the challenge with Erik Bøgh's *En Caprice*, a vehicle created for Pepita but danced for Ibsen by Bianca Bills. It played twenty-three times in succession; but success came at the price of a betrayal of the theatre's nationalist ideals, for with a single exception all the characters in it spoke either Danish or German. *Morgenbladet* was moved to ask its readers what the point of having a Norwegian-language theatre was? 'We cannot conceive what purpose is to be achieved by such a repertoire of triviality upon triviality; we cannot conceive why the whole theatre

78

is permitted to wander ever further in the direction of Danish non-sense – under the leadership of a Norwegian dramatist.'[11]

The Norwegian dramatist responded by employing a second dancer, Madame Dobson St Louis, and presenting her in another of Pepita's vehicles, *De to Kometer* (*The Two Comets*). But accusations that the theatre was degenerating into a sort of 'fun-house for the lower-classes, a vaudeville theatre' stung. Holberg's *Jean de France* was one of the more successful 'legitimate' pieces of theatre Ibsen put on that year; but even that ran for only six performances. Of genuine foreign dramatists Ibsen risked only Calderon, Molière's *Les Fourberies de Scapin* and de Musset's *Un Caprice* during his tenure. Kotzebue and Scribe were well-represented, Scribe especially so; but there was no place for Oehlenschläger. In the spring the theatre succeeded with Hans Christian Andersen's *Ole Lukøie*, but failed with D'Ennery's *Herren ser dine Veie*, described by one hostile critic as a tearjerker to compare with Munch's *Lord William Russell.*

Ibsen's annual report to the committee on 29 September was the by now familiar tale of good ticket sales but a continuing overall loss. Three times in the course of that season he had petitioned the government for state support, urging the importance of dramatic art as an edifying force in the life of a country and asking for personal sponsorship for a six-month trip to London, Paris, Germany, Denmark and Sweden 'to develop my knowledge of the literature and art of drama'. Ibsen complained that while the government willingly recognised in the form of sponsorship, scholarships and travel grants the role of arts like literature and painting in creating a national culture, the role of the theatre was severely undervalued:

> In this country the drama is marginalised and left to fend for itself. The reason for this cannot possibly be a denial or even simple undervaluing of the importance of this particular art form on the part of the government; for it has already recognised the importance for the nation of poetry, painting, sculpture and music, and can therefore not possibly deny the validity of the actor's art. Indeed this art must by its very nature be regarded as a higher synthesis of all the individual art forms, unifying as it does the qualities of poetry, painting, sculpture and music.[12]

It seems curious that his application stressed the importance of the art of acting when it was for himself, a dramatist, that he was requesting the money. The application was not successful, however. Another disheartening setback was the loss of Madame Hundevadt, the diva, to the Christiania theatre after a break with the rest of the cast over alleged favouritism by the management, involving free dancing lessons. Jomfru Berg, another actress popular with the audiences, followed her. Their departures were to some extent counterbalanced by the arrival from Bergen of the Isachsens, husband and wife; but the real significance of the moves was that the Christiania theatre was now of its own accord moving away from its Danish profile and cultivating a more Norwegian one.

Boldly, the Norwegian theatre committee decided to go ahead that year with its plans to buy the theatre, and to carry out a complete refurbishment programme. They borrowed 2,500 speciedaler and work began. It was supposed to be finished by the autumn; but in the event the opening of the 1860–1 season was delayed until 11 October. Goodwill towards the undertaking on the part of the press remained, and there was praise for the improvements, though disappointment that Ibsen failed to mark the occasion with anything more exciting than H. Ø. Blom's old vaudeville warhorse *Tordenskjold.*

But though it was not immediately apparent, the provision of greater comfort in the theatre, and in theatres in general during this decade, had an impact on the development of Ibsen's writing. As director he had already noted the liberating effect on acting styles of the arrival of good gas lighting, enabling companies to dispense once and for all with the ritualised, gestural style associated with the theatre of Goethe and Schiller; and the trend towards comfort in the auditorium, part of the process of attracting the bourgeoisie, created audiences that would, in due course, be prepared to sit and meditate on the relatively static, intellectual form of drama Ibsen was gradually working his way towards.

But such audiences were still twenty years away, and for the time being Ibsen was obliged to follow a play for which he had respect, such as Karl Gutkow's historical five-acter *Haarpidsk og Kaarde,* with a trifle like Sardou's *Et farligt brev* (*Les Pattes de Mouche*). The pattern of alternating the relatively sublime with the banal must have frustrated Ibsen as much as it did his critics in *Morgenbladet* and *Aftenbladet;* but with the huge debt the theatre had now incurred box-office successes were becoming their only hope of survival. Probably at Ibsen's instigation a dancing school was opened for the company, and on 1 January. the first 'Dansedivertissement' was staged. But the hit of the season was *Mursvendene* (*The Masons*), adapted by Isachsen from Cogniard and Clairville's *Les Compagnons de la Truelle*, which ran for twelve performances. Yet again an attempt was made to transfer the action of the play to Kristiania. *Morgenbladet*'s always conservative critic conceded that 'there is a certain attraction for the masses in seeing and hearing themselves portrayed on stage', but he still favoured the ideas of the French classicists that life on stage should be idealised, and ended his review with a complaint about the 'verbal photographing of reality'.

By the spring of 1861 the Christiania theatre appeared to have seen off the challenge from Møllergaten, where the refurbished rows and boxes remained empty as the public flocked to Bank Pladsen to see Pepita in a revival of *En Caprice*. A wit compared a visit to Møller-gaten as 'a sort of aesthetic sickbed visit'. The repertoire was blamed, Ibsen was blamed for choosing it, and he was blamed for the gener-ally poor level of performance, although in truth the company never recovered from the loss of Madame Hundevadt.

Ibsen spent much of that spring fruitlessly expending his time and wit writing responses in the newspapers to criticisms of his incompetence. *Morgenbladet* accused him of delaying the production of two new Norwegian plays, offered to the theatre in 1859 and still not performed by 1861, reminding Ibsen of his own outrage when *The Vikings at Helgeland* was similarly treated by the Christiania theatre. A member of his own company, the actor Døvle, criticised him in a public lecture. No doubt angry at a decision forced on the company in February, either to take a wage-cut or face closure in April, Døvle did not forget to tell his audience that in the midst of all these problems Ibsen's annual wage was a healthy 1,000 speciedaler. There were calls for Ibsen to be sacked and the job given to Bjørnson. For the first time the idea of merging the two theatres was aired.

In his annual report Ibsen offered several excuses for the poor season, reminding the members that the Isachsens, his 'reinforce-ments' from Bergen, had not arrived until late September, making good casting difficult. The departures to Bank Pladsen had severely curtailed the number of the plays the company was able to perform at any given time, and he complained that the rebuilding of the theatre had rendered the existing decor unusable.

Among those closely involved in the undertaking there was little doubt that Ibsen's lukewarm interest and general neglect of his professional obligations were major factors in the theatre's decline. Knud Knudsen, the theatre's language consultant and one of the shapers of modern Norwegian, wrote in his memoirs of how he had had to deal with Ibsen as though he were a schoolboy. He complained of his 'tardiness and his resistance to pressure from above', echoing an observation Ole Bull had made, that one had to deal firmly with Ibsen if one hoped to get anything out of him. The general dissatisfaction was summed up by the committee chairman Hansteen, who complained that 'the artistic director has not shown as much initiative as we had hoped'.

Under the circumstances, Ibsen's enthusiasm for the job waned rapidly, and the theatre entered a terminal decline. He did not turn up for committee meetings, and on one occasion it was the committee who had to go and meet him, in a back room at L'Orsas café. For another season he continued to make gestures towards his mandate, mounting productions of two plays by Bjørnson. But directors at both theatres were desperate for new plays, and at one point the absurd situation arose of the same play – *I Dynekilen* (*In Dynekilen*) – occupying both stages simultaneously. Building work on the theatre continued, apparently unsupervised, and by season's end the debt had mounted to 28,000 speciedaler. 'The treatment for the theatre's ills and woes – the rebuilding – turned out to be worse than the sickness,' wrote Knudsen.

In June the committee voted to suggest formally a merger with their rival. Bank Pladsen replied on 21 June, reminding Møllergaten that they themselves had first suggested this in 1860; then, when the Norwegian theatre was flushed with optimism by the enlargement of the stage and refurbishment of the interior, the offer had been rejected. Bank Pladsen now returned the compliment, unwilling to assume the burden of debt, more ominously claiming that they were now so Norwegian in their profile that the Møllergaten venture was redundant. The company had little option but to declare itself bankrupt, wind up its affairs, and sack everyone, including the artistic director, with effect from 1 June 1862.

Knudsen, in his disappointment, laid the blame for the failure of the enterprise squarely at Ibsen's feet. Probably suspecting that their director's commitment to the development of nationalist drama could not compare with his committment to his own development, he declared him to have been a disaster, worse even than his

Danish predecessor Cronborg: 'Ibsen had done his bit and sowed the seeds of its failure over the last five years'.

Certainly Ibsen's work load was too great, his responsibilities, ranging from the artistic to overseeing the building work, were too varied. Possibly a return to the 'Danish' arrangement such as the one at Bergen with Laading, might have worked better. The brave new venture had needed a director of exceptional talent, and as a director Ibsen was generally recognised to have been of below-average ability. For all his growing knowledge and understanding of the dramatic art he was too introverted, too shy to stamp his authority on the company.

His dismissal marked the end of his ten-year career as a theatre director. It had proved a more than adequate replacement for the university education he never acquired. The much-derided 'low-brow' repertoire taught him vital lessons, fruitfully compromising the high-minded æsthete he was by temperament, and instructing him in the techniques of gripping, holding and entertaining an audience. Close, daily association with a company of actors taught him the importance of good casting, and the limited financial resources at his disposal that imagination must respect the realities imposed upon it by technical limitations. But that Ibsen despaired of the job is no surprise. A few years later he warned Bjørnson against attaching himself to a theatre:

> Are you really going to join a theatre again? Of course there is a task to be done there, but you have a more pressing one still in your own writing. Sure, if it were just a question of putting in the time it wouldn't matter too much. If all the good literary ideas, moods, images could be put aside and simply taken up again later. But that is not the way it works; others come along, but those inbetween die unborn; work in the theatre for a writer is a series of such abortions, repeated on a daily basis. Society punishes such transgressions.[13]

Several times, as his star gradually rose in the years to come, he would be invited back to take over as a theatre director in Kristiania. But he had taken what he needed from the job and never seriously considered the offers.

6

The Ring of Thumb and Forefinger
Love's Comedy · The Pretenders

Frustrated at the theatre, with no time to write plays, Ibsen turned increasingly to poetry during these years. Most of it was occasional, and most of it doggerel. It seems no request for a prologue to open a sports meeting or shooting competion, to celebrate a wedding, ennoble a death or hail a professor's anniversary, was too small for him. In the more militantly public-voiced of these he often fell back into the tone that characterised his earliest Grimstad poems, hectoring the non-participant:

> Woe to the man who offers only words
> to help his brother in need,
> his grave in oblivion lies waiting.

Such poems and threats were addressed in part to himself as he continued to struggle against the dreamer, the thinker, the watcher he was by nature. Bjørnson saw through the pose. Writing in 1859 to Clemens Petersen, the leading Danish critic of his time, he explained Ibsen's poetic aggression as his way of compensating for inadequacies in other departments. With the self-assurance of a man who had both a big chest and a big bottom he described Ibsen as 'a small, scruffy man, with no arse and no chest, nor any talent for public speaking, which is why he feels compelled to write so fiercely. On top of that he doesn't write what he really wants to, i.e. what he is capable of writing.'[1]

Some of the overtly nationalist poems of the period may have sprung from a feeling that his nationalist credentials were being questioned during the rowing over his conduct of the theatre. One such is the long ballad 'Terje Vigen', printed as a supplement to the first issue of *Illustreret Nyhedsblad* in 1862, about a seaman in a southern coastal town during the time of the Napoleonic wars who tries to break the British blockade to get food for his wife and child. He is captured by a British man o' war and despite pleading for his family is held for five years in jail. When he returns he finds they have died in his absence. Some time later, working as a pilot, fate puts the former captain of the man o' war, and his wife and child, at Terje's mercy; determined to take his revenge he hears the mother calling the child's name, Anna, the name of his own lost child, and at the last moment desists and forgives.

'Terje Vigen', which rapidly became a national treasure in Norway, is essentially a simple, heroic ballad with a working man as its hero. An oddity is the presence of Christian morality in Terje's forgiveness, for in times to come it is Jehovah rather than Christ who emerges as Ibsen's nearest spiritual relative. The poem symbolised his range, mixing naïvety and sophistication, and his desire, despite frequent signals to the contrary, to remain in dialogue with the ordinary man and woman. Hans Jacob Henriksen, during periods when he took to the road drinking, armed with his birth certificate and introducing himself as an Ibsen, would often identify himself as the original of Terje's abandoned child.

Two great poems, meditative and deeply personal, that appeared in the same year, 1859, provide the most striking contrast imaginable to these ballads, patriotic and occasional verses. One was 'In the Picture Gallery', referred to earlier, relating his discovery of great art as a replacement for religion during the study trip abroad in 1852. The other was 'Paa Vidderne' ('On the Heights'), for the inspiration of which he credited Suzannah, calling it one of the first fruits of his maturity as a married man.[2] This remarkable poem seems to begin in Bunyan, proceed through Byron's *Childe Harold*, and end in an anticipation of Nietzsche's *Zarathustra*. Its sixty-nine verses tell of a poet who leaves home, mother and sweetheart to wander on the heights alone. He meets a tempter up there, a man with a dog, whose aim is to persuade him to forget about his past, his home and his life 'down below', 'above' and 'below' seeming to symbolise the contrast between the spiritual and the sexual life.

There is a distinct syncretism to the persuasions of this tempter. In part he is a pantheist who urges on the poet the literal superiority of the church of nature over the church built by man; but he is also an indoors man, a man with an almost pathologically overdeveloped aesthetic sense. From their vantage point on the heights the two see below them the house of the poet's mother going up in flames.

The poet's companion, Ibsen's detached, watching *alter ego*, observes:

> He made the ring of thumb and forefinger
> to improve the perspective;
> a song drifted up to us,
> and I knew that my mother
> was with angels.

The gesture of aesthetic detachment, the painter's ring of thumb and forefinger (Ibsen was still painting at this time) recurs as the poet watches from his great height the wedding procession of the young woman to whom he was engaged to be married before his flight to the mountains:

> I stood on the brink, my soul steeled,
> high above the summer.
> The procession was like a glinting ribbon
> as I made the ring of thumb and forefinger,
> to improve the perspective.

The notable feature of 'Paa Vidderne' is the poet's acceptance of what he thinks of as his 'new wisdom', this newly-discovered ability to accept his own detachment, unmoved even by the death of his mother and the loss of his promised bride, at the same time as he conveys a despairing hatred of this detachment. It reminds Ibsen again of the image of himself as a man trapped inside himself, a man slowly turning into a statue. Rejecting the offer of further help from his mentor he says:

> No thanks, now I can manage alone,
> though the offer is appreciated;
> no more river floods through my veins,
> in the vault of my chest,
> I sense my turning to stone.

In trying to face up to his guilt and pain about the absence of contact with his unknown son and the break with his family in Skien, the poet concludes in an uneasy self-acceptance, an assertion of Nietzschean superiority over the common herd that is only half-convinced and half-convincing.

> Now I swopped my last rhyme
> for a higher view of things.

> Now I am steeled, I obey the call
> to wander on the heights!
> I'm done with life down below;
> up here on the mountains are freedom and God;
> down below the others just stumble.

This was perhaps one of those self-revealing verses he was thinking of when he described his poems as 'little devils' that should never have been published.

Ibsen would probably not have recognised it at the time, but the pressures of working for five years at the Møllergaten theatre were beneficial to his real writing, forcing him into thinking, taking stock, allowing ideas to mature instead of, as in Bergen, having to produce plays almost on an assembly-line basis. *The Vikings at Helgeland*, though it was the first play he wrote which can still be performed on its own merits, is not an outstanding piece of work. The other two plays from this period, *Love's Comedy* from 1862 and and *The Pretenders* from 1863, can both be described as near-masterpieces. *Love's Comedy* was, according to Ibsen, along with 'On the Heights', another of the fruits of his marriage to Suzannah. Both play and poem describe the clarifying in their central characters of a philosophy of life based on withdrawl and self-denial. Ibsen made the connection explicit in a biographical note of 28 October 1870: 'That need for liberation which runs through the poem did not find full expression until *Love's Comedy*. The book was much debated in Norway, where people related it to the circumstances of my personal life. I lost a great deal of face. The only one who liked it then was my wife.'

The bulk of the play was written in the summer of 1862, shortly after losing his job at the theatre. In verse, it builds on a prose fragment *Svanhild* in one act and four scenes from 1860. Svanhild, like Hjørdis, is based on Suzannah. She meets a young writer, Falk, a scoffing observer of his friends as one by one they drift away from the idealism of their youth into the banalities of marriage and daily life. Falk falls for her; in a speech which links the couple directly to Ibsen's final couple, Rubek and Irene in *When We Dead Awaken*, he warns her away from those rivals and plagiarists of God who will form and sculpt her in marble, and then stand back marvelling at the normality they have imposed upon her. Instead he recommends

87

himself, telling her that with her assistance he will be able to spread his literary wings and leave the earth. Svanhild responds with a brilliant attack on his assumption of her role in his life. Far from seeing him as a falcon (many of the characters have the names of birds) she sees him as a paper dragon, drifting without purpose in the wind, his wings bright epigrams that flutter and flail everywhere but hit nothing and no one.

Falk sees the truth of this at once and the speech marks a turning-point in his life. Where before he hid behind irony when criticising those who abandoned their idealism he is now openly serious in what he says. In a short space of time he breaks with all his friends and upsets his landlady so much that he is evicted from his lodgings. He orders the porter to burn his poems and give away his books. Henceforth he is committed to a life of action and unbending opposition to the lie that the highest goal of marriage is domesticity.

Yet there is also recognition on Ibsen's part that there is something inhuman about Falk's fanaticism, and that he is stealing a form of life-lie from those he attacks for having 'betrayed' their idealism. Pastor Straamand, once a man of fiery dedication to his call, is now married with twelve children and spends much of his time thinking about how to provide for them. The pastor pleads with Falk to withdraw his criticism, but Falk is adamant. 'There is a Nemesis in life', he warns him, 'No matter how late it comes its aim is true', and 'It is given to none to flee from it'.

The play's crucial scene follows shortly after this. Falk has a rival for Svanhild, an affluent older man named Guldstad. He presents his case in front of both of them. Romantic love doesn't last, he tells them. Not even love based on idealism. Pastor Straamand's wife was once the love of his life. Seeing her again recently after many years he failed even to recognise her, and when told who she was he felt nothing of his former love. What he offers Svanhild is a relationship based not on love but on friendship, respect and protection; implicitly he will also spare her the pain of waking one day to discover she no longer loves him, since he does not even require her to love him at the outset.

His intervention has a dramatic effect on the young couple. Falk furiously denies the truth of it, but when Svanhild asks him how long he will love her for, he cannot in honesty reply 'for ever' but only 'for a long time'. It is then that Svanhild proposes the insane, heartbreaking solution that will permit their love to live on for ever:

a complete break between them, and her acceptance of Gulstad's proposal. In the play's final scenes Straamand, seeing that the couple have now parted, reflects on Falk's own words to him about Nemesis; and Falk repairs the broken friendships of the day, likening himself to Erasmus Montanus, who finally sees the point of abandoning his position of knowing best to admit that the world is, after all, flat. It is our knowledge that he is lying, that he and Svanhild voluntarily turn to a future with this mad act of emotional self-mutilation at its core, that gives *Love's Comedy* its extraordinary poignancy and makes it Ibsen's greatest love story.

That he should return to verse after the mixtures of verse and prose used in the Bergen plays and after the prose of *The Vikings at Helgeland* suggests Ibsen intended the play primarily for reading. It was published in Kristiania on 31 December 1862 but not performed there until much later, in November 1873. Once he had achieved fame it became one of his most popular plays among nineteenth-century audiences, with performances in Copenhagen, Stockholm, Berlin, Paris and at the Theatre Studio in Moscow, where it was directed in 1906 by Vsevelod Meyerhold.

In March 1862, just before writing the final draft of *Love's Comedy*, Ibsen applied to the Academic Collegium* for a state grant of 120 speciedaler to enable him to travel in the Norwegian interior as a collector of folk tales. His application was successful, and in June that year he set off. Recent years had seen the publication of M. B. Landstad's collection *Norske Folkeviser* (*Norwegian Folk Ballads*) and Asbjørnsen and Moe's *Norske Folkeeventyr* (*Norwegian Folk Tales*). Asbjørnsen was a friend of Botten Hansen's, a sort of auxiliary member of the Holland, and it may have been in discussions with him that the idea for the trip arose in Ibsen's mind. The urban, intellectual fascination with *bonderomantikken* (the romance of the peasantry), part of that process of almost deliberate creation of a distinctive 'Norwegian national identity', was still vivid and Ibsen clearly hoped to capitalise on it.

Leaving Kristiania on 24 June 1862 his trip took him via Eidsvoll, Hamar and Lillehammer, up through Gudbrandsdalen, Ottadelen and over the mountains and down to Vadheim in Ytre Sogn, ending at Ørskog in Sunnmøre on 16 July. He travelled variously by boat,

---

* This was the name of the administrative board of the University of Kristiania.

on foot, by ferry and by horse-drawn wagon. This was a long
expedition, but it was not virgin territory for collectors, and most
of the stories Ibsen collected had been collected and published
before. Nor did his introverted nature suit him to the collector's
role. At the parish priest's house in Lom a situation arose in which
the presumptive oral sources found the roles reversed and themselves straining to persuade their collector to open up to them: 'Our
guest was silent and sealed, and all our efforts to get him going
were in vain.'

Ibsen, who for part of the journey was accompanied by the actor
Andreas Isachsen, kept a journal for a few days. At the outset of the
journey there was some thunder about, and Ibsen noted that he
was 'Nervous. Drank a tankard of beer.' Later, after he and Isachsen
had parted company, Isachsen to walk over Hedalen, Ibsen continued along Vaagedalen to See, 'where I sit now alone and
depressed'. This was about as personal as he proposed to be, and
for the most part the journal consists of unexceptional descriptions
of nature and the arrival and departure times of stage-coaches and
boats. There are occasional bursts of activity, such as their encounter
at the staging post at Holmen with two men, both of whom wore
knee-breeches. The detail did not escape the fashion-conscious
Ibsen. Many years later Isachsen met one of the men again and it
reminded him of how struck Ibsen had been by these breeches:

He thought much about this practical improvement in travelling
clothes, and when we reached Vågå he made up his mind to
adopt it. The long trousers he had on were already so worn at
the bottom that it seemed to him the logical thing to do was to
cut the lower part of them off completely and turn them into
knee-breeches. No sooner said than done. Thus Henrik Ibsen was
the modern tourist in at least part of his attire during his wandering over Sognefjell.[3]

Ibsen raised little dust in his travels, and the anecdote is typical of
those he left behind him, refreshingly dull, and gentle in its lack
of consequence. Twice, during the course of their journey, they
were temporarily joined by young Swedish men whom for no given
reason Ibsen believed to be the poet Carl Snoilsky, whom he had
heard of but never met. Neither were. Elsewhere he wrote of 'the
long and boring sail up to Lillehammer', and in his description of

the great lake Mjøsa he seemed to be offering a mild rebuke to God as artist:

almost nowhere does one encounter elements that harmonise artistically; the lines are monotonous and without expression, and the jumbled mixture of forest, field and heath give the landscape a disturbing appearance which can never make pleasant appeal to one's sense of colour. A few miles further on, Gudbrandsdalen has almost the same character, although here the river adds a llittle variety.

Even when literally 'on the heights' Ibsen still, like the narrator of his poem, had a tendency to look at nature 'through the ring of thumb and forefinger'. One senses that the real pleasures of the trip were stories such as the one he heard at Vestnæs involving a priest who organised a collection for a needy local widow, which he related for the sophisticated readers of *Illustreret Nyhedsblad.* The joke was that the woman already had four suitors and to celebrate her new-found wealth had brought a little heir into the world to share it. The priest involved rebuked Ibsen for recycling the gossip, calling it a shameful misuse of his public funding as a 'collector' of folk tales; the upshot was that Botten Hansen printed a retraction and an apology for the article. Ibsen loved any such tales in which trusting idealists were duped by the worldly. Another was a more authentic 'folk tale', the Holbergian saga of Kristen Kulbrænder, a man of neither education nor spirituality who tricked the learned into appointing him a priest.

On his return from the trip to Kristiania Ibsen reported to the Academic Collegium that he had already found a publisher for the 'seventy or eighty different and previous unpublished folk tales' he claimed to have collected. The book never appeared, however, and the only published results of the trip were the four tales and as many landscape sketches published in the pages of *Illustreret Nyhedsblad.*

One story he noted down at length concerned the heathen belief in rocks and hills and mountains as dwelling places of supernatural beings. A fiddler of renown who fell asleep one day in open country was spirited into a hillside by a supernatural girl. She handed him a fiddle and asked him to play on it for her. He could not bring himself to touch it; and yet the world of her rock-home fascinated him:

Inside the hill he saw strange carvings in wood, and other curious artefacts, and all he could think of was whether he might not be able to make similar things himself. He could not say how he got out of the hill, and he was never the same again afterwards. He would never join in the work of the farm but spent most of the time on his own, thinking and trying to reproduce what he had seen inside the hill. He made fiddles which were supposed to be like the fiddle the girl in the hill had shown him, each one different in some detail or other from the ones used in the local villages. He spent most of his time up in a little loft at home, which was always full of all sorts of finished and half-finished carvings, the purpose and use of which no-one knew. Mostly he worked on a carving of a doll which was supposed to be the girl he had seen in the hill. He said that even the clothes he made for her were like the ones she was wearing; but he never managed to make it to his complete satisfaction, and would always begin the work over and over again.

Ibsen's interest in the story is instructive, for the fiddler seems a sort of folk-tale version of himself; in his apartness, in his lonely struggle to reproduce images from a hidden world that had been revealed to him alone, in his fascination with the mysterious woman and his endless attempts to reproduce her in a carving.

For the last two years Ibsen had been in deep financial trouble and the failure of the trip to produce a book was a disaster for him. In a contract drawn up with the man he hoped would publish it, Christian Tønsberg, he had even made arrangements for the advance to be paid directly to one of his creditors, a lawyer named Jacob Nandrup.

The trouble had been brewing since before his marriage, and grew worse with family responsibilities. In his impatience to put behind him the days at Grimstad when he had to thank Schulerud for the gift of a pair of trousers he adopted that flamboyant style of dressing which made him such a remarkable sight in Bergen. With no personal outgoings other than clothes, books and food, money was not a problem; yet he left behind a debt to a shoemaker, dating from September 1852, when he departed for Kristiania in 1857. The debt was small, only about four speciedaler, and was not pursued until 1861, when the shoemaker reappeared as one of ten creditors who took Ibsen to court that year, nine of the ten cases being heard within a five-month period, indicating perhaps that Ibsen's parlous financial state had become a subject for anxious gossip in the two cities. In addition to the Bergen creditor there was the licensee of the bar at the Christiania theatre; an authoress, Fru Marie Colban, who was suing for unpaid rent on an apartment at Nedre Bakkehuset 73; three tailors, two soft furnishers and a second shoemaker, all waving unpaid bills signed by Ibsen. Two *examiniti juris* chased him for unpaid loans.

The case involving a builder, C. A. Grosch, was particularly time-consuming. For a few months in 1860 the Ibsens lived in one of Grosch's newly built apartments on Bogstadveien, moving to Nedre Torvegade 17 on 29 September and leaving unpaid rent behind. Ibsen responded to Grosch's court action with a counter-claim that the building was only half-finished, the walls and windows ill-fitting, the steps up and down simply planks and the promised supply of fresh water non-existent, obliging them to walk some distance for their water. It shows the relative nature of the Ibsens' poverty that one of the witnesses produced to substantiate these claims was their maid, Johanne Johannesdatter. The court found for Grosch in most instances and awarded him 100 speciedaler, after a round of some twenty hearings between October 1860 and August 1861.

The debt of about forty speciedaler to Johan Olsen, licensee of the bar at the Christiania theatre, spanning the period October 1861 to May 1862, also tells its own tale and explains why Daae felt obliged to deny rumours that Ibsen was 'degenerate' during this period. Degenerate or not, many of his debts were humiliatingly small, five of them less than nine speciedaler,[4] indicating the degree of his indifference to the good opinion of others and perhaps also his general personal and professional despondency at the turn his life had taken since coming to Kristiania.

Part of the problem was that the Norwegian theatre's economic fortune was also his. Labouring under debt for most of its existence meant that the company had to learn to live with wages paid late, or only in part, or in exceptional circumstances not paid at all. Even so, the wage-receipts Ibsen signed monthly between, for example, June 1860 and April 1861, were with two exceptions all well in excess of his monthly basic of fifty speciedaler. He was living above his means, in which Suzanne, with her 'almost violent hatred of all petty considerations'[5] perhaps abetted him.

At some point Ibsen seems to have hit upon the idea of taking out a single large loan to clear all of his debts and leave him with just one major creditor. To this end he borrowed another 400 speciedaler from Nandrup. Inevitably, when the time came, he found himself unable to pay back this loan either. Nandrup sued him, and at a court hearing on 12 May 1862 Ibsen gave his word to pay the debt. Two days later he wrote a desperate letter to J. B. Klingenberg, a member of the Norwegian theatre committee. Married and with a two-year-old child, he was just two weeks short of being without a permanent job:

> If you have, as I hear, had a meeting with any members of the committee, or are willing to act on your own initiative, you would be doing me the greatest favour imaginable if you would send a messenger to me with however much of the money as goes to me. I am being sued for last years' tax (11–12 speciedaler), and today they threaten to come and take my things. This is a harsh fate, when such a large part of my hard-earned annual wage is still owing to me, and I put my faith in you, being the only one I can turn to.[6]

On 24 May Ibsen found himself re-enacting the humiliations of his father Knud thirty years earlier and submitting a detailed list of the personal property he was offering as security for the payment of his debt. Fortunately for him, Nandrup did not press his claim at once, giving Ibsen breathing space in which to plan his flight from what had become an impossible situation. Attachment from 1 January 1863 as a part-time literary consultant at the Christiania theatre at a wage of twenty-five speciedaler per month kept the wolf from the door; but his most realistic hopes were now set on further, and if possible permanent, state funding. Encouraged by his success with the Academic Collegium he again applied to them on 6 March 1863 for a grant to travel further afield in search folk tales and ballads. Again he was successful, to the tune of 100 speciedaler. The trip was a ruse, however, and Ibsen used the money to support himself and his family while working on *The Pretenders*.

The Pretenders was written in bursts during 1863 – Ibsen recalled specifically one of six weeks in the summer – but he had the historical sources and presumably the idea for it back in 1858. A five-act play in prose set in the first half of the thirteenth century, its direct inspiration is conventionally ascribed to the rivalry between Ibsen and Bjørnson for a role something like that of our poet laureate, with Bjørnson at the time of writing as the holder of the title. Their literary doubles are Skule, the pretender, and Håkon, the king, but *The Pretenders* is so well realised and timeless that it requires no biographical subtext. Its only real faults, which are usually corrected in modern productions, are the introduction of too many minor characters imparting too much history; Bishop Nikolas, an Iago, steeped in Machiavelli, who draws Skule into the corrupting attempt to usurp the throne, is too obviously evil in the first two acts and does not become a real character until his deathbed scene in the third. Ibsen makes use of three conventionally 'significant' letters, but does so with such skill that disbelief remains in suspension.

Its great strength is the character of Earl Skule, a talented and brave man hobbled by self-doubt, bitter to the point of corruption over the arbitrariness of human nature which curses him with this useless complexity while appearing to leave his friend and rival Håkon entirely free of it. Urged on by Nikolas, his demon personified, he seizes the crown of Norway and for a while becomes King Skule. But his doubt only increases. He remains tormented by the instinctive certainty that Håkon is the natural king, the one intended by God. He once heard him express a thought which he immediately recognised as a *kongstanke* (kingly thought): 'Norway was a kingdom. It shall become a people.' King Skule makes the thought his own, but is corrupted by the plagiarism.

One of the finest scenes in the play, and one in which his self-doubt emerges as more truly kingly than Håkon's simple self-certainty, is that between Skule and his skald Jatgeir at the beginning of Act Four in which Ibsen seems almost to be conducting a dialogue between his private, writing self and his worldly, ambitious self. Skule complains of the hell of public, 'kingly' life, of being scrutinised at all times; but Jatgeir never reveals himself in public. He speaks of 'the modesty of his soul', and of the skaldic art as incommunicable. 'The skaldic art cannot be taught,' he says. Its origins are in sorrow, and 'I was given the gift of sorrow'. The lines echo irresistibly Ibsen's to Carl Anker on how he once longed for some great drenching sorrow to enter his life. Jatgeir is Ibsen's conscience, Skule's purer self.

Skule is finally punished for usurping power and plagiarising another's thought. Having long believed that one sign of God's indifference to his ambition is that he never had a son to succeed him, he suddenly learns that he is the real father of the son of a former lover, now grown up and training for the priesthood. He binds the boy to him in love and admiration by means of the stolen king-thought; but in the final scene confesses the deception and father and son go to meet their death at the hands of the victorious King Håkon's supporters. Afterwards Håkon delivers an epitaph for him: 'Skule Bårdssøn was God's stepson on earth; that was his riddle'. This gracious salute to the mystery of a great human riddle is valid. In the plays of his middle years, from *The Pillars of Society* in 1877 to *Hedda Gabler* in 1890, Ibsen tended to neglect the psychology of his male characters for a concentration on the females; but in Skule Bårdssøn he created a character as fascinating and complex as Hamlet or Macbeth, and offered meditations on the nature of power scarcely less rewarding than Shakespeare's.

The Pretenders was published in Kristiania on 31 October 1863 by Johan Dahl, who paid him 150 speciedaler for the rights. The author received twenty free copies. Then and henceforth it was always a matter of concern to Ibsen to get his new plays published some months in advance of their first performance, and if possible in time to catch the Christmas-present market. *The Pretenders* had its première eleven weeks later at the Christiania theatre on 17 January 1864, with Ibsen himself directing.

The pittance he earned as consultant to the Christiania theatre did nothing to alleviate his economic *misère* and on 10 March 1863 he wrote a long letter to the *Storting*, detailing his life and achievements so far, adding that an edition of collected poems was forthcoming, and applying for an annual grant of 400 speciedaler to enable him to continue to write full-time. None of his plays so far had earned money for him, he explained. Even his most successful, *The Vikings at Helgeland*, on which he had spent the best part of a year, had brought him only 227 speciedaler. Towards the end of the letter he stated the problem baldly: 'To live entirely or even chiefly from one's literary activities in this country is an impossibility.' He confessed to debts of 500 speciedaler and threw himself on the mercy of the *Storting*'s awarding committee.

His timing was not good, however. Bjørnson was home again after a three-year *bildungsreise*, in the course of which he had written the historical trilogy *Sigurd Slembe* which established his pre-eminence as the country's great nationalist writer. As a mark of gratitude and an encouragement the *Storting* awarded him an annual grant, the first time such an award had been made to a writer.* With state support of individual writers such a rarity at this time it was a tactical mistake for Ibsen to have applied for two large, separate grants in the space of one week. The committee knew that the Department of Ecclesiastical Affairs, which handled such matters, had already decided to approve his previous application of 6 March for a travel grant, and so turned down Ibsen's second application. It was almost certainly not ill-will but simply ill-luck that the applications had been decided in that order.

Undaunted, Ibsen tried again on 27 May, suggesting a travel grant to spend a year in Rome and Paris to study art, art history, and literature. Bjørnson had enthused him with the idea when the two met up again at a music festival in Bergen in the summer. This time Ibsen was successful and was awarded 400 speciedaler.

Daae has left a description of Ibsen's last home before his departure for southern Europe. The family were living at Oslo Strandgate 33: 'He was living on the road to Old Town, by the railway line, in a rundown house, a real dump. Many times his wife had a struggle even to get them their daily bread. He really was so poor that he was starving.'[7]

Professionally the humiliations of life as a debtor had a lasting effect on his work, notably in the preoccupation with money, promissory notes, debt and the horror of public shame that is such a feature of later plays like *A Doll's House* and *John Gabriel Borkman*. Personally it was perhaps at this point that Suzannah began to assert herself in the marriage; that she began the process of which Sigurd later spoke, of giving Ibsen the backbone she found him lacking in if he were ever fully to do justice to the talent she knew he possessed. Ibsen, with his strong self-dramatising element and his desire to be considered an outsider, always contrived to convey the impression that his departure from Norway was enforced. Summarising the experience in his autobiographical letter to Peter Hansen he wrote of being 'made an outcast; everybody was against me'. But it was a pose he could sustain only by ignoring the extent to which he had

---

* The playwright Andreas Munch had received such an award in 1860, but with a nominal duty to lecture at the university attached. Bjørnson's was the first unconditional literary award.

been indulged and encouraged by his fellow-countrymen over the course of the last ten years, before debt, Bjørnson and the desire to travel turned his thoughts towards Rome. Botten Hansen had recently been appointed librarian at the university in Kristiania and the Holland arranged a supper in his honour at the Hotel du Nord, and this doubled as a farewell to Ibsen. The Oslo fjord was still iced up, so he travelled by small boat down the fjord to Drøbak, where the ocean-going *Kronprindsesse Louise* awaited, sailing for Copenhagen on Saturday, 2 April 1864 and arriving the following evening.[8]

7

The Prophet
Brand

The four years of Ibsen's first sojourn in Italy were to be the most intense creative period of his life. By the end of it he would be wealthy, with a fame throughout Scandinavia that was beginning to spread into Germany, whence it would go on to occupy the whole western world. He also underwent a radical process of self-reinvention to create an outward image that would become – through the Victorian fashion for portrait photography – the agent of this spreading fame.

His journey south began with a fourteen-day stopover in Copenhagen, where Suzannah and Sigurd would be living whilst he was away for the projected year his funds would last. Suzannah's stepmother, Magdalene Thoresen, was then living in the city with her four children, having moved back to Denmark from Bergen after the death of her husband. On 18 April Ibsen left his family, boarded the steamer to Lübeck, and travelled by train through Germany and into Italy. Some forty years later, speaking at a dinner to honour his seventieth birthday in Copenhagen on 1 April 1898, he recalled his first, glowing impressions of the country in what was probably a conscious image of rebirth. Passing beneath a dark curtain of cloud over the Alps the train entered the tunnel, 'and suddenly we found ourselves by the Mira Mare, where the beauty of the south, a strange, bright sheen, shining like white marble, suddenly revealed itself to me.'[1]

Rome, a city of some 200,000 inhabitants,* was at that time still an independent state under Pope Pius IX, protected from Garibaldi's army of nationalists by French troops supplied by Louis Napoleon. It had for several decades past attracted a colony of Scandinavian artists and writers keen to follow Goethe in his *Italienische Reise*. A generation of Danes including Carsten Hauch,

* The population of Kristiania in 1859 was just under 47,000.

99

Ingemann, Oehlenschläger, Hans Christian Andersen, Paludan-Müller and the influential sculptor Bertel Thorvaldsen had opened up the cultural links between north and south, but for Ibsen the single greatest influence was Bjørnson, who spent two years there between 1860 and 1862 and sent home ecstatic letters about the street-life and café-life, the architecture, Michelangelo's paintings, Palestrina's austerely beautiful church music, about the hugely broadening effect the whole experience had had on his life.

Activities in Rome centred on an expatriates' club in the north of the city, the Circolo Scandinavo in the palazzo Correa in Via de' Pontefici, a baroque building at the entrance to Cæsar Augustus's mausoleum, functioning in those days as a combination circus, open-air theatre and concert hall for the inhabitants of the densely populated area. The club was established in 1860 as the Scandinavian Society for Artists and Scientists in Rome under the stewardship of Johan Bravo, whose wages were paid by each of the three Scandinavian lands. Its only other official was Bravo's secretary and the club librarian Lorentz Dietrichson. In lieu of wages Dietrichson had a free apartment on the premises plus light and fuel. He lived with a cat, and was fond of saying that the chairman and the cat were the only paid employees of the club, since the cat kept the place clear of mice and rats in return for a weekly allowance of four *bajocchi* towards its tripe.

Ibsen presented himself in the palazzo Correa on the morning of Sunday 19 June, ringing loudly on the bell. Dietrichson sprang from his bed with a cry of *'Chi è?'* ('Who is it?'), Ibsen was admitted, and sat in the reading room and read the newspapers while Dietrichson dressed. Afterwards they went out to explore the city together. Their day mingled modern and ancient tourism, with a trip to St Peter's during Mass and visits to the Forum Romanum and the Janiculum before relaxing with a carafe of wine in an open-air café in Trastevere with the river flowing right by its walls. Travel and the change of scenery had worked an instant wonder on Ibsen and Dietrichson found him very different from the beleaguered theatre manager he had last met three years previously in Kristiania.

It was the custom of expatriates and tourists to leave the city for the summer months, to avoid the heat and the outbreaks of malaria, and in late June Ibsen, the Dietrichsons, and a Finnish sculptor named Walter Runeberg departed for the town of Genzano, in the Alban Hills, some twenty kilometres south-east of Rome. Runeberg and Ibsen took a room together in the local café, situated behind the billiard room. Ibsen, the bohemian dandy, habitually wore a broad-brimmed hat with a light blue lining which the other Scandinavians called 'the blue grotto'. The local residents in Genzano referred to him as *Capellone* (Big Hat).

The little group spent the early part of the day working, and in the late afternoon would all meet for a meal and a drink in a dark wine-cellar, sharing the place with a large basket containing a bitch and her pups. Now and then the light in the room would disappear completely as an ass positioned himself in front of the window to scratch his rump against the wall. After the meal they would lie reading or chatting together beneath the trees on a hillside overlooking the *Lago di Nemi*, once the centre of the cult-worship of the goddess Diana. Dietrichson, a classical scholar, was reading Ammianus Marcellinus's description of the campaigns of the Emperor Julian the Apostate at the time and, on one such evening, he and Ibsen fell into conversation about Julian. Ibsen was at once fired with the ambition to write a play about him, and expressed the hope that no one else would tackle the subject before him.

He then tempted fate by setting the plan aside for nine years, turning instead to an idea that seems to have come to the surface during his journey across Europe, as the direct result of an experience during a few days spent in Berlin. Germany had just defeated Denmark in the decisive action at Dybbøl which gave the Germans possession of the disputed territories of Schleswig-Holstein, and Ibsen arrived in time to see the victory parade at which the captured Danish cannons were displayed. He saw some among the crowd riding on the gun-carriages and spitting into the mouths of the cannons. As a keen pan-Scandinavian Ibsen found the experience acutely distressing and since his arrival in Rome had lost no time in revealing to his fellow Norwegians and Swedes the extent of his disgust at their failure to go to Denmark's aid. In his memoirs Dietrichson recalls Ibsen talking about the war and what he had seen in Berlin. He grew impassioned, and when he was finished no one spoke, no one touched their drink. 'I think', wrote Dietrichson, 'that all of us there that afternoon felt we were hearing the Marseillaise of the north, heard only by a small band of us there in the Roman night . . . and I know that I have never since been even remotely as moved by the power of the spoken word as I was on that evening.'[2]

Since many of Ibsen's negative attitudes towards his own countrymen were ostensibly shaped by this particular event in history, and his anger on the issue has been routinely admired, it is worth examining the situation in some detail. Schleswig-Holstein was the region comprising the southern part of the Jutland Peninsula that joined Denmark and Prussia. Though the population of Holstein was entirely German (in 1815 Holstein became a member of the German Confederation) and that of Schleswig partly so, the duchies had been united for several centuries with the King of Denmark as their duke. In 1848 a Danish nationalist movement sought to annex them to the crown of Denmark, a move resisted by the inhabitants with the support of Prussian troops. A compromise was reached in 1852, but the Danish crown continued to try to acquire the duchies. In the brief summer war of 1864, the aftermath of which Ibsen witnessed in Berlin, the Danes were defeated and Schleswig-Holstein ceded to the German states.

Any dispassionate analysis of the situation will not find Ibsen's fury over Norwegian and Swedish refusal to participate sympathetic. The Danish soldiers themselves were not keen on the war. Christopher Bruun, sometimes mentioned as one of models for Brand, was one of the eighty-nine Norwegians who did volunteer to fight. He wrote in one of his letters home after the fall of Dybbøl that 'The soldiers say that it's the gentlemen in Copenhagen, the "posh folk", who are to blame for the war and the defeat; They aren't afraid, they're tough, calm peasants and not easy to scare; but it is probably no easy matter to drive them to accomplish great deeds.'[3]

Bruun's mother Lina, his sister Thea and brother Peter happened to be among the Norwegians staying at Genzano that summer, and Lina Bruun carried on a correspondence with her son that in perhaps surprising detail concerned itself with Ibsen's enigmatic character:

Henrik Ibsen has arrived in Genzano. His genius needs to accuse, something to complain about; but since there is not really enough to complain about he first has to create a Norway so dreadful that there is not a shred of hope left for it, so that gives him something to warrant his great punishment. He has sworn never to set foot in this wretched land again, where evil-eyed people stare at him through their lorgnettes, where all he has asked for is a quiet room in which to write – and even this apparently proved impossible. Petty bourgeois behaviour persecuted him wherever he went; but of course it's a great honour for poor old Norway to have a son who sees things so plainly (. . .) The government of Norway is dishonoured because it doesn't precipitate us into a war with Prussia and Austria. Those who gave their personal promise of help to Denmark but couldn't keep their word find themselves martyred. As to what their sufferings might be I have no idea. And I have to listen to all this.[4]

Ibsen was already thinking of extending his exile from Norway beyond the one year, for on a couple of occasions he seemed to be looking to use his indignation over Dybbøl to make his return home a moral impossibility. At Fru Bruun's birthday party on 30 June he announced to anyone who cared to listen that he did not wish his son to grow up a Norwegian, that he had no wish for the boy to grow to manhood among a people whose highest aim in life was to be little Englishmen. Fru Bruun, who lived in constant fear of news of the death of her son, became so incensed by his armchair sword-waving that when he requested permission to come to her house one evening to read some poems she blankly refused.

Their relationship continued for a while on what she called a footing of armed neutrality as she resolutely rejected all his attempts to associate himself with those who, like her son, had actually volunteered to fight for Denmark. On one occasion Ibsen announced that in the event of Christopher dying in battle he would personally erect a memorial to him in the form of a poem which would stand as a permanent monument to the shame of the Norwegian people who had broken their word. In fury Lina Bruun replied that if he did she would with her own hands make sure that any such monument was buried deep underground. It is said that Ibsen's eyes filled with tears at this, perhaps one of the few times when the horrific reality of war penetrated the halo of disappointed glory with which he was surrounding it.

And during the course of the two summer months in Genzano Lina Bruun began to realise the extent to which Ibsen's posing was not to be taken too seriously. Her other son Peter, who was suffering from tuberculosis, told his mother that at times Ibsen spoke quite differently about his homeland, so that she was soon admitting herself that 'Ibsen, for all his hatred of Norway, is so thoroughly

Norwegian that I cannot help but like like him anyway.' Writing to Christopher on 5 August she told him: 'A double nature like his is not easy to understand. In daily intercourse he is the most sociable, amusing and friendly man you could imagine.' Runeberg the sculptor and he could play together as harmlessly as boys, she said, until suddenly the devil got in him and his only wish was for one single hour of power in which to change the world. At the age of thirty-six this involved his standing up on Monte Cavo and ordering the entire population of the world (with the exception of Danes and Poles) to walk into the sea and drown themselves. Runeberg would be his second in command on the great day. Fru Bruun, Peter and Thea would fly away like white doves. Later on Ibsen met and became friends with Christopher Bruun. Once Bruun asked him why, if he felt so strongly about it, he had not volunteered to fight himself. 'We writers have a different call; we sing for you,' replied Ibsen. 'Oh thanks very much,' replied Bruun, 'you sing about it, and we're supposed to do it.' But Bruun understood Ibsen. 'Poor man!' he wrote to his mother once, 'he deserves your pity more than your anger. His attacks on Norway are probably just expressions of his own unhappiness, so one shouldn't pay too much attention to them.'[5]

Lina Bruun's account of Ibsen's fantasy in free flight in Genzano is in sharp contrast to the accounts from his theatre-managing days of his morose and taciturn ways. The new and exotic surroundings were intoxicating, as was the wine, and Lina Bruun marked his pleasure in life. He was no drunkard, she said, but 'he is very fond of a glass of wine, which livens him up, and since he's lively enough anyway it means that he is easily *misunderstood*'. When he was writing, she added, he drank nothing but tea.

Writing at this time meant the first attempts to make his anger over Dybbøl work for him in the form of *Brand*. In his autobiographical letter to Peter Hansen of 1870 he described how he kept a scorpion in an empty beer-glass on his desk during these days. Now and then it would become sick, he wrote. Then he would drop it a piece of soft fruit into which it would ejaculate its poison. Aren't we poets the same? he wondered. Don't the laws of nature also apply in the spiritual realm? His point was clear enough, despite the dubious zoology. It was Thea Bruun who captured the scorpion for him, an extremely large one she found above her brother Peter's bed one morning. Lina Bruun made Ibsen promise he would not dip his pen in it, to which he replied, ambivalently, that he intended it strictly for private use.

On one of their days off Dietrichson and Ibsen decided to go to Castel Gandolfo to witness the arrival of Pope Pius IX as he took up his summer residence there. They hired two asses for the purpose and set off. On arrival they found the main street so tightly lined with waiting crowds that they had no option but to ride with as much dignity as they could muster down the middle, to the great amusement of the locals. Stage-fright presently overcame the asses, which first bolted and then, to wild applause, lay flat on their stomachs in the middle of the road, whence they had to be hauled away, neighing and braying as the papal procession appeared through the town gates. Ibsen, with his horror of appearing ridiculous, was mortified.

In the late summer they returned to Rome and Ibsen was joined by Suzannah and Sigurd. Dietrichson, one of Suzannah's childhood friends from Bergen and an admirer of her character, accompanied him when he went to meet them, and recorded the long and tender kiss which they exchanged after the six-month absence. Their first address was a small flat on the corner of Due Macelli and Via Capo le Case. Ibsen continued in good spirits throughout the winter, but his pleasure during these first months in Italy, the invigorating surroundings, the companionship and the intense excitement of creating a character like Brand (in this earliest incarnation still known as 'Koll') were darkened by a companion sense of humiliation, best illustrated by the fact that the passport on which he had travelled, issued to him at Kristiania Police Station on 31 March 1864, shows that he was misrepresenting himself to be 'Doctor. phil: og Stipendiat Henrik Ibsen' (Doctor of Philosophy and scholarship holder Henrik Ibsen).

The causes of this feeling of lack of self-worth were rooted in his family's social decline, in the 'fall' with Else Sophie Birkedalen, and now in his inability or unwillingness to meet the debts he had accumulated during his last few months before leaving Kristiania. On his own initiative Bjørnson had organised a collection among his acquaintances for Ibsen, raising the sum of 700 speciedaler, which Ibsen could add to the 400 speciedaler already granted by the goverment. This was a handsome gesture; yet coming from his only serious literary rival in Norway it left him squirming. A mutual acquaintance, the lawyer Berhard Dunker, was to administer the fund for Ibsen, sending him money as and when requested. Dunker and Bjørnson were also Ibsen's agents in dealing with Nandrup, to whom Ibsen still owed 400 speciedaler.

Ibsen wrote a number of long letters to Bjørnson after his return to Rome from Genzano that first autumn, full of the same sort of self-doubt that Skule in *The Pretenders* discovered whenever he compared himself with King Håkon. The mere thought of Bjørnson intimidated Ibsen, devastated his self-confidence, aroused his love, his admiration, his fear, his guilt. In effect he sent Bjørnson reports on himself, on the spiritual and educational progress he hoped he was making, as though unable to shake off the feeling that Bjørnson now owned him. In his letter of 16 September 1864 he told Bjørnson that Suzannah and Sigurd would be arriving later in the autumn: 'I hope you approve of this arrangement. From the purely practical point of view, let me just remark that it will be cheaper for us all to live here together than for me to continue to keep a second household in Copenhagen.'[6] And in terms recalling the letter to his walking-companion C. J. Anker in Bergen in 1858 he confessed his enduring sense of unease about his personality:

> I know that this is a failing of mine, this inability to approach intimately and openly those people whose nature requires such absolute giving; I am a bit like the Skald in *The Pretenders*, I can never bear to reveal myself completely, I feel that if I try to express myself I only ever manage to give a false impression of what I am really like deep inside, the real me, so I prefer not to, and this is why sometimes it seems as though we two have as it were stood observing one another at a distance.

To another of his more extrovert, self-confident correspondents, his mother-in-law Magdalene Thoresen, he expressed something similar in a letter of 3 December 1865:

> I have been meaning to write to you for a long time; now finally I am able. Up until now I have never been able to be myself with you, either in person or in writing. Whatever innermost things I wished to say achieved only a false expression, and since I knew this only too well I preferred to close myself off.

Yet as he told Bjørnson, he firmly believed, or willed himself to believe, that exile would change him, had indeed already changed him. He analysed the change as the driving out of an addiction to the aesthetic, 'distancing' response to life which he had cultivated since the *Andhrimner* days and all through his association with Botten Hansen and Vinje in the Holland:

> I have purged myself of aestheticism, that before laid claim to a self-sufficient existence within me and had me in its power. Aestheticism in this sense seems to me as great a curse for poetry as theology is for religion. You have never been burdened with aestheticism in this sense. You have never looked at life through the circle made by the artist's thumb and forefinger. – Isn't being able to write the most wonderful and happy of gifts? The accompanying responsibility is great, but I now feel I possess the necessary seriousness and ability to be hard myself. Once when I was in Copenhagen I heard an aesthete say: 'Christ really is the most interesting phenomenon in the history of the world.' – The aesthete in him savoured Christ as the gourmet savours the sight of an oyster.

The credit for this liberation he gave to Bjørnson. But does a person really change? Perhaps the claim only shows that he remained as romantic as he had ever been. In his letter to C. J. Anker in 1858 he referred to his own former longing for 'a great sorrow' that would fill his days and give his life meaning. It was a silly phase of his life, he confessed, and he had left it behind him. But his monomania on the subject of Dybbøl shows that this was not the case. Jatgeir told Skule that it was the gift of sorrow that made him a poet, and Ibsen had realised instinctively that in order to write *Brand* he needed that gift too. Having no sorrow of his own to hand he borrowed Dybbøl from the Danes, turning himself into an honorary Dane in the process. He identified the state of affairs very specifically for Magdalene Thoresen: 'We (Norway and Sweden) have nothing that unites us, no great sorrow, such as Denmark has, because our people lack the kind of spiritual elevation necessary to be able to grieve.'[7] At times Ibsen's fury tipped over into the irrational. He wrote approvingly to Magdalene Thoresen of the Italian mothers in Piedmont, Genoa, Novara, Alessandria who took their fourteen-year-old sons out of school so that they could join Garibaldi on his march to Palermo: and how many of our members of parliament, he asked rhetorically, do you think would do the same thing if the Russians were to invade through Finnmark?

The other side of this danophilia was his cultivation of a hatred of Germans. On 1 January 1865 he submitted a resolution to the committee of the Circolo Scandinavo in which he proposed that the constitution be amended on two points, one to allow 'Danish Schleswegians' to be members, and a second to impose an outright ban on members bringing German guests into the club. At an Extraordinary General Meeting on 6 February the first suggestion was accepted, the second rejected.

Socially speaking Ibsen's life in Rome remained insularly bound by the Circolo Scandinavo throughout the four years of this first stay in the city, and though he began a vocabulary book of Italian words he seems to have made no progress with the language and to have had little or no contact with Italians. By early April 1865 he was signing as a member of the club committee himself, a role he continued in with obvious enjoyment for almost two years.

Some of his most frequent contributions as a club member during these years were as a regular user of the complaints protocol, in which he drew the attention of fellow-members to such matters as the poor quality of the reading lamps. Entries for 14 March 1865 include his comment on a cast of Thorvaldsen's sculpture *The Dancer* which stood in one of the club's rooms: 'A packet of adhesive has been lying on the dancer's pedestal since the New Year. Hereby suggest it be removed.' And in November of the same year: 'Propose the dancer's left toe be restored.' A little later he suggested that a large map of the papal state be purchased and hung in the club as soon as possible. It was an almost Pooterish existence, with time and mental energy expended on matters that scarcely seemed to warrant it and the dividing line between mock-pedantic humour and genuine pedantry often hard to discern. Sometimes a ferocious feud would break out over something as apparently trivial as the choice of newspapers available. For some three years, at Ibsen's suggestion, the club subscribed to the Vatican newspaper, *L'Osservatore Romano*. Early in 1868 the subscription was cancelled without warning, and in the ensuing argument Ibsen forced an opportunity to unite his hostility towards Germans with his displeasure over the cancellation of the paper. He claimed that the committee's action compelled those Scandinavians who wished to read *L'Osservatore Romano* to do so – for a reason he did not detail – in some nearby German artists' bar. The committee declined to resubscribe to the paper, describing it as 'servile, shabby and unreliable'. On 10 March Ibsen replied: 'I remain insistent that the subscription to the newspaper *L'Osservatore Romano* be continued. The cancellation of the newspaper was an act of *stupidity*; likewise the committee's reply'.[8] In response the committee expressed dismay at Ibsen's use of language: 'the honourable member's language will not be tolerated'. Ibsen would not be cowed: 'That is as may be; but it must be tolerated, since it is the truth. If neither the complaints protocol nor the copy of the Society's rules had been illegally removed from the premises for a period of one and a half days I should already have obliged by explaining my description of both the committee and its reply. I now hasten to do so.' Two days later Ibsen offered a compromise to the committee: he would remove the offending phrase if allowed to replace it with the words 'extreme thoughtlessness'. There the matter appeared to rest.

Perhaps he felt such an attitude of mingled responsibiliy and irritation was necessary to keep the club from descending into chaos; but his adherence to such Protestant qualities so far from home did not make him popular. The Swedish painter Georg von Rosen used to amuse himself by attending the club in company with a 'Herr Sverdrup' who was in fact a young woman dressed as a man. No one minded particularly once the deception was revealed, save Ibsen, who inundated the complaints book with entries on the affair and succeeded in making the atmosphere so unpleasant that in the end a dozen or so Swedish members and friends of Rosen began spending their evenings elsewhere.

The majority of anecdotes of daily life involving Ibsen passed down to us in the memoirs of such as Frederik Knudtzon show him in a generally unflattering light, as a testy, irritable man, with a tendency to be aggressive when drunk. In terms of good stories the amusing times, of which there must have been many, have to be taken as read, for in later years Ibsen spoke of this first stay in Rome as a happy time. He had friends, and a sense of mischief of his own, milder than Rosen's and inevitably coloured by seriousness. It showed itself in one occasion when he was caught defacing one of the club's magazines containing a portrait of Manderström, the Swedish foreign minister whom he held chiefly responsible for deserting the Danes in the Prussian war. Ibsen drew a noose around his neck. Unfortunately a relative of the minister, the poet Carl Snoilsky – the young man whom Ibsen kept thinking he had met during the folk-tale collecting trip in 1862 – was in Rome at the time. He saw the drawing and demanded to know who the culprit was. Ibsen owned up, and the matter was smoothed over (unlike Bjørnson, Ibsen never came to blows with anyone).[9] Indeed he and Snoilsky afterwards struck up an enduring friendship of the long-distance type that suited Ibsen best. In later years he recalled the incident in a letter to Dietrichson, referring to those days, apparently without irony, as his *Sturm-und-Drangperiode*.[10]

Dietrichson was one of those Ibsen adressed in his letters as *Carissimo!*, coming from Ibsen a mark of rare intimacy. Another whom he wrote to in this fashion was a Danish lawyer, Anton Klubien, a bluff, extroverted Bjørnson-type whose company he greatly enjoyed. Klubien was part of a shifting Scandinavian community that ebbed and flowed with the Roman seasons, and it was here that Ibsen found the kind of company he appreciated most. Besides Klubien and Snoilsky there were a number of young sculptors – Bergslien, Prior, Kiellberg and Runeberg – all attracted to Rome by the opportunities to study as well as the ready availability of marble. This large crowd would gather in the early evenings to drink wine at a bar they called *Tritonekneipen*, not far from Ibsen's apartment on Due Macelli. These *osterierne*, as they were called, were favourite features of the tourist landscape in Rome. During the 1860s the city still boasted its *Goethekneipe* and its *Thorvaldsenkneipe*. Drinking dens of a primitive sort that appealed particularly to Norwegians escaping the pietistic, guilt-laden drinking culture of home, Dietrichson described them as little more than black holes, with a chimney at the back and a fire tended by an invariably fat hostess. Seating was at rude benches placed along either wall, and the feeble light from a smoking oil lamp heightened the general atmosphere of dim romance. The possession of a good knowledge of these places, of where the wine was good and where merely cheap poison, was, says Dietrichson, valued as highly as a knowledge of history or of art. Customers bought their own food with them, ham or sausage or whatever, and lettuces which could be washed in the nearest fountain. During the first winter in Rome, when *Brand* was still growing inside Ibsen, Dietrichson noticed how time and again during these gatherings Ibsen would work the conversation round to a discussion on one of the major themes of *Brand*, the morality of 'the spirit of compromise'. In later years he would irritably deny that the play was necessarily about a priest, saying that his hero could equally as well have been an artist, and the topic of key-swallowing to which he so frequently reverted during these conversations bears out his claim. The circumstances of the death of the Rowley-poet Thomas Chatterton at the age of eighteen, which Ibsen perhaps knew of from Alfred de Vigny's play about him, fascinated him. Ibsen believed that Chatterton died because he had swallowed his latchkey in an attempt to stave off hunger and keep writing poetry rather than get an ordinary job, and the discussions would concentrate on the correctness of this attitude. The connection with Brand and his motto 'All or nothing' is clearly discernible. Ibsen's goal would be to flush out some hapless bourgeois willing to protest that Chatterton should certainly have got a job, as a shop assistant if need be, rather than die for his writing, and then to disagree with him, passionately urging that any real artist would always swallow his latchkey rather than sell out, and suggesting that this would have been his way too.

Ibsen was a diligent and observant cultural tourist in Rome, and Dietrichson an ideal companion in this respect, with his wide knowledge of the art and architecture of antiquity. In Ibsen's first winter there he had the opportunity to follow a course of twenty lectures his friend gave on the archeology and topography of ancient Rome, delivered to his Scandinavian audiences from a variety of sites – the Forum Romanum, Palatine hill, Caracalla's baths and Titus's thermal springs. This was a period in which some of the most exciting archeological finds were taking place, and hardly a week went by without some important new statue or site being unearthed. Ibsen's mysterious relationship with stone, from his early fascination with folktales about supernatural rock-dwellers and mountains that swallow up human beings to the fear of his own petrifaction, was already well-established by this time. From his earliest writings it is clear that the sculptor's art – the carving of human beings from blocks of stone – was for him the art form most closely related to his own – the creating of temporary statues made of flesh and blood. So it is not surprising that sculpture and contrasting sculptural styles were the dominant feature of his response to wandering through what was for him essentially a city-sized museum. In letters home and discussion there are no references to great paintings, to great works of Italian literature or music. Sculpture alone preoccupies him. Again Dietrichson was a stimulating companion in this respect, though of course what he stimulated to, Ibsen being Ibsen, was disagreement. Dietrichson recalled their visiting the Vatican gallery together, where a discussion arose as to the respective merits of

Greek and Roman portrait busts. Dietrichson urged the superiority of the Greeks, who worked the head and bone-structure of the face in the direction of the typical and the general, while Ibsen favoured the Roman way, of individualising the heads by the inclusion of detail, like the furrowing in the brow of the Marius in the Museo Chiaramonti, on the grounds that this conveyed more about the spirit of the subject than the idealised Greek method. Indeed, this was one of his first impressions of the art of antiquity, a feeling of disappointment at the absence of a sense of individuality in the work and in the artist. He compared the state of affairs to the heroic ballads of the north, which also seemed to him the diffuse products of a people and an epoch rather than the unique works of individual artists.

His prejudices did not leave him unable to appreciate classicism, however, and one piece that he must have contemplated at length – and perhaps even fallen in love with – was the Melpomene, the Muse of Tragedy in the Vatican. A long letter to Bjørnson described the almost visionary effect the statue had on him, revealing to him the essence of what Greek tragedy was: 'that indescribably elevated, great and peaceful joy in the facial expression, the richly leaf-crowned head, with its unearthly quality of the luxuriant and the bacchantic. The eyes, that look within at the same time as they look through and far beyond what they are looking at – that is what Greek tragedy was like.[11] He was deeply struck by the persistence through time of these pieces of stone, acquiring from them an understanding of what 'imperishability in beauty' really means. 'If only I too, in my particular field, can make use of this understanding,' he told Bjørnson.

Almost godless by now, Ibsen was yet god-fearing, if we can allow the paradox. Lazing about, relaxing, drinking wine in the sunshine, enjoying oneself, these were all obscurely tainted pastimes. In one of his early 'reports' to Bjørnson he wrote: 'Often I lie half the day out between the excavations on the Via Latina or on the old Via Appia, and though it is an idleness yet I do not think it can be called time-wasting.' This he could write because he had come to Rome to work, and it never seriously occurred to him to do anything else.

He mentions *Brand* for the first time in his letter to Bjørnson of 16 September 1864, where he praises the peaceful suroundings of Rome as conducive to writing and refers to 'a longish poem' and 'a tragedy on Julianus Apostata', both of which he hoped to complete by the following spring, at the latest by the following summer. In its original form *Brand* was to be an epic poem, using iambic pentameters in verses of eight lines. He worked hard on it throughout the winter of 1864–5, setting aside the tragedy as well as a plan brought with him from home to write a five-act drama about a sixteenth-century adventurer named Mogens Heinessøn.*

In July 1865 the Ibsens moved for the summer to Ariccia in the Alban Hills, helped by another award of 100 speciedaler from the Royal Scientific Society in Trondheim. They remained there until September. Ibsen's day would begin sometimes as early as four a.m. with a walk in the nearby tree-filled Chigi Park. Sigurd Ibsen, revisiting Ariccia in later years, called it 'a strange, dreaming landscape, with an unforgettable atmosphere mingling ancient myth and heathendom'.[12] Opposite the Chigi Park was an old church with stone benches in front where Ibsen would sit sometimes in the evenings after the day's work was done, often in the company of Lars Hansen, a Danish painter living locally.

Ibsen was not satisfied with the work he had taken to the country with him. His sense of unease continued to bother him until he was released from it one day in dramatic fashion. As he wrote to Bjørnson in September 1865:

Everything is all right now, and in truth has been all along, apart from those times when I did not know what I was going to do next, not only as regards money but also in my work. Then one day while walking in St Peter's – I had some errand in Rome – all at once I had a very clear image of what it was I wanted to say. Now I have jettisoned all the material of the last year that plagued me but never seemed to get anywhere. In the middle of July I started on something new, and it flowed for me in a way nothing has ever flowed for me before. It is new in the sense that I then began writing it down, but the material and the mood have hovered and brooded over my mind ever since all those unpleasant experiences back home which forced me to look inside myself and our lives there, and to think deeply about things which before I had only lightly touched upon, not having then the necessary seriousness.

* At one point in his career Heinessøn had to flee the country from an accusation of incest, a crime that held a lifelong fascination for Ibsen.

The major difference was that he reconceived *Brand* as a drama instead of a verse epic. A change of name for the main character symbolised the clarity of vision he acquired that day in St Peter's, the Koll (hill) of the former becoming the Brand (fire) of the latter. Little of the epic survives – indeed the little that survives may be all he actually wrote of it – but there is enough to see that the drama acquired a great deal more value from the fact of Brand's being a priest than did the epic, a circumstance perhaps confirmed by the fact that Ibsen borrowed a copy of the Bible from the library of the Circolo Scandinavo, in Kalkar's translation, on 16 August that year. 'I read nothing but the Bible,' he wrote to Bjørnson, 'It is powerful and strong.'

Ibsen gave no details of the precise nature of the revelation in St Peter's. It may have been an abstract realisation through the cathedral of the sheer size of vision possible to the human mind. It may have been the feeling, reflected by Brand in the play about the church he himself builds, that on the greatest scale even something as magnificent as St Peter's is puny to its purpose. Or it might have been a quite concrete realisation: for his later plays Ibsen made no secret of the fact that he always required living models as a base on which to improvise, and perhaps the great moment in St Peter's was the realisation that he could base Brand on Gustav Adolf Lammers.* He had never met Lammers personally but knew of him as a charismatic figure who from his post as parish priest in Skien led the religious revivalist movement which swept southern Norway in the 1850s. Ibsen's brother Ole Paus followed Lammers when he left the state church in 1856 and started his own evangelical free church, and even submitted to adult baptism. Ole Paus described Lammers as 'a giant of a man, very handsome, with a voice that carried from the pulpit right out into the market square. A real hell-fire preacher whose motto was "all or nothing".' So powerful was Lammers's charisma that a number of the women who fell under his spell believed him to be the returned Christ. Hedvig also joined the movement, which at its height had some 200 members in Skien. The majority of them were women.

Lammers proved the key into the work, and Ibsen soon found himself for the first time able to write 'both mornings and after-

---

* Ibsen several times emphatically denied that Brand was based on Kierkegaard. He told his biographer Henrik Jæger that 'Kierkegaard was too much the armchair rebel. Lammers, on the other hand, was just the kind of open-air preacher that Brand is.'

1 Ibsen was born in Stockmann's, the house next to the church. To the right of the church were the stocks and to the left the town hall, with prison cell and 'loony bin'

2 The house at Venstøp, just outside Skien, where the family lived after Knud Ibsen's economic ruin in 1834

3 A painting by Ibsen from Grimstad, depicting Elijah under the juniper tree. Ibsen wore a full beard from his earliest youth and the painting hints at his notion of the muse of poetry as a combination of the erotic and the abstract

4 Ole Schulerud, who tried to get *Catiline* published in Kristiania and ended up paying for publication himself

5 Christopher Due, who made the fair copy of *Catiline*, 'a duty he performed so conscientiously that he included every single one of the innumerable dashes left littered across the manuscript at those places where I had been momentarily unable to find the right word'

6 Goethe, the only figure in European literature with whom Ibsen was inclined to compare himself

7 Ludvig Holberg, the father of Scandinavian drama. He was one of Ibsen's earliest inspirations and remained a favourite throughout his life

8 Adam Oehlenschläger, the Danish poet and dramatist whose literary explorations of Scandinavia's heroic past strongly influenced the young Ibsen

9 The prolific French dramatist Eugene Scribe. Though Scribe's themes were too banal to make much impression on him, Ibsen learnt a great deal about practical stagecraft from Scribe's plays

10 The room in the dispensary at Grimstad where Ibsen slept and where he wrote *Catiline*

11 Rikke Holst, whom Ibsen courted in Bergen. He wrote several love-poems to her, but was driven off by her father

12 The company at the Norwegian Theatre in Bergen. *Top row, from the left*: Benedicte Hundevadt, Marie Midling, Ole Bull, Louise Brun, Lucie Johannesen. *Middle section, upper row*: Johannes Brun is on the far right, with Andreas Isachsen standing next to him. Ibsen's job was to 'assist the theatre as dramatist'

13 Magdalene Thoresen, Suzannah's stepmother. Ibsen admired her for her spontaneity and independence. He used elements of her personality for Ellida Wangel in *The Lady from the Sea*

16 *Opposite*: The Norwegian Theatre in Møllergaten, Kristiania, which Ibsen led from 1857 to 1862. The theatre is the building on the right

14 Suzannah Thoresen, whom Ibsen married on 18 June 1858. 'My marriage brought a new seriousness into my life'

15 Ibsen in Napoleonic pose in the early 1860s. Borkman is discovered in a similar pose in *John Gabriel Borkman* as he waits for Foldal, 'standing by the writing-desk with his left hand on the tabletop and his right inside his jacket against his chest'

17 Bjørnstjerne Bjørnson, the poet, dramatist and short story-writer. He was Ibsen's friend, benefactor and rival

18 Paul Botten Hansen, founder-member of 'The Learned Holland' and, as editor of *Illustreret Nyhedsblad* 1851-66, a faithful supporter for Ibsen during his difficult years

19 Lorentz Dietrichson, the secretary of the Circolo Scandinavo, who introduced Ibsen to Rome in 1864. He and Ibsen conducted a minor feud in 1885 but were later reconciled

20 Frederik Hegel, the publisher of *Brand* and all Ibsen's subsequent works. He was also Ibsen's economic advisor: 'I have now – thanks to you – become a capitalist!'

21 The critic Clemens Petersen (*centre*) was the arbiter of literary taste in Denmark in the 1860s. His reservations about *Peer Gynt* infuriated Ibsen. Petersen fled to America in the wake of a homosexual scandal in 1869. Bjørnson is standing on the right

noons'. Looking back on it later he recalled the ecstasy of those days: 'I felt a crusader's joy in me, as though there was nothing in the world I did not have the courage to fight against.'

It must also have helped his state of mind to know that he already had a publisher waiting for the play. This was as a result of another favour from Bjørnson, who spoke enthusiastically of his talent and of his work in progress to his own publisher in Copenhagen, Frederick Hegel, head of the house of Gyldendal. Under Hegel, Gyldendal was in the process of becoming the largest and most influential publishing house in Scandinavia, and Hegel, after Suzannah, probably deserves to be called the greatest influence on Ibsen's professional life. He was born in Fredensborg on 11 May 1817, the illegitimate child of a maid and the young son of the master for whom she worked. His biological father, who later qualified as a doctor, did not marry his mother but helped him at various important stages of his life, and was instrumental in apprenticing him to the publishing house of Gyldendal, under the guidance of its owner Jacob Deichmann. A great friendship developed between the two men, and in 1850 Deichmann handed over ownership of the company to Hegel. It was a financially sound business, but not much more than that, and it published little or no serious literature. The establishment of such a list was the making of Hegel's fortune, as well as that of many a Danish and Norwegian author. He discovered important or popular new Danish writers like Vilhelm Bergsøe, H. V. Kaalund and Christian Richardt, as well as attracting established names like Meir Goldschmidt, C. Hostrup and Vilhelm Topsøe. Hegel was a good judge of literature, had the right personality for dealing with writers, was scrupulously fair in dealing with them, and though personally conservative had the business acumen that enabled him to see the profit in controversial and even scandalous books. Most of the writers associated with Georg Brandes and the breakthrough into modern times in Danish literature that took place in the 1870s and 1880s were his, and he also provided the Danish public with translations of important contemporary European thinkers and writers like Taine, Heyse and Darwin. In a business sense he was a visionary, the first publisher to take account of the close similarity between written Danish, Swedish and Norwegian to treat the whole of Scandinavia as a single potential market. His association with Norwegian writers began in 1858 when he was approached by Camilla Collett, whose feminist novel *The District*

Governor's Daughters had originally been published anonymously in Norway in 1854.* His Danish edition of 1860 was a success and encouraged Hegel to build a list that presently included every major Norwegian writer of the period, among them Bjørnson, then Jonas Lie and later Alexander Kielland, the three writers who, along with Ibsen, came to be known as 'the four great ones', all of whom went on to enjoy big European reputations and become wealthy. Ibsen's mother-in-law Magdalene Thoresen, who was half-Danish anyway, was another writer who did well for him.

But none of them did anything like as well for him, or for themselves, as Ibsen. By the middle of September, on Bjørnson's recommendation, Hegel had already agreed to publish Ibsen's book unread, in an edition of 1,250 copies, and sent him an immediate advance. The first third of the manuscript went off to Copenhagen on 7 November, and the remainder on 15 November. Hegel, anxious as always to have his strongest new books on the market in time for Christmas, sent it straight to the printer. Ibsen, adaptable and anxious for a big Scandinavian readership, readily concurred with the suggestion that the printer ignore his Norwegian orthographical trait of doubling the consonant to indicate the shortness of the preceding vowel.

A hiccup occurred when Hegel actually read the manuscript. What he believed he had bought was the historical tragedy *Julian the Apostate* which Bjørnson had mentioned to him. It was, after all, for this 'large dramatic work on a theme from Roman history' that Ibsen had applied for his grant from the Royal Scientific Society in Trondheim, and this was the play everyone assumed he was writing. Not for the first time, his secretive personality caused confusion around him, for now when Hegel read the unfolding tale of Brand he felt growing doubt about its commercial viability. In the end he wrote to suggest to Ibsen that their agreement on royalties remain in force, but that he would in the first instance publish a first edition only half as large as originally planned. Ibsen, keen for his book to appear in time for the Christmas market, wrote back agreeing. His letter was lost, and both he and Hegel spent the next few weeks in a limbo of ignorance concerning each other's plans.

Ibsen passed the time, among other things, in writing a letter to Clemens Petersen, soliciting a review and flattering Petersen with

* Most publishing in Norway was done by booksellers.

the news that his opinion that Ibsen's natural form was 'verse, with a symbolic underlay' had made him think deeply. The critic, it seemed to him, was right, as the work he was drawing to his attention would shortly demonstrate. Ibsen's desperation to succeed drove him time and again to undertake such manoeuvres, shamelessly flattering his correspondent, usually at the expense of his own countrymen: 'Your criticism will be decisive for the reception my countrymen give the play, and the truths I have been unable to refrain from uttering; but naturally, I would prefer to avoid martyrdom for as long as possible. The newspaper scribblers who call themselves critics in Norway do not understand this.'[13] Thus, from the moment of his first contact with Hegel and Danish Gyldendal, did the once-patriotic Ibsen transform himself into the flirt beneath the stairwell at a party, whispering into the ear of the object of his desires his variation on the oldest betrayer's plaint in the world – *my country doesn't understand me.* But one wonders if Ibsen had selected the right recipient for such a confession. Petersen, who within three years would have to flee Denmark after a paedophile scandal, was hardly the man to respond to Ibsen's fear of martyrdom. In his own way he would have understood better Ibsen's concluding remark to him: 'I have an unendurably oppressive feeling of standing quite alone.'

As it turned out he scarcely needed Petersen's support, for when *Brand* was eventually published on 15 March 1866 – owing to the lost letter in the full edition initially agreed upon – it was an instant success, commercial and critical. A month after publication a correspondent from Copenhagen wrote to the Norwegian *Morgenbladet:* 'Of works of literature recently published here, Henrik Ibsen's *Brand* occupies a position of unique pre-eminence. It is read with the greatest interest, its praises are everywhere sung and its powerful words weigh on all minds.' Two months later Hegel printed a second edition of 500 copies, a third in August, a fourth in December.

Ironically, in view of the fact that Ibsen felt he had chastised his country and its leading men so severely in the drama that such *Sjæle i Lommeformat* (pocket-sized souls)[14] could not possibly look favourably upon him, he received over the next few months repeated indications of the country's pride in him. On 30 April the Royal Scientific Society in Trondheim granted him a further 100 speciedaler, and on 12 May the government voted, with only four against, to award him a lifetime writer's grant of 400 speciedaler per annum;

on 28 July the government also awarded him another travel grant of 350 speciedaler. This grand total of 850 speciedaler, added to the royalties accruing from the four new editions of *Brand,* signalled the end of his poverty. Indeed it all meant that he suddenly had so much money he was able to ask Hegel to hold on to his royalties for the time being. For a while at least, his banking remained attractively primitive: the writer Kristofer Janson, who borrowed a small amount of money from him at about this time, wrote that he kept quantities of it wrapped in a sock.

Brand is a priest. As the play opens he is passing close to his childhood home on a pilgrimage in search of a higher connecting of himself with God. He becomes involved in an incident in which he shows great bravery by crossing stormy waters to hear the last confession of a dying sinner, a man who has in anger murdered his own child. No one else dared make the crossing, and Brand's courage, built on his faith in God, wins him the admiring love of a young woman, Agnes. She deserts her boyfriend Einar, an artist, and marries Brand. They have a child. Brand abandons his personal mission to remain as pastor to the local community. He is a severe leader, an Old Testament prophet. Then his baby son falls ill and needs a warmer clime in order to survive. Brand sees this as a test of his faith and will not move. The child dies. A year or so later Agnes dies of grief. Brand pays for the erection of a magnificent new church, yet once it is finished it does not seem to him magnificent after all. He leads the people up into wilderness high above the town on a pilgrimage without physical goal, with the only aim of enduring suffering in the name of God. Enthusiastic at first, the people soon tire of the pilgrimage. They turn on Brand and drive him away with stones. In the final scenes he is visited by the spirit of his dead wife who tempts him to seek his own ease. He rejects her, and his only companion at the last is a mad girl, Gerd. She fires a rifle-shot at a hawk, precipitating an avalanche. As the mountain buries Brand a voice is heard, crying, 'Han er deus caritatis' (He is the god of love).

Brand's physical origins may have been, as Ibsen himself suggested, in his experiences while passing through Berlin, of seeing vulgar displays of triumphalism directed against a people for whom he had always felt friendship and admiration. And in his own delicate humiliation it is easy to see how he could project the vulgar triumphalism of the crowd on to his own situation, leading him to reassert himself by furious displays of righteous anger over the 1864 war. It was probably during the writing of *Brand* that he discovered the value of anger itself as a creative fuel, for the majority of the plays he later wrote would be born from similar clouds of almost self-consciously cultivated anger. Even when the success of *Brand* was an established fact he continued to give vent to his curiously treacherous anger, in a letter to Hegel relating his hope 'that I may in the future enjoy the honour and pleasure of being associated with you as an author, as it is my purpose as firmly as possible to associate myself with Denmark. Norwegians and Swedes owe a terrible debt of blood to you which must be washed away.'[15]

Yet like all great art *Brand* effortlessly transcended the author's own immediate understanding of it. It was more than anything else a Herculean effort to be done once and for all with the hated aesthetic response to life, by an act of will to peel off the mask of detachment, cynicism, sarcasm and irony behind which he had been shelting for so many years. His anger over Dybbøl was action for him. It was involvement, it was daring to be openly serious, to care deeply about something outside his own skin. Brand, that lonely, passionate tower of a man, was a statement of the hero he wanted to be, a man exploding through that prissy circle of thumb and forefinger described by the poet of 'On the Heights', not a man of God but a man *part*-God.

Of earlier work it is *Love's Comedy* which best predicts *Brand.* The marriage between Brand and Agnes is based on the same mutual spiritual admiration that brings Falk and Svanhild together. *Brand* shows what happens when the idealistic couple involved take the risk of marrying, as Falk and Svanhild did not. Brand and Falk have much in comon, notably the angry, fundamentalist contempt for the spiritual shabbiness of ordinary people and the spirit of compromise. The advance involved in *Brand* is that, while in the earlier play Falk swallows his fundamentalism in order to rejoin his friends, Brand remains intransigent in his opposition to the spirit of compromise and tries to wrench the community over into his fundamentalism. Ibsen had used his motto 'All or nothing' earlier as a characterising position in *The Pretenders,* where it is Skule's response to the suggestion that he and Haakon might share the kingdom. One could almost say that without realising it, Skule – and Ibsen – had found there that 'kingly thought' which both of them longed for so much, for 'All or nothing' is Brand's very own 'kingly thought'.

Humanity is not a godly quality in Brand's eyes. He asks 'Was God humane towards Jesus Christ?' What he neither realises nor accepts is the purpose of Christ's death, that Christ died *for* us. He is determined to rival both God and Christ in his willingness to sacrifice, and Brand's Promethean dimensions are referred to on the title page of the earliest extant manuscript of the play, which has beneath the title the words 'And he created Man in his own image' carefully crossed out. For some Brand – and through him, Ibsen – became a religious hero. But perhaps it takes an atheist to write a great play about God, and Ibsen was very close to atheism by the time he wrote this play. Not long afterwards he began, to the great disappointment of some of his readers, the process of distancing himself from its overtly religious theme. To a young novelist Laura Kieler who had written a 'sequel' to the play, entitled *Brand's Daughters*, he wrote that *Brand* was 'in every respect a work of art and nothing but'. That his hero was a priest was merely a detail. He made the same disavowals to Georg Brandes in 1869, and in 1873 replied to a letter from a reader who wished to know whether his purpose in *Brand* had been to confirm the biblical truth 'that man cannot be the justifier of his own deeds' and that, on the contrary, his only purpose had been 'to depict a person of great energy.'[16]

Evidence of the narrow but real distance Ibsen observed between himself and his creation is the even-handedness of the treatment of those opposed to Brand. Einar, the artist who loses Agnes to Brand, is treated with respect by Ibsen. So is the Sheriff, the pragmatist who gives the hungry people food instead of appealing to their spiritual vanity, as Brand does, by telling them that man does not live by bread alone. In later plays Ibsen tended to neglect this even-handedness in the treatment of antagonists. Brand himself is the subject of a monumental ambivalence which sounded echoes throughout its first Scandinavian readership: was he a hero or a villain? Was he to be admired and copied or despised as an anti-Christ? Ibsen was able to achieve this range of debate because he contained the range of paradoxes within himself. It is an extraordinary thought that he could commute between the creation of this titan during his days and in the evening join battle with fellow members at the Circolo Scandinavo over such matters as the provision of new carpets, better oil lamps and Italian newspapers. More-over the tendency to separate out Ibsen's later plays from *Brand* is only an example of historical packaging, for the ethics of the play were every bit as much the debated topic of the hour in mid-nineteenth-century Scandinavian society as were the institution of marriage, local government corruption, and hereditary sexual disease for his later audiences.

What is one to make of Ibsen's passion in the name of religion? On one level *Brand* shows the technical mastery of the writer able to give massively credible expression to a position he does not hold personally. But there is more to it than that. Ibsen may have lost his faith; but the social visionary in him read the signs of a new age dawning in the sensational success of *On the Origin of Species*. He sensed the imminence of the great challenge to God from Nietzsche, Rutherford, Freud and others, and in his conservative anarchism cried out for *others* to resist it, as though what he wanted was not change in the world at all but a titanic revival of faith that would ensure the survival of a revitalised past.

After *Brand* Ibsen carried out an extensive programme of self-reinvention which began in the spring and summer of 1866 and continued for the next three years. He risked a partial exposure of his face, abandoning the full beard he had worn since puberty and shaving his upper lip and chin to cultivate a priestly ruff of hair under the jawline and thick, bushy sideburns. This new beard had the effect of heavily weighting his face, accentuating the downward curve of the lips. In contrast to the bohemian style which had charac-terised his last years in Kristiania he began dressing with neat, almost pedantic care in the manner of a London businessman. Thus did he announce to himself and his surroundings his re-entry into the middle class from which he had been in exile since his childhood in Skien and his father's financial ruin. With great deliberation he created an image of himself somewhere between businessman and high-church priest that he would maintain for the remainder of his life; and that would in its consistency presently make him one of the most easily recognisable celebrities in Europe. In the set of photographic portraits with which he documented his life from this time onwards, the public image ages, but does not change.

Psychologically the image brought him close to the state of human statue which was the ideal of Victorian self-certainty. He had the deeply Victorian desire to seem to be in complete and knowing charge of himself. Marx was perhaps the only philosopher of note from this period who understood that progress is haphazard and moves in jerks and fits. Ibsen cannot have liked the idea. As he insisted in a letter to Lorenz Dietrichson: 'My development has been absolutely and wholly consistent.'[17] He willed it to be so, edited his personality until it was so, shaped his appearance until it was so, until he could claim, in the spirit of Taine, to have colonised himself.

Ibsen's process of self-reinvention penetrated even to his handwriting, and over the course of the same two- or three-year period he began whipping its formerly uncertain loops and straggles into a punishingly upright legibility. In time the eradication of spontaneity would lead him to write letters by hand with justified margins, even splitting words in the middle to give his handwriting something of the impersonality and authority of the printed page. It is natural to presume that the nature of the change in his handwriting amounted almost to a psychological statement about the new certainty of purpose and direction in his life after *Brand*; yet one should not lose sight of the practical aspect involved. Ibsen lived a thousand miles from his publisher. The post between Denmark and Italy took between fourteen and sixteen days to arrive, and it was not uncommon for it not to arrive at all. This presented obvious difficulties for a writer, particularly at the proof-reading stages of proceedings, and Ibsen discovered that to make his handwriting as legible as possible was one very sensible way of minimising the number of misreadings the printer might make.

If the outer man was under control it was a long time before the inner man followed suit, and he remained at the mercy of a delicate sense of *amour propre* which at times led him into slightly disgraceful behaviour. An incident that took place about a fortnight after the publication of *Brand* seems to show him trying to force recognition of an authority he perhaps thought he ought now to possess. The young Edvard Grieg was in Rome briefly that winter, and on 6 April received news of the death from tuberculosis of his close friend Rikard Nordraak at the age of twenty-four.* Three days later a concert was given at the club by a quintet of Italian musicians. Ibsen was present, and later on in the evening demanded that there should be dancing. News of Nordraak's tragically early death had affected

* Nordraak was a cousin of Bjørnson's and composer of the music to the national anthem.

1845

1860

1868

1872

1877

1884

1899

As part of his metamorphosis after the success of *Brand* and *Peer Gynt*,
Ibsen changed his handwriting

the whole Norwegian colony and the suggestion was greeted in
silence. Undaunted he merely repeated his demands for the floor
to be cleared for dancing. Grieg, a dismayed witness to the scene,
records that Ibsen became absolutely furious at his failure to command obedience.[18] Later in the year a rather dull party was in progress at the Circolo Scandinavo's premises. As the speeches flagged
someone rose and called for glasses to be raised in a toast to the
two arrangers of the evening, Lars Hansen and Henrik Ibsen. Ibsen
rose angrily to his feet and halted proceedings, saying that he
refused to allow his health to be drunk on the grounds that he was
a member of the Food Committee.[19]

And towards the end of the year he received a piece of long-
delayed news that more than anything else must have reminded
him of how hard it was to slough off an old and rejected self. He
learnt, apparently for the first time, that a matter of days after his
departure from Norway two years earlier his creditor, Nandrup,
had applied to Bernhard Dunker, then managing Ibsen's funds, for
repayment of the debts to him. Dunker had declined to let him
have the 500 speciedaler he was owed and Nandrup, seemingly

unaware of Ibsen's intention to leave the country, had thereupon officially requested that the property held by him as security for the loan be sold by auction. It was duly announced in both *Morgenbladet* and *Christiania Intelligenssedler* that an auction of Henrik Ibsen's property was to be held at Møllergaten 7. The list included mahogany chairs, a sofa, a divan, a bed, a writing desk, armchairs, mirrors, coffee tables, buckets, bedclothes, rugs, blankets, paintings, vases, cutlery, a terracotta bust, more mirrors, a dozen punch glasses, ditto wine glasses, a bookcase, a cot, curtains, kitchen equipment – an abandoned family life for sale.

The auction was held on 2 June 1864 and raised 131 speciedaler and 41 skillings, less than a third of what Ibsen owed Nandrup. A lot of the stuff went to Nandrup himself, including six of the twelve mahogany chairs, the armchair, the mahogany ottoman, the drop-leafed table and the commode, and the oak desk.[20] As well as the silverware Ibsen's personal papers were supposed to be kept out of the sale; but the precaution was in vain. When he received the news Ibsen took it stoically. He wrote to Bjørnson in October:

> I don't bemoan the loss of the furniture and suchlike; but to think of all my private letters, papers, drafts etc in the hands of rank strangers was extremely vexing, not to mention the loss of so many things that had a value very different from market value.[21]

Bjørnson replied on 20 January 1867:

> Next, on the day that your furious letter arrived, I went to see Nandrup. I made him come with me to where all the rest of your things were stored; because he maintained that all the paper and the bed linen and so on were quite secure. But the stuff was in an unlocked store, and he said most of it must have been stolen, there was almost nothing left! Who on earth had the key, who was supposed to be looking after it?[22]

It was as a result of this diaspora that Ibsen's birth certificate surfaced as wrapping paper in a watchmaker's shop in Bergen some thirty years later, and his university examination results among the papers of a ship's engineer on a steamboat in the Canary Islands. One can hardly blame him for keeping his jacket buttoned so tightly.

8

The Clown
Peer Gynt

Sigurd was a pretty, soft-skinned boy. Photographs show that he resembled his mother more than his father. He was a precocious child, able to read by the age of four, and by the age of six an avid reader of the historical novels of B. S. Ingemann, a sort of Danish Sir Walter Scott. In the early days Ibsen enjoyed baby-talking him. He was his *Kikkidorian* and his *Grimme-Grimme*. In Italy, where Ibsen was *Capellone* (Big Hat), Sigurd was *Picerillo*, meaning 'Tiny One' in the Neapolitan dialect. Suzannah was, presumably depending on her mood, Ibsen's Cat or his Eagle. He was himself, on the home-made cards in the form of large bank-notes he gave her on her birthday each year, variously the Tiger, the Bear, as well as *Ragazinos yderlig skjønne Papa* (Ragazino's – i.e. Sigurd's – unusually beautiful Papa), *Den kjære Persaun* (the Dear Person), *Den geistlige Milchbauer und Oberst* (a nonsensical military title) and *Den pragtfulde*, meaning something like 'the Perfect One'.

One of Suzannah's main functions was to provide him with the optimum conditions he needed to write, which included staying out of the way when necessary. 'I work a lot and stay indoors,' he wrote to Magdalene Thoresen on 3 December 1865, 'Suzannah and Sigurd roam all over the city, through the ruins, the museums, the galleries and collections.'[1] In the days before the success of *Brand* and Ibsen's connection with Hegel at Gyldendal brought them economic security, she had to manage the household budget very carefully. The humble living conditions endured by Brand and Agnes were a true reflection of the family's own circumstances at the time of the composition of *Brand* in Ariccia, and in a letter of her old age to her daughter-in-law Bergljot, Suzannah recalled details of their simple life there that summer in terms that show how much she had enjoyed the struggle:

Sigurd can tell you how he used to go every afternoon and buy three soldis' worth of bread and cheese for us. Along with a half foglietta of red wine this was our supper. I cooked the main meals myself down in the kitchen with a baking oven heated to 30 degrees, so I never froze. There was coffee in the house, and every morning Sigurd went down and ordered *café au lait* and bread. He had a little red shirt, cut low at the neck, with short sleeves, white shorts and bare legs. Yes, that simple, quiet lifestyle was what enabled Ibsen to write his great work . . .[2]

She was a firm disciplinarian. They had no nanny, and if she had to go to town for some reason and leave Sigurd alone she would place a wad of cotton wool on the floor and tell him that he was not to go beyond it. In later life Sigurd recalled that wad of cotton wool, how it hypnotised him, so that he remained staring at it until his mother came back. He had something of his father's nature, mixing an instinct to obey with sudden gestures of impatient unrestraint, such as pushing pot plants off the windowsill into the street below. On one occasion, when travelling, he was compelled to wear a sailor's hat which he detested. He threw it from the carriage taking them to the harbour. It was retrieved. On the boat-trip he threw it into the water. Someone rowed after and retrieved it. Completing their journey by train he finally succeeded in ridding himself of it permanently by hurling it from the compartment window.

'Sigurd can read now, he reads folk tales and fairy stories every day,' Ibsen wrote in his Christmas letter to Magdalene Thoresen, and it was perhaps his son's enthusiasm that revived his own former interest in the world of trolls, princesses, magic bears and talking animals: Asbjørnsen's *Norske Huldre-Eventyr og Folkesagn*, published in a second edition in 1866, contained two stories under the title *Tales from the Mountains* which provided him with the inspiration for his greatest play, *Peer Gynt*. He began work on it in Rome on 5 January 1867, finishing the first act on 25 February. Act Two was begun on 3 March, and five days later he was halfway through it.

In May the family moved to Casamicciola, on the island of Ischia, where he continued work on the third act. They lived in the Villa Pisani, and from the balcony of his room on the second floor he had a view of vineyards that stretched out from the walls of the villa and extended all the way to the sea. To the right of the Villa Pisani was the ancient clifftop fastness Castello Aragonese. The summer of 1867 was hot, with temperatures between thirty and forty degrees for most of June and July.

His nearest neighbour and walking companion that summer was Vilhelm Bergsøe, a young Dane. Bergsøe's original interest in life had been zoology, but he had to abandon it when his eyesight began to fail. He turned to writing and his novel *Fra Piazza del Popolo*, a series of linked short stories about life among the Scandinavian colony in Rome, based on his earlier stay there in 1863, was one of Hegel's successes in 1866. In 1867 he returned to Rome with his brother and sister, and on revisiting the Circolo Scandinavo encountered Ibsen for the first time:

> Our old club had never been notable for its luxury, the government grant made sure of that. But in the four years I had been away the old place had really gone down hill, I could hardly recognise it. The staircase was scruffy, the sofa-cover in rags, the curtains faded, and instead of familiar Scandinavian faces all I saw was one stranger, a dark-haired man sitting so deeply buried in the newspapers that he did not even register my presence.[3]

A few days later he was accosted by a sociable Ibsen walking in the sunshine along Capo le Case. Bergsøe, who later became vain about his literary talent, wrote in his memoirs that Ibsen said, 'Now I know that you are Wilhelm Bergsøe I greet you doubly', while he himself casually failed to recognise the author of *Brand*. Ibsen had to tell him who he was, adding the Gyntian remark, 'Yes, indeed, I am who I am, and I presume you are too?'

On Ischia they resumed their cordial relationship. Ibsen had delivered an oblique warning that Bergsøe must not expect to see too much of him that summer, saying, 'Well, now I am going to work. I feel like a rearing stallion getting ready for the race', and work is what he did. Bergsøe called his discipline *kontormæssigt* (office-like), and noticed that his habits were so regular one could tell the time of day merely by observing him. He would rise at dawn, take a walk, drink coffee out on the terrace, and at ten o'clock begin writing, continuing without stop until two. During this session Suzannah and Sigurd would invariably leave the house and spend the time down by the beach. After a siesta and the main meal of the day Ibsen then reread and revised what he had written in the morning, hiding away the fair copy so that no harm should befall it. Then, feeling the need for male company, he would call on Bergsøe, who lodged next door and invite him out for a walk.

Setting off in the direction of the little town of Forio the conversation would begin in lively enough fashion. But as soon as they had left Casamicciola behind Ibsen would descend into a deepening silence, into which Bergsøe was inexorably drawn, so that most of their company passed in absolute silence, until they reached Forio, where, with a glance at the sea, Ibsen would suggest they turn round and go back. 'So I can't really say that these walks were all that much fun', Bergsøe wrote later. Ibsen was, of course, still writing in his head, as one of their rare conversational exchanges showed. Admiring a certain view in the course of the walk he exclaimed, 'My, look at those beautiful hop gardens!', at which Bergsøe protested that they were not looking at hops but at grapes. 'Quite right!' said Ibsen. 'Sometimes I have to pinch myself to remind myself that I'm not in Norway.'

Other conversations Bergsøe found memorable indicate the simple, violent cocktail of paranoia and ambition that still burned inside Ibsen. Imagining from such exchanges about the hops that he was suffering from homesickness Bergsøe asked why he did not simply return home, at which Ibsen rounded on him, eyes blazing. 'Do you think I will allow myself to be trampled to death by geese? – *I* don't go back to Norway until Norway calls for me.' He openly confessed that he hoped his writing would last for all eternity, and when Bergsøe protested that this was something that would certainly be denied even the greatest of all writers, Ibsen turned on him in something close to anger: 'Get away from me with your metaphysics! Deprive me of eternity and you deprive me of everything.' It was still the Grimstad apprentice speaking, the deeply religious but godless young man who had hitched his wagon to the most god-like of earthly goals, the eternal fame of the skald in Valhalla. It was a goal that these years in Rome, with its statues of the long-dead great, must have done much to render tangible.

But if Ibsen was unsociable on these afternoon rambles he made up for it in the evenings when, with the day's work behind him, he would again rouse Bergsøe with a Holbergian cry of, 'Hey, Jacob Shoemaker! Now we'll damn well have us a drink!' 'Only then did Ibsen become himself,' said Bergsøe. He would even toy with his self-discipline, broaching the subject of winding up for the night after two *fogliette* had been consumed and allowing Bergsøe to overrule him and order a third. 'If only I dared drink for just another farthing, for just one last little farthing; but I mustn't! I'll have an accident – damn, my feet just won't get up from this chair. Hey, Jacob Shoemaker, another one over here, chalk up another farthing or two on the slate, eh?'

Describing another occasion on which he and Ibsen drank together Bergsøe touches on a most sympathetic aspect of Ibsen's character; his willingness to take time to encourage those trying to write or whose already published work had been mistreated by a critic. Bergsøe had followed *Fra Piazza del Popolo* with a collection of poems which had been poorly received by the Danish critics, notably and painfully by Clemens Petersen. Early in their acquaintanceship Ibsen had promised Bergsøe that in time they would set Petersen's review in its proper perspective.

The hour for this arrived in the course of an outing the two men took together to the summit of Epomeo, the extinct volcano which rose behind Ibsen's villa to command a magnificent view of the whole island and beyond to Naples and Sorrento. A hermit lived near the top. They began the ascent at five a.m. to avoid the worst heat of the day, walking on an empty stomach, for at that hour they had been unable to rustle up more than some black coffee and dried bread. Presently they came to a hostelry, where the smell of the garlic-laden egg-pudding the host offered them put them off all thought of food. The local wine proved excellent, however, and they sat drinking for some time. At Ibsen's invitation Bergsøe then read out the offending review, interrupted by Ibsen at its worst moments with a loud cry of, 'Cheers, Jacob!' He took a paper bag, blew it up and popped it – a trumpet blast for Petersen, who had blown so many loud trumpet blasts for his rival Bjørnson. Then he bought them each a cigar to smoke the critic's health. Bergsøe noted that he carefully recorded the purchase in a note book. Enquiring about this he learnt that personal bookkeeping was a relatively new habit that Ibsen was self-consciously cultivating, presumably in the effort to control that instinctive tendency to live beyond his means that had landed him in so much trouble during his final years in Kristiania. Like all good hermits, the Epomean monk was not at home when they reached his retreat, and Ibsen and Bergsøe never did reach the top, being interrupted by a minor earth tremor which sent them scurrying down to Casamicciola again.

Bergsøe was amused by Ibsen's extreme concern for his personal safety. If in his writing he sent Peer inside a mountain, he had no wish to duplicate the feat in real life, and one day when Bergsøe tempted him down into a crater with volcanic springs boiling in its basin he lost his nerve and turned for home. 'Are you trying to get me inside the mountain?' he cried. ' We could be crushed by falling rocks!' In a similar story Bergsøe and Ibsen climbed the peak known as Punto Imperatóre as a great sirocco storm was brewing. Bergsøe stood enjoying the wild motion of the sea below them; Ibsen lay flat with both arms clasped around a rock, accusing Bergsøe of trying to kill him and swearing, 'This is the last time I come with you on your so-called nature rambles!' As the Taoists would say, he was utterly fearless in being timid.

Ibsen seemed to thrive in the exceptionally high temperatures that exhausted his fellow-Scandinavians, and despite the ravages of the sirocco. It returned at the beginning of August, driving temperatures up to thirty-seven degrees and discouraging people from even attempting to leave their houses. Then one night the island was shaken by an earthquake. Going out to inspect the damage in the morning Ibsen discovered that the bell-tower in the local church had a crack in it large enough to accommodate his hand. Clearly it was impossible to continue to write in such uncertain surroundings, and the next day the family left Ischia. During his three months there he had completed the first three acts of *Peer Gynt* and sent them to Hegel. They had been profitable and enjoyable days, and he later wrote a glowing testimonial to the Villa Pisani and its owner, Signor Crescenzo Pisani, for him to use as he saw fit.* And the village remembered his visit on the occasion of his death in 1906, erecting a plaque commemorating his stay there, its wording an unhurried resumé of the plot of *Peer Gynt* and a tribute to the love of the 'immortal Solveig'.

Eighteen sixty-seven was known as the Great Cholera Year in Rome, and as it was unsafe to return to the city the Ibsens and the Bergsøes spent the remainder of the summer and the autumn in Sorrento, lodging on the second floor in a modest rooming house for artists on via Umberto I, (now the Corso Italia nr. 170) known as 'Rosa Magra's', after the thin proprietress. Ibsen resumed work on *Peer Gynt*, and the evening strolls with Bergsøe:

I had to smile when I saw where he was taking us. It was a broad,

---

* The villa is now known as the *Villa Ibsen.*

dusty country road which led to a pine forest in the vicinity of the village of Massa. It had in every respect the greatest similarity to the road to Forio, with this undeniable advantage, that there was no danger of highway robbery here, for the road between Sorrento and Massa was much used.

The relationship between the two of them was one of convenience rather than friendship, for they were temperamentally very different from one another. Ibsen's letter of 21 October to the Danish zoologist and literary man Jonas Collin shows the touching ambivalence of his need for company and the difficulty he seemed to have in attracting friends to whom he was himself attracted. 'There can scarcely be any question of our having a closer relationship. We're both to blame for this,' he conceded. Collin was not Bjørnson, however, nor Carl Anker, and there was no mention of the 'repellent cold, which makes close association difficult'. 'I have no wish to go into detail about what the impediment is from my side', was all he would say. With the years the buttons – and the lips – were tightening.

Not surprisingly, most of Bergsøe's anecdotes of their fellowship in the summer of 1867 are on the cool side. One can, after all, be fascinated by someone one neither likes nor admires personally. Drinking wine with the family one day in Rosa Magra's he witnessed an unpleasant scene between the couple. Suzannah began to speak well of the Swedish people. Ibsen, still nursing his fierce disapproval of Swedes as well as his hatred of Germans, presently rounded on her and attempted to demolish her position. Suzannah persisted in her folly. Ibsen, heedless of company, beat the table with his fist and roared: 'Be quiet! I will not hear anymore of this! You make me sick!' Bergsøe was distressed on her behalf, but he may have judged the situation too conventionally. In his memoirs he wrote that Suzannah 'happened' to begin praising the Swedes; yet she must have known full well the reaction she would get from her husband. Perhaps she judged that his writing had left him stranded in a scorpion mood that afternoon and so offered herself as his piece of fruit. Sigurd, having observed the scene, responded with the tact of the diplomat he would one day grow up to be: 'Father doesn't like Swedes, and I don't either. If I could I would claw their eyes out. Because there's a troll in me!' This latter was one of Ibsen's favourite boasts about himself, and Sigurd's loyal response no doubt pleased him.

And despite their precaution the cholera showed up in Sorrento, though not in their quarter of the town. Ibsen arrived one morning outside Bergsøe's apartment in great alarm, saying that Suzannah was ill and he didn't know what to do. Bergsøe told him to fetch the doctor, which meant a trip into the area where the disease had established itself. 'No, no I'm not going up there,' he cried. 'If I catch it, what will we do then? And what about Sigurd!' Someone else went for the doctor, who examined Suzannah and found her suffering from the mild sickness known as sporadic cholera. She was fully recovered within a week.

By 15 September the fourth act of the play was finished, and the fifth on 14 October. Four days later these were sent off to Hegel, and the Ibsens left Sorrento and set off on a roundabout trek back to Rome, spending two days in Pompeii before moving on to Naples and then heading for Rome.

A background event to the carefree lives of foreign artists in Rome all throughout this decade was the progress of Garibaldi and his red-shirts in his quest for the unification of Italy, with Rome as its capital. As a poet Ibsen found the campaign stirring. As a traveller he viewed events much as any other tourist or foreign resident, finding the insurrection a colourful irrelevance which could develop into an inconvenience. As a result of the revolution the railway connections to Rome were closed between 2 and 12 November and the Ibsens found themselves stranded for ten days at San Germano. Writing to Consul Bravo on 4 November Ibsen enthused that there was nowhere they all felt more at home than in Rome, adding with unrevolutionary fervour, 'Let's just hope there are not too many changes made to the usual way of things.'[4] This time his luck was in, and when they eventually arrived back, their old rooms at Capo le Case 55 were waiting for them.

'Could I not, like Christoff in Jakob v. Tyboe, point to *Brand* and *Peer Gynt* and say – look, wine did this?' Ibsen wrote to Peter Hansen, and if one can't quite see the connection between *Brand* and wine, as motif for the mood and atmosphere of the whole of *Peer Gynt* it could not be improved upon. Not the least astonishing thing is the speed with which Ibsen wrote the play. It seems to appear without a history, to have sprung as a fully formed intention into his mind and then to have been written with an ease he had not known since *Catiline*.

Asbjørnsen's folk tale collection gave him a head start in the form of some of the most characteristic episodes used in the play, particularly the magnificent lie with which Peer introduces himself to us – the story of the thrilling ride over Besseggen on the back of a reindeer.* This was actually the deed of one Gullbrand Glesnes, borrowed by Ibsen's Peer in the spirit of this passage, from *Tales from the Mountains*: 'That Peer Gynt, there was nobody like him, said Anders. He was a real spinner of yarns and a good rhymer, you would have enjoyed him. He used to claim that all the stories people used to tell from the old days had actually happened to him.'†

To Hegel Ibsen wrote on 5 January 1867 that his main character was 'a figure from the recent past of the Norwegian peasantry, a half-mythical adventurer'. Later in the year he seemed more inclined to assert Peer's real-life existence, telling Hegel that Peer was a real person who lived in Gudbrandsdalen, probably at the close of the last or the beginning of this century. 'His name is still familiar among the common people up there, but not much more is known about his escapades than is written in Asbjørnsen's *Norwegian Folk Tales* (in the piece called 'Mountain Pictures'). So I haven't had much to build on, but on the other hand it has given me a lot more freedom.'[5] In fact Peer was more mythical than Ibsen thought, and his name a byword for human fecklessness and the easy way out among Norwegians even in Holberg's day. Holberg had used him in 1744 as an archetype of the man always in search of the short cut, in an essay in which women were praised for their innate diligence, conservatism and shunning of the short cut.[6]

Ibsen's more orthodox literary influences include the second part of *Faust*, from which Peer casually and humorously misquotes, for the structure of a spiritual journey that traverses the world and ends at home, and for the Gretchen figure he turned into Peer's Solveig; Swift and *Gulliver's Travels* for Peer's passages of disgusted intercourse with the trolls and the huldre (part cow and part woman) which recall Gulliver among the Yahoos, as well as for the social satires; Holberg's comedies, for his insolent, folksy playfulness; the *Baron Munchausen* stories, one of which is quoted by Peer – an obvious literary brotherhood of tellers of tall tales; the Dane Frederik Paludan-Müller's epic poem *Adam Homo*, about an unprincipled

---

* The Norwegian novelist Jan Kjærstad has compared this to the freefall scene with which Rushdie's *Satanic Verses* opens as an example of the 'magical realism' of *Peer Gynt*.
† Woody Allen's *Zelig* has much in common with Peer.

and ambitious opportunist who sacrifices true love for his career but is redeemed by the forgiving and limitless love of a true woman; and for the sheer creative exuberance of the whole, Oehlenschläger's delightful verse-drama *Aladdin*.

In his autobiographical letter to Peter Hansen Ibsen tried to explain the liberating effect of life in exile on the writing of the play. 'So far away from one's potential readership one grows heedless. This poem contains much that derives from things that happened to me in my own youth.' In the self-assertive but unpopular young Peer as he makes his entrance at the wedding feast he was perhaps recalling his own status among the youth of Skien and Grimstad, where his nicknames were first *Styggen* (Ugly) and then *Spætus* (Weedy); yet his difference and apartness are grudgingly recognised by all. Persuasively autobiographical too is the relationship between Peer and his mother, Åse, especially their comradeship in the face of his father Jon's drinking habit.

One grows heedless . . . and in this play, for the first time since Julian Poulsen in *St John's Night*, Ibsen uses the distorting and disguising prism of his talent to take another look at the effect of his youthful 'sin' with Else Sophie Birkedalen in the episode involving Peer and 'a woman in green', the hag-princess daughter of the old Dovregubben who almost traps him into marriage. The most poignant description of the persistence of the memory is the scene in which Solveig comes to Peer at his new home in the woods, offering her unconditional love and devotion after he and his mother have lost everything at the auction caused by Jon Gynt's profligate ways, and Peer has been declared an outlaw. He goes out hunting, delighting in her, his princess, found and won, until in the woods nearby he encounters his troll family, the Dovregubben's daughter with their ugly son in tow. 'Even as your house was being built', she tells him, 'mine went up alongside it,' announcing her intention to ride like a permanent nightmare over his happiness with Solveig:

> THE WOMAN: In the autumn, when I gave birth, it was the devil
>   held my back;
> so it's no wonder you find me ugly.
> If you want to find me lovely as you once did before,
> – that girl that's in there with you, show her the door.
> Drive Solveig out of your sight and your mind,
> and this ugly nose of mine will disappear, you'll find.

PEER GYNT: Away from me, you troll-witch!
THE WOMAN: Yes, just see if I do!
PEER GYNT: I'll smash your head in - !
THE WOMAN: Yes, just see if you dare!
   Ho ho, Peer Gynt, I can stand a thumping -
   You'll never get rid of me.
   I'll spy at your door, I'll visit the pair of you.
   When you sit with your girl on your bench made for two,
   when you tickle her, Peer, and nibble her ear
   I'll be there, beside you, claiming my share.

'After *Brand*, *Peer Gynt* just seemed to follow by itself,'[7] he once wrote. For Peer was always Brand's bright twin, and at each step Ibsen plotted for Brand along his hard, decisive way he must have heard too the skipping echo of his magnificently irresponsible other self. For among the thousand other things it is, *Peer Gynt* is also an outstanding demonstration of the artist's power to deny his audience the right to categorise him – indeed, to claim and exercise a contrary right to categorise his audience as an audience to whom anything may be said. *Peer Gynt* and *Brand* form a beautiful complementary pairing that is perhaps unique in literature, the one a delirious and reckless response to the act of writing the other – and not least a comment on the public's reception of *Brand*. Ibsen reveals both plays to be equally dazzling acts of literary imposture. It is as though he were saying to his audience, 'Look – I can do *this*! And I can do *this* too!'

The simple contrast between the heroes is encapsulated in their respective mottoes. In the world in which Peer meets the Dovre-gubben, Brand's exalted 'All or nothing' does not exist. For trolls the motto of the world of man is, 'Man, be yourself' (*Mann, vær deg selv*), which they have adapted for their own purposes to, 'Troll, no need to be more than – a troll!' (*Troll, vær deg selv – nok!*) Peer's flirting with this reduced level of self-expectation and its promises of constant self-forgiveness goes on throughout most of the play, and the exuberant sympathy with which Ibsen describes the flirtation is the clearest sign of his complicity in the failings of his hero. At the level at which he is addressing his newly acquired readership he is saying, 'I am not Brand.' To mark the distance between himself and the hero of the earlier play he introduces the scenes in Egypt (perhaps plotting a contemporary reference to the Suez Canal, the great engineering feat of the time, no doubt also attracted by the anagrammatic relation between 'Peer Gynt' and 'Egypteren', 'the Egyptian') in which Peer is taken for a prophet and fraudently goes along with the charade in hopes of a sexual adventure with Anitra. The great thing about being a prophet, says Peer, is that 'if you catch on, then it's *yourself* that gets the glory, not your pounds, shillings and pence'.

Appreciation of *Peer Gynt* is also enriched by the knowledge that Ibsen was, throughout work on both it and *Brand*, engaged in researching his long-standing plan to write a play about Julian the Apostate, for just as Peer's performance as a prophet is a grotesque parody of the tragic prophet Brand, so his clownish Emperor foreshadows the tragic Julian, with the singing statue of Memnon as a comic harbinger of Julian's dark communications with the oracles in the later play. *Peer Gynt's* joyous syncretism anticipates Julian's darker attempts to bring about the Third Kingdom, mingling Heaven and St Peter with Soria Moria,* whence Peer and Mor Åse ride on a coach drawn by Grane, Odin's son.The Memnon statue reminds the irreverent Peer of Dovregubben, as the Sphinx reminds him of the Bøygen, which is a sort of folk-tale version of the Hydra, as Peer himself is a bucolic and anti-heroic Ulysses. In later years Ibsen's extensive extra-literary posturing as a sage could easily get out of hand; everywhere in *Peer Gynt* he gloriously mocks the traps of pomposity and even pretension which he later had such difficulty in avoiding, as well as some of the most cherished romantic illusions of his earlier, 'sensitive' period. Peer mocks his creator's own long-held belief that a great grief makes the man in the scene with Anitra where he cries out for one – 'A terrible one, but keep it short, just a two-day wonder!' This is in the same spirit as his misquotation from *Richard III*, offering his kingdom for a horse, at once reducing the offer to half the kingdom. In the same way the scene in which he hatches a plan to become a historian and 'skim the cream off history' is a relaxed sidelong glance at his own urgent educational tourism as well as a refreshing corrective to the impression given, in his application for government grants, of a man offering his own wandering among ruins and statues as activity of a somehow higher order than that of the other participants in the wave of mass tourism of which, at that time in Rome, he was simply a part:

* In Norwegian folklore *Soria Moria* is a mountain castle in a magic land where the hero finds the lost princess.

> It's true – my learning on the subject isn't deep,
> and history's inner workings far from clear;
> but what the hell – the crazier your starting-point,
> the more original your findings.

Ibsen's humour is never far below the surface here and in its literary self-consciousness it is often startlingly modern: from 'the Strange Passenger' reassuring the drowning Peer that 'one doesn't die in the fifth act' to Peer's mutter, as he slips off into the dark, 'There it popped out of him at last – he was a tiresome moralist'; and Peer's last meeting with the wandering old Dovregubben, who complains that 'people say I only exist in books.'

But perhaps Ibsen is most modern in his depiction of Peer's search for the 'real self' and his discovery that for humans there is no such thing. Peer recognises that only animals, in their non-verbal innocence, can truly be said to be themselves. What Ibsen does is make his journey towards this realisation the fascination and joy of life itself. Literal and mythical images of search speckle the book, from the reference to Baron Munchausen's fox whipped out of its skin through a hole in its forehead, to the macabre literalness of 'the Strange Passenger's' request for Peer's body in the event of his death, and his talk of the autopsy he will carry out on it, cutting it open in search of the seat of dreams.

This image of an autopsy as a literal image of the search for self sheds light on a macabre letter Ibsen wrote to Georg Brandes in April 1866,[8] with *Brand* just published and *Peer Gynt* already 'following along by itself'. Ibsen had not met Brandes yet, and in this, probably the first and certainly the first surviving letter to him, he described in painstaking detail the exact circumstances surrounding the death of a young friend of Brandes' named Ludvig David. David was living in an apartment near the Ibsens in Rome, and one day dived to his death from the second-floor window in delirium or suicide. (Ibsen believed that in his sweating delirium the young man imagined he was diving into a refreshing sea.) Ibsen had made it his business to be present at the autopsy and gave a vivid account of the state of the corpse, with the skull crushed at the top, the bloody scrape marks across the face, 'the arms and legs whole, but several ribs crushed and the lungs torn, which caused a considerable amount of blood to flow'.[9] Of course, he makes no mention of seeing the seat of dreams, nor of hearing an upward-rushing whoosh as the real self escaped from the body; yet one feels he was half-hoping he might, for the fascination was with *what is inside us.* It was a literal fascination, operating on a literal level, and as such it may even explain something about his attraction to the idea of trolls, with their two and sometimes three heads, for three heads must mean three selves – the old beliefs make modern approaches to the problem of the self seem dull by comparison.

Peer Gynt is Ibsen's greatest play, one of the greatest plays ever written. In its sheer range it far outstrips anything else he had written before or would write in the future. Never again was he able to play so fruitfully with the burden of consciousness, never again did he dare so openly to implicate himself in all his glorious, generous and instructive satires on human frailty and folly. And the end of all the searching is perfect. Brand was punished for not knowing that God is love. To Peer it is given to know this, through the love of Solveig. The endless quest for the chimera of the real self, symbolised by the stripping of layers from an onion, is resolved in this realisation, that we are truly ourselves only in the love of the Other. The warm and beautiful conclusion banishes with insouciant, Gyntian brilliance the dark world of Greek tragedy as the hero returns to the woman's arms, no god-destroyed Oedipus but a transfigured Peer '(a shower of light falls over him): My mother; my wife; purest woman!'

Hegel published *Peer Gynt* on 14 November. The success of *Brand* had aroused great interest and the first edition of the new play sold out almost at once. Hegel published a second edition of 2,000 copies within fourteen days. The two critical responses Ibsen most eagerly awaited were those of Bjørnson in Norway and Clemens Petersen in Denmark. As one might imagine Bjørnson loved the play. It seemed literal proof of the claim Ibsen had made in those early letters from Rome, that he had liberated himself from the distant, aesthetic response to life and managed to melt that layer of protective ice that coated him. In his review for *Norsk Folkeblad* Bjørnson wrote that 'Time and again I found myself roaring with laughter, positively bellowing with laughter, and thanking the writer inwardly, as I now take the opportunity to thank him publicly.' Yet even Bjørnson was so in thrall to the nationalist obsession of contemporary Norway that he assumed *Peer* to be not primarily a personal statement with strong autobiographical elements but a satire directed towards other people, Ibsen's own countrymen, a satire 'on Norwegian self-love, smugness, narrowness'.

Norwegian *Morgenbladet* and *Aftenbladet* both carried long and largely favourable reviews. The Swedish critics too were favourable, and it looked to Ibsen very much as though he had managed the difficult trick of following up a breakthrough with another success and maintaining his whole Scandinavian audience. But Denmark was the most valuable market both economically and in terms of status, and he was particularly vulnerable to reaction there. When it came, Clemens Petersen's lengthy review in *Fædrelandet* on 30 November was a major disappointment. The essence of his critique was that *Peer Gynt*, despite many good qualities, was to be considered a failure, since it broke too many of the aesthetic rules that he, as a critic, believed it was every dramatist's duty to observe. He wrote that it was 'not poetry' because 'it lacks an ideal'. The play's free drift between reality and fantasy or dream was also offensive to him.

Petersen's sterile and mechanical analysis offended Ibsen. It also indicated the failure of his campaign of letter-writing, and to realise that Petersen now possessed these letters and still dared to criticise their author must have humiliated him profoundly. That same day he wrote to Bjørnson to rebuke him for having failed to safeguard his interests:

> What the hell is it that at every point seems to come between you and me? It's as if some personal devil had made it his job to shadow us. I got your letter. When someone writes the way you write there then there cannot be any thought of treachery. Certain things cannot be counterfeited. I wrote you a reply from the depths of a grateful heart, not for the praise, but for the under-standing, that is what makes one so indescribably grateful. Now I have no use for my reply. I have torn it to pieces. One hour ago I read Hr. Clemens Petersen's review in *Fædrelandet*. If I reply to you now I'll have to begin in a different vein; I must respectfully acknowledge receipt of the favour of your letter of the something something inst. enclosing copy of review in aforementioned paper. – If I was in Copenhagen and there was someone as close to me as Clemens Petersen is to you then I would have knocked him senseless rather than allow him to commit such a crime against truth and justice.[10]

'My book *is* poetry' he continued; 'and if it isn't then it will be. In our country, in Norway, the definition of what is poetry will bow to my book.' Ridiculing Petersen's description of 'the Strange Passen-

ger' as 'symbolising *angst* (I just slipped the scene in on a whim)',
he insisted that Peer was 'a personality, complete, individual':

> As a matter of fact I'm happy to have been treated so unjustly.
> God's purpose and will are in it, because I feel my powers growing
> with my anger. If there is to be war, then so be it! If I am not a
> writer, then what have I to lose? I'll try my luck as a photographer,
> and I'll take all my contemporaries up there (i.e. in Scandinavia)
> one by one, the way I did with the language reformers.* I shall
> not spare the child in the mother's womb, not the thought nor
> the intention behind the words of any living soul who deserves
> the honour of being taken.

His fury shows something of the impotence he must have felt at the
thought that the most influential critic of the time was in the pocket
of his greatest rival, Bjørnson. From that point of view Petersen's
fall in the scandal two years later, in March 1869, and his subsequent
departure for America was a piece of unlooked-for good fortune.
Overnight Petersen became a non-person, and in the ensuing
struggle for cultural authority Georg Brandes began his rise to prominence. Ibsen conveniently forgot his flattering words to Petersen
when the scandal broke, claiming in a letter to Hegel that he had
'always had strong suspicions about his character; but something
like this –!!'[11]

Ibsen left Rome in the spring of 1868. He may possibly have been
worried that the imminent arrival of Garibaldi in Rome, the departure of the French troops who had been protecting the papal state
since 1867, and the prospect of wholesale change in the city was
too disturbing a prospect to contemplate. In his memoir *Days of
Youth* Frederik Knudtzon gives an account of Ibsen's behaviour that
also suggests he was becoming dangerously bored at about this time.
A group of Scandinavians had spent the afternoon drinking
together. Afterwards:

> Ibsen's brain was working better than his legs were. If we had
> been thinking straight we would have ordered a cab. But it never
> occurred to us. Off we went in procession, with Fru Ibsen in front
> with old Hansen and Fladager. Some distance behind came Ibsen

---

* Ibsen is referring to the scene with Huhu in Peer Gynt, intended as a satire on his old
friend Vinje, who was very radical in language matters.

with Stramboe and me, one on each side of him. We held him firmly under the arms as we marched along, slow and stately. But after we had gone about a third of the way, something on the pavement on the other side attracted Ibsen's attention. It was a large dog, behind an iron gate in the wall that ran round one of the huge villas. It directed a loud 'woof' in our direction. Ibsen became agitated – he wanted to cross the road, so that meant we *all* had to cross the road. So we stood by the wrought-iron gate the three of us. Ibsen had a stick in his hand, which he began to jab in the direction of the dog. It was one of those huge stately-home type dogs, that look like little lions. It came closer, and Ibsen jabbed at it and struck it, trying in every way to aggravate it, and succeeded in arousing it to such a pitch of fury that had not the iron gate separated us he would have torn us to pieces ... I should think Ibsen stood there teasing the dog for something like six or eight minutes.[12]

And there was another factor to take into consideration, one that would figure increasingly in Ibsen's plans as the years passed: Sigurd's welfare. The boy was now ten years old. During his first months in Rome it had been an easy matter for Ibsen to speak of sacrificing his son as a way of demonstrating fidelity to his principles over Dybbøl and his disgust with his own countrymen. But with the passage of time it became apparent that Sigurd, though not growing up among a people 'whose highest goal in life was to be English-men', was in fact growing up with no sense of belonging to any people at all. For the first time, Ibsen considered the prospect of a return to Norway in the not too distant future.[13] Yet he disliked the thought, so much so that he swallowed down his prejudices and settled instead on a trip to Germany as a compromise. He wrote to Hegel asking him to send out a parcel of textbooks for Sigurd and on 9 May 1868 they left the city, making a holiday of the move and travelling for some five weeks, spending eight days in Florence, two in Bologna, and eight days each in Venice and Bolzano before crossing the border in late June into Germany, where they settled for the summer months in the town of Berchtesgaden, in the Bavarian Alps. Ibsen was delighted with it: 'This is the most beautiful place I have seen north of the Alps, cheap, accessible, in every respect pleasant ... The people here are excellent, both the residents and travellers.'[14]

He had the beginnings of a new play, *De unges Forbund* (*The League of Youth*), with him, and looked forward to finishing it during the course of the summer, in which he was, as usual, slightly optimistic. A favourite technique in the compositional phase of writing was walking, both obsessively pacing up and down in the writing room, and long country rambling. Here he had the mountains, and an eight-day trek over them to Gastein must have helped him achieve clarity about the plotting of the new play. About his personal plans he was still undecided: on 28 July he wrote to Hegel 'we will spend the winter in Munich and Dresden, and probably after that set off for home.'[15]

In the event he decided to settle in Dresden, probably because of the reputation of its international schools and its relative proximity to the baths at Bohemia, which Suzannah had been advised to try as a cure for her rheumatism. After a brief visit to Munich, where they 'savoured the real artistic treasures to be found here, as well as the inhabitants' hatred of the Prussians, the degree of which people back home cannot possibly imagine', they moved at the beginning of October into a rather featureless apartment block at An der Frauenkirche 6.

Sigurd began attending school a one-hour walk from where they lived, Dr Elbe's Institute, a school for the children of foreign residents, with pupils from America, England, Russia, Poland. Tuition was in German and French. He was of necessity good at languages and was soon speaking German like a native. Ibsen carried on with *The League of Youth*, and Suzannah read, treated her rheumatism, and looked after them. Ibsen missed the fellowship of the Scandinavian community in Rome and was delighted when Hegel began sending him Danish and Norwegian newspapers. He told Hegel that the play he was working on was 'written for the theatre, and completely realistic, a product of the heavy German air'. It was a social and political satire with a contemporary setting, and the sense of contact with conditions and developments at home in Norway that he acquired from newspaper reading was invaluable. He also mentioned that with all their moving about since leaving Rome the package of textbooks Hegel had sent for Sigurd so many months ago had still not turned up. The saga of the missing package was, he said, 'a long and remarkable story' and he promised one day to relate it for him at length.

Hegel, no doubt, could hardly wait. By now he had become Ibsen's main correspondent; but it was a permanent source of disappointment to him that nothing like real warmth or friendship ever developed between them. A few years later, in 1881, he characterised their relationship thus: 'Ibsen is an extremely polite man and a pleasure to do business with; but very cautious and reserved, and I have a feeling that I am no closer to him now than I was in 1866, when I had the honour of publishing *Brand*, - and to be honest it hurts me.'[16]

Later in the year they moved again, to Königsbrückerstrasse 33. 'We live comfortably and pleasantly here,'[17] he wrote to the sister of his old friend Ole Schulerud. 'We have a floor to ourselves in an area that resembles Homansbyen in Christiania.'

Though he was now doing reasonably well and still receiving his annual grant of 400 speciedaler from the government Ibsen applied on 16 February 1869 for another large government grant, 400 speciedaler 'to enable him [*sic*] to conclude his journeying abroad with a stay of one year in Sweden, chiefly for the purpose of studying the state of affairs respecting the culture, art and literature of the Swedish people'. Meanwhile, he had been invited to Stockholm, to participate in a conference on the planned development of the three written Scandinavian languages.

Success had changed much for him, snipping away prejudices that had outgrown their usefulness. His hatred of Germans failed to prevent him from settling among them in Germany, and now that the Swedes were beginning to take note of him as a major dramatist he prepared to abandon his anger at their cowardice over Dybbøl, in the throes of which he had once expressed the view that 'the Swedes are, inevitablity, on the basis of their culture, our spiritual enemies'.

The plan to remain in Sweden for one year prior to returning to settle in Norway was grant-speak. He had no intention of returning home and once the committee had awarded him 300 speciedaler he sent Suzannah and Sigurd to live out in the German countryside for the summer while he left for Stockholm, where he remained for ten weeks, much enjoying the company of old friends like Knud Knudsen, the Hollander Jakob Løkke, Carl Snoilsky and Lorenz Dietrichson, now professor in art history at the Art Academy. He wrote to Hegel: 'My stay in Sweden has been and still is one long celebration; on all sides I encounter a courtesy and a goodwill I can scarcely describe.'

A five-day Nordic universities' conference on languages was in session at which Ibsen participated. The aim of the conference was to try to control the development of the written languages of the three Scandinavian countries in the direction of uniformity. Ibsen the nationalist might have struggled fiercely for the preservation of uniquely Norwegian elements in the written language; Ibsen the professional writer was another animal altogether and he keenly endorsed every suggested reform in the direction of uniformity. He had already, at Hegel's suggestion, begun the task of removing local linguistic anomalies from his plays, and the only real changes made to a revised edition of *Love's Comedy* in the spring of 1867 were to make the language more accessible to his new post-*Brand* Danish readership. After the conference Hegel sent copies of his plays to Ibsen with a request to implement for the benefit of his typesetter the changes agreed on, a task which Ibsen entrusted to Sigurd. Bjørnson by contrast remained the intransigent nationalist, emphatically rejecting Hegel's suggestion that he change his spelling with the complaint that 'the Danes have seduced the Norwegians by dragging them before the German Delilah'.[18]

By 1869 the post-*Brand* metamorphosis from insecure, slightly bohemian, gaze-averting failure into the outward image of entrepreneurial self-certainty was almost complete. In June he sent a photograph of himself to Lorenz Dietrichson with the inscription, 'I enclose as requested a picture of my snout. I don't know whether you recognise me from my bearded days.'[19] It was probably the last time he permitted himself the Gyntian liberty of a laugh at his own expense. Shortly afterwards the metamorphosis received its finishing touch in the form of the award, in September, of the Vasa Order from the union king of Sweden and Norway Karl XV, and an invitation by the grace of the king to attend the opening of the Suez Canal in Egypt as one of the two Norwegian guests of the Khedive Ismail Pasha.

Some time before he had broken the news of the Egyptian trip to her Ibsen received a rather wan letter from Suzannah. She thanked him for a recent letter, adding, 'Sigurd says, Papa can of course stay on in Sweden when he has no need to be there, but it's so much better when you are home!' And, a little later that summer, Sigurd wrote to his father 'I am pleased you are going to so many dinners and eating so much fat'. The words sound a forward echo of the scene Ibsen later described in *The Wild Duck*, between the solitary and precociously sad Hedvig and her boastful, self-centred father Hjalmar, when Hjalmar proudly returns from dining at the Werles' and presents Hedvig with the souvenir of his great social triumph, the menu of his evening meal.

Ibsen learned of the death of his mother that summer, on 3 June, aged seventy. He had not seen her since that last visit to Skien in 1850, nor had there been any correspondence between them. While he was still living and working in Kristiania in the late 1850s and early 1860s Marichen fell ill, and believing she was about to die sent Ole Paus to ask him to visit her. Twice Ibsen promised to come, but he never made the journey. Since 1865 she and Knud Ibsen had been living apart, he on his own in rented accommodation, she with Hedvig and her husband. The precise reasons for their separation are not known, but Knud Ibsen's drinking grew worse with the years and this may have been a factor.

On 26 September, four months after receiving Hedvig's letter, during which time he wrote at least twenty other letters, chiefly to business associates, theatre managers, translators and critics, Ibsen responded to her news:

Dear Hedvig!
It has been months since I received your kind letter – and only now do I answer. But there is so much that stands between us, between home and me. Understand this, and do not think that through all these long years, and now this summer, I have been silent through indifference. I cannot write letters; I have to be there in person to give myself completely. You, on the other hand, you can write. Do it, do it often! I shall respond with at the least an affectionate greeting, with some message that, I hope, will not depress you.

I look inside myself. There is my battleground, where I experience both triumph and defeat. But such things cannot be described in a letter. Do not try to convert me. I want to live in truth. What happens afterwards will happen anyway.

So our dear old mother is dead. Thank you, for so lovingly bearing the responsibility of this for the rest of us. You really are the best of us!

I travel widely in the world. Who knows, maybe next summer I might come to Norway, and then I will revisit the old home, where I still feel I have so many roots. Give Father my affectionate greetings. Explain to him about me. You understand, but perhaps he does not.

I have been here in Stockholm since the middle of July; now I leave, via Dresden and Paris, for Egypt, where, as you may have read in the papers, I have been invited by the Vice-Regent. I expect to be back in Dresden by mid-December, to rejoin my wife and my little son, who goes to school there. I have just the one child.

I enclose a portrait of myself. If you have a picture of you and yours, send it to us. I do wish you could meet my wife; she is ideal for me. She asks me to say hello. Our address is Königsbrücker-Strasse no.33.

This is a short letter, and I seem to have avoided mentioning what you perhaps especially wanted me to mention. At the moment this is how it must be. But don't think that I am lacking the warmth which is above all necessary where a strong and truthful spiritual life would thrive.'[20]

'Now I leave, via Dresden and Paris, for Egypt, where, as you may have read in the papers, I have been invited by the Vice-Regent' – it is almost as though he is offering his sister this degree of fame, this degree of recognition as an excuse that reasonably overrides and overrules any expectations that might be made of him as an ordinary human being, as someone's son, as someone's brother. Even at such a critical juncture in life as the death of his own mother, Ibsen remained possessed by the demons of achievement. His indulgence of them, his absolute submission to their power, would return to haunt him in old age.

9

Green in the Buttonhole
The League of Youth

The Khedive's guests assembled in Paris and travelled by train to Marseille, sailing on the *Moeris* on 9 October for Alexandria. Ibsen's Norwegian companion was a young Eyptologist, J. D. C. Lieblein, who had arranged to provide *Morgenbladet* with a series of travel-pieces. Ibsen regarded Lieblein with mixed feelings. Wearing his other hat as the newspaper's drama critic Lieblein had praised Ibsen's *The Vikings at Helgeland* as 'a genuinely national play', but condemned the much more considerable *Brand* as the way of the lunatic. Ibsen's other travelling companion was a Swedish military man, Captain von Knorring, whom he had met in Stockholm.

The Mediterranean crossing was rough for most of the four days it took the *Moeris* to reach Alexandria. There the party was received by the engineer of the canal Ferdinand de Lesseps before being transported to the Hôtel d'Europe. They spent two days sight-seeing, then moved on to Cairo where they remained for five days before embarking on what was, for Ibsen, the high point of the journey, a three-week cruise up the Nile.

The journey brought home to him 'for the first time' the advantages of belonging to a small nation, for he observed with annoyance and disapproval that 'Europeans take their quarrels with them wherever they travel, and here is no exception'. He was presumably reflecting on an incident that occurred on 22 October, the morning they set off up the Nile on board the steamer *Ferus*. Ibsen, von Knorring and Lieblein along with a Dutchman and a Swiss, were heavily outnumbered by their seventeen German companions who, appealing to the pan-Germanic solidarity of the others, tried to insist that the trip be made under the German flag. In this they were thwarted and, as Lieblein reported, they were unhappy at the prospect of the French hearing of their failure. In his despatches to

Kristiania Lieblein noted for *Morgenbladet*'s readers the considerable tensions between the German and French guests. He made no secret of his own preference, finding the Prussians intolerably arrogant. Ibsen, pragmatic, ambitious, professional, busied himself making useful contacts for the day when *Brand* would appear in German translation.[1]

Ibsen intended to publish a full account of the trip and made sporadic notes which show him to have been very much the tourist, with little interest in penetrating beneath the visible surface of Egyptian society, though there was probably little opportunity for this anyway. He later wrote of how he had 'during my stay in Suez lived among Hindus for several days'. It seemed to him that these 'mild, silent people resemble the vegetation in their own world.'[2]

Here, in another world of ruins, he was struck by the ephemerality of life. In a bazaar he found a seller of mummified parts and purchased for a kroner a female hand with a scarab ring on it, wondering if it had once belonged to some royal Egyptian – a very Gyntian way to win the hand of a princess. Ephemerality was still his overriding impression of the trip many years later, as he recalled the arrival of the Empress Eugénie at Thebes on 31 October on a large, roseate Nile boat, dressed in white, as lovely as Cleopatra, with the setting sun blazing across the banners and carpets and silken tents – 'within a year she would be no more powerful than the kings whose guest she had lately been'.[3]*

Abydos, the fragment which was to be the basis of his travel book, is an addition, after the truncated short story of his adolescence and the incomplete notes from the early 1860s on his folk-tale collecting trip, to the small corpus of prose literature Ibsen left behind him. As a Victorian believer in progress, for himself and for others, some of his first thoughts were on the problem of civilising the Egyptians, in the course of which he displayed little patience with the idealism of liberal objectors:

> For the chief task is not the introduction of modern improvements to something which already exists; the task here involves nothing less than a reshaping of the whole spiritual environment in which the individual lives, the breaking down of a thousand years of prejudice, – indeed, to exercise a degree of violence upon

---

* In March 1871 she fled to Chislehurst in Kent with her husband, Napoleon III, after his defeat by the Prussians in the Franco-Prussian war.

its very nationality. Such a project can only be carried through by a fearless and absolutist government. A government by the people along European lines would inevitably end in a lot of gentle twaddle about 'human rights'; like the flooding Nile it would put the whole project under oratorical water, and when it departed leave nothing behind it but words.

But his commitment to these colonial instincts was not complete, for as the days went by it became easier for him to recognise a respectable social order and culture among the local people, and his meditation concluded with what amounted to a colonial heresy, the realisation that 'nations are, in their essence, nothing like as different from one another other as one is inclined to imagine they are'.

The best writing in *Abydos* is its few moments of unguarded self-revelation, as when comparing the effects on his mood of sunsets at home with those in Egypt:

Never have I experienced the peace at sunset as here in Egypt. Back home it always brought with it an unease that depressed me and drove me to seek company. Here, in the land that gave birth to the concept of hermitage, here one can understand the idea, just as in Italy one learns to understand how it is that a man can enter a monastery and feel happy there.[4]

There was also his discovery, on a donkey-ride, of a place called Bardies, where the overgrown whitewashed houses appealed to him so much that he thought he could happily live there. But the most memorable moment in his account comes with another image of ephemerality, a burst of perverse aesthetic enthusiasm for the sight of some vultures, atop a sandbank, tugging at the carcase of a dead camel: 'They looked magnificent, sharply silhouetted against a background pregnant with light.'

How remote such exotic images must have seemed to him twenty years earlier, as he sat in the Grimstad dispensary with Schulerud and Due discussing the trip to the Orient they would one day make with all the money Ibsen would rake in from *Catiline*.

Something of his enduring sense of disbelief concerning the whole trip emerged in the fulsome nature of the thanks he offered to von Knorring afterwards. Attributing his invitation to join the party to von Knorring's influence on the king he described the trip as 'the richest episode of my life, and I know I will never be able to thank you as much as you deserve. I could have travelled to many countries in the world; but without your help I would never have come to Egypt.'[5]

The highly structured nature of the experience – essentially a diplomatic package tour – suited his temperament, and it is no surprise to find him a little later in a letter to Hegel recalling, perhaps not entirely without self-irony, 'Among the Danes I have met are P. Hansen and Robert Watt; we lay in a tent in the desert and read Danish newspapers.' He reiterated that it had been one of the most memorable experiences of his life, but concluded that 'best of all is to sit here quietly at home and look back on it all'.[6]

By the middle of December, after spending a few days alone in Paris going round the art galleries, he was back in Dresden doing just that.

In one of those Danish papers he sat reading in the desert he might have read an account of the rough reception given his new play, *The League of Youth*. Finished early in May, before his departure to Stockholm, it began its long life as nineteenth-century Norway's most popular Ibsen play at the Christiania theatre on 18 October. First, however, it had to survive a couple of *pibekonserter*, more or less organized sessions of booing, jeering and whistling intended to disrupt or even curtail performances.

The booing was not for aesthetic reasons but because the un-principled main character was given mannerisms of speech and behaviour very obviously based on Bjørnson. Bjørnson, entering into the spirit of the father confessor role allotted him by Ibsen after his departure for Rome, had been urging him ever since *Brand* to write a light entertainment, presumably as a sort of therapeutic device. Ibsen agreed with him. But aspects of his accelerating distrust of Bjørnson as friend and professional rival complicated the project, notably in that intemperate letter of rebuke to Bjørnson for his failure to knock Clemens Petersen senseless as punishment for his review of *Peer Gynt*. In that wild moment, it seems, several important elements of the new play were born.

In the letter he threatened to try his luck as a photographer, and in *The League of Youth* he was as good as his word. He gave Bjørnson his light entertainment and into the bargain a large, portrait-sized photograph of himself, taken from his worst side. Everyone knew that 'Stensgaard' was supposed to be Bjørnson, and with Bjørnson already a charismatic leader of political opinion in Kristiania his young supporters made their objections to the cynical gesture as fiercely as they could. The first night went off quietly enough. On the second the whistling and shouting were so loud the director had to take the stage to plead for calm. Fighting broke out once the performance was over and the gas lights had to be turned out in the theatre before the audience would leave.[7] The brawling continued in the streets outside. There was more rioting on the third night before it settled in for its long and successful run. In a poem 'At Port Said', written in November 1869, Ibsen bemoaned the philistine reaction of his fellow-countrymen; but his pleasure at the success of his provocation shines through every line. For his future career as a professional *provocateur* the whole affair was extremely instructive.

Ibsen's plays can be linked in many different ways, but one of the most durable is the history they tell of his thoughts on the nature of ambition, from Catiline's reformism to the Shakespearean rivalry between the earls in *The Pretenders*, on through Brand's spiritual rivalry with Christ in 1866, through the ambitious materialists of *The Pillars of Society*, the self-deluding nobility of Hjalmar Ekdal in *The Wild Duck* and the successful, world-weary artist-entrepreneurs Solness, Borkman and Rubek of the last plays. *The League of Youth*'s role in this analytical chain is unique in that it wilfully reverses the idealised portrait Ibsen gave of Bjørnson in *The Pretenders*. Posing as a young political idealist Stensgaard gathers a new party around him, The League of Youth, with the aim of eliminating corruption and bringing his new radical group to power. In his machinations to achieve election he indulges in sexual and social manoeuvring of such great and finally unmanagable complexity that in the end all the various women he has at one time or another planned to marry reject him, and all his political ambitions end in ruin.

The plotting shows Ibsen still making use of Scribean conventions of misunderstanding (Stensgaard's speech against the old aristocrat Brattsberg, which Brattsberg mistakenly believes to refer to his rival Monsen) and accidental confusions over letters leading to them being delivered to the wrong person. The great joy of the play, a natural successor to *Peer Gynt*, is Daniel Hejre, a hilariously irresponsible old gossip modelled to a degree on Ibsen's father, Knud. One exchange seems to mingle elements of both father and son, the Ibsen of the year of the many court cases:

> BASTION: Is it true what people say, that you once summonsed yourself to appear before the court of settlement?
> HEIRE: Myself? Well, yes; but I didn't turn up.

The lack in *The League of Youth* of the kind of serious 'infrastructure' that would characterise Ibsen's later plays has the effect of liberating the dialogue to be natural and witty to a degree not possible later on, when his fascination with the potential of symbol and his professional determination to make every line relevant to the main issue deprived him of this freedom. After *Peer Gynt, The League of Youth* is the most purely entertaining of all the plays of Ibsen's maturity. Despite its roots in domestic contemporary issues its cynical humour and farcical intrigue still work today. That it should retain its popularity all through the period of Ibsen's canonisation was due perhaps to the fact that actors and audiences alike could enjoy the play without the lurking fear that they did not fully understand it. This is Ibsen's most Holbergian play, a comedy on human weakness which does not, like some of his later plays on weakness, end in the punishment of the weak.

Christopher Due, his friend from the days in the dispensary in Grimstad, recalled in his memoirs a double-cartoon Ibsen once showed him. In the first drawing a fat man slumped snooozing and pot-bellied in an armchair. Above him, the hand of God appeared through the clouds holding a medal in the form of a star on a ribbon. The second drawing described the fat man's surprise on awakening to find the decoration pinned to his chest. Momentarily baffled he puts a hand to his head: 'What? A decoration? Why? How?' Then it dawns on him: 'But of course – I have *Slept*!'

Due comments that Ibsen hated the honours system; but by the age of forty Ibsen had changed his mind on the subject. Much as it pleased him, the award of the Vasa in 1869 can have come as no great surprise, since he had actively solicited it. In his journal entry for 22 September the king's chancellor, Erik af Edholm, refers to an evening at the Dramatiska Theatern after which Ibsen and others were invited to take punch with the king and his courtiers. During the course of this audience, writes af Edholm, 'I.(i.e. Ibsen) hinted to me that "something green" to put in the buttonhole would look good in Egypt, where he is now bound.'[8] A few days later the chancellor raised the matter with the king, 'who at once wanted to give Ibsen a Vasa'. On breaking the news to him Erik af Edholm found Ibsen 'childishly happy about this', adding laconically, 'because, I imagine, he is such a rebel.'

The Vasa was the first result of what rapidly became a concerted campaign to acquire as many such honours and medals as possible, resulting in five more within the next six years. The second of these, the Commander Third Class of the Turkish Medjidjie Order, was awarded him in Egypt by the Khedive, though it took months of anxious correspondence before the medal was safely on his chest. A scandal arose on the subject of some reciprocal orders taken out to Egypt by the man in charge of King Karl XV's horses, Ohan Demirgian, an Armenian who exerted what many Swedish courtiers felt to be a Svengali-type influence on the king. Demirgian and his party had gone laden with medals for their hosts, but in the opinion of many he went too far in personally presenting the Khedive's mother with an order. When the Swedish party returned to Stockholm there were dark mutterings about Demirgian and talk of a coup to get rid of him. Demirgian, getting wind of it, was reluctant to return home and lingered in Egypt, with a resultant delay in the delivery of the Khedive's medals.

Ibsen was informed of the reason for the delay in receiving his medal by von Knorring. Aware of the unusual importance Ibsen was attaching to this award, and aware too that Ibsen was possibly overestimating his, von Knorring's, importance in the matter, he used Ibsen's anxieties to further a plan of his own. In a series of letters in which he never failed to address Ibsen as 'Dear Friend in Honours' and to reassure him that he need not worry, the order was his already, von Knorring put forward a suggestion for the two of them to co-operate on a play about the trip to Egypt. Such an approach to Ibsen from a man who was not even a writer would normally have been dismissed out of hand. Extraordinarily, in von Knorring's case, Ibsen showed enthusiasm for it. He even sketched out an idea for a plot. Von Knorring worked on the joint enterprise, at the same time writing his own account of the two-month stay in Egypt.

On 23 November, on the advice of von Knorring, Ibsen wrote to Demirgian, 'innocently' enquiring what was delaying the despatch of the order. He complained he had so far been neglected in his own country when the medals were being handed out, 'and this in spite of the fact that I am always firmly on the side of the government and support it with my pen and with all the energy at my disposal'.[9] Finally however, on 10 May 1871, he was able to tell von Knorring the good news:

> Yesterday I received the Commander's Star and diploma! Thank you, thank you, you who conveyed me to the land of Egypt! You of course will have received your order a long time ago. Lieblein I hear received an Officer's Star, which of course is a lower award. Which other of our countrymen received decorations?[10]

The lesser award to Lieblein was gratifying to Ibsen not least because of Lieblein's lukewarm review of *Brand*; but as awards go it was slightly devalued anyway by the fact that members of the Swedish government delegation had refused to accept the Khedive's decoration.

Von Knorring and Ibsen met again while all this was going on in the summer of 1870, when Ibsen visited Copenhagen; but their correspondence ceases not long after this, with no more mention of the comedy about Scandinavian tourists in Egypt. The flamboyant Turkish medal remained one of Ibsen's favourites, and is the one he is wearing in Julius Kronberg's famous painting of him from 1877.

Anxieties concerning whether or not he would ever receive the Turkish decoration perhaps lay behind the next stage of Ibsen's campaign. He badly wanted a domestic award, and in a letter of 9 September 1870 charged Anton Klubien, his old friend from Rome, with getting him one. In particular he wanted the Danish order known as the *Danebrog*. This had recently been given to two of his fellow-countrymen, the writers Andreas Munch and J. S. Welhaven. To Klubien Ibsen complained that Welhaven had only published one volume of verse in Denmark whereas he, over the course of the preceding six years, had given them five editions of *Brand*, a new edition of *Love's Comedy*, two editions of *Peer Gynt*, two of *The League of Youth*. He also mentioned the imminent new edition of *The Pretenders*.

Welhaven was now an elderly man nearing the end of his life and career. Andreas Munch too was considerably older than Ibsen, yet Ibsen's intriguing mind persisted in seeing the awards as political rather than literary: 'I have, when the hour beckoned, fought for

Denmark with my pen, just as bravely as Welhaven'. He confessed that he was 'frankly greedy for any recognition which might come my way from Denmark'. 'From your own experience as a diplomat in Paris you know as well as I do that it is necessary to drop a little hint, *and I do so here.* After all, you know ministers who are, I think, well-disposed towards me. Take care of this business for me. An award from Denmark would impress powerfully in Norway. I need hardly urge that you observe a diplomatic discretion in the matter.'[11]

On 8 January 1871, some four months after his first approach to Klubien, Ibsen wrote to him again on the subject of decoration. The letter gives a unique insight into the long, slow swings his self-image described between the polar extremes of greedy Peer Gynt and noble Brand:

My dear Klubien!
There is nothing else for it. I must write to you while there is yet time.

When I was in Copenhagen this summer, so close to my own country, it seemed to me a matter of overriding importance to be able to return home under conditions that I regarded as so necessary that I expressed a wish which I, on mature consideration, would like to retract.

It seems to me now that the matter such as I presented it to you can only have left you with the impression of me as a quite commonly vain person. And that obviously you, under the circumstances, could not but present me as such to the opinion of others.

For this reason the matter has plagued me ever since; I feel as though I have gone unwashed into the street.

I cannot endure this. I must raise myself up again in my own estimation. Therefore I beg you, drop the whole thing, and help me rise again in the estimation of those men who are of real importance to me. Nothing is as important to me as this.

The confession brought him huge relief:

There now! That feels better. Consider me once again your old Roman *carissimo* and devoted friend.

And almost as a reward for his honesty he found that he was too late, Klubien had already given the necessary nudges and winks, and on 24 January 1871 Ibsen was awarded the Danebrog medal.

He closed the subject with a letter to Klubien of 13 February:

> If only I could thank sufficiently those men who have used their influence in this matter! If I could have my wish, I would sing the praises of each one of them on their respective diamond jubilees. As this point lies in the relatively distant future, I would ask you confidentially to be my agent in this matter for the time being. As for you, I need hardly express what I feel like. . . .
>
> Thank you and thank you again! This show of honour is a matter of great importance for me, greater than I can really say!
>
> At the moment I am completely occupied with the publication of my collection of poetry, which will appear shortly in a huge edition, with an advance on royalties to match. I shall make quite certain that *carissimo* is among the book's first readers.

At the simplest level this love of honours casts a glancing light on the superficially unlikely attraction of such a serious man to the world of the theatre by appealing to his love of dressing up. One of his pleasures as a child in Skien was to be allowed to watch the dressing rituals of an elegant old villager named Lund. Lund's finery consisted of velvet breeches, a silk waistcoat trimmed in brown and gold, brown coat, starched neckcloth and buckled shoes, and little Henrik never tired of watching the transformation from man into peacock.[12]

But if he loved these medals and ribbons in his childish vanity he also needed them psychologically as part of the unfolding of his deeply-ambiguous attitude towards bourgeois society. On the one hand he was still determined to exact his revenge upon it for the twin humiliations of his childhood (family ruin) and adolescence (Else Sophie Birkedalen); on the other he was firmly determined to be accepted as one of its most respectable members. The awkward paradox he personified, particularly in the later stages of his career, as a state-supported and state-rewarded rebel, is illuminated by an exchange of letters with Bjørnson on the subject of honours back in 1867, when Bjørnson asked for his support in a proposal to decline in solidarity any offer of honours that might be made to them, as a way of ensuring the independence of their pens in matters of nationalist interest.

Ibsen turned his proposal down flat. He pointed out that he was a confirmed monarchist, not a republican; that both he and Bjørnson were in receipt of annual government grants and that, where honours were awarded by the king, this was 'a mark of honour, because he responds to a mood which he recognises is present among the people. Why reject one expression of this when we don't reject the other for the same reason?' Mindful of the potential compromise to his freedom of speech he added: 'If I had had any positive desire for such decorations I would naturally have avoided appearing in the role of "state satirist"; but should they arrive – then no rejection!'[13]

Yet as he showed shortly afterwards, he had a positive desire for them. The resultant unease he dealt with by adopting a posture of impossible radicalism, exemplified in his poem 'To my friend the revolutionary orator', written in 1869. He addresses an unnamed critic: 'You say I have become 'conservative', but 'I am what I have been all my life':

> I'm not interested in moving the pieces;
> knock the whole board over, then I'm with you.
>
> There's just one revolution I remember
> that wasn't the work of a half-hearted bodger
>
> Its glories are the mark, even today.
> I mean, of course, the Flood.
>
> But even then, Lucifer was tricked
> for it was Noah who emerged as dictator.
>
> Let's do it again, more radically -
> but for that we need both men and leaders.
>
> You irrigate the world with your flood-water
> I would prefer to torpedo the ark.

To lay claim to a fundamentalism so profound offered him permanent protection from the prospect of involvement in social revolution at the trivial level in Norway – the struggle for extended democratic rights. There is a touch in it too of the old 'aesthetic' arrogance with which he had distanced himself from the Thranites in Kristiania back in 1851. Revolutions had to be floods; nothing less would do. It left him free to think of himself as a ferociously rebellious man betrayed by the banality of everyday life; and yet free to accept medals from the very forces that kept it banal.

* * *

Over the same period of time as he was pursuing these orders Ibsen was also cementing his friendship with the young critic most frequently credited with giving him the courage and intellectual encouragement he needed to face head-on the difficult challenge of putting the modern world on his stage. Five years after Ibsen had opened their correspondence with his long report of the suicide in Rome of Brandes's friend Ludvig David, Georg Brandes finally called on Ibsen at home in July 1871 to make his personal acquaintance. Brandes was twenty-nine years old.

He found Ibsen handsome, with 'a most unusual forehead, clear eyes and long, curly hair', and to his surprise wearing his Vasa order and ribbons. In a gesture of intimacy so uncharacteristic as to suggest either that Brandes was exaggerating or that Ibsen had been drinking, he recalled that Ibsen 'hugged me to his breast, almost suffocating me'.[14]

Brandes, like any literate young Scandinavian, had been interested in Ibsen's plays for several years, and it was an interest that may have extended to a curiosity about the the writer himself, for in 1864 it was his turn to be the latest interesting young man in the life of Ibsen's mother-in-law Magdalene Thoresen, unmarried since the death of Prost Thoresen in 1858 and enjoying her freedom to the full. After abandoning a course in law he had taken up the study of æsthetics, won the gold medal at the University of Copenhagen and obtained his PhD in 1870 with a paper on Taine. He had published two critical works, *Aesthetic Studies* and *Criticisms and Portraits*, and was already committed to some of the most important ideas behind what would become his major work, the multi-volumed *Main Currents in 19th century European Literature*.

A *bildungsreise* through France, England and Italy between April 1870 and July 1871, in the course of which he met Taine, Renan and John Stuart Mill, had turned him into an æsthetic heretic keen to impose his ideas on European culture. His new literary heroes were those writers who, as he phrased it in a lecture at the University of Copenhagen, 'set themselves the task of debating problems', exemplified by George Sand on marriage, Voltaire, Byron and Feuerbach on religion, Proudhon on property, Dumas the younger on the sexual relationship, Emile Augier on social conditions. Concluding his trip in Germany and Dresden, it was natural for him to call on Ibsen, the leading Scandinavian dramatist of the younger school (though Ibsen was by now forty-three years old).

The tone of their meetings in July 1871 may perhaps be inferred from the letters they had already exchanged. It was at once intimate, relaxed and bantering. The received wisdom is that Brandes influenced Ibsen in the direction of his later writing, those plays from 1877 onwards that did indeed debate the problems of the day; but the impression one gets from the early letters is rather that what was involved was a crash-course for Brandes in Ibsen's own anti-democratic radicalism, the so-called 'aristocratic radicalism' that Brandes made his own some fifteen years later. In the spring of 1870 Ibsen was almost paternal in his advice to the younger man:

> You say you have no friends at home. I have long thought that must be the case. When one's life and work are in such intimate relationship to each other as they are in your case then one cannot expect to keep one's 'friends'. But I think actually it is good for you to have travelled away from home without leaving any friends behind you. Friends are an expensive luxury; and when one invests all one's capital in a call and a mission in this life, one cannot afford to have friends. The expense of having friends lies not in what one does for them but what one out of consideration for them does not do. This can stunt one's spiritual development. I have been through this, and that is why it took me several years before I succeeded in becoming myself.[15]

Brandes became and remained fascinated by Ibsen's personality. In 1875 he wrote to the novelist Paul Heyse that Ibsen was 'reserved, somewhat shy and taciturn, a very eccentric and bizarre Norwegian'.[16] Much of Brandes's fascination must have derived from the obvious enjoyment Ibsen took in proposing and embodying paradoxes. He had become himself, he told Brandes; but if the self was a Gyntian onion, what then?

If bizarreness and eccentricity were the dominating impression of the first visit, a degree of genuine affection appeared following a second visit, in the autumn of 1872. On 29 September that year Brandes wrote to his mentor Hans Brøchner, professor of philosophy at Copenhagen University:

> I have spent the past few days together with Ibsen. It often worries me that I was so thoughtless as to repeat to you my impression occasioned last year by that little bauble in his button hole. I. no longer wears decorations at home. But only now have I really

become acquainted with him. He must give everyone the impression of being a man of very great note, so serious that a smile is rarely seen on his face; he has the rather awkward characteristics of the autodidact, but at the same time there is something menacing and imperious in his person, as with someone demanding obedience. He is strict in his views, including those on himself. He is most retiring in his manner of life, and devotes himself entirely to his work. . . . Politically he is very conservative, or rather absolutist; he is convinced that political liberals are almost always intellectually highly illiberal, saying that it is better to be subject to one powerful ruler than many lesser ones. Finally, he naively says, political oppression leads to such a wonderful longing for true freedom and the struggle to achieve it.[17]

The developing relationship between writer and critic was much more successful than the one Ibsen had attempted to build between himself and Clemens Petersen. Where before he had openly courted Petersen prior to the publication of *Brand* and *Peer Gynt* he adopted towards Brandes an almost Confucian display of sensitivity to protocol. After the publication of his collection of *Poems* in 1871 he wrote to Brandes apologising for having delayed so long in answering an earlier letter. He explained:

Since the publication of my poems was imminent, I did not want to take any step that might look like an attempt to court favour with you before you had read the book. I am very well aware of the fact that your opinions are not for hire; but a certain tact prevented me from taking any such calculated action. My dear friend, this you will understand.[18]

This was just a few weeks before their first meeting. In the same letter he thanked Brandes for enclosing a photograph of himself, 'it has been of enormous value to me in the understanding or more correctly in the appropriation of your innermost personality', a daunting thought for the potential visitor, and evidence too of Ibsen's extreme social caution, for this was also about the animal's dream of seeing without being seen. There was, too, a mystical side to Ibsen to which the miracle of photography evidently appealed. In this letter he also responded to an earlier criticism Brandes had offered, 'that I have not assimilated current scientific thinking', by suggesting that such study was not necessary, since the *zeitgeist* was something one simply inhaled, like the air – 'Have you never noticed in a portrait gallery from some bygone century the remarkable family likeness between the different people of the same period? This observation is also true in the mental sphere.' Again, the thought suggests the mystic in Ibsen, the proposal of an agnostic still on the lookout for magic in an age of rapidly advancing rationalism. Ibsen later conceded that Brandes had been right in his suggestion, and in a range of plays from *A Doll's House* onwards made extensive use of 'current scientific thinking' for his plotting. He also valued and was prepared to act on Brandes' literary criticism, since Brandes answered his demand that a good critic should attempt to offer the writer constructive solutions to the shortcomings he was exposing. Shortly before their first meeting, with Brandes' photograph in front of him, Ibsen wrote to him expressing the faith that they would 'find themselves able to agree about a great many things besides a shared love of velvet overcoats',[19] and so it proved. A non-practising Jew with an outsider's perspective on Scandinavian society, Brandes became in years to come one of Ibsen's most valued intellectual allies and supporters.

The visits of a lively and intelligent young literary man like Brandes were rare highlights in a daily life which was, as Brandes noticed, entirely dedicated to work. After Brandes's second visit to Dresden, in the summer of 1872, Ibsen told him how he 'daily recalled those few weeks last year, when you brought life and variety into our lonely existence.'[20] And urging von Knorring to continue corresponding with him he wrote that 'under the circumstances I am even more lonely than usual,'[21] – the circumstances being the gloomy atmosphere in Dresden occasioned by the Franco-Prussian war and the presence in the city of wounded German soldiers and captured Frenchmen. There were occasional visits from old friends and acquaintances – Lorenz Dietrichson, Andreas Munch and family – and some contact with Norwegians living locally like Karl Bomhoff, a trained pharmacist like Ibsen, who worked in the chemical department of a local factory. Bomhoff returned to Norway in 1870 to start his own business in Trondheim, and in a moment of homesickness Ibsen and Suzannah prevailed upon him to send over a consignment of the rosefish of which Ibsen was so fond. On the same errand they got Suzannah's brother Herman to send them a carton of Norwegian brown cheese.

Social life itself was not really a problem for Ibsen. At home his only interest was work, and if he wanted to go out for a drink there were several cafés nearby – the *Brülsche Terrasse, Wildruffersplatz,* and the *Café Français,* where there were even Scandinavian newspapers to read. His need for literary companionship was met by his membership of the Dresden Literary Society. He went with Brandes in September 1872, and together they heard lectures on Tieck's study of *Hamlet,* and on a book by one of the members, *Jesus und die Frauen.* The death of the philosopher Ludvig Feuerbach was also remembered, with a reading from *Das Wesen des Christentums* that brought tears to the eyes of some of the older members. Brandes mentions as a highlight of this stay in Dresden his meeting with Herman Hettner, the literary theorist whose 'very interesting and stimulating book'[22] *Das Moderne Drama* Ibsen had come across during his first trip to Dresden in 1852. Brandes socialised extensively with Hettner, but Ibsen seems not to have been present on these occasions – surprisingly, perhaps, for Hettner must surely have been a member of the Dresden Literary Society.

Another writer who visited Ibsen that summer was Hans Christian Andersen. One who did not visit was Feodor Dostoevsky, who from August 1869 to July 1871 lived not far from the Ibsens. He was unknown outside Russia at this time and the only book of his translated into German, *From the House of the Dead,* had failed completely. The two writers were both gambling but there was a difference between the two Danish lottery tickets Hegel regularly bought for Ibsen at his request and Dostoevsky's wilfully ruinous sessions at the roulette tables. In 1898 Ibsen singled out *Raskolnikov,* as *Crime and Punishment* is always known in Norway, for special praise; but that he met the author of the book is unlikely.[23]

As companion Suzannah had her unmarried sister Marie, who joined them early in 1870 and stayed for some eighteen months. Another visitor from home was her young half-brother Thomas, determined to emulate his mother Magdalene and brother-in-law Ibsen and become a writer himself. He visited in the summer of 1872, again in the summer of 1873, and spent the winter of 1874–5 in Dresden.

Sigurd continued at Dr Elbe's, where he had the misfortune to be bullied. Dearly as she loved him it was not sensitive of Suzannah to send him to a posh school wearing hand-me-downs from his father, left on the large side so that he could grow into them. Boys ran after him in the street, calling out and laughing at him as he trod on his own trousers. Ibsen, blithely ignorant of the situation, told him one day he was welcome to bring some chums home from school if he so wished. Sigurd said he preferred not to. The situation worsened in 1870 with the outbreak of the Franco-Prussian war. Sigurd, apeing his parents' prejudices, advertised his sympathies for the French side, with predictable results. Ibsen was away in Copenhagen at the time and Suzannah had to deal with the problem. In her letters to Ibsen she referred to 'these terrible weeks here' in Dresden, but reassured him that 'Sigurd is now, with the help of the headmaster, protected from bullying at the school; but for two weeks he was regularly beaten up because he would not support the Germans.'[24]

The outbreak of the war on 19 July was a disturbing element in Ibsen's environment and for several weeks he found himself irritable and unable to work. He chanelled some of his energy into a feud with a Kristiania publisher, H. J. Jensen, formerly the owner of *Illustreret Nyhedsblad*, the magazine in which he had published regularly in the 1850s and 1860s. In its day *Illustreret Nyhedsblad* had included the texts of both *Lady Inger of Østråt* and *The Vikings at Helgeland*. Jensen was in financial trouble and had hit upon the idea of republishing these two plays in order to take advantage of the fame Ibsen had lately achieved. He sent copies of the new editions to Ibsen in Dresden in September 1871 for Ibsen to proofread and correct if he so wished. In reply he received a small masterpiece of personal and professional vituperation:

> With the greatest surprise I received today your insolent and shameless letter, from which I gather that you intend to publish new editions of my plays *Lady Inger of Østråt* and *The Vikings at Helgeland*. Naturally I oppose in the firmest possible manner this planned assault on my purse. You have not even the remotest right to the works in question, which were sold to me at that time solely for use in *Illustreret Nyhedsblad*. I will have you know, furthermore, that both books are about to be published by Gyldendal in completely revised form, and that the public will be informed of this at once, so that your intended swindle will bring nothing but shame and disgrace upon you. Furthermore, I have today put the matter in the hands of my lawyer, and if you persist

in your adventure, then I shall in the press and through the courts show you just exactly what the consequences of such rascally behaviour can be. Your package is hereby returned un-opened.

Undaunted, and certain that he was the legal owner of the two plays, Jensen proceeded with the publication of *The Vikings at Helgeland*. In one of the many letters he wrote in connection with the case Ibsen complained that 'the law protects the salmon in our rivers and the game in the mountains; authors, on the other hand, are classified with vermin, we do our best to exterminate them'.[25]

The Jensen business dragged on for almost five years before settlement, and covered the period of intensive writing on *Emperor and Galilean*, so it also provided Ibsen with a source of anger to keep him going through the long, hard task. Jensen became the fruit into which he injected his venom, and some of his responses were so insulting that Jensen contemplated suing him for libel. Ibsen, for his part, indulged his paranoia and saw the episode as evidence of his native country's imagined hostility towards him – 'every bad thing that comes my way comes from Norway'.

It was in this sort of mood that he made, in a letter to his old Hollander friend Michael Birkeland, the first of what became his numerous threats to 'cut every tie with Norway, and never again set foot in the country' should Jensen triumph over him. He believed this particular example of malice towards him was indicative of a prevailing climate of socialist and democratic sympathies in Kristiania which obviously he found unsympathetic. Suddenly anxious at the prospect of a libel suit from Jensen he wrote to Birkeland that now he understood why his comments on Jensen's 'swindling' and his 'rascally ways' might prove dangerous to him, for 'if Jensen were a senior civil servant, a professional man or any sort of refined person at all there would be no danger; but a dirty scoundrel, who precisely because of his dirtiness is "one of the people", may not, naturally, be dismissed with scorn.'[26]

But it all ended well for him: in April 1876, before Jensen could proceed with his plans for a new edition of *Lady Inger of Østråt*, the case came to the High Court. Jensen was fined, ordered to pay Ibsen damages, and had his remaining copies of *The Vikings at Helgeland* confiscated.

*   *   *

It was a novel experience for Ibsen to be suing rather than sued, and another indication to him of how much his situation had changed over the previous ten years. To his relief his outstanding debt to Nandrup was finally settled by December 1873. He wrote to Herman Thoresen, who was now also handling his financial affairs in Norway: 'I am debt-free and have several thousand invested in shares which Hegel has been buying for me over the years and which increase steadily in value, so I look forward to a time in the not-too-distant future when we can live from the interest alone plus my stipend.'[27] To Hegel he wrote, 'I am now, of course, – thanks to you – a capitalist!'[28]

Ibsen had good grounds for his cautious financial optimism, for after Scandinavia the rest of Europe, with Germany in the vanguard, was beginning to open up to him. In February 1872 Siebold's translation of *Brand* appeared, and later in the same year Strodtmann's *The Pretenders* and *The League of Youth*. Both wrote biographical and literary articles on Ibsen, Siebold in March 1870 in *Illustrierte Zeitung*, and Strodtmann early in 1873 for a Hamburg paper. Ibsen wrote to thank Strodtmann for his support and inform him of more acclaim – three lectures on *The Pretenders* and *The League of Youth* delivered to the Dresden Literary Society.[29]

At about the same time the first English notice of his work appeared, in the form of a review in *The Spectator* of March 1872 of *Poems*. The reviewer was Edmund Gosse, then working as assistant librarian at the British Museum, who had come across Ibsen's work while travelling in Norway in 1871. He sent a copy of his review to Ibsen, with an accompanying letter. Prior to this England and Englishmen had been, if anything, a term of abuse in Ibsen's literary vocabulary. The English were everything the Brand in him despised – a nation of shopkeepers, crass materialists, world-polluters with their great smoking chimneys belching modern times out into the world. His boy Sigurd would never be allowed to grow up in a world of craven anglophiles. Like his prejudice against the Swedes, his anglophobia proved fleeting and not strong enough to survive the sweetness of a little attention. Replying to Gosse he told him that the English were a nation 'whose characteristics are practicality and efficiency, united in remarkable fashion with a pure and dignified emotional life and a nobility of bearing that makes yours a nation of aristocrats, in the best sense of the word.'[30]

The volte-face in regard to Swedes and Englishmen did him no professional harm at all; but in due course his more extensively documented irritation with Germans would pose a slight threat to his growing reputation there which he would have to deal with.

10

The Apostate
Poems · Emperor and Galilean

In his first period in Dresden there is a sense of Ibsen slowly imposing order on his life, tidying up the past (the end of the Nandrup debt) and organising the future. ('On my Egyptian trip,' he told Hegel, 'I have made many useful German contacts, particularly in the literary world.') The mood is symbolised by the effort he now made to collect, revise and publish a volume of his favourite poems. In a practical sense, too, the undemanding nature of such work suited him, for the Franco-Prussian war and the depressed atmosphere in Dresden continued to make it hard to concentrate on anything as substantial as *Julian*, the play which had now been waiting patiently almost six years for its expression.

It was his old Hollander friend, the school teacher Jakob Løkke, who did the spadework. Ibsen had renewed personal contact with him at the language conference in the summer of 1869 in Stockholm, where Løkke had volunteered to scour the various newspapers and magazines in which Ibsen's poems had appeared over the years and make copies of them. Fortuitously, at about the same time Hegel had suggested an edition of his collected poems to Ibsen.

In January 1871 Ibsen received the fruits of Løkke's industry – 'a thick book; but for the moment at least I am scrapping three-quarters of it and rewriting the rest'.[1] He also wrote new works especially for inclusion, the long 'Balloon Letter to a Swedish Lady', the lady in question being Fru Limnell, with whose family Ibsen had stayed in Stockholm in 1869 before leaving for Egypt; and 'Verse Letter to Fru Heiberg', for the actress and director whose production of *The Pretenders* had recently enjoyed great success in Copenhagen. The selecting and rewriting occupied most of January, and on 21 January Ibsen sent off part of the manuscript to Hegel.

Poems, a collection of fifty-five poems, appeared on 3 May 1871.

The earliest included was 'Fiddlers', a revised extract from his 1851 poem 'A Saturday Evening in Hardanger'. There were poems from *Love's Comedy, The Pretenders, Brand,* and *The Vikings at Helgeland,* as well as some of the best of his early long poems such as 'On the Heights', which he allowed to stand in its original 1859 form, and 'Terje Vigen', likewise unchanged save for amendments made to adapt the spelling to the recommendations of the Scandinavian language reformers. A notable absentee was 'In the Picture Gallery', present in *Poems* only in the fragmentary 'In the Gallery'. The collection contained many of the 'public-voice' poems inspired by his reaction to the 1864 war over Schleswig-Holstein, including 'Grounds for Belief', 'A Brother in Need!' and other politically inspired poems such as 'The Murder of Abraham Lincoln' and 'To my friend the revolutionary orator!' Poems such as these rely for their drama and effect on Ibsen's love of the consonantal alliteration or initial rhyming of Old Norse skaldic verse, so declamatory in their style that they really need to be read aloud for their full force to be experienced. In terms of content, however, they are of little interest.

Poetry at its best should tease us forward by the mysterious logic of its syntax and vocabulary into the understanding the poet wishes to convey to us, tricking us out of the illusion of understanding brought on by our endless familiarity with words. The highlights and memorable moments of *Poems* are not the large and self-consciously clear public-voice verses but those short, private poems like 'Gone' and 'From my home life' which perform this magic. 'Gone' is almost Japanese in its mystery and brevity:

> We followed the guests
> to the gate.
> The night breeze took
> the last of our farewells.
>
> Great desolation
> over the garden, in the house
> where lately sweet music
> had enchanted me.
>
> It was only a party
> before the coming dark night;
> she was only a guest;
> now she is gone.

Ibsen told Jakob Løkke that 'Gone' was inspired by the early death of Christopher Bruun's sister Thea, whom he met during his first summer in Italy at Genzano in 1864, but here our appreciation of the poem positively discourages such biographical connections. The revised 'The Miner', however, seems to have acquired an almost programmatic significance in the years since its composition in 1850, and appreciation of the poem is only enhanced by our knowledge of Ibsen's life and personality. Similarly 'Building Plans', whose simple metaphor of the writer as builder stretches from 1853 into 1892 and *The Master Builder*. 'From My Home Life' is a remarkable snapshot of the writer at his desk suddenly emerging from his literary trance into a paralysing self-consciousness of the strangeness of what he is about:

> All was still in the house, the streets quite dead.
> I sat by the shaded lamp;
> the room was swathed in soft shadow;-
> the children entered, with sweet greeting
> behind the veil of my Havana.
>
> They came to me one by one, my winged children,
> playful boys and girls
> with cheeks shining, as after a bath.
> Oh how wild and happy was our playful romping
> through all the sweet kingdoms.
>
> But just as our joy reached its heights
> I happened to glance in the mirror.
> There stood a sombre guest
> with blue-grey eyes and buttoned coat,
> wearing, unless I am mistaken, felt slippers.
>
> And a weight descends upon my wild children;
> one puts a finger to his mouth,
> another stands frozen and clumsy;-
> for in the presence of strangers, you know,
> bright boys grow wary.

The poem 'Thanks' gives voice to the enormous respect and gratitude Ibsen felt towards Suzannah for her selfless support over the years of their marriage:

> Hers were the sorrows,
> that confounded my path, –

hers the joys
that helped me by them.

Her home is out here
on freedom's sea,
where the poet's craft
is reflected.

Her brothers and sisters
are those shifting forms
that march with banners waving
through my verse.

Her goal
is to fire my vision,
yet none must know
who lit the flame.

She wants no thanks
and just for that reason,
I sing her this song
of thanks.

When *Poems* was published Suzannah searched it in vain for the poem in her honour which Ibsen told her it contained. Finally he told her she must read the titles backwards, which gave her 'Kat', one of his pet-names for her.

The last poem in the collection, and deliberately so, was another love-poem, the newly written 'Burnt Boats'. This time the addressee was his native land:

He turned his craft
away from the north,
sought the playful tracks
of lighter gods.

Beacons in the snow
extinguished in the sea
ancient gods of the south
made their demands.

He burnt his boats;
blue smoke
like smoke from a railway bridge
hurtled behind him.–

To snowbound huts
from sun-rim's brushland,
a rider comes riding
each single night.

Concluding thus, Ibsen managed to make the collection a personal history. Hegel forwarded a package of reviews to him in July 1871 with which Ibsen expressed himself satisfied. Brandes's response, which he had been particularly anxious to hear, was a mixture of enthusiasm (the most important aspect of the collection was that 'it exceeds its own limitations, bringing word from a spirit with the rare quality of being able to aspire, both as an artist and and as a human being') and rejection ('My young Wine', 'Album Rhyme' and 'To H.Ø.Blom' were 'misconceived and despicable'). True to his credo, Ibsen did not take umbrage at what he regarded as contructive criticism. Moreover his own attitude towards the collection was ambiguous and he had already, in a letter of 17 February to Brandes, written something curiously close to a disclaimer, describing the editing of *Poems* as a 'damned difficult piece of work, having to go through all those numerous standpoints with which I was done long ago.'[2] He suspected himself that he was now effectively finished with poetry, and Brandes' mixed response must have confirmed him in his suspicion.

Poems proved popular and went through five editions between 1871 and 1886, with small alterations each time. Composers have not shown great interest in the poems, though Edvard Grieg's *Six Poems* have proved as durable as his orchestral music for *Peer Gynt*. Delius' dramatic treatment of 'On the Heights' for solo voice and orchestra is particularly successful.

One poem that was not included in *Poems* was 'Judas':

Among the twelve he was a rare bird –
literally the wagon's twelfth wheel.

What drove him on remains a riddle;
history tells us only the facts.

We know that in the sleep of conscience
he stepped forward and kissed the Saviour.

Heaven and Hell were victors both then;
– But what if Judas had said no?

171

A similar thought is expressed in a note made for *Kejser og Galilæer* (*Emperor and Galilean*):

> If Jehova had said to Cain: go forth and murder your brother, and Cain had answered, Lord, should I lose my eternal soul? And the Lord had answered, do as I bid you – what then? If the Lord had said to Judas, I need you to betray my son so that the Creation may be perfected, and Judas went forth and betrayed his master and lost his soul in the act of obedience – what then?[3]

Individually and together these two pieces of writing show how far Ibsen's religious doubt had travelled since 'Doubt and Hope' in 1849 and the flirting with syncretism in *The Warrior's Barrow* as he sought for solutions to the sense of being morally excluded from Christian society by the adolescent indiscretion with Else Sophie Birkedalen. The profundity of these naked formulations of the question reveal perhaps more clearly than anything else he wrote the absolutely fundamental nature of his scepticism. To be an atheist is one thing; to suggest, as Ibsen does towards the end of the play through the mystic Maximos, that Julian's apostasy was an historically necessary 'sin' forced upon him by the needs of Christianity, as the sins of Cain and Judas were forced upon them by the same 'prodigal God', is a position beyond atheism. 'Judas' was never published, perhaps because Ibsen felt he was trying to say something so controversial that he dare not risk it in such unadorned form; hence, in its stead, the enormous ten-act *Emperor and Galilean*, the play in two parts which stands almost at the chronological heart of his career.

Dietrichson's account of Ibsen's response in 1864 to Ammianus Marcellinus' description of the campaigns of Julian the Apostate suggests that Ibsen experienced the same sort of instant identification with the Emperor as he had done sixteen years earlier on first coming across Catiline. His intention was to write the play immediately, but *Brand* overtook his thoughts. In 1866, after a forty-year gestation period that makes Ibsen's delay seem the merest pause, Carsten Hauch's tragedy about Julian appeared. Hauch was Oehlenschläger's successor as professor of aesthetics at the University of Copenhagen, a pedagogically idealistic novelist who had become concerned in his old age with asserting the inevitable final harmony of God and the golden age with progress in the natural sciences, a reassuring thought to those frightened by the heresies of evolutionary theory: 'just wait until science has finished, then we will see that the essence of the biblical account of Eden is in full accord with the conclusions science arrives at'.[4] Ibsen, who never felt the need of this kind of reassurance, did not trouble to read his book. He knew the material was his by divine right anyway.

After *Brand* his purpose was once again deflected, by *Peer Gynt,* and after *Peer Gynt* by *The League of Youth.* Evidently, as he wrote to Peter Hansen in March 1869, Julian was 'a man and a material that I find myself drawing back from'. But once *The League of Youth* was out of the way he wrote on 28 May 1869 to Lorentz Dietrichson, 'I intend to get to grips with Julian this autumn', and a few days later he told Hegel, 'I feel that the material has now become sufficiently clear to me, and that when I finally begin the work will go swiftly and smoothly'. The socialising summer in Stockholm and subsequent trip to Egypt yet again delayed things; but with his decision not to expend effort on writing up his travel notes on his return from Egypt the committment to tackle *Julian* was made.

The poverty of source material on the historical Peer Gynt had liberated him from the demands of pedantry to write what he liked; and one obvious explanation for the continuing delay with *Julian* was the amount of research he felt obliged to carry out in dealing with such a well-known historical figure with a well-documented life. His failure as a classical scholar in 1850 rankled, and a lesser aim of the play was perhaps also to transcend the memory of this failure. The sources he consulted included Ammianus's *History of Rome* in a German school-edition, perhaps Julian's own writings in Latin and his *Misopogon* (the beard-hater) in German translation, and August Neander's *Über den Kayser Julianus und sein Zeitalter.* In July 1871 he wrote to Hegel asking for copies of three biographical articles that had appeared in *Fædrelandet* some years earlier. His only concern was to acquire accurate background detail, and he was in the main unimpressed by the theories of Julian's personality he came across. He had read a lecture by David Strauss, *Der Romantiker auf dem Throne der Cäseren,* but found it to contain 'only disputational lunacies, and I am quite capable of providing those myself'.

The sheer volume of material presented him with problems of form. His first solution was to write a sort of trilogy. The first section, *Julian and the Friends of Truth* in three acts, was ready by the end of

1871. The second, *Julian's Apostasy*, also in three acts, was written largely in the summer of 1872 in Berchtesgaden. He was engaged in making his fair copy by 8 August and anticipated starting work on the third part, *Julian on the Imperial Throne*, imminently. It would be in five acts, he told Hegel, and his preparations were so well advanced that 'it will take a lot less time than the preceding acts'. Though each part could be published and appreciated as an entity in itself, he hoped Hegel would agree to publish all three simultaneously.

Returning to Dresden, at the beginning of September he began work on this final part. Then a sudden change of mind led him to rewrite the entire second section and reconceive the work as a double play, with five acts in each part. This process was nigh complete by the time Brandes visited him later in the month. In his letter of 29 September to Hans Brøchner, professor of philosophy at Copenhagen University, Brandes was able to tell Brøchner that '*Julian* will consist of two long dramas, each of five acts; the first is already finished, the second exists in a detailed draft scene by scene'.[5] To Gosse, with whom he had struck up a correspondence after the *Spectator* review, Ibsen related with his customary precision that the second of the two linked dramas had been written between 21 November 1872 and 16 February 1873.

Brandes felt sure that *Julian* would be an 'extremely significant work', and Ibsen too was in no doubt about the status of his double play. Well before he had written it, in July 1871, he announced it to Hegel as 'my major work'. He made the same claim to his old Hollander friend Ludvig Daae, whom he contacted in a last-minute flurry of correspondence over details he was unsure of, such as the correct forms of personal names in Greek and information on whether the Greeks grecianised Latin names. (A sample question: did the Greeks write Basilios, Basileos or Basileus? Is the name Cæsarius the same as Cæsarion?) To both Hegel and Daae he explained the significance of his subtitle, 'a world-historical drama'. He told Hegel he had invented the term by analogy with 'folk-drama, family-drama, nationalist drama etc'.[6] To Daae he summarised its theme as a version of the Manichæan heresy: 'The play discusses the struggle between two incompatible forces in the world which will repeat itself eternally, and because of this universality I call the book "a world-historical drama" '.[7]

Finally, content that his book was secure from the assaults of malevolently learned pedants, he despatched the manuscript to Hegel, who published *Emperor and Galilean* on 16 October 1873 in an edition of 4,000 copies.

In his play Ibsen followed the known events of the historical Julian's life fairly closely. Thus his adolescent Julian finds something lacking in the Christian religion in which he has been brought up and begins to take an active interest in the heathendom that preceded it as the state religion. Rising, almost against his will, to become Emperor, he believes himself to be a reincarnation of Alexander the Great, and that his destiny is to complete Alexander's world conquest. He converts wholly to heathenism, but proclaims religious toleration. But the decree of the God of the Christians is 'thou shalt have no other Gods but me'; Julian's Christian subjects reject tolerance and begin destroying heathen temples. Julian retaliates by persecuting them.

His sense of historical mission grows; yet his military prowess and powers of decision are compromised by a scholarly, reflective side to his personality. Like Skule, he is unable to prevent this element from leading him into self-doubt. Deep into his campaign he is tricked by a Persian double-agent into burning his fleet. His megalomania increases as he comes to believe himself a god. He orders ikons of himself to be set up at all pay-stations in the military camp. The gesture alienates the Christians among his soldiers. Julian falls in battle with the Persians, but the Persian army is routed because the Roman soldiers, led now by the Christian Jovian, believe that Christ is with them. Julian, wounded in the side by a spear, cries out, 'You have triumphed, Galilean,' and dies in a manner recalling Christ's death on the cross, with the words, 'Sun, Sun – why have you betrayed me?'

The central relationship in the play is that between Julian and the heathen priest Maximos, 'the Mystic'. Their exchanges are at times on the same intimate level of private understanding as those between Skule and his skald Jatgeir in *The Pretenders*; but Maximos's necromantic power and esoteric knowledge give him greater authority over his master than Jatgeir had. The crucial scene in the play – one of great drama, mystery and power – is the seance arranged by Maximos at which the spirits of the three greatest negative powers in human history are to be conjured. Julian is here Faustian in his determination to know these three and to talk to them. Cain speaks, then Judas. The third of the three cannot, it seems, be contacted; but it is evidently Julian himself who is fated to join this company of damned souls. Returning to this mystical theme late in the play, after Julian's death, Maximos voices Ibsen's most unusual and dramatic idea, that none of these three deserves contumely. He absolves them of personal responsibility for their murders, betrayals and blasphemies. He sees them as simply living out their destinies, likening them almost to actors obediently playing the parts assigned to them by a cosmic director. Julian, he says, is 'necessity's sacrificial victim'. During work on the play, Ibsen wrote to Georg Brandes that he had 'to a certain extent become a fatalist', although he also made it clear that his play had no 'moral' as such. Maximos bemoans the fact that he was deceived by the gods over Julian, so that he mistook him for the prophesied agent of a synthesis between the old and the new religions. Yet he retains his faith in the necessary arising one day of a new moral and intellectual understanding which he calls *det tredje rike* (the third empire). When that time comes, the true nature of the role of these three negative forces will be recognised, and incense will be burned at ceremonies to honour their contributions to the unfolding of world history. Though he sees it purely from the Christian perspective, Basilios comes close to expressing the same idea when he reflects on the Emperor's life: 'The Emperor Julian was a rod for our backs – not to beat us to death, but to bring us to renewal.'

Julian, Catiline and Skule, all three are joined in self-doubt, all contain elements of the self-portraiture Ibsen confessed to when he told Daae that the play contained 'more evidence of my own spiritual journey than I am willing to admit to in public'. Perhaps he was referring particularly to the parallel between Julian's religious journey and his own, from the loss of childhood faith in Christ to the search for something to replace it. What Julian rejects in Christ is His monopoly on value judgements:

If my soul cringed and twisted in hatred for the killer of my family, the commandment was: love thine enemy! If my mind in its thirst for beauty turned to the ways and images of the ancient Greeks the Christian message burst in upon me with its: seek only what is the only necessity! If I felt the sweet pangs of lust for this or that object of desire, I heard the words of the Prince of Fear: you must die here to gain life in the world to come! – Humanity was outlawed the day the Galilean victor became ruler of the world. He has turned living into dying.[8]

As the poems of his adolescence show, Ibsen and Julian shared a more natural sense of kinship with heathendom and polytheism than with Christ and monotheism. Yet Julian's apostasy fails to deliver him into the freedom of polytheism; his Christian upbringing leaves him too firmly attached to a stark either-or position and he cannot adopt the true flexibility of the polytheist for whom the lack of such a dichotomy allows the freedom simply to incorporate Christ into his pantheon as just one more god among many, with his own special skills in special situations. The classic example is that of the Icelandic settler Helgi the Lean, who believed in Christ, but made sacrifices to Thor or Odin before important sea-journeys, reasoning that Christ was an oriental god who could know nothing of the vagaries of the weather off the coast of Iceland. This kind of god-dominating freedom is what one imagines Ibsen really wanted for himself. But he could only create a Julian in his own image, as an oak, not a willow, a man who must confront Christ in the form of single combat – hopeless odds, as Ibsen himself admitted: 'Once a man has been been under his rule, such a man can never completely free himself'.[9]

It is often thought that Ibsen wrote *Emperor and Galilean* only to be read. Indeed it has been performed in its entirety just once since publication, in an eight-hour marathon directed by Sam Beskow in Oslo in September 1987. Yet there is ample evidence that Ibsen was thinking dramatically in constructing the play, with techniques including the interruption of vital scenes before critical information can be divulged, and certain effects that can be appreciated in reading but which require performance to achieve their full effect, like that in which Julian's cries to Helios down in the sacrificial chamber are counterpointed with the singing of a group of Christians. Moreover there is an absurdity involved in stipulating that certain characters sing verses if the intention is that such singing shall only be imagined by a reader. In addition the play has scenes of great visual potential, notably the seance with Maximos, and the closing scene of Part One in which Julian emerges from the sacrificial chamber with blood smeared across his face and body.

On the other hand it has major drawbacks as a piece of theatre, principally its length, a piece of Victorian giganticism that must test

177

the patience of both perfomers and public (there was a break for dinner in the Beskow production). Another difficulty is that Ibsen was too concerned to display his mastery of the historical sources, so that the information-divulging scenes at the opening of each section drag. Julian's speeches are also generally speaking too long, and Ibsen is especially indulgent towards him as the end approaches and fate closes in on him. Ibsen's underestimation of his audience/ readership also led him to accentuate certain events unnecessarily, as in the scene towards the end where he signals the parallels between the deaths of Julian and of Christ. Agathon, crying, 'With Christ and for Christ,' hurls the spear which fatally wounds Julian in the side. The intention is obvious enough without Agathon's then crying out 'The lance of the Roman from Golgotha!'*

Another major drawback to a successful adaptation of the play for the stage is that despite the battle scenes the conflict between heathendom and Christianity remains an abstract, intellectual conflict. At times it seems as though what is being debated is really no more than the relative aesthetics of the ceremonials of the two religions. Christ's truly revolutionary thought was that a man must not seek to revenge himself when wronged but instead turn the other cheek and forgive his enemy. The overt perversity of this great thought is the main reason Julian gives for his rejection of Christianity; but the play offers no display of moral conflict at this level between the two religions, only affirmation and counter-affirmation.

Ibsen said of *Emperor and Galilean* that it contained 'the positive world-view which the critics have for so long demanded of me'. Some readers found it to contain this, though not in the way Ibsen had intended. The young Norwegian sculptor Christen Magelssen, in conversation with Ibsen, surprised him by naming this as his favourite play. Ibsen asked for an explanation. Magelssen said it was simple enough, it was because the play provided 'such a superb account of the triumph of Christianity over heathendom'.

'Really,' replied Ibsen. 'I can't in all honesty say that I had thought of that as the heart of the work.'

'I don't see how it could be thought of any other way', responded Magelssen. Ibsen's reply to this seemed to him almost too indecent

---

* The wound in the side is also a feature of the Odin myth. Odin hung from a tree for nine days in order to acquire divine insight.

to repeat; but his trust in his confidant (Francis Bull) was such that he eventually revealed it: 'Can you imagine, he went on to speak as though he were a downright atheist!'[10]

The anecdote illustrates Ibsen's knack of writing finished works of art that were capable of thoroughly contrary interpretations. Bjørnson took the opposite view to Magelssen, found the work 'atheist' and as such no more than might be expected of a man like Ibsen. To Brandes Ibsen wrote in dissimulating vein that recalled the pre-empting and rejection of attempts to abstract unambiguous meanings from *Brand*: 'I can't be bothered to analyse what the book may or may not be about; all I know is that I saw in vivid fashion a fragment of human history and I tried to reproduce what I saw.'[11]

Emperor and Galilean was awaited with enormous interest. On 2 October Hegel, with his usual winning respect, wrote to Ibsen that orders for the book were so numerous he was having to put back his planned publication date:

Dear Hr Ibsen!

Some 10–12 days ago I sent to you in a sealed package a clean proof of your *Emperor and Galilean* fresh from the printers. I am now extremely keen to hear whether you are happy with the printing and the quality of the proof-reading. For the cover I have commissioned a portrait of Julian after an original in the possession of Prof. Ussing. Following a circular which I had distributed to all the bookshops in Scandinavia the response was so great that I am having to print no less than 800 extra copies of your latest work, and this will take so much time that it will not be possible to get it into the shops before Friday October 17. (. . .) For the time being I have added your royalty of 3200 Rdl to your account. – Do you want me to put it in the savings bank, or would you like me to invest it for you?[12]

There was also American interest to look forward to with the appearance of Catherine Ray's translation of *Emperor and Galilean* – the first time Ibsen had appeared in English. He wrote to Hegel: 'I am particularly pleased to hear that the market in America has now opened up for us too.'[13]

Critics have puzzled over what Ibsen meant by the claim that the play offered 'the positive world-view which critics have for so long demanded of me'. A possible explanation is hinted at in an autobio-

179

graphical summary he wrote some years later for his German translator, the Dane Julius Hoffory:

> Then I experienced the great time in Germany, the war and the subsequent developments. All this brought about a profound change in so many of my views. Up to that point my view of world history and human life had always been a nationalist view. Now it developed to become tribal, and this is what enabled me to write *Emperor and Galilean*.[14]

He explained that *Emperor and Galilean* was not the first play he had written in Germany, 'but probably the first written under the influence of German spiritual life.' Earlier, in a letter to Edmund Gosse in October 1872, he had claimed that 'the historical theme in question has a closer connection with events in our own time than one might at first sight realise',[15] something he repeated after publication to Georg Brandes. The claim for contemporary relevance can only logically refer to the proclamation of the German Empire at Versailles on 18 January 1871, where the rulers of the various German states chose King William 1 of Prussia as their Emperor, thus creating the second German Reich. This state was simultaneously a nation, and thus a solution to the 'German question' that had dogged European politics for decades; it was a great military and economic power situated at the heart of the European state system; and it was an Empire, with all the ambition such a name implies. It seems that Ibsen, with his belief in Germany's 'world-historical mission', was hinting strongly that Germany was the promised land in which the 'the third kingdom' prophesied by Maximos in *Emperor and Galilean* would arise.

Another element in Ibsen's sudden promotion of himself as a prophet of pan-Germanism is that, while living in Dresden and working on *Emperor and Galilean*, he had become involved in an unpleasant literary argument with his hosts that forced him to some energetic deconstructionist wriggling in order to survive with the goodwill of his German translators and literary contacts intact. Ever since Dybbøl and the war of 1864 he had continued to cultivate his public dislike of Germany. The 'Balloon Letter to a Swedish Lady', written in late 1870, contained warnings to Prussia about the fruits of her militarism and expansionism.

But Ibsen was now on the verge of a literary breakthrough in Germany, and instead of standing by his poems he wrote a long

The cartoonist in the satirical magazine *Vikingen* viewed Ibsen's poem 'On the Millenial Celebrations' as an advertisement for himself rather than his country

rationalisation of his position for *Im neuen Reich*. In documenting his fondness for Germans he related that during the recent war with France he had financially supported a local widow whose two sons were involved in the fighting, and after it paid for the schooling of a war-orphan.

Shortly afterwards he even rehabilitated Bismarck, a target of earlier poems, with 'On the Millennial Celebrations', written to celebrate in July 1872 the anniversary of the battle of Hafrsfjord. Here he urged his fellow-countrymen to 'Read the law of the day! It will not be denied. Cavour and Bismarck wrote it for us as well' – the 'law' being, presumably, the inevitability of race-based nationalism.

Bjørnson too had undergone a change of heart about Germany. One must let bygones be bygones, he was now urging, forget about 1864, Dybbøl and narrow pan-Scandinavianism: pan-Germanism was the doctrine of the future, and the new Germany its heartland. Ibsen reacted with contempt in a poem, 'Signals from the North', that mocked Bjørnson for his inconstancy:

There's a change in the weather! Let's hear the big speeches!
The weather-cock has changed his direction.

Yet in a letter of 20 March 1873 to Adolf Strodtmann, the German translator of *The Pretenders* and *The League of Youth*, he could write:

Like the majority of Norwegian pan-Scandinavians, I am a pan-Germanist. I regard Scandinavianism as merely a staging post on the road to full unification of the whole Germanic tribe. If I thought the aim of it all were simply an isolated Scandinavian union, I would never dip my pen into an inkwell to promote such a goal.

He continued:

That I remain true to my belief in Germany's world-historical mission in this century will be obvious from the enclosed poem,* which is less than eight months old. What I have expressed there I stand by and am willing to repeat whenever necessary.[16]

Such inconsistencies embarrassed him little, and at about the same time as he was busily husbanding the growth of his own reputation in Germany he found time to complain to Hegel that Bjørnson was doing exactly the same thing – 'but of course he has never allowed a sense of moral obligation to trouble him'.[17]

In the absence of more dramatic personal vices Ibsen's great joy was travel, and he was fortunate after the labours on *Emperor and Galilean* to be invited to participate in the World's Fair in Vienna, representing Norway and Denmark as a member of the jury judging the painting and sculpture. He left Dresden on 12 June, remaining in Vienna until 1 August while Suzannah and Sigurd took the one-hour steamboat ride from Dresden to spend the summer in Pillnitz.

As one would expect in an undertaking that involved the awarding of medals, Ibsen took his obligations seriously. In a 'Letter' to *Morgenbladet* he warned against the futility of reading too much into a bare league table of awards. The English, for example, had paid little attention to the stipulation that medals would be awarded only for works by living artists created after 1863, with the result that though their exhibition consisted almost entirely of masterpieces, they received very few medals. He was favourably impressed by the

* Presumably the poem he enclosed was 'Ved tusenaarsfesten'. ('On the Millennial Celebrations').

contributions from Russia and Belgium, and in general felt that the exhibition offered 'a wealth of material that illuminates our contemporary culture and history', and that it would do much to wipe away erroneous prejudices. He scotched the myth that 'the Slavic tribe contribute little or nothing to the great common enterprise of civilisation'; on the contrary, as the exhibition demonstrated, Russian painters were every bit the equal of those in Germany, France 'or any other country'.

Socially Ibsen had a quiet time. Thomas Thoresen had travelled with him from Dresden but he seems to have asserted his independence from his uncle as soon as possible. He returned to Dresden after a fortnight, with Ibsen complaining that he had been 'invisible throughout the last days and left without saying goodbye'. Ibsen must have been a difficult travelling companion for a restless young writer. He took with him the same clockwork approach to existence as ruled his working life at home, so Suzannah will not have been surprised to receive a letter like this:

My time is divided up thus: in the morning I rise at 6 a.m. and between then and 8 a.m. I wash and dress, eat breakfast, read the paper and smoke my morning pipe. Then I go down to the Exhibition, where the deliberations of the jury on painting last from 9 a.m. to 12 a.m. As soon as these are completed I make my way to a nearby restaurant, where I eat a good meat meal with a tasty glass of beer. At 2 p.m. the jury for the sculpture meets and these meetings last until 4.30 or 5. But these meetings are not all just sitting down; at the moment, we go to the massive exhibition buildings in order to study the works of art. Naturally, since my arrival in Vienna, there has been no question of a lie-down after the main meal. As you can imagine, I am tired by the time the jury meetings are over. I then take a seat in one of the many open-air restaurants in the Prater and watch the thousands of carriages in the allée while eating my supper, which consists of my cheese and bread with an excellent beer. At 9 I go home and go straight to bed. Life down here suits me extremely well. So far no social life for the jury members; they say this will begin later.

The description of Fritz von Dardel, a Swedish military man and fellow jury-member, reinforces the picture of Ibsen as a shy man who preferred to keep his own company:

Ibsen was the Norwegian jury member for fine art. The black clothes and the white cravat he always wore, and the searching, penetrating gaze behind his spectacles gave him the appearance of a French notary rather than an artist. He remained completely silent during all our meetings, spoke to no one and avoided every opportunity to make the acquaintance of his comrades, who were for the most part well-known people.

While the rest of us ate a communal breakfast in the restaurant, Ibsen made his way to a beer-hall, where he sat quite alone and emptied his beer glasses. I accompanied him there on a couple of occasions and found his conversation very interesting.

Von Dardel relates that his fellow jurors were astonished to discover that their 'French notary' was the well-known Norwegian dramatist Henrik Ibsen.

Ibsen returned from Vienna at the end of July and joined Suzannah and Sigurd at Pillnitz. The great beast of *Julian* had finally been wrestled to the ground, but the intellectual, moral and spiritual problems it dealt with lived on inside him as vividly as ever. Like the spiritual thief-catcher he was becoming, he had begun to resemble his enemies more and more with the passing of each year. The Swedish theatre director Ludvig Josephson visited him at Pillnitz that summer and was amused to hear of the confusion his appearance had caused among young Tyrolean girls during his stay in Berchtesgaden the preceding summer. Taking him for a Catholic priest they had kissed his hand and asked him to bless them.

11

'Papa had a Strange Dream'

On a number of occasions since leaving Norway in 1864 Ibsen had spoken of returning. He remained a presence in the country despite his absence. During two periods of leadership crisis, in 1867 and again in 1870, the board of the Christiania theatre offered him the post of artistic director. The offers may have satisfied his vanity, but he considered them only briefly before declining. His feelings towards living at home again remained ambivalent. Replying to a letter from the widow of his good friend Ole Schulerud from Grimstad he told her that despite his travels in Italy and Germany, despite having sat by the Red Sea and seen Mount Sinai, 'In my mind I feel more Norwegian than I ever have before.' He wanted to come home, but was afraid of the consequences of permanent return: 'I feel it will cramp me in my work. We human beings are long-sighted; we see best from a distance; when one is in the middle of the crowd all the irrelevancies, all the purely ephemeral and temporary things acquire a quite unwarranted importance.'[1] So strong was this ambivalence towards Norway that neither in 1869, when on his lengthy summer visit to Stockholm, nor in Copenhagen the following summer, did he make the short trip to Kristiania. In this he ignored the advice of Suzannah, who wrote to him from Dresden urging him not to put it off for another year, 'for that will definitely look like indifference, and I am afraid it might harm you.'[2]

What held him back? Anxiety, predominantly, at the prospect of once again exposing himself to view in that tiny society, of walking the soil where his unknown son walked; of perhaps, now that he was so famous, being approached by the boy. In at last deciding to overcome his unease he may have been influenced by a gesture that meant much to him: at the crowning of Oskar II, the new king of the Swedish-Norwegian union, at Trondheim on 19 July 1873 he had been created a Knight of the Order of St Olaf for 'services to literature'. Only two Norwegian writers had previously been so honoured, Andreas Munch and P. A. Jensen, and Ibsen's pleasure at this, the first such award from Norway, was evident. As he had done with previous awards he at once ordered a miniature to be made up by his silversmith.

He arrived at Kristiania, with his family, on 19 July 1874, on board the steamer *Århus*. They stayed for ten weeks, living at Henriette Hofgaard's private hotel, at Pilestredet 7. Ibsen made it clear from the start that he wanted the visit to go off as quietly as possible. Many of his old friends were dead by now – Schulerud, Botten Hansen, and Vinje, with whom he had edited *Manden* back in 1851. Birkeland, Løkke and Daae were still around, however, and Ibsen saw something of these former members of the Holland. But he was no longer Gert Westphaler, 'the talkative barber'. The seriousness suggested by the formal, dark apparel did not belie the inner man. The novelist Jonas Lie, a former *batofil* or auxiliary member of the Holland, met him several times that summer. Ibsen, now aged forty-six, had become, as Lie put it in a letter to Bjørnson: 'a man somewhat advanced in years with firm opinions and a firm sense of self, someone thoroughly at home with Bismarck's social and disciplinary theories, as he has a perfect right to be; there is a logic to it, just as there is in his writing.'[3]

The visit was the low-key affair Ibsen had wanted it to be. Declining an invitation from Birkeland to join a bathing-party out in the woodlands near Maridalen, he told him it was his intention 'as far as possible during my stay here to avoid every kind of official function'. He told Birkeland that he would instead call on him at home unannounced one day, and that he hoped to see a few old friends there. He also spent a weekend as a house-guest of Ole Bachke, with Jakob Løkke. Together they visited Eilert Sundt, the first sociologist in Norway, married to the daughter of one of Ibsen's earliest literary influences, Mauritz Hansen.[4]

Ibsen's homecoming left little mark on Kristiania's literary history. Of the few surviving anecdotes two are almost identical, the memories of young men, P. A. Rosenberg and Gunnar Heiberg, both of whom recall answering the door at their respective fathers' homes to discover Ibsen on the steps wearing his full Ibsen-outfit. On hearing who the visitor was, both young men experienced the pangs of disappointed hero-worship. Heiberg recalled:

There stood a small, broad-shouldered man with a halo of dark hair round his face. He leaned against the wall as he waited. There was something stooped and hunched about him. His clothes were strange. He wore a velvet jacket, white cravat and a Decoration. I thought it looked very imposing, and yet not very imposing at all. I thought it was magnificent, and I also thought it was a little ridiculous. He asked for my father, and said his name was Henrik Ibsen. Then I recognised him from his photograph.

One of his few public appearances was to attend the performance of *The League of Youth* with which the Christiania theatre opened its 1874–5 season on 10 September. After the performance the students marched in torchlight procession for him and Ibsen gave a speech. His horror of public speaking was one reason he could hero-worship an effortlessly natural public man like Bjørnson (when he wasn't busy hating him). He regarded it as a god-given gift and, to a journalist who protested that it was simply an art that could be learnt, he retorted 'I could never in this world learn to speak in public, no matter how hard and how long I might try.' It shows how much the affection and good opinion of his young countrymen meant to him that in response to the students he delivered what was probably the longest public speech of his life. It was both moving and revelatory, nowhere more so than in the concluding lines, in which he referred to what he probably thought of personally as the Emperor Julian's real tragedy:

When the Emperor Julian reaches the end of his road, and everything collapses around him, there is nothing that causes him more pain than the thought that all he has achieved is this: to be remembered with respect and recognition by the sober and the reasonable, while his opponent enjoys a place in the warm, living hearts of people. This theme is something I came across on my spiritual journey. It has its origins in a question I sometimes posed to myself down there, alone, in the south. Now this evening the youth of Norway comes to me and gives me my answer in words and in music, gives me an answer that is warm and unconditional in a way I had never expected. When I leave I will take this answer with me as the richest prize of this trip home among my countrymen.

Here he sounded an echo of the rivalry between himself and

Bjørnson, and of his nagging fear that he would lose in the struggle for the hearts and minds of the nation's youth against his charismatic opponent. The definitions and descriptions of a writer's life he offered his audience were intimate in a way that a more calculating speaker like Bjørnson might have avoided:

> And what does it mean, to write? It took me a long time to discover that to write is essentially to see – but, mark this well, to see in such a way that what is seen is understood in the way in which the writer meant it to be understood. But this can only happen when what is seen has been truly appropriated by one's under-standing. This appropriation is above all the secret of the writing of our new age. Everything I have written over the past ten years has been a result of this act of spiritual appropriation. But no writer experiences life in isolation. What he sees, his contempor-aries among his own countrymen also see. Of course, for were it not so, then how could a bridge ever be established between the one who brings forth, and the ones who receive?

Conceding the extent to which he had used himself as a model in his writing he spoke of the great range of qualities incorporated within a single human being. If he had based Brand on himself in his best moments, as he once said, he confessed here that he had also 'written out of the dregs and the sludge of one's being. In such cases, writing has been like a bath for me, from which I have emerged cleaner, healthier and freer.' He articulated too the great conflict of his own life, 'the conflict between word and deed, between will and duty, between life and learning'.[5]

The reception the students gave him, his reception generally, exceeded all his expectations. A week later he wrote to Hegel that he had been 'received with overwhelming goodwill by all' and that 'the ill-will of old is now history'. In his enthusiasm he was even seriously considering buying property in Kristiania, 'Several of my friends have made a lot of money in this way, and I do not see why it should not also work for me.'[6] Of his past economic *misère* there was but one slight reminder when a creditor from his Bergen days threatened him with court action over a trifling debt. Peter Blytt, his former boss at the theatre, took care of the matter for him.

The greater difficulties stemming from the troubles of his boy-hood and early manhood he dealt with by ignoring them. His mother was now dead and his father and sister the only members of his immediate family still living in Skien. The Lammers' revivalist movement which he had once hinted to Bjørnson was the direct cause of the break with his family, had run out of steam several years earlier. Lammers himself, not, finally, Brand, had rejoined the state church in 1860. The state church did not welcome his return, and in his last years – he died in 1878 – he closed his mind to religious questioning and turned instead to the study of painting. None of this was enough to tempt Ibsen to visit or even write to his father in Skien. Guilt and the fear of imminent revelation haunted him throughout the visit. Later he recalled the physical distress that had accompanied him throughout the entire stay, the tightness in his chest, the sensation of nausea. He imagined 'cold and uncomprehending eyes in the windows and on the pavements' that followed him wherever he went.[7]

Shortly after the Ibsens returned to Germany in September word came that Marie Thoresen was dangerously ill. She had left Dresden and returned to Norway in May 1872, with the aim of establishing a life of her own as a schoolteacher. Ibsen had written to Herman Thoresen urging him to support him in his opposition to her plans:

> Isn't it much to be preferred if she remains here with us? When we move to Norway perhaps she can get some information about teaching jobs in Kristiania, and when she doesn't have board and lodging to worry about then she doesn't have to overstrain herself. That we really do not want to lose her goes without saying. But I do assure you, it is first and foremost her own good I am thinking of when I put the matter to you like this.[8]

Her attempt to achieve independence came too late, however. In an effort to cure her tuberculosis she tried the sea-air by the fjord in Drammen, and the mountain air in Valdres, to no avail. She had been staying with her half-sister Sara Ludvigsen in Copenhagen, but was now so ill that the Ludvigsens had put her in hospital. Suzannah travelled back to Scandinavia alone to be with her. 'Dear Ibsen' she wrote *en route* from Lubeck, 'Thank you, thank you for allowing me to travel.' In Copenhagen she moved into the hospital and sat with Marie round the clock. 'She is, thank God, no longer alone in the hands of a professional sitter'. But her sister's distress was extreme: 'Dear Ibsen, how I long to hear from you, perhaps Sigurd at least could send me a few words, I am in such need of support, poor

Marie's sufferings are beyond all description.'[9] Not even morphine helped, she wrote, but she was praying for her suffering soon to be over. In the midst of her distress Suzannah also found time to worry about the well-being of her husband and son – 'I hope Lina is airing and cleaning properly' – and urge Sigurd in her absence to show that 'he was grown-up and very sensible and practical'. Sigurd duly wrote and told her that father did not eat much during the day, but dined heartily in the evening.

Marie lapsed into unconsciousness during her last days, and died at six o'clock in the evening on 10 November. Suzannah stayed all night with her. Hegel accompanied her to the funeral. Ibsen wrote:

> Naturally you will see to it that Marie's letters etc do not fall into the hands of others, and by others I mean first and foremost her Danish relatives. Take as much travel money as you need, and equip yourself well for your journey. The trip south will be bitterly cold. Travel second class in a Ladies' carriage, and be sure to have a bottle of good quality Port with you. I gave you your itinerary in a previous letter. I am writing this on Sunday midday. Sigurd is at Thomas's. Be sure to let me know, if possible, when you will be leaving Copenhagen. I do not know yet if we can meet you here at the station, because it will be difficult to know exactly which train you arrive on.

Ibsen's concern at the death of Marie showed itself in several ways that mark a contrast to his reaction to the death of his mother. He insisted on paying the funeral expenses and provided money for the care and upkeep of Marie's grave for the next twenty years, and angrily accused the Ludvigsens of having treated her shabbily by having her taken to hospital. Suzannah tried to protest that Sara had treated her half-sister well, but Ibsen dismissed the claim as 'silly and hysterical nonsense': 'If Marie had been in Bergen, the Baars would not have had her put in a hospital but kept her at home with them. The same would have been done in Kristiania; and we would have done the same too.'[10]

He was also much preoccupied with the fact that Thomas Thoresen had failed to visit his dying half-sister when in Copenhagen. Thomas was in Dresden the winter Marie died, and when Ibsen put the matter to him he claimed that Sara had told him Marie was too weak to receive visits: 'find out if he's telling the truth,' Ibsen instructed Suzannah. All in all he made, in his own curious way, a unique fuss over the death of Marie. A letter Sigurd sent to his mother while she was watching over Marie, offers a strong hint as to why:

Papa had a strange dream recently, which he described to me one evening. It seemed to him that he was standing in an open garden, with a great, broad stairway going down from it and an even bigger one leading up from it. You and a lot of other people Papa knew were standing on the downward steps. Then Aunt Marie arrived on a steamship or something and walked to the downward steps and shook hands with the people who were standing there. Then she walked across the grass to where Papa stood, alone, took hold of his hand and said: 'We do not need many words.' It seemed to Papa in the dream that he should just act normal, and he answered: 'No, we really do not.' Then Aunt Marie stepped on to the upwards stairs, where there were many people whom Papa did not know, and then she disappeared.'[11]

That he should think, in his dream, to 'just act normal' when spoken to by Marie is an enigmatic detail. Marie, forty years old at the time of her death, had never married, and spent much of her adult life living with members of her family, with the Ludvigsens in Copenhagen, with her uncle Captain Daae in Solnor, and for much of the last five years of her life with the Ibsens. The relationship between the sisters was strong. Two years older than Suzannah, she was said to have been very different from her, more conventionally feminine in her manner, gentler, a dove to Suzannah's eagle. She looked up to her tough little sister, loving and admiring what her sister loved and admired. It was an innocent, beautiful love and extended naturally to include her sister's husband. In her letters to Suzannah in Rome, Marie wrote of how she longed to hear from Ibsen, and used the same pet names for him as husband and wife used. 'I really long to see that absolutely outrageous *persaun*,'* she wrote in one letter. And during the months before her final collapse, while she could still write, she used another of Ibsen's silly names, underlining it for the humour as she asked Suzannah for news of 'the dear, high Reverend'. In return both Ibsens fondly referred to her as *Strilen*, a comic name for a native of Bergen. Ibsen became, vicariously, the husband she never had. When he was away in Stockholm and Egypt

* Øyvind Anker suggests credibly that this spelling mimics the word 'person' spoken in Marie Thoresen's Bergen accent.

in the summer and autumn of 1869 Sigurd wrote to tell his father that 'Aunt Marie cannot sleep, she is uneasy since you left and afraid you might have an accident'.[12]

Ibsen was open about his disappointment when she returned to Norway against his wishes, and in his letter to Herman Thoresen wrote that she was always welcome back to their household. Ibsen's first note to Suzannah after hearing of her death was as close as a man like him dared come to expressing grief: 'Ah well, she is then no longer with us in person; but we will preserve her in loving memory.' His romantic dream of her death, and the poem he wrote for her, 'With a Waterlily', were other expressions of his love for her. Some twenty years later, in *John Gabriel Borkman*, he took an artist's elliptical look at the mysteries and sorrows of the triangular relationship, borrowing for the study elements from his own experiences in Dresden with his wife and his wife's sister.

Emperor and Galilean had been a great success for Ibsen and Hegel. Hegel wrote to him on October 17 1873: '*Emperor and Galilean* was sold out here in the day of publication. In my experience, and probably in the whole history of the firm this is unique, and must be very encouraging indeed for you.'[13]

The massive play had functioned as a centre of gravity for Ibsen throughout the decade of self-imposed exile. Conceived during his first weeks in Rome, it fertilised and enriched his imagination during the writing of *Brand, Peer Gynt* and *The League of Youth* while awaiting its own full expression. But having finally divested himself of its intellectual and moral weight he found himself without any obvious literary road forward. He had made his name at home as a conservative voice from the right: *Brand* was perceived as a salutary call for renewed spiritual rigour in a backsliding age; *Peer Gynt* was an uncontroversial fable on the triumph of true love; *The League of Youth* was an attack on the advocates of the party political system and on the party system itself. He was a favourite of the union king Karl XV, whom he met in Stockholm in 1869. 'I got on particularly well with the king,' he wrote aferwards to Herman Thoresen. He had become an even greater favourite of Karl's successor Oskar II, a poet, biographer and translator of *Faust*. He was a favourite of the people, and it was said that every Norwegian schoolboy could recite 'Terje Vigen' by heart. In this perspective his return to Kristiania had been a return in triumph. He had reached a peak. The problem that faced him on his return was how to proceed from there.

Back in Dresden, with his thoughts on love and family relationships perhaps even more sharply focused by the slow and painful death of his sister-in-law, he allowed himself the indulgence of looking back on his life so far. Unable to get started on anything new he kept his talent ticking over with revisions, revisiting *Fru Inger til Østråt* and *Peer Gynt*. Late in the year he wrote to Hegel, noting that in March 1875 it would be twenty-five years since his first play appeared and suggesting that they celebrate the occasion jointly by publishing a revision of *Catiline*, which he proposed to send out to all those whose contribution to his success over the years he particularly valued.

Hegel concurred, and on 10 March 1875 Ibsen wrote eleven letters to accompany copies of *Catiline* that had been sent out. First on his list were King Oskar and Frederik Stang, the Prime Minister of Norway, followed by seventeen names, including Herman Laading and Peter Blytt in Bergen; Michæl Birkeland; Ludvig Daae; Hegel himself; Erik af Edholm, Hartvig Lassen and Edmund Gosse. His tribute to Laading, his mentor at Bergen, was particularly generous, and sounded again that touching note of fatalistic acquiescence in his own crippling inhibitions as a person:

> Yes, those years in Bergen really were my apprenticeship! I was in a ferment at that time, and found it hard to be open and trusting with people. I did not know myself either, and that probably explains, if it does not excuse, my strange behaviour as well as a lot else. You on the other hand were a mature man, and that created a distance between us; but often you showed me a trust that nullified the distance, and I was grateful to you for that, though I did not have the power to express this feeling properly.[14]

But the most striking result of his winter of self-scrutiny was that he wrote a letter to his father, Knud Ibsen, now living alone in rented accommodation. Ibsen's letter has not survived, but his father's reply has:

> My dear son,
>   I have had the pleasure of receiving your welcome letter of 25 February, it was a rarity indeed, for as you say in your letter I haven't seen you or heard from you in twenty-five years, all the same I have heard from you in your writing: *Brand, Peer Gynt,*

Love's Comedy, The League of Youth have all been given to me.
Brønlund let me have *Emperor and Galilean*, but I don't know if
I'm allowed to keep it.

It is a trial to write a letter now, I wrote quite well when I was
young, but now age takes it toll, just think, I'll be eighty in two
years' time, so writing tires me out, and I have seen my best years
and now just wait for the end. You're coming to Norway in the
summer and so I expect we'll hear from you in Skien, I would
like that very much. Hedvig has probably given you the family
news in her last letter, so I won't repeat it, everything is just the
same as usual. But I have got some news, Peder Lendsmand who
went up to Confirmation at the same time as you got married a
few weeks ago. First he was engaged to the sheriff's daughter,
but she changed her mind, so he had to make do with something
awful – one of his own servants. Now I must cease this chatter
and stop bothering a learned son with all my nonsense.

I tried to read your letter, but I couldn't understand it, I felt
ashamed and so end here simply with a friendly greeting to you,
your wife and son from your affectionate old father.

Knud Ibsen.[15]

Ibsen must have read the letter many times, brooding over possible
interpretations of its superficial naiveties. You haven't written to me,
his father says, but I've heard from you all the same through your
plays. These he doesn't get from his son, their famous author – he
has to get them from his neighbours, 'but I don't know whether or
not I'm allowed to keep it'. He meanders into a patch of gossip, an
apparently guileless story about the marriage of one of Henrik's old
acquaintances. It returns Henrik to the scene of his confirmation
back in 1843, and Knud Ibsen's theory that his son's third place
among the confirmants was a deliberate slight on the whole family,
and that the fathers of the first two boys had bribed the priest with
veal. The point of his tale is that people who cheat the Ibsens don't
prosper. If it takes thirty years, a boy who cheated his way to first
or second place at a confirmation ceremony ahead of an Ibsen will
get his punishment in the form of a disappointment in love and a
public humiliation – 'something awful, one of his own servants'.
Marrying a servant isn't everyone's idea of Nemesis. It isn't even
everyone's idea of 'something awful'; but perhaps it was Ibsen's,
and perhaps in reading the letter Ibsen found himself wondering

again, as he must have done so many times, what his 'other' son was doing. Then, having tweaked his son's shame like this, there is the shrugging and mock self-rebuke: 'well, I mustn't waste my learned son's time with a lot of nonsense'. This is Rasmus Berg's father, addressing the son who left home to go to university in the city, chopped over his roots, Latinised his name to Erasmus Montanus and came back bulging with self-important contempt for his family and for the ways of ordinary people. A devout admirer of Holberg, Ibsen cannot have missed the reference.

The curious statement in the last paragraph – 'I wanted to read your letter, but I couldn't understand it' – must be sincere, for somewhere along the way, in the years between 1850 and 1875, Ibsen lost the power to express himself in a personal way. Faced by an emotional situation he could only respond with a fog of abstract formulations devoid of real content. To tell Hedvig, in the letter on Marichen's death, that 'I look within myself; there is my battleground, the scene of my triumphs and failures' may sound magnificent, but it says nothing about the death of their mother and offers no comfort to his sister. The letter to Knud Ibsen must have been in this same vein, abstract almost to the point of incomprehensibility.

Later in the spring of 1875 the Ibsens moved from Dresden to Munich. Again Sigurd's schooling was one of the main reasons for the move. Dr Elbe's Institute had run into financial trouble towards the end of 1873. Ibsen was away in Vienna at the time, but Sigurd kept him posted, in his laconic way informing him that the proprietor owed huge debts and had sold off the school's equipment, that it was quite some time since he had had any lessons, and that the last time he went to school the police were there too. The school survived, but only by dropping its two classes for older pupils, and Ibsen felt that the remaining schools in Dresden were not suitable for the education of foreign students.

Another consideration was tax. As a foreigner living in Munich he would pay tax only on what his writing earned him in Bavaria, and as he wrote later 'that was really not such a large amount'.[16] There was also a larger Scandinavian colony in Munich which he felt the need of. A repeated complaint in his letters from Dresden is of the lack of company and the fact that so few people visited them. The move to Munich took him further from home, but it also brought him closer to Italy, and offered the additional benefit of living among Catholics, 'which here in Germany is unquestionably better than living among Protestants.'[17] Finally, as he told Daae, 'the wanderlust has come over me again'. So there was a general mixture of reasons in play when, in May, he moved his faithful family into their new apartment at Schönfelderstrasse 17. The expenses were defrayed by a gift from Oskar II of 1,000 kroner*, as thanks to his skald for the copy of the revised *Catiline* which Ibsen had sent him.

* About £4,000 in present day terms.

PART TWO

THE PRESENT

12

Modern Times
The Pillars of Society

On 23 October 1875 Ibsen wrote to Hegel that he was making good progress on a new play, and expected to finish the first act in a few days' time. It was to be called *The Pillars of Society* and would be in five acts. Ibsen described it as complementary to *The League of Youth*. It would 'deal with several of the most pressing problems of the moment.' He was pleased, for the first act was 'always for me the most difficult part of a play'.

One of the wonders of Ibsen's later life was his ability to produce a new play every two years. But this only holds true for the plays after *Emperor and Galilean*; prior to this there is no discernible work pattern. They might appear every year, as they did in Bergen in the 1850s under the pressure of his contractual obligations, but there were four years between the last Bergen play, *The Vikings at Helgeland* in 1858, and *Love's Comedy* in 1862. A year separated this from *The Pretenders*, three years later came *Brand*, one year after that, in 1867, *Peer Gynt*, two years after that *The League of Youth* and four years after that the long-gestated *Emperor and Galilean*. During the four years between this and the appearance of *The Pillars of Society* in 1877 Ibsen produced no new dramatic work of importance.

The best explanation for the gap is simply that Ibsen was thinking. Ten years is a long time to be away from home. Though he read his *Morgenbladet* and *Dagbladet* assiduously, his personal experience of the increasing industrialisation of life during his trip to Norway in the summer of 1874 must have been striking. The new play was not, like the best of his earlier plays, an organic eruption from his own psyche. It was a deliberate attempt to write a modern play, his first play about *other people*, and probably the most objective play he had worked on since the forcing-house days in Bergen in the 1850s. The very impersonality of his theme laboured his progress, and two full years and numerous rewritings would pass before *The Pillars of Society* appeared in the bookshops and on the stage.

The national romanticism that had exercised him and his fellow Norwegians in the 1850s and 1860s was cultural history now. Modern times had arrived. A self-confident professional class had appeared, country-dwellers left their roots to work in the factories, capitalism was a fact of life. *Das Kapital* appeared in 1867, the year of the deceptively bucolic *Peer Gynt*. Magdalene Thoresen, writing to a friend in 1866, enthused about the excitements and challenges of being 'a child of the century of electricity, steam-power and photography'.[1] The so-called 'engineer's conception of life' became dominant. There was a power shift, from men in dark coats – priests, lawyers – to men in white coats: doctors, engineers, chemists, agronomists with their natural sciences became the new oracles. Money, time and hygiene were their slogans. The industrial revolution had established itself, symbolised in the case of Norway by the inauguration of large-scale plans for the building of railways in 1872.

Successful professional people built their homes in pleasant surroundings, far from the ugly and odoriferous production sources of their wealth. The end of textile working at home meant the coming of rugs and plush curtains. Flowers appeared in the windows, yet clothes were no longer the bright colours of the peasants but rather the dark suits deemed more suitable to the new business world of brick and steel. In the home tables and chairs advanced from their former modest place along the walls and took up position, brooding and sombre, centre-stage.

No longer bound in work and the rough intimacy of farm-life, families were able, as a luxury of civilisation, to practise formality towards one another.[2] This luxury of privacy within the home gave impetus to the cultivation of individualism, and this in turn caused an evolution in the sexual relationship. In many of the customs associated with the old, predominantly rural culture, men and women typically functioned as groups and not individuals. In church women would sit on the left of the aisle, and men on the right. This had given way to the appearance of men and women sitting together as married couples.

Norwegian women were making rapid social progress. In 1876 they entered the field of higher education when a young woman, Ingeborg Poulsson, received official permission from the Department of Ecclesiastical Affairs to sit the secondary school examination, and by a massive majority of 114 to 1 in 1882 they received the right to enter university.

Sociology, a growing interest of young Sigurd Ibsen, had consolidated its claims to be take seriously as a tool for cultural analysis and the idea of an objective and rational approach to solving the problems of human happiness. The first Norwegian sociologist, Eilert Sundt, whom Ibsen met during his visit to Norway in 1874, had already been carrying out his extensive demographic and ethnographic studies of the Norwegian people for some twenty years past.

The technological achievements of the age had consequences for its arts. Fox Talbot's discovery in mid-century of a technique for making negatives of photographs made possible the multicopying of portrait images, a process that appeared to involve a mysterious statement about the nature of the soul. Ibsen had already, in *Peer Gynt*, shown himself willing to use its imagery: 'Remember, there are two ways to be yourself; the right way and the wrong way round. You know, in Paris recently they discovered how to make portraits with the help of the sun. There's the portrait as it really is, then there's its so-called negative.' And in the wake of Clemens Petersen's review of *Peer Gynt* he had used the idea again in his letter to Bjørnson, threatening to become a sort of literary photographer and take pictures of all his enemies at home in Scandinavia.

Theatres had become more comfortable and sophisticated places, and Richard Wagner's innovation of turning down the house lights during performances encouraged the development of audiences more receptive to plays with an intellectual content without demanding, as formerly, regular doses of farce to take their minds off their aching feet. But as yet, no playwright had given them such plays, where conversation replaced action and where the flow of conversation, followed in silence, a unique experience for each individual member of the audience and yet essentially also a shared experience, *was* the plot.

This developing world, capitalist, rationalist, inventive, yet mistrustful of spontaneity, sombre and massive in its ambition, was Ibsen's world. By 1875 he had written himself away from the most threatening psychological dangers of his past. He was only just forty-seven years old. In *Brand* and *Peer Gynt* he had taken verse-drama, intended primarily for the theatre of the mind, to a level it was hardly possible to improve upon. Now, having thrown off the burden of *Emperor and Galilean*, having decided that he would write no more poetry, he found himself in mid-career faced with the problem of how to renew his talent. He was well aware of the writer's need to find fresh and unexpected perspectives if he wished to continue in dialogue with his audience. Concerning his contemporary Jonas Lie he had written to Hegel in 1874 of Lie's need to 'broaden his field, if he is to remain in the public's favour for any length of time'.[3]

Several times in recent years he had given voice to a controlled creative impatience with the prevailing aesthetic in drama. His response to Edmund Gosse's criticism of *Emperor and Galilean*, that it would have been better had it been written in verse, expresses this impatience clearly. He thanks Gosse for a copy of the review

to which I would like to add a few words of comment. You believe the play should have been written in verse and it would have gained thereby. Here I must disagree with you, for as you will have noticed, the play is presented in thoroughly realistic form; the illusion I wished to create was the illusion of reality. I wanted the reader to feel that what he was reading was the history of something that had actually taken place. To have used verse would not have served this purpose of mine. The many ordinary and minor characters with which I deliberately spiced the play would have lost their individuality and disappeared into each other if I had obliged them all to speak in metric rhythms. We are no longer living in Shakespeare's time, and among sculptors there is already talk of painting statues in realistic colour. That is a matter which is open to discussion. I would not like to see the Venus de Milo painted, but on the other hand I would prefer to see the head of a negro sculpted in black than in white marble. In general the form of language used must be in accord with the degree of idealism involved in the play as a whole. My new play is not a tragedy in the older sense of the word; my purpose was to depict human beings, and for just that reason I did not want them to speak 'the language of gods.'[4]

Ibsen's way to self-renewal was slow and arduous, and he turned to it only after he had exhausted the possibilities of the past. When John Adams writes operas about Nixon in China or the hostage-taking on board the *Achille Lauro*, part of the interest these works arouse stems from our surprise at the choice of today's news as fit subject matter for art. Modern times seem banal by comparison with history. Familiarity prevents us from seeing our politicians, our entrepreneurs, our artists even, as great in the same way that such figures from the past seem great. It takes a certain kind of daring, one which came more easily to the Victorians than it does to us, to erect monuments to ourselves and our ways while we are still alive. Ibsen possessed that daring. He knew that *Brand* and *Peer Gynt* were timeless creations that transcended concepts of 'modernity'; yet he was also equipped with a sense of destiny that led him to believe he was living in an age of unprecedented change that carried with it a demand for the documentation of a uniquely 'modern' art. It was this sense of being a vital element in the destiny of his age that persuaded him to embark, with *The Pillars of Society*, on a long series of cultural analyses, in dramatic form, with the aim of finding out why, in the midst of their wealth, comforts and rationalism, his audiences remained unfulfilled and unhappy.

Ibsen lived in Munich much as he had done in Dresden. When not working or walking he visited places like the Café Probst in Neuhausergasse, which subscribed to Scandinavian newspapers for the benefit of the large Scandinavian artistic community in the city. The painter Marcus Grønvold compared its function and atmosphere to that of the Greco in Via Condotti, one of Ibsen's favourite haunts in Rome. The community of about fifty also included the painters Eilif Peterssen, Rusti and Ekenæs, in whose progress Ibsen took a fatherly pride. For a while the Ibsens held open house once a week but, according to Bergljot Ibsen, this stopped when Ibsen heard rumours that their guests spoke slightingly of their hospitality.

He preferred the company of a German literary circle, known as 'the Crocodile', whose members gathered informally around midday, once a week, to drink a beer at the Achatz, a hotel in Maximiliansplatz. The presiding genius of the Crocodile was Paul Heyse, a prolific novelist and dramatist much admired in his time but little read now. Ibsen admired Heyse and wanted to meet him, but with his usual caution wrote first to their mutual friend Georg Brandes to request a letter of introduction. Brandes mentioned the fact to Heyse, referring in passing to Ibsen's expressed fear that someone might 'work against him' with regard to Heyse. The comment reveals the considerable streak of paranoia in Ibsen's personality. Some three years earlier, in Dresden, Ibsen had confided to Brandes a suspicion that 'there was someone here who seemed to go out of their way to make sure you did not visit us too frequently on your own'. However, once contact between the two men had been established they took to each other, and Heyse mentioned Ibsen by name as a 'faithful Achatzer' in a light verse he once dedicated to his companions in the group. Ibsen also attended the club's annual suppers held in honour of the Keiser's birthday, tacitly reinforcing his claim that the hostility expressed towards Germany in the poem 'Signals from the North' had been misunderstood. The small storm occasioned in 1872 over the publication of that verse had not, as he feared it might, harmed his career in Germany.

In June the following year Ibsen travelled to Berlin at the invitation of a German nobleman and patron of the arts, Duke Georg 11 of Saxe-Meiningen, whose passion was theatre. His private theatre group *Die Meininger* performed in Europe throughout the period 1874–90, observing a set of aesthetic principles which accentuated the importance of good scenery, good lighting, and good quality acting in the supporting roles. In eschewing the 'star' system the group also emphasised the idea of performance as a joint enterprise. Their scenery was historically accurate and realistic. Iron, wood and stone were used instead of canvas backdrops and papier-mâché props. The costumes were made of silk and velvet, the spears and swords heavy and appropriately noisy. The extras, who were often soldiers of the duke's army, were taught to act in a relaxed, natural manner and coached in what to say when a script called for crowd reaction. Roles were discussed and analysed, and rehearsals might go on for months. In short, their commitment was to quality and seriousness of purpose, as Ibsen's had been during his own periods as a director. They exerted a powerful influence on a new young generation of theatre enthusiasts like André Antoine and Konstantin Stanislavsky, whose application of their techniques of realism to Ibsen's dramas of modern life would shortly play such an important part in the explosive spread of his reputation through Europe.

The duke was an early enthusiast for Ibsen's work and among the group's first productions were *The Vikings at Helgeland* and *The Pretenders*, the choice of Ibsen's most 'Germanic' plays reflecting the enthusiasm for the cult of pan-Germanic brotherhood prevailing in the newly unified Germany at the time, with the new emperor as its most passionate advocate. On 13 August of the same year, 1876, Wagner's Bayreuth Festivals were inaugurated with a performance of *Das Rheingold*, which launched the first-ever complete performance of the *Ring* cycle. In this atmosphere of cultural and racial excitement Norwegians, with their Viking ancestry and rich literary heritage of Germanic myths and legends, were regarded by the racial fashions of the time as the most Germanic of the Germans. It does not in any way belittle the achievements of Ibsen, Bjørnson, Munch, Grieg, Hamsun and the other Norwegian artists who enjoyed such success during these first decades of the German empire to note that their road to German and European fame was considerably aided by this perception.

The Pretenders already existed in a German translation by Strodt-mann, but *The Vikings at Helgeland* was newly translated, ostensibly by Ibsen himself, actually by a professional German translator, Emma Klingenfeld, as *Nordische Heerfahrt*. As Ibsen's reputation began to grow in Germany it irked him not to receive the money from performances which, in the absence of copyright protection for Norwegian writers, went to the translators or the theatres. He therefore hit upon this idea of translating several of his own older plays into German so that when performed in Germany they would be paid for as original, German works. By late 1876 he could report that Vienna, Dresden and Leipzig were all planning performances of *Nordische Heerfahrt*, 'and in Munich it is still playing to great acclaim'. He wrote to Herman Thoresen: 'At all theatres in Germany and Austria the royalty is 10 per cent of the gross income of each performance during the lifetime of the author and the same to his heirs for the first fifteen years after his death. So you see, it pays to write for the stage here.'[5]

The visit to Berlin was a great success. Though the German theatre critics were not particularly enthusiastic about the play (Ibsen attributed this to the fact that most of them were dramatists themselves) he was delighted by the public's reception of *The Pretenders*. It played for nine nights in succession and, by his own account, was greeted with numerous demands for curtain calls for both performers and author. Afterwards the duke invited him to his country palace of Liebenstein for a few days. On his departure the duke made him a Knight First Class of his own Saxe Ernestine Order.

Ibsen was by now operating in a new dual role as his own literary agent. The juggling with the new translations of his old plays into German, his attempts to place them and the need to write numerous business letters in connection not only with these but also with his own domestic theatres in Scandinavia, consumed a great deal of his time. Given his experiences with someone like the publisher Jensen, it is easy to sympathise with Ibsen's insistence on being the main beneficiary of his own success; but in one instance his rigour showed an automated unwillingness to distinguish between cases.

The Bergen theatre, after its collapse in 1863, was preparing to rise from the ashes in 1876. In an atmosphere of uncertainty concerning their economic viability the board approached the two leading Norwegian dramatists of the time, Ibsen and Bjørnson, and asked for their indulgence: would they allow their plays to be performed for the first year without payment of a specified fee, accepting instead a fee to be agreed upon at the close of the season when the board would have a better idea of how the books balanced? Both writers dismissed the approach. Ibsen accused the board of a lack of patriotism, asserting that the risk in such 'experiments' should be borne by rich citizens of the town, not by writers. To an acquaintance he complained of Norwegians that 'it seems natural for them that a stevedore gets paid, but that an artist should get paid for his labours too is something our national consciousness seems not quite ready for.'[6]

On 21 October he sent the theatre a contract of his own devising, offering them the right to perform any of his plays at a fee of 400 kroner for each première, forty kroner for each of the next five performances, twenty kroner for performances over and above that, Catiline and The Feast at Solhaug to be paid for at half these rates. Statements of earnings and payment were to be submitted to him at the end of each financial year, and failure to do so would invalidate the contract. Ibsen's status was such that the terms were accepted without further argument, but there was bitterness towards him in Bergen. The town had given him his earliest opportunity to work in the theatre, and had even subsidised his artistic education in the form of the European trip of 1852. During the absence of a permanent Norwegian stage in the town a travelling Danish theatre company under August Rasmussen had several times visited Bergen, and when it became known that Ibsen had only months previously given Rasmussen the right to perform The Vikings at Helgeland as often as he liked for a mere 100 kroner, the bitterness tipped over into something close to contempt. A writer in Bergens Tidende meditated morosely on the fact that Ibsen had made a career out of exposing his own countrymen to ridicule and that a little charity towards them might be timely. Bjørnson, by contrast, after initially dismissing the approach, had relented: 'I'm always all right again once I've had my little moan. Take the plays, pay me what you can!'

'Sentimentality' was a term of abuse in Ibsen's vocabulary. In *Familien Pehrsen (The Pehrsen Family)*, a *roman à clef* about the three Ibsens by the young Bergen writer John Paulsen, Fredrik Pehrsen's stock rebuke to any show of emotion from his son Sverre is 'Are you being sentimental now?' One explanation for Ibsen's lack of charity is probably his desire to avoid behaviour that might be construed as sentimental. Moreover a matter of principle was involved, though the sarcastic and bullying tone of his letter would have been avoided had he been writing to a Swedish or Danish theatre on a similar matter.

His attitude was probably also influenced by events after the death from TB on 9 April that year of young Thomas Thoresen, Suzannah's half-brother. Two of Thoresen's vaudevilles, *Hos kaptejnen* and *På bygden*, had proved very successful crowd-pullers, and the board of the renascent Bergen theatre had obtained Magdalene Thoresen's permission to perform them on the same terms as those offered to Ibsen and Bjørnson. Ibsen's alert sense of professionalism at once quashed the initiative. His urgent concern to protect Magdalene Thoresen from the consequences of her own generosity; his offer to take over negotiations with the theatre on her behalf; and his offer to contribute financially to a memorial stone for Thomas 'on condition', as he wrote to Herman Thoresen, 'that your father's grave is well-maintained' – these were all Ibsen's way of showing that he was sorry Thomas was dead; that he pitied Magdalene; that he wished to extend his condolences to Herman. But for him to have said so in as many words would have been 'sentimental'.

On 3 August Ibsen, Suzannah and Sigurd left to stay for two months in the Tyrol at Gossensass, a small mountain town in the Brenner Pass between Brenner and Sterzing. The railway, that quintessential symbol of modernism, burst its way into the Brenner Pass in 1867, making Gossensass a magnet for summer tourists from the large European cities. The travellers from Munich went via Rosenheim and Innsbruck, from where Gossensass lay a mere three- to four-hour ride.

Gossensass became Ibsen's favourite summer residence, and he would return in 1878, 1882, 1883, 1884, and for a last time in 1889. Each stay lasted on average two to three months, so that between 1876 and 1884 Ibsen spent over a year there, writing during the same period *The Pillars of Society, A Doll's House, Ghosts, An Enemy of the People* and *The Wild Duck.*[7] By this simple act of geographical repetition Ibsen was able to reduce his life to a condition of almost idealised uniformity which one suspects had long been his permanent goal: a world of pure work, with flowers that came and went in the fields outside the windows and a view all around of snow-capped mountains, in which his life could approach the condition of unintelligible sameness. People visit. They walk the lowland paths together. Suzannah and Sigurd conquer some of the nearby peaks. Ibsen contents himself with the view from the bench atop Malerhügel, a rock some twenty metres high not far from the hotel. It means he can remain Henrik Ibsen all the time, he doesn't have to change out of his Ibsen-clothes. To Herman Thoresen he wrote:

> As for Suzannah and Sigurd, they are enjoying themselves greatly; a fortnight ago they climbed from Gossensass in Eisach Valley the famous Hühnerspiel, an Alpine peak of about 9,000 feet, and yesterday they left to climb Monte Roën, I expect them back hopefully in good condition later this afternoon.[8]

The anecdotes of daily life wash placidly back and forth across these Tyrolean summers. Ibsen buys and wears a pointed hat with a feather. It bounces in time with his tripping steps as he walks along. He is seen fishing. The local children notice him and call him *das Bachmandl* (the River Man) from his habit of halting on one of the bridges over the Eisack to gaze down into the waters. The family stay at Gröbner's Hotel. They eat not in the main dining room but in a smaller, adjoining room. Ibsen is always first down and manages to drink at least one schnapps before Suzannah and Sigurd join him. He says little, discourages contact with strangers, and works.

Later that summer they were joined by the composer Edvard Grieg, on his way back from Bayreuth, and Grieg's compatriot from Bergen, John Paulsen. *Peer Gynt*, in Ibsen's adaptation with music by Grieg, had been the hit of the season at the Christiania theatre earlier in the year, and Grieg's visit seems to have been partly holiday and partly to discuss the possibility of further collaboration. In this he was disappointed. Ibsen tried to interest him in working on an adaptation of *Olaf Liljekrans* he had carried out some years previously, but what Grieg wanted was an original libretto, and Ibsen was simply too busy with his own plans to oblige. Some years later the two again broached the idea of a collaboration, this time using Ibsen's libretto based on *The Vikings at Helgeland*. On reading it, however, Grieg found it unusable.

In an unexpected way the relationship between Ibsen and young John Paulsen proved the more interesting. Paulsen arrived with a letter of recommendation to the Ibsens from a mutual acquaintance in Bergen, but found himself so warmly received that he deemed its presentation unnecessary. Paulsen was to achieve and sustain a remarkable closeness to Ibsen and his family over the next six years, until he destroyed it all with the publication of *The Pehrsen Family* in 1882. A writer of modest ability, he had a talent for meeting people and his friends, acquaintances and correspondents included such luminaries of the period as Grieg, Georg Brandes, Jonas Lie, Alexander Kielland, Amalie Skram and Paul Heyse. Ibsen was his biggest catch, however. Personable and sociable, Paulsen was able to reminisce with Suzannah about Bergen and bring Ibsen the latest gossip from Copenhagen and Hegel's stable of Norwegian writers. He was also close enough in age to Sigurd to be a suitable companion.

In September, when fresh snow fell on the surrounding mountains and the air grew cooler, Ibsen suggested they follow the sun to Kaltern bei Bozen, a small town in the south Tyrol close to the Italian border. Grieg returned to Norway, Paulsen accompanied the Ibsens. His two books dealing directly with this six-year period of his friendship with the family were written many years after the scandalous *roman à clef* and present a more charitable portrait of Ibsen than that of *The Pehrsen Family*. In them he relates the words and opinions of a great man on a wide range of subjects. He records an after-dinner discussion on the subject of life after death. Grieg and Dietrichson, another visitor that summer, gave their views, whereupon Ibsen gave his: *if* there were a life after death, he said, it could not involve the kind of large scale impersonal dissolution into universality imagined by the Buddhists. To have value, life after death must involve a conscious, personal memory of life before death. Several of Paulsen's accounts, of life in Gossensass and later in Munich, display Ibsen's elusive sense of humour, and describe his particular enjoyment of a description Suzannah brought back with her from the Oberammergau Passion Play, of how during a break in the performance she happened to see backstage the actor playing Judas enjoying a drink with the actor playing Christ.

Ibsen's views on the use of language were sometimes strikingly personal, as when he pointed out to Paulsen the implication of the biblical statement that when God created the world he 'looked and he saw that it was good'. Clearly, he observed, God must have been in some doubt about the value of his creation. The observation suggests neatly the condition of doubt on the subject of everything, which was his own natural state. It also sheds light on a letter he wrote to Georg Brandes in the early years of their relationship,[9] when he attempted to comfort Brandes at a time of intellectual and personal isolation by recommending the cultivation of 'a really full-blooded egoism, that for a time forces you to prize yourself and what is yours as the only thing of any importance, and everything else as non-existent'. This piece of unguarded personal wisdom was justified because 'there really are times when the entire history of the world seems to me like one great shipwreck, from which the only imperative is to rescue oneself'. It is as close as Ibsen ever came to an open confession of the personal anarchy that was his only reliable navigational aid through life.

There was something about Brandes which inspired Ibsen to continue to offer him such confidences. For three years, between October 1874 and September 1877, Brandes edited a literary journal called *Det nittende Aarhundrede*. Writing to him at the birth of the magazine[10] Ibsen urged Brandes to avoid the trap of making it too narrowly Danish in its appeal and to concentrate instead on reaching a broad, Scandinavian market 'if it is to achieve for your ideas the distribution they deserve and ensure for you a pleasant and troublefree existence.' Brandes took offense at this last part, but Ibsen was unrepentant, responding that he could not see how it was insulting to suggest to someone 'that he should expect to make a living out of what it is he lives for.' Such misunderstandings were bound to arise as long as he insisted on looking like Brand but allowed himself the liberty of sometimes acting like Peer Gynt.

Brandes, like most intelligent people who met him, remained fascinated, repelled, attracted and utterly baffled by Ibsen. His mysteries, and the sense he gave of being hermetically sealed within himself, brought out the anthropologist in people. Not long after their first meeting Brandes observed the curious aura of anxious threat he exuded. He never smiled, Brandes wrote, 'not even when the person who was talking to him smiled first'. Alcohol, the light Frascati wine he drank in Italy and the dark Bavarian beer in

Germany, was a good friend to him in this respect, helping him to relax, smile and enjoy company.

Other diversions, at least during the Gossensass summers until 1882, included lecturing Paulsen. Paulsen is told that his character will improve if he makes a point of brushing his own shoes. He is advised to prune his vocabulary of dialect words which none but the natives of Bergen will understand. He is scolded for vulgar behaviour, in particular for laughing at the story of an outdoor toilet that collapsed and spilled its contents over a footpath where moments before the widow of the Duke of Tuscany had been walking. News of the disaster was much exaggerated and when the story reached the castle a carriage was urgently despatched to rescue the duchess. Paulsen's enjoyment of the story was too much for Ibsen:

> He was red in the face and gave me a contemptuous, grey, icy look. 'Your behaviour is that of a fool,' said Ibsen. 'A woman with the status of the widow of a duke ought to be spared your stupid and inappropriate humour. Is she not a member of one of the most respected Royal Houses of Germany? And here you, in my presence, have the cheek to make jokes to the other guests about this unfortunate incident which is now the talk of the whole town! It is outrageous!

Paulsen's mischievous personality upset Ibsen on another occasion. He was visiting Jonas Lie's apartment one day when one of Lie's sons and John Paulsen returned from a walk carrying what looked like a snake. Ibsen, who was present, vented his wrath on Paulsen: '"How could you", he burst out, "bring a dangerous snake into this house? What on earth did you think Fru Lie would say? It is unmannerly. You are yourself a guest in this house. It is outrageous, utterly shameless!"' In vain the two young men protested that it was only a slow-worm. Ibsen disliked being wrong, and so a dangerous snake it remained. Paulsen and Mons Lie got rid of it by stuffing it into the village chemist's letter-box.

Nor did he find respite from his painful fear of ridicule. He and the Lies decided to visit a local salt mine. The trip underground, partly by miniature railway and partly on foot, necessitated wearing protective clothing over their ordinary clothes, a leather helmet and a leather patch to protect their bottoms. As Ibsen was tying the leather bottom-protector around his waist another member of the party, a painter from Munich, burst out laughing and said, 'The doctor should have his picture taken in that outfit – it would go round the world!' Without a word Ibsen began removing the outrageous clothing. In vain did the Lies try to persuade him that they all looked ridiculous. Ibsen returned alone and fuming to the hotel. According to Erik Lie, he was not seen for several days afterwards. He was happiest when alone, or in a setting in which he was suddenly not 'Henrik Ibsen' for those around him. Erik Lie saw him in Gossensass once, on his own, among a crowd of children watching a puppet show behind Our Lady's Church, polishing his spectacles incessantly with a silk handkerchief and laughing as the puppets beat one another over the heads with their sticks.

In 1876 the phenomenon *Peer Gynt* began its journey out into the world. The transformation of a Norwegian national epic into one of the best known music-dramas in the world was, paradoxically, the responsibility of a Swedish director, Ludvig Josephson.* The long fight to establish a cultural identity with which Ibsen had been involved as director and writer at the theatres in Bergen and in Kristiania was almost over by this time. The Danish actors at the Christiania theatre, tiring of the hostility towards them, had begun drifting home to Copenhagen. The nationalist ventures in both Norwegian cities, despite economic and artistic problems, had come a long way towards achieving their goal, and the Christiania theatre, revitalised by an influx of Norwegian actors after the folding of Ibsen's old Møllergaten theatre in 1863, became and remained until the end of the century, in fact if not in name, a 'national' theatre. But for some the sheer nationalism of the theatre remained the object of the whole exercise, and the employment of Josephson as its new artistic director in 1873 had proved highly controversial.

Josephson had achieved European recognition in 1867 with his production of Meyerbeer's *L'Africaine* at the Stockholm Opera. He thrived on adversity and challenge, and by his own account enjoyed the outcry from disgruntled nationalists that greeted his engagement. He found the artistic level at the theatre 'mediocre, in fact downright depressing', and a dispiriting attitude towards the challenges presented by Ibsen's three great early works, *Love's Comedy*, *Brand* and *Peer Gynt*, all still unperformed: 'When the subject of

* Ludvig Josephson's 1893 portrait by his nephew Ernst Josephson, one of the fruits of the painter's mental illness, was one of the most influential modernist images in Europe.

Ibsen's great works came up ... they shrugged their shoulders, almost complaining at the bother to which he was putting the theatre'.[11]

Josephson was a music-lover and in the second year of his engagement he brought the unheard-of sophistication of opera to Kristiania, opening with Mozart's *Don Giovanni* in November 1874. Well before this he seems to have had a dream of staging *Peer Gynt* as a music-drama and enthused a fellow-Swede, August Söderman, to write music based on the play. Söderman wrote a number of settings for piano and voice in the late 1860s and there were plans to perform them at a concert at the Stockholm Opera in June 1871 to celebrate the opening of the railways between Stockholm and Kristiania. Nothing came of the plan, Söderman died in 1876, and his music was not performed publicly until many years later, in 1892.[12]

Josephson began his engagement knowing that he would be producing Ibsen's work extensively at the theatre and so made it his business to get to know him. He travelled to Pillnitz in the late summer of 1873, where Ibsen was staying with Suzannah and Sigurd after his summer in Vienna. As the little steamboat approached the quay Josephson saw Ibsen waiting for him, 'a man walking up and down by the water's edge on his own, dressed in black, with an order pinned in his buttonhole, kid gloves and a tall black hat'. Josephson recognised him, as everyone recognised him, from his pictures.

No doubt the purposeful nature of the visit eased their intercourse, for the two men got on well. Of the famous men whom he had met, Josephson found him one of the most normal, unpretentious and kindly; but he could not overcome his sense of wonder at Ibsen's formality and pedantry. Once he accompanied him to a tailor's shop to buy a velvet topcoat and waited, listening incredulousy as Ibsen discussed in interminable detail with the tailor the exact cut and styling of the coat he wanted.

During this stay Josephson must have mentioned his idea about *Peer Gynt*, for in February 1874 Ibsen wrote to thank him for a previous letter and informed him that he had spent much of the winter adapting a version of *Peer Gynt* for the stage. He had offered the task of composing the music to Edvard Grieg. As a mark of his respect for Josephson Ibsen declared himself willing to accept whatever additional changes the director might want to make to his script. Josephson then produced a version in which the first three acts remained more or less as Ibsen had written them. In the fourth the scene involving the four foreign businessmen was cut and the scene in which Peer plays a prophet was drastically shortened. The practical difficulties of the sudden change of scene from the Egyptian desert to a Norwegian valley where Solveig sits waiting for Peer were solved by presenting it as Peer's dream in the desert. The burial scene in the fifth act disappeared. Ibsen approved the changes, and this was the version, lasting four and three-quarter hours, that was staged. T. Blanc, the historian of the theatre, wrote that it was the costliest and most extravagant production yet seen at the Christiania theatre.[13]

The music-drama was performed twenty-five times in its first season and eleven times in the winter of 1877. Then in January a fire broke out that destroyed or spoiled the costumes and scenery and temporarily put paid to further activity at the theatre. In an attempt to cut their economic losses the board made use of a contractual clause relating to outbreaks of fire to rescind the contracts of all the opera performers. They offered them continued engagement on standby at reduced rates. The performers refused. Josephson was also offered the chance to continue in his post after the winding-down of the opera, but refused, leaving the theatre at the end of the season. With his departure Ibsen lost a great supporter in Kristiania, but his position in the rest of Scandinavia, his growing recognition in Germany, and the special contract agreed the year before with the Bergen theatre left him free to speak his mind on the turn of events. He wrote to the theatre's artistic advisor and censor, Hartvig Lassen, that rather than sacking Josephson the board should have sacked itself, that if it was a question of economy then Lassen should have resigned rather than allow a director as talented as Josephson to be seen off. He accused the board of functioning *kollegialt*, as a clumsy cross between a democratic grouping and an old boys' club, and feared for the future of the theatre. He had come across Josephson's appointed successor, Johan Vibe, in Munich in the summer – 'he spoke like a five-year-old child about the post he was about to take up. How long do you think you can go on with such a pathetic and completely useless individual? You won't last the season.'[14]

Early the next year, on 27 February, Ibsen wrote to ask Hegel for an advance on the new edition of *Love's Comedy* to help defray the costs of a move from Schönfelderstrasse 17 – 'the main thing for me is to find somewhere I can work undisturbed; in that respect the current apartment leaves much to be desired' – and on 1 May the family moved into a new apartment on Schellingstrasse 30, on the first floor. In their memoirs both John Paulsen and Josephson praise Suzannah's ability to make a home, and remark especially on the large number of oil paintings, covering the walls from floor to ceiling. Some of the paintings, by artists they knew personally like Julius Kronberg and Marcus Grønvold, Ibsen had assembled during his years in Rome.

Here Ibsen set about finishing *The Pillars of Society*. On 29 July, at about the same time as Suzannah and Sigurd were departing to spend the summer months in Norway, he sent the first batch of material to Hegel, expressing his usual optimism about its prospects, and perhaps a little more than that: 'I think I am safe in saying that we will both be satisfied with the results of this piece of work. In every respect it is new and timely, and of all my works perhaps the most skilfully composed.'[15] He then went on to excuse his illegible handwriting: 'I have been working since five this morning, and now it is dusk.' There were four more letters to Hegel – beyond all comparison the most regular recipient of letters from him – and on 20 August Ibsen sent him the final pages. The resolutely business-like tone of the letters to Hegel, from which it appears that Ibsen's only concern was whether or not he would finish in time to hit the Christmas market, is in striking contrast to the more conventionally sensitive relationship to his writing revealed in a letter to a female correspondent, Elise Aubert: 'I have tried to hold it back for as long as possible; because each time a new book is about to appear in the bookshops I have a feeling like that I imagine parents have when they are about to marry off a daughter; it is almost a kind of jealousy. It is as though you do not really own something once you no longer own it alone.'[16] But after this indulgence the gloves were straight back on. As punishment for their treatment of Ludvig Josephson, he told Hegel, he was boycotting the Christiania theatre. The play was not to be offered there.

The Pillars of Society was published on 11 October 1877 in an edition of 6,000 copies. This quickly sold out and a second edition of 4,000 was published in November. The première of the play took place on 18 November in Copenhagen. The practice of reading plays with

the same care and interest with which one reads novels has died
out now, but as these figures show it was common in Ibsen's time,
and was one of the factors which made it natural for him to think
of his plays as if they were similar to novels, incorporating complex
metaphors and imagery which almost demanded a prior knowledge
of the text from a theatre audience.

As early as the last weeks of 1869 Ibsen had written to Hegel: 'I
am thinking of writing a new, serious drama with a contemporary
setting in three acts.' Notes from about 1870 (dateable from the
change in orthography he adopted after the Stockholm conference
of 1869), seem to show that Ibsen already had the genesis of *The
Pillars of Society* in mind as a kind of 'follow-up' to *The League of
Youth*. In the event it had to bide its time until he had worked out
his obsession with Emperor Julian. The essence of this early sketch
proposes a play in which 'the keynote that sounds through the whole
will be the so-to-speak 'shy' presence of women in the midst of the
male whirl, with its narrow aims and a self-assured pretention to
competence which is at once provocative and impressive.'[17] He made
notes for six major characters, of whom four are identifiably early
images of the constellation of relationships that centre on Karsten
Bernick in *The Pillars of Society*. A heroic mother-figure 'with the
calm strength that derives from the struggle of life' was dropped
completely.

What decided Ibsen to use the business world as a fitting environment for his play was probably his own increasing activity as the
capitalist Hegel had made of him. On his instructions Hegel had
long been making regular purchases of shares in railway companies.
A typical representation of the period was Ibsen's letter of 12
October 1873: 'For the amount owing to me might I ask you to
purchase shares in Swedish State Railways at the current price? I
believe that these are certainly the best investment one can make
if one is not interested in taking risks.' He was active again in 1875,
buying shares in the new Kristiania railways project, and taking his
fee for the revision of *Catiline* in the form of shares in the Zealand
railway. He also bought shares in the Norwegian steamship *Dronningen* that year and in the Kristiania tram cars which he paid for
out of his annual government grant.[18]

During the years Ibsen had been living abroad, Italy and Germany
had both been opened up geographically by new rail links; and in
Norway itself, after preliminary discussions in 1869, serious building

projects had started in 1872. In the opinion of Halvdan Koht[19] Ibsen was possibly also influenced in his choice of plot by Samuel Plimsoll's campaign in the British House of Commons between the years 1868 and 1875 for legislation on the subject of unseaworthy shipping, which eventually resulted in the adoption of the Plimsoll Line. The debates were reported in the Norwegian press as of particular interest to a seafaring nation like Norway. By coincidence, in August 1876, Ibsen received a letter from a company run by K. L. Daae and Partners, informing him that they had bought a new ship, a long-distance freighter weighing 260 tons, and requesting his permission to call it the *Henrik Ibsen* as a mark of gratitude and respect for the honour which his work reflected on the country. Ibsen consented, and the ship was duly registered with this name, a fact that conceivably actuated in him some sense of responsibility for the unimpeachable seaworthiness of the *Henrik Ibsen.*

With great artistry Ibsen then laid these global, capitalist concerns across the microcosmic framework of a small Norwegian coastal town. This was recognisably the Grimstad of his adolescence, a town in which most inhabitants, regardless of class, were small investors in the shipping trade. A railway is being built nearby and a branch line will connect the town to the network. Karsten Bernick, a prominent local shipowner, and a consortium of three partners have secretly bought up the land through which the line will pass and will be able to demand a vast sum from the railway company to part with it again. No one suspects Bernick because of his high moral standing in the town. He is also relying on this perception of him as a pillar of society to silence critics when the deal becomes public knowledge. The unexpected return from America of two former inhabitants threatens his plans, for these two alone know the true story behind a sexual scandal that took place fifteen years earlier. Johan Tønnesen took the blame for his friend Bernick and emigrated to America, never thinking that he would need his good name again. But returning to Norway, he falls in love with a local girl and the rumours surrounding his name have persisted. Bernick thinks hard, desperate to hang on to his reputation and protect his scheme. Act Three is an hypnotically natural account of his deepening dilemma. One of his ships is due to leave for America. Knowing it to be so unseaworthy that it cannot possibly survive the long journey, he makes no attempt to detain Johan from boarding when the latter plans to return to America, with the intention of selling his farm and returning to Norway to claim Dina Dorf's hand. One of the intricate subplots now sends Bernick's own son Olaf, aged thirteen, as a stowaway on board the doomed ship. This Grecian twist and the impending tragedy is averted by his wife, whose intuition leads her to the docks. The doomed ship returns to port. Bernick has already seen the only evidence definitely linking his name to the old sexual scandal ripped to pieces before his eyes by Lona Hessel, the other returned emigrant. She implies by this that his moral destiny is now in his own hands. The next move is up to him. The play's climactic scene is a gathering at the Bernicks' house to honour his example and achievements, and in his speech of thanks he makes a partial clean breast and confesses to his dishonesty over the railway land.

The first act proceeds smoothly and decisively. Information is imparted in a natural way, conversations are interrupted, thoughts change direction. The only false note is struck by the schoolteacher-moralist Rørlund, who is too blatantly being set up as the play's spiritual hypocrite. This problem recurs in the third act. This is unimpeachable in terms of its growing tensions and excitement and the gripping depiction of Bernick's conflicts as his options close and force him to contemplate the murder of his brother-in-law. But Ibsen, having made the artistically brave decision to break with the past by writing a serious play, in prose, about ordinary people, could not liberate himself completely from its conventions. In the third act Bernick and Rørlund in particular, Hilmar Tønnesen to a lesser degree, all deliver dialogue that has a false ring to it. Bernick's hell is obvious enough to an audience without his assertion that 'I cannot tolerate any burden on my conscience', a villainous aside which should properly be delivered with the back of the hand shading the mouth. Rørlund is similarly addressing the audience rather than a fellow-character when he remarks in conversation, 'In that case I would be a poor servant of the society whose morals and decencies I am employed to guard.' In a theatre review earlier in his career Ibsen had considered the dramatist's problem of how far to trust an audience to understand his meaning, criticising the over-explicit dramatist who was driven constantly to remind his audience, 'Look here, this is the meaning, this is the import of what you see in front of your eyes', and defining the cause as an 'unwarranted lack of confidence in the public's ability to assimilate poetry.'[20] Twenty years on he found that it was, after all, probably better to under- rather than over-estimate them. Whether his fears were justified or not is hard to say. At a distance of 120 years it is difficult to judge the sophistication of a typical mid-Victorian theatre audience. But enough of Ibsen's Norwegian contemporaries, including his fellow-writers Alexander Kielland and Børnstjerne Bjørnson, commented on the crudity of such underlinings in his writing to suggest that his audiences would have been even more impressed by his talent had he managed to avoid them.

The perception of Ibsen as a social critic, teacher and moralist stems from this play, and yet *The Pillars of Society* has its moral oddities. The plurality in the title refers both to Karsten Bernick and to his foreman, Aune. Aune is rebuked by Krap in the play's introductory scene for lecturing his fellow-workers and for agitating against the introduction of labour-saving machinery in the shipyard. He retorts that he does so 'to support society' (*for å støtte samfunnet*). This class-struggle sub-plot gets lost in the play's more dramatic events, but is revisited in the closing minutes when Bernick magnanimously concedes that he was wrong to force Aune to skimp on the repair work; the job must be done thoroughly. 'Aye aye, Herr Consul – and that with the new machines!' is Aune's happy response. Thus Ibsen effects a symbolic reconciliation between employer and worker, 'pillars of society' both of them, opposite sides of a moral equation whose sins and follies cancel each other out.

Except that it is not quite that simple. Bernick's sins are of a different order from Aune's. Power is his demon, not Aune's basic need to hold on to a job and keep a roof over his head. Ibsen's meditations on the nature of power so far, in *The Pretenders*, in *Brand*, in *Emperor and Galilean*, had not been dispassionate. Skule, Brand and Julian are all heroes, their desperate strategies dignified and rendered sympathetic by their ultimate failure. But by 1877 and Bernick, Ibsen's attitude towards success was more darkly ambiguous. *The Pillars of Society* shows evident sympathy for the plight of the man of power who abruptly finds himself in a situation in which his achievement is threatened. The sympathy extends to an acceptance of the fact that a man might kill under such circumstances. Fortunately murder is not necessary. Bernick's only problem as the end of the play approaches is how to react to Lona Hessel's challenge, that he assume responsibility for his own moral destiny.

How he does this is an object lesson in opportunism and finely judged business acumen, for in his speech in response to the torchlight procession and Rørlund's fulsome words of praise, he requisitions 'honesty' as though it were a commodity. Unhesitatingly he dumps his three fellow-speculators and announces that the option to buy shares in the land will be open to all, by making the offer seem magnanimous and personal neatly turning the confession to his advantage. By the end of his speech he possesses the commodity so completely that he is advising each of his listeners to 'go inside yourself – compose yourself – look inside yourself'. His implication is that they will find he has probably acted no worse than anyone else under similar circumstances. This is a cynical view of human nature, Ibsen's as well as Bernick's; and it does not even take into account how close Bernick came to committing murder in his anxiety to hold on to power. In the final tableau Bernick basks in the admiring embrace of three women and announces himself cleansed and saved by their loving forgiveness. Bernick knows how to manipulate his audience. A hundred years on he would be a television evangelist and make himself a great deal more money out of religion than ever he made out of shipping.

The theatre of social debate, urged by Georg Brandes in his lectures and writings since the early 1870s, had in fact already been essayed by Bjørnson in *The Newly Weds* as early as 1865. Two more plays by Bjørnson in 1875, *The Editor* and *A Bankrupt*, consolidated the appeal of the new direction. Brandes hailed the plays with the comment that 'those two great powers, time present and reality', had finally been accorded their dues. Strindberg later called Bjørnson's two plays 'signal rockets' for a whole new generation of dramatists. While Ibsen was working on *The Pillars of Society* both *The Newly Weds* and *A Bankrupt* were performed in Vienna, under the direction of Heinrich Laube, to a public and critical acclaim that must have both encouraged Ibsen and, given his competitive relationship with Bjørnson, urged him on to even more meticulous efforts.

It was the technically superior Ibsen, with *The Pillars of Society*, who made sure that the two 'great powers' had come to stay, for if the play fails to convince as a moral fable for its capitalist audiences – it must have left them feeling too comfortable for that – as a piece of practical theatre it remains a stunning achievement.

The play was a success in Germany, and turned Ibsen from an admired dramatist into an influential one. An early disciple was Otto Brahm, who was just twenty-one when he saw it. He later founded Freie Bühne, a German version of Antoine's Théâtre Libre, to perform modern dramas of the type Ibsen now began writing. The dramatist and theatre historian Paul Schlenther, another of Freie Bühne's founders, was another who later testified to the liberating and modernising effect of the play on his own outlook. Perhaps it took someone from outside Germany to dispel the shadow cast by a great genius like Goethe over the efforts of his successors, for paradoxically Ibsen's own great genius and success cast a similar debilitating pall over the efforts of subsequent generations of young Norwegians to find acceptance for a contemporary drama of their own creating.

The didacticism and problematic moral tenor of *The Pillars of Society* were avoided in a poem, also based on a maritime metaphor, which Ibsen wrote in 1875 for Georg Brandes's magazine *Det nittende Aahundrede*. 'A Letter in Rhyme', the last important poem Ibsen was to write, was also included in the slightly expanded second edition of his *Poems* which Hegel published in 1875. With its uneasy, dream-like atmosphere it suggests the Conrad of *The Shadow Line* or *The Nigger of the 'Narcissus'*, and has something of the mood of existential mystery Sartre tried to explicate some sixty years later in *La Nausée*. The poet writes a letter to his friend the reader from aboard a ship. All seems well. The compass works, the cargo is secure, the engine thrums strongly; yet something is definitely not right, 'there is a queer, oppressive heat'. The explanation is revealed to be the suspicion among the passengers that there is a corpse on board. Ibsen's determinist contemporaries were certain this corpse was a symbol for something, that Ibsen knew what it was, and that in his usual riddling fashion he was advising them to get rid of it. Christianity was the popular choice of many. But it is more likely that Ibsen meant the past in general, for the image of history as a literal burden was one that he returned to often in his writing. Sometimes he seems to be referring to a personal history, as in the 1875 revision of *Catiline*, where Catiline begs Furia to kill him and release him from his burden: 'Can't you see, I bear the corpse of Catiline on my back?' Elsewhere the thought is given more general application, as in the scene with the Fellaheen in the lunatic asylum in *Peer Gynt* who carries the mummified body of King Apis on his back. He asks Peer how he can more nearly resemble his hero. Peer advises him to hang himself, then they will both be dead.

'A Letter in Rhyme' has enduring power and permanence

precisely through its mystery; but Ibsen profited greatly from the
self-confidence of the Victorian world, where scientific advance led
to the belief that everything had an explanation, and that the explanation could be found. Ibsen was half-implicated in the belief and
liked to pretend that he was toying with his readers and audiences
and knew the answers to his riddles himself.

Almost immediately after finishing *The Pillars of Society* Ibsen left
Munich for Uppsala, where the university was celebrating its four
hundredth anniversary as the oldest university in Scandinavia. On
the recommendation of Lorentz Dietrichson Ibsen had been invited
to attend and receive an honourary doctorate. The separation of
the Ibsen family, with Suzannah and Sigurd in Norway and Ibsen
in Sweden, occasioned one of their all-too-rare series of exchanges
of letters. Much of Ibsen's side of the correspondence consists of
routine boasting: 12 September, '*Vikings*' performed this Monday;
full house; huge enthusiasm, the author repeatedly called to take a
bow'; 23 September, 'You have probably read in the newspaper of
how extravagantly I have been fêted in Sweden. The Danish papers
too write that I was the most fêted of all the guests at Uppsala, and
it really is true.' The love he expresses for his wife and son is elliptical, coded love, as though he is not quite sure he wants to expose
himself, even to them. It takes the form of an absurd anxiety for
their safety. 'Be very careful both on land and at sea; the slightest
carelessness can have the most terrible consequences,' he warns
Sigurd, then eighteen years old. 'Don't spend too much time on
the water, and absolutely no sailing boats!' Later the message is:
'Do not take the risk of bathing up there, because the water is
cold and can easily induce a state of deadly cramp.' Sigurd casually
ignored such warnings and replied with more conventionally 'newsy'
letters, often finding gentle amusement in observing his mother.
Of their six-hour tourist trip to visit Ringdalsfossen, a well-known
waterfall, he wrote:

> Our guide soon exerted the authority of his tyranny over Mama,
> simply by not saying a word to her the whole way and by ignoring
> every attempt to start a conversation.
> Mama found this unpleasant, and her displeasure was increased
> by the steep, desolate mountain way and the man's own dark and
> unhappy countenance.

So she gave him almost all the rum and beer we had with us and most of the food, all of which he accepted as his natural due.

Today when we went into the store to buy something Mama thought the storekeeper, who looks very like the guide, actually was him. It terrified her, and she acted so humble and feeble and polite towards him that it mystified me.

... When we go on trips I often row out on the fjord. Mama always comes along and is usually so afraid she spends all her time flattering me, praising my rowing but in the next breath begging me to keep as close as possible to land, 'for', she says, 'the better one rows, the closer to land one rows.'

Even so, Suzannah possessed greater physical courage than her husband. When she decided on an ascent of Folgefonden everyone warned her against it because of the weather, 'but as each day passed it drew me more and more, and yesterday we climbed it'. She described the weather, the snow-storm, the thick mist at the top, the seven hours it took to descend in driving rain. Elsewhere she wrote that she had visited her father's grave and seen old family friends, the Dahls, who wept with joy to see her again after almost twenty years. She told Ibsen that all the Norwegians she met were as though taken straight out of *The Pillars of Society*, and that of her old friends only the Baars impressed her – the rest had abandoned themselves to 'bourgeois refinement'. Sigurd visited Ibsen's old boss at Bergen, Herman Laading, who spoke the entire time about the letter Ibsen had sent him along with his copy of *Catiline* in 1875. Suzannah enjoyed this trip back to Norway, her second in three years. There would be other trips without Ibsen. She never hid her enthusiasm for home and her love of being in Scandanavia. Most of her letters calmly and consistently urge it on her husband.

On the way back from Sweden Ibsen stayed a few days in Copenhagen as Hegel's guest at the Hotel d'Angleterre. An undated anecdote of the period may well stem from a garden party Hegel gave in his honour, at his country house Skovgård. Another of the guests, the Danish novelist Sophus Schandorph, tried to kiss and embrace Ibsen, precipitating Ibsen's early departure from the table. He was back in Munich before Suzannah and Sigurd, and wrote a final letter to them before they returned, implying that he missed Suzannah and wished she were home by complaining that he did not like having to eat out every day, and that he was off his food anyway. The evenings were long, cold and sad. He ended on a practical note, requesting Suzannah to buy him six new pairs of leather gloves from a shop on the corner of Østergade, next to Kongens Nytorv. Thin, preferably dark brown, size eight and a half, should cost one krone seventy øre a pair. In case of customs inspection she was to be sure to pack them at the bottom of her bag.

The honorary doctorate Ibsen acquired that summer was of huge importance to him. He was henceforth, regardless of context, always Doctor Ibsen. The vanity emphasises how deep-seated his sense of shame was, at his father's degeneration from a pillar of local society into a bitter near-alcoholic, at the accidental establishment in his eighteenth year of the hidden troll-family with Else Sophie Birkedalen, at his humiliations as a debtor in Kristiania. These memories must have haunted him, burdened him over the years with a feeling of personal worthlessness from which this heap of honours must release him. There must have been relief too, for the award turned his long-standing deception into prophecy: the Munich city address register for 8 May 1875 shows that eleven years after leaving Norway, and two years before the grant of the honorary doctorate at Uppsala, he was still inaccurately claiming to be a PhD.[21]

Knud Ibsen died on 4 October 1877 at the age of eighty. His death was not mentioned in the local Skien press, but the national *Morgenbladet*, to which Ibsen subscribed, carried a small notice on 30 October announcing the death of 'the writer Henrik Ibsen's father, with neither sickness nor pain'.

On 11 November *The Pillars of Society* had its première at the Royal theatre in Copenhagen, and on the same day – perhaps for that very reason feeling strong enough to tolerate the pyschic disturbance that any thought of home caused in him – Ibsen wrote one of his rare letters to Skien, to his uncle Christian Paus:

Dear Uncle Christian!

Though one of your closest relatives, I fear and not without good reason that I shall seem half a stranger to you when you receive these lines from over here. Because obviously in the eyes of outsiders it looks as though I have deliberately cut myself off from my family once and for all and wilfully made myself a stranger. But I believe I can say that inevitable circumstances and states of affairs have from the very beginning been the main cause of this.

My reason for writing to you today, dear Uncle, is something you will readily understand. From foreign newspapers, and lately via a letter from Hedvig, I gather that my old father has passed away, and I feel a need to express my heartfelt thanks to all those members of the family who lightened his burden through so many years of his life, and who thereby, on my behalf or in my place, took upon themselves those responsibilities which I, until the very recent past, would not have been in a position to discharge.

From my fourteenth year I have had to look after myself. I have struggled long and hard to make my way in the world to the position I have now reached. That I, in all the years of this struggle, so very rarely wrote home, is chiefly to be explained by the fact that I was not able to offer my parents any support or assistance; it seemed to me futile to write when I could not offer practical assistance. I hoped always that my situation would improve; but this happened very lately and very recently.

It was therefore a great comfort to know that my parents, and now most recently my aged father, were surrounded by loving relatives. And when I hereby offer my thanks to all those who extended a helping hand to the late lamented, these thanks cover also all the help and support this gave me on my journey through life. Yes, dear Uncle, I say to you, and to the rest of the family, that their loving assumption of my duties and obligations has been a great support to me in my striving and has assisted me in achieving what I have achieved in this world.

During my last visit to Norway I had a strong desire to visit Skien and my relatives in particular; but I felt also a strong antipathy to the thought of any closer contact with certain dominant spiritual tendencies there, for which I have no sympathy at all, and over which a disagreement could easily have called forth unpleasantness or at least created an uncomfortable atmosphere which I would rather avoid. I have not, however, permanently abandoned the thought of at some point seeing my childhood home again. Next year my son will be a student here, and we will then be free to choose to live wherever we like. Probably we shall spend some time briefly in Italy, and after that settle in Kristiania, though I doubt whether in the long run I could be happy or work in Norway. My living conditions here, in the atmosphere of the outside world, where there is freedom of thought, and people take a broad view of things, are much to be preferred. On the other hand, living like this demands many sacrifices of many different sorts.

I enclose a photograph of myself. It is now twenty-seven years since we last saw each other, and it is obvious that you will not recognise me. But I hope the day will come when the family will have the opportunity to see for themselves whether the picture is a good likeness or not.

With that, dear Uncle, I will close. My warmest greetings to you and the family from
Your devoted and grateful nephew
Henrik Ibsen.

The mingled tone of guilt and pride tells its own tale, of problems and pains too great to confront anywhere but in the world of art.

13

A Doll's House

The immediate and widespread success of *The Pillars of Society* put Ibsen in the pleasant position of being able to carry out his boycott of the Christiania theatre after they left Ludvig Josephson with little option but to resign as director there in the aftermath of the fire in 1876. Within a year of publication it had been performed at five theatres in Berlin and at twenty-seven court theatres throughout Germany. It had been premièred in Swedish and Danish; and in Norwegian at Bergen. It had even been premièred in Kristiania, but in Swedish and under a Swedish director, Gustaf Keys, at the Møllergaten theatre, now re-opened and operating as a purely commercial theatre with no nationalist brief. Ibsen had single-handedly surrounded the national theatre with his play, and before long the theatre was asking him for mercy. A new manager, Harald Holst, opened negotiations with a letter asking Ibsen for the right to perform the play. In his reply Ibsen took an obvious pleasure in the situation, and the exchange of letters that followed illustrates how seriously he pursued his campaign for decent treatment and recompense for dramatists. He demolished the credentials of the theatre's current artistic director, Josephson's successor Johan Vibe; complained of lack of protection when his copyright was infringed by actors who made use of his material for their own benefit performances (his former friend Isachsen was the greatest sinner in this respect); reminded the theatre of the obstacles they had placed in Josephson's way when he first mooted the plan of staging *Peer Gynt*; and regretted personally that Josephson's departure meant the end of his ambitious plans to stage both *Brand* and the first part of *Emperor and Galilean*:

> But as long as there exist certain earlier, stageable dramatic compositions by me, while the theatre expresses no interest in these,

227

it would not occur to me to offer it something new. Nor has the theatre ever, as your worship notes, expressed any desire to obtain my latest play, a fact which I, considering the repertoire chosen by the artistic consultant and artistic leader, find only too easy to understand.[1]

He then went on to state his conditions. Artistically, these were that Vibe should not be allowed any part in the production, and that the replacement director's casting should be subject to his approval. Financially they were detailed, and showed the results of Ibsen's experiences in Germany:

In the matter of the fee, I leave it to the discretion of the honourable directors to decide which it prefers of the following two alternatives: the theatre pays me the sum of 2.500 – two thousand five hundred kroner – and thereby acquires the right to perform the play forty times, – or it pays me 2.000 – two thousand kroner – for the right to perform the play twenty-five times. In both cases the whole amount to be paid to my agent in Kristiania the day following the date of the first performance. (...) As from and including respectively the forty-first or twenty-sixth performance, and for a period of time equivalent to that laid down by the laws governing the provenance of literary copyright as regards an author's ownership of his own writings, I shall be entitled to 2 1/2 per cent – two and a half per cent – of the gross receipts each time my play is perfomed. These percentage royalties to be paid to me in a lump sum each season and at the latest fourteen days after conclusion of same. In the event of incomplete payment or of late payment the theatre loses all further rights to perform the play.[2]

Concluding, Ibsen wrote that it had been 'an especial pleasure for me to receive the honourable gentleman's most gracious communication', and we believe him. Holst and the board capitulated on all points, and Johannes Brun, who was also to play Aune, was appointed director. Ibsen was happy enough with this arrangement, but memories of his own frustrating years as a director surfaced in a letter to Holst in which he urged that Brun 'ensure from the outset that the parts have been thoroughly learned, if not the ensemble playing necessary for the play will be impossible'.

Further instructions show the extent to which Ibsen had been encouraged by his experience of Georg von Meiningen's ideas to begin making specific demands on the subject of practical stagecraft:

I permit myself the suggestion that the tempo throughout the entire performance, with especial reference naturally to the most emotional scenes, be somewhat more sprightly and swifter than is normal at the Christiania theatre. Groupings and positioning must be given the necessary thought. All positioning stage centre front of the main characters should be avoided, the positions vis-à-vis each other to change as often as is natural; in general, every scene and every tableau ought as far as possible to reflect reality. The less thoughtful players may be tempted to caricature certain of the characters in the play. I hope that this does not occur. What I would hope for is an even and steady naturalness.[3]

The net result of Ibsen's stand was the modernisation and professionalisation of the theatre in Kristiania, and with that the fruition of the work for a national theatre of stature begun so modestly in Bergen in 1851. His complaint that the Christiania theatre was being run by an 'old pals' network' was properly addressed a few months after the first Norwegian performance of *The Pillars of Society*, on 9 March 1879 when, in recognition of the fact that democracy and aesthetic judgement do not mix well, an artistic director, Hans Schrøder, was elected with sole responsibility for the artistic side of the theatre's activities. Henceforth the committee would confine itself to practical matters, predominantly financial, connected with the running of the theatre. Ibsen wrote telling Schrøder that he was sure that the new arrangements 'will prove themselves to be of great benefit to the theatre'.[4]

The Pillars of Society had achieved great success in Stockholm, and as early as March 1878 Ibsen wrote to Erik af Edholm at the Kungliga Dramatiska Teatern 'I have already begun making plans for a new play from contemporary life.' The requirements of Sigurd's education were again the formal excuse for a move to Rome in the late autumn of that year, after another summer in Gossensass. Here the Ibsens lived in an apartment at Via Gregoriana nr.46, within easy walking distance of the Spanish Steps and Café Greco on Via Condotti. Sigurd studied law at the university and Ibsen worked on his new play. A first statement of the theme of *A Doll's House* occurs in a note dated 19 October 1878:

There are two kinds of spiritual law, two kinds of conscience, one in a man and a quite different one in a woman. They do not understand one another; but the woman is judged in practical matters by the man's law, as though she were not a woman but a man.

The woman in the play ends with no idea about what is right and what is wrong; her instinctive feeling on the one hand, and her belief in authority on the other bring her into complete confusion.

A woman cannot be herself in contemporary society; it is exclusively a male society, with laws written by men and with prosecutors and judges who judge women's behaviour from the male standpoint.

She has committed a forgery and she is proud of it, because she has done so for love of her husband, to save his life. But this man in all his daily living adheres rigidly and honourably to the code of law and regards the matter with male eyes.

Spiritual battle. Oppressed, and confused by her belief in authority, she loses faith in her moral right and ability to raise her children. Bitterness. A mother in contemporary society like certain insects that crawl off and die once they have done their duty for the furtherance of the race. Love of life, of home, of husband and children and family. Typically female turning aside from the thoughts. Sudden, recurring bouts of anxiety and fear. Everything must be borne alone. Irrevocable approach of catastrophe, inevitable. Despair, battle and defeat.

But the sympathetic understanding expressed here and in the final version of *A Doll's House* was something Ibsen came to slowly. Perhaps, in his youth and early manhood, he had derived such comfort from women as adorers that he was loth to promote the notion of equality. Marichen seems to have treated him as her confidant; Hedvig admired and looked up to him. The company of the maids at the Grimstad dispensary, especially during his first two lonely years there, was perhaps the only sympathetic company he had at the time; and in Suzannah he had found a wife happily selfless in her devotion to his talent. The image of the woman as self-effacing support is central to what Ibsen was trying to say in both *Peer Gynt* and *Brand*.

In his personal life too Ibsen's behaviour was paternalistic.

Though intrigued by Magdalene Thoresen, his mother-in-law, and in his letters to her adopting a noticeably virile tone, she remained to him a woman who had to be accorded special treatment in money matters. Writing to Herman Thoresen in March 1872 he referred to a debt of thirty speciedaler that Magdalene owed him: 'This matter was completely unknown to me, until you informed me of it.' He assured Thoresen that had she asked he would have given her the money anyway, and concluded 'it is not necessary to specify that not a word of this must come to the attention of any third party! If the slightest whisper of this should reach your mother's ears it would render impossible all open and free intercourse between us; – so, silence!'[5]

On a similar errand to protect the 'weaker sex', in his letter to Bjørnson after receiving the long-delayed news of the auction of their property that had taken place not long after the Ibsens' departure for Rome, Ibsen told him that, should he happen to meet Marie Thoresen, he must ask her not to mention 'the auction or any of that sort of thing' in her letters to Suzannah, 'which I know would cause her great distress'.[6] Here he resembles his own Erik Brattberg in *The League of Youth* and to some extent Karsten Bernick in *The Pillars of Society*, both of whom are upbraided by their wives for failing to share their troubles and difficulties with them.

His line towards Marie Thoresen was also firmly traditional. By the time she had expressed her desire to become a teacher she was already one of society's spinsters, a 'maiden aunt', and as such a figure on whom was focused much of the growing agitation in Norwegian society of the 1860s and onwards for legal reforms affecting the rights of women.[7] Neither wives nor mothers, such women – particularly those of the middle and upper-middle classes – presented a special social problem, and many of the changes in the laws relating to the rights of women before the 1870s were spurred by the need to provide such 'useless' women with a degree of dignity and independence. Thus the right to practise a handicraft was extended to women by law in 1839, but only to 'infirm women over the age of forty who are unable to sustain themselves by any other means'. Not until 1866 did women acquire the right to practise on the same terms as men. An unmarried woman required special permission to undertake the simplest legal function, until 1845 when a law gave to women over twenty-five the same rights as 'male minors'. Other legal milestones occurred in 1854 with sisters gaining the same rights to inherit as their brothers,* and in 1865 when a law was passed making the coming of age twenty-one for both sexes. But Ibsen did not encourage Marie in her bid for independence, and even wrote in confidence to Herman Thoresen to solicit support for his opposition.

Intellectually Ibsen was a latecomer to the idea that social and legal change was urgently needed in order to improve the social lot of women. Georg Brandes' translation into Danish in 1869 of John Stuart Mill's *The Subjection of Women* had struck an immediate chord in Scandinavia among radical women like the Danish writer Renna Hauch, and the Norwegians Camilla Collett and Aasta Hansteen. Brandes' translation was a labour of love, specifically his love for a married woman named Caroline David, who had passed on to him her own hatred for the institution of marriage. In his Foreword to the translation he railed against 'the crudity of society's current attitude towards women'. Bjørnson hailed the book and *Norsk Folkeblad*, the radical newspaper he edited between 1866 and 1871, devoted several articles to it, informing readers that it deserved their 'closest attention and praise'.[8] But Brandes failed to carry the sceptical Ibsen along with him in his belief in Mill. Of his translation in 1872 of Mill's *Utilitarianism* Ibsen wrote:

> I will therefore in all honesty confess to you that I simply cannot understand that the Stuart Millsian is the way of progress or of the future. I cannot comprehend why you have given yourself the bother of translating this essay, which in its philistine 'sagacity' reminds me of Cicero or Seneca. I am convinced that you, in half the time you spent on the translation, could have written a book that was ten times better.[9]

In conclusion he added: 'I think also that you do Stuart Mill a grave injustice when you doubt the truth of his assertion that all his ideas come from his wife.'

But if Ibsen's nature was such that he could not be approached directly, Brandes had exerted a powerful elliptical effect on him in a review of *The League of Youth* in which he had suggested that one of the minor characters, Selma Brattberg, was interesting enough to warrant a play of her own on the strength of a single outburst that occurs halfway through the third act:

* This was as a result of a campaign by the writer Camilla Collett.

A Doll's House

ERIK BRATTSBERG: Selma, come on, let's go. You're the only one I have left now. We'll face this misfortune together.

SELMA: Misfortune? Face it together? (with a cry) Am I good enough now?

THE CHAMBERLAIN: Good Lord!

ERIK BRATTSBERG: What do you mean?

THORA: Control yourself!

SELMA: No I will not! I can't keep quiet and pretend and lie any more. Now you shall know. I am not going to face anything.

ERIK BRATTSBERG: Selma!

THE CHAMBERLAIN: Child, what are you saying?

SELMA: Oh how you have mistreated me! Disgraceful, all of you! I'm always supposed to take, never allowed to give. I've always been the poor one among you. You never came and demanded any sacrifice of me; I have never been good enough to face anything. I hate you! I loathe you all!

ERIK BRATTSBERG: What on earth is it?

THE CHAMBERLAIN: She's not well. She's not herself at all!

SELMA: How I have longed for even one drop of your troubles. But if I asked, all you had to offer was some joke as you turned me away. You dressed me up like a doll. You played with me the way one plays with a child. Oh but I longed for some heavy burden; I was serious. I longed for storms that would raise me up high. Now I'm good enough, now Erik has no one else. But I refuse to be the last straw. I don't want any part of your troubles.

The Pillars of Society, appearing eight years after *The League of Youth,* had a strong feminist element, activated by Konsul Bernick who repeated Erik Brattsberg's mistake by trying to shield his wife Betty from his troubles. Her response when these are revealed to her is: 'Do you know, Karsten, that you have now opened up to me the happiest prospect for many years?' Bernick is astonished. She explains: 'For years I believed that I had you once and lost you again. Now I know that I have never had you; but I shall win you.' As the play moves towards its conclusion it is peppered with feminist statements. Lona Hessel, Betty Bernick's half-sister, wears the uniform of radical women of the period, cropped hair and boots. When Consul Bernick confesses that he has never really seen his wife in all the years of their marriage, it is Lona Hessel who extends his

233

confession: 'I can well believe it; your society has the soul of a bachelor; you do not see the woman.' And in the play's penultimate speech Bernick proclaims 'It is you women who are the pillars of society', at which he is once again corrected by Lona, who twists the play away from the directly feminist statement it suddenly threatens to become: 'No, truth and freedom – *these* are the pillars of society.'

What focused Ibsen's interest in the social status of women, turning it from one of sympathy to one in which it seemed to him a social problem most urgently in need of attention, was probably the effect of the conversations he had with Suzannah on the subject, and also with their mutual friend, the novelist Camilla Collett. Collett's novel *The District Governor's Daughters*, published in 1854–5, was in many ways the inspiration that generated a movement for change in the status of women that, in Norway at least, has not ceased since. The movement had two distinct sides: one was the legalistic, social side, in which Ibsen became involved; the other was the erotic side, the question of free love and of the double standard which, among male writers, was more Bjørnson's *forte*. The immediate inspiration for Collett's novel was her unhappy love for the poet J.S.Welhaven who, with her own brother Henrik Wergeland, made up the first great pairing of literary rivals in Norway, a situation that found its later echo in the rivalry between Ibsen and Bjørnson. It seemed to Collett that her life had been blighted by the conventions that prevent a woman from inaugurating a relationship with a man and condemn her to wait to be asked. If Welhaven reciprocated her feelings he was too shy to do anything about it, so the pair never found each other.

In the autumn of 1871, when the Ibsens lived in Dresden, Collett was a regular visitor. In the course of her visits she soon discovered that Ibsen, the creator of the valkyrie-like Hjørdis in *The Vikings at Helgeland* whom she so greatly admired, was in person a quite conventional upholder of the prevailing relationship between the sexes. In a letter to her son Alf on 23 February 1872 she wrote:

He is an egotist from head to toe, and above all as a man in his relation to women. His situation at home has had no influence at all on him. Note all his heroes: *despots* every one of them in their dealings with women. Even for that repulsive creation Peer Grynt some noble woman has to stand by ready to drag him up out of the muck, i.e. sacrifice herself for him. Imagine our arguments, Alf! He'll remember it for sure, I don't think anyone, not even men, have ever said to him the kind of things I wasn't afraid to say. He listened ... I can't make him out. For me he's the one among our geniuses whose life has had the *least* impact in bringing him to a truthful way of looking at things. Because of this and despite all his talents, he's on the wrong track. He's always lived like a hermit.

She dreaded the prospect of Brand, 'that egotist', achieving recognition as a manly ideal – 'God save us from that becoming a reality at home, where what we really miss is tenderness, and everything that is gentle or refined gets repressed.'

That Collett should criticise Ibsen for egoism was audacious, for she was herself, by all accounts, a monstrously self-centred woman; but during these years, and later in 1876 when she lived in Munich at the same time as the Ibsens and was again frequently in their company, she managed to convince Ibsen of the importance of what she was saying. In the 1870s she published four books of polemic on the theme of the subjection of women, with explanatory titles such as *From the Camp of the Mute* and *Against the Current* and while it is unlikely that Ibsen read these himself Suzannah surely did, and acquainted him with their contents. *From the Camp of the Mute* contains a brief poetic tribute from Collett to Suzannah, a mark of the common views the two women shared. In a letter written to her many years later Ibsen paid an unusual tribute to Collett's influence on his writing: 'It is some years ago now that you, in your spiritual progression through life, in one form or another began to have an effect on my writing.'[10]

None of this would have mattered much had Ibsen not discovered a plot around which to twist his ideas on the position of women in society in a natural and gripping fashion. This he found in the shape of Laura Kieler, the young woman who had first come to his attention some years earlier when she sent him a copy of her 450-page novel *Brand's Daughters*. On the strength of their correspondence Kieler visited Dresden in 1872, stayed for a month and visited the Ibsens regularly, receiving further literary encouragement from Ibsen and establishing an almost confessional relationship with Suzannah.

In 1873 she married a Danish teacher, Victor Kieler, and the following year they started a family. The marriage was stormy but loving. The specific situation Ibsen made use of in *A Doll's House* arose when Kieler contracted tuberculosis and the doctor advised that only a trip to southern Europe could save him. Laura Kieler secretly borrowed money in order to finance the trip they made to Italy in 1876. Victor Kieler recovered, and on their way home through Europe the couple visited the Ibsens in Munich, where they were then living. Here, it seems, Laura poured out her heart to Suzannah, who in due course passed the details on to Ibsen.

After the Kielers returned to Denmark Laura's attempts to pay off her secret debts became increasingly bizarre and desperate. In 1878 she sent a manuscript to Ibsen, *Ultima Thule,* asking him to recommend Hegel to publish it – anonymously – and to persuade him to pay the inflated sum of thirty riksdaler. At the same time she wrote to Suzannah, and received in reply a note that said: 'Believe me, I feel so worried and sorry for you, for having to bear such a great burden on your frail shoulders, and you must believe me, I have done all I can to interest Ibsen in your case. God help you!'[11]

Ibsen was sympathetic but not sentimental in his response to Kieler. His letter of 26 March 1878 is worth quoting at length. Although the circumstances involved were crucially different, it shows that the expectations of chivalrous behaviour Nora had of Torvald in *A Doll's House* – old-fashioned, patriarchal and romantic – were Ibsen's own towards Laura's husband, Victor Kieler:

Dear Fru Kieler,
   Only now do I find myself in a position to answer the letter you sent to us – for I assume of course that the intention was that I should read it.
   I neither can nor will in any way recommend the enclosed manuscript *Ultima Thule* to Hegel. In a small literary community like Denmark's you could not long remain anonymous, and such a disastrous and in every respect ill-conceived and slapdash piece of work will certainly, and rightly, destroy your literary reputation and credibility for a considerable length of time to come. Your description lacks any trace of credibility and reality. I can certainly understand your having written it all down, but why your husband has not expressed his firm opposition to its publication is incom-

prehensible to me. For he must inevitably feel it his duty and his responsibility to shepherd your talent; and naturally he does feel this; he must have urged you to work slowly and self-consciously, and only to embark on plans that have matured fully. But in that case you are behaving irresponsibly towards yourself by not following his advice.

You refer in your letter to circumstances that compel such haste. I do not understand. In a family in which the husband is alive it can never be necessary for the wife to – as you are doing – drain her own spiritual blood. Nor do I understand why no-one prevents you from doing so. There must be something you are not telling me in your letter, something which radically alters the situation. I have this distinct impression, having read your letter several times now. If I am mistaken in this, and if matters really are just as you describe them, then you must pull yourself together and put a stop to it. It is inconceivable that your husband knows the full story. You must tell him. He must assume the burden of all the worries and problems that are causing you such pain and anxiety. You have already sacrificed more than is defensible. *Everil* is not what it could have been if you had given your work time to mature. This careless haste does you a great disservice. I cannot believe it is anyone's fault but your own.

It is most regrettable that you find yourself confined in such a small and narrow-minded provincial circle. You are too good for this. Your place is in Copenhagen, I doubt if anywhere else would suit you. Could your husband not bring himself to live in the capital? Consideration for you and your spiritual vocation must after all be dominant. And no matter what, remember that you have a natural talent for which you will be held to account.-

I shall send your sketches to Hegel.* What his decision will be I have no way of knowing. Do not raise your expectations. But place all your troubles in your husband's hands. He is the one who must bear it all. Do write back, if you find it necessary.[12]

In despair at this response Laura Kieler burnt the manuscript of *Ultima Thule*. She then attempted to pass a forged bank draft, which was rejected. Shortly afterwards she was confronted with this document. She lost her self-control and indulged in bizarre behaviour, on one occasion purchasing a very costly and unwanted piece of

---

* He is referring to *Everil*.

furniture, a sort of cry for help in an era that did not yet know the phrase. She suffered a nervous breakdown and was committed to an asylum, from which she was mercifully released after four weeks. The couple separated, and remained apart for two years, at the end of which time, at Victor Kieler's initiative, they resumed family life.

Ibsen saw at once the dramatic potential in this story of an unhappy marriage. An innocuous-seeming postscript to his first letter to Hegel after returning to Rome shows that the dog had already spotted the rabbit. Thanks for the money, he writes. Thanks for the new edition of *Vikings*, we've found a nice place here, not too dear, but it's almost too hot at the moment, best wishes to you and your family. Oh and p.s. – 'Should you, when you next write to me, have any more information concerning Fru Kieler, it would interest me greatly to hear it.'

This was on 8 October 1878, just eleven days before that first dated 'note for a tragedy of modern times'.

After that it was just a matter of writing the play. But its parturition had an interesting counterpoint in the affair of the female librarian at the Circolo Scandinavo, an episode that seems to confirm that Ibsen needed present feelings of anger and aggression as fuel to keep him writing once the minimal nutritional value of his early morning slice of bread and cup of black coffee had worn off. At a committee meeting in the club on 28 January 1879 Ibsen expressed his regret at the disappearance of yet another librarian, and asked his fellow-members 'if it were unthinkable, that a lady should be our librarian', referring them to 'the change in the situation of women back home' (i.e. in Norway).

He was thinking of one lady in particular, Frøken Fanny Riis, one of the Ibsens' acquaintances from their days in Bergen in the 1850s. Riis, from a literary family, was a 'new woman' who wore her hair short and smoked Havana cigars. She was a regular visitor to the Ibsens' house on Capo le Case. Ibsen's campaign to get the rules changed so that she could have the job alarmed the more traditional members of the club. The Danish consul asked whether such a female librarian would also be a committee member. Ibsen, an unpredictable negotiator, replied, 'No, a purely advisory capacity'. When the matter came up again for discussion on 8 February Ibsen presented formal proposals to the committee. Point (a) read: 'In filling the post of librarian suitable women candidates ought to be considered preferentially, if such submit an explanation.' Point (b) suggested an amendment to an existing regulation that permitted Scandinavian women to use the facilities freely but denied them the right to sit on committees and cast votes. Ibsen's recommendation was that anyone, regardless of sex, could acquire these privileges by the simple act of paying a separate annual subscription.

Much of the subsequent debate centred on the use of the word 'preferentially', which was quite simply an attempt at positive discrimination. In giving his reasons for this Ibsen was carefully pragmatic. Young men abused the post of librarian by staying only as long as it suited them before continuing their European travels. The collection was in disarray and needed someone who was willing to stay for years and more or less make a life's work of it. It seemed to him that a woman would be much more likely to do this: 'a female librarian might be expected to remain in the post for some considerable length of time; for women there is no civil service post waiting for them at home, and it is contrary to their nature to give up a steady position in search of the new and the unknown.'

Defending his suggestion that women be allowed to vote he said that women, like students and artists, had the happy knack of arriving at a correct decision by instinct. The discussion on the voting rights was the more controversial of the two suggestions. To calm the most conservative elements in his audience Ibsen insisted that he only wanted the vote for women, that he was not proposing that women could stand as candidates for election to various posts and committees. This was too much for the young radicals, among them the sculptor Christen Magelssen (a distant relative of Suzannah's), who declared that such a ruling would be an insult to women. One man nervously asked if the acceptance of such changes as were being proposed might not alter the character of the club so greatly that the Danish government would withdraw its financial support. Ibsen replied, with a unique and no doubt extempore show of faith in the liberalism of his own government, that a *rejection* of his proposals would entrain a similar response from the Swedish-Norwegian government.

A vote was taken on the removal of the word 'preferentially' from Ibsen's proposal. Sixteen voted for, five against. On the amended proposal to open the post of librarian to women on an equal footing with men the final vote went twenty for and six against. Shortly afterwards Fanny Riis took up the post, and confirmed Ibsen's rationale by remaining in it for many years.

There was also a clear majority – nineteen for and eleven against – for the proposal to give voting rights to women members; but this fell under a club rule that demanded a clear two-thirds majority.* Ibsen was extremely annoyed with those who had failed to support him. He confined his company for the rest of that winter to those who had voted for his proposal and would not even greet on the street those who had opposed him. Yet he might have been grateful to them, for their obstinancy was surely what thereafter fuelled him through the great burst of activity on *A Doll's House* that saw a draft of the first act finished by 25 May, of the second by 14 July, and of the third by 3 August of that year.

Most of the work on the first draft of *A Doll's House* was done in Amalfi, where it was cooler than Rome, cholera-free, and offered the pleasures of sea-bathing, which all the Ibsens enjoyed. They left Rome on 5 July, travelling by rail to Naples and then by diligence along the coastal road through Sorrento to Amalfi. Here, in the Hotel Luna, a converted Franciscan monastery, they rented two rooms on the second floor, high above the sea, with a magnificent view across the Gulf of Salerno. The hotel also provided Ibsen with ample scope for his meditative pacing, in the peaceful surroundings of the flower garden in the hotel courtyard or through the narrow streets of Amalfi itself. Sometimes, on his afternoon rambles, he took the hotelier's small son with him. One day he came home and told Suzannah that he had just *seen* Nora. Suzannah, whose interest in Madame Blavatsky's theosophy must have begun at around this time, calmly asked Ibsen how she was dressed. 'She was wearing a simple blue dress,' he replied.

The revision followed closely upon the heels of the first draft, and the final version was finished by 20 September. Shortly afterwards the Ibsens left. Passing through Sorrento Ibsen wrote to Marcus Grønvold in Munich announcing his attention to return to Germany: 'Soon we will have been away for fourteen months; I am tired of this wandering life and feel I want to settle for the winter.'[13] His tiredness is understandable, for Ibsen was a neurotic traveller. According to John Paulsen he would begin packing for any trip at least a week in advance, and was so determined not to be late that

---

* At the general meeting on 7 November 1879 female artists were by a large majority given the vote.

he would present himself at points of departure one clear hour before the time of leaving.

Grønvold helped them to find an apartment in Munich, close to the university, at Amalienstrasse 50a, on the second floor, where they were to remain for just over a year. There was a maid by this time – Helene – followed by Antonia, both young and pretty and both chosen by Ibsen himself. John Paulsen was a frequent visitor to the apartment and later published a description of it.[14] Albums and books were laid out on tables, and there were numerous small wood-carvings the Ibsens had brought back from Sorrento. Hanging among the paintings on the wall was a small study of Ole Schulerud, Ibsen's friend and supporter from the days of *Catiline*.

Germany was now Ibsen's most important market. Though the closet sensualist in him missed the sea-bathing in Italy, logistically Germany was the most sensible place for him to live when a new play was to be launched and he needed to be easily contactable. Hegel, whose commercial instincts were as sharp as Ibsen's, published *A Doll's House* on 4 December in what he himself described as a 'very big edition' of 8,000 copies. This sold out quickly, to be followed by a second edition of 3,000 copies in January and a third in March. The play was equally successful. It had its world première at the Royal theatre in Copenhagen and was still playing to full houses on 5 March 1880, when Hegel wrote to inform Ibsen of its huge earnings. It played to full houses in Stockholm, Kristiania, Bergen, Munich, Berlin, Hamburg, Hanover, Moscow, Warsaw, and has scarcely stopped playing to full houses since.

In practical terms the most immediately noticeable difference between *The Pillars of Society* and *A Doll's House* is in the number of characters, nineteen with names cut down to just six with names. For the remainder of his career Ibsen would stick to this chamber format, and it is this more than anything that gives the later plays their characteristic quality of intimacy. *A Doll's House* is also the first time Ibsen made extensive use in one of his plays of current theories of determinism and genetic heritage as a structure to underpin the psychology of his characters: Nora behaves as she does because she is her father's daughter. In this he was belatedly responding to Georg Brandes's injunction to him in the 1870s that he should, as a modern writer, assimilate 'current scientific thinking'. But more importantly the move also represents the latest turn in his long, slow search for meaning in life without God. The determinist psychology of *A Doll's House* is a statement of belief in a 'something' having the same pretensions to expose an underlying order as the lost Christianity had once had. At the same time it offered a fatalistic imperative to behaviour of which, as a dramatist, he realised he could make excellent use.

As an attack on marriage *A Doll's House* is no longer of relevance for the grandsons and granddaughters of those for whom it was written. Separation, divorce, children who grow up recognising one, three or more parents are commonplaces of western society. On the other hand it has propagandic relevance for societies aspiring to reform the terms of the sexual relationship. It has acquired notable appeal for advocates of an Islamic reformation, and has twice in recent years been performed in Oslo by visiting and native Islamic theatre groups. An adaptation of *A Doll's House* has also recently been the subject of an Iranian film.

Ibsen can scarcely have imagined such a history for his play down through the ages. As a man he would be delighted; as an artist his feelings would be ambiguous. He was unhappy with any suggestion that what he had written was propaganda and not art. In a distancing manoeuvre reminiscent of that carried out involving Brand, when he told Laura Kieler 'the fact that Brand is a priest is incidental', he later claimed that the liberation of women was of no interest to him, that he did not, in fact, know what was meant by the term, and that he had certainly never worked to bring it about. His real aim, he stated, was the liberation of human beings.

But for all its remarkable qualities, *A Doll's House* remains essentially a piece of propaganda. As a work of art it fails to surmount the author's evident contempt for Nora's husband, Torvald Helmer. She, who is so vividly and recognisably a real person, is given as her deuteragonist someone who is little more than a caricature. Ibsen misses no opportunity to turn the audience against him. Early drafts of the play show how consciously he worked on this. In the penultimate version, when Krogstad the blackmailer returns the incriminating document to Nora to do with as she pleases, Torvald burns it with the happy cry to Nora, 'You are saved, you are saved!' Nora would still have found his response to her plight troubling had Ibsen not changed this in the final version to 'I am saved, Nora, I am saved!', for this is not the behaviour of a misguided man but of a repellent human being.

Another piece of irresistible weighting is the flirtatious relation-ship between Dr Rank and Nora. This does not exist in the earlier version. When Ibsen introduces it into his final version it is to turn the audience against Torvald. Torvald considers Rank his best friend; yet when Rank discovers he is dying it is Torvald's wife he confides in, not Torvald. The message is clear: not even the man's friend really likes him. Even more effective in this respect is the scene in which Nora confides to Dr Rank her secret desire to swear some harmless oath in front of her husband. Torvald duly enters, Dr Rank laughs and urges Nora to indulge herself. She does not, of course, and what we as an audience experience is the faintest sensation of our 'ganging up' on Torvald. We have our little secrets from him. We change the subject of our conversation when he enters the room. It is not a pleasant feeling.

Yet Torvald is so evidently monstrous that we soon forget our guilt. Ibsen equipped him with the same tendency as Hilmar Tønnessen in *The Pillars of Society* to claim a sensitivity amounting almost to an allergy in the presence of 'immoral' people or in an atmosphere of 'lies'. This is exaggerated to a degree that makes it seem merely ridiculous. Yet that Ibsen did not regard Torvald as a caricature is evident in a note he wrote on the casting for the production at the Royal theatre in Stockholm, in which he urged that the part be given to Gustaf Fredrikson because of his ability to play 'an elegant and lovable lightheartedness'. There was a dusting of crude inno-cence across Ibsen's sharp, cynical intelligence.

Ibsen once confided to John Paulsen that 'a man is easy to study, but one can never completely understand a woman'. But it was only in recent years that he had discovered for himself the complexity of women, after having contented himself for so long with female characters like Agnes and Solveig who were, perforce, clichés in their relationships with their self-obsessed men. Having seen the light after his conversations with Suzannah, Camilla Collett, Laura Kieler and others, all his psychological energies were then expended on creating Nora. Until she changes personality towards the end of the play, when she ceases to be the individual 'Nora' and lectures Torvald impersonally as a representative 'woman', Nora has all the complex charm and attractive human foibles of Ibsen's greatest character, Peer Gynt. But in the excitement of creating her he neglected to make a believable human being out of Torvald. The same brusqueness affects the Helmers' children, brought on stage largely to give them a living presence in the audience's mind as part of Nora's dilemma as mother. But their lines are perfunctory and their presence invariably a crude flaw in the illusion. Fassbinder omitted them altogether from his television film on the grounds that Nora was, anyway, an egocentric who did not really care about them.

The great moment in *A Doll's House* comes with that last stage direction – 'From below the banging shut of a door is heard' – which tells us that Nora has left husband and children. Dramatically it is necessary. Psychologically it is not. Nora has already proved herself the stronger, and Torvald's re-education has begun. But Ibsen clung to the fiction that somehow it was still Nora who needed the education. Writing to Erik af Edholm in January 1880 he called her 'a big, overgrown child, who must go out into the world to discover herself and so may one day be, in due course, fit to raise her children – or maybe not. No one can know. But this much is certain', he continued, 'that with the perspective on marriage that has opened up to her in the course of the night it would be immoral of her to continue living with Helmer: This is impossible for her, and this is why she leaves.'[15]

Perhaps Ibsen needed Nora to leave for another reason, for in the autobiographical half-light which glows faintly beneath everything he wrote her story is also his: that of someone prepared to sacrifice his or her own children, defenceless and precious, for the goal of self-realisation. Ibsen needed to present the actions of such a person as being above the claims of conventional morality. This trawls the dangerous edge of his gospel of self-realisation, and sheds light on why a play on such a controversial theme yet enjoyed such astonishing and instant success among its contemporaries.* For beneath its sexual politics *A Doll's House* was a hymn to individualism, that *sine qua non* of industrial capitalism and the market economy. Nora was not only a woman, she was also an advocate of the same 'thoroughgoing egotism, that for a while leads you to look upon yourself and what is yours as the only thing of any value and meaning, and on everything else as non-existent' that Ibsen himself once recommended to Brandes as the only sure navigational tool through life.

* For all his admiration for *A Doll's House*, Georg Brandes could not accept the conclusion: 'The ending is impossible,' he wrote. 'There must be a lover. No woman goes off to the country in search of self-improvement.'

So publicly did Ibsen identify with the moral courage, for good and ill, of characters like Brand and Nora Helmer and the mighty absolutism of their demands ('all or nothing') that it remains a puzzle why he was willing to write the soft, alternative ending to *A Doll's House*, the so-called 'German ending'. On one occasion he said that it was in response to a warning from his German translator, Wilhelm Lange, that those theatres not happy about the radical ending might compose a more acceptable ending of their own. In anticipation of this he provided an ending in which Torvald leads Nora to the door of the bedroom where the children are sleeping, at which she sinks down in a faint and agrees to stay, for their sake. Elsewhere, writing to Heinrich Laube, director of the Vienna State Theatre, he said that he had written the new ending at the request of a German theatre impresario 'and an actress who wants to make a tour of northern Germany'. The actress was Hedewig Niemann-Raabe, who had declined to play the part as written, on the grounds that '*I* would never leave *my* children!'

Ibsen himself called the change 'a barbaric act of violence'.[16] But his willingness to provide it shows how far he had travelled since the days of *Brand* and his proud boast to Bjørnson that he would rather be a beggar for life than change a line of it at the behest of the 'pocket-sized souls' in the Norwegian *Storting*.

Since the author himself had written it, many German theatres used the new ending. Hedewig Niemann-Raabe performed the barbarism in Flensburg, Hamburg, Dresden and Hanover. She also performed it in Berlin, where there was such an outcry over the dishonesty that shortly afterwards the play had to be performed in its original version. This in turn provoked a second outcry, and a third version was performed, incorporating a putative 'missing' fourth act in which Fru Linde and Krogstad are discovered a married couple, with a restless Nora their guest. Torvald arrives. Nora looks up at him and whispers 'Have you then quite forgiven me?' Helmer gives her a mysterious but affectionate look, takes out a large bag of the forbidden macaroons and pops one into her mouth with a smile. 'The miracle of miracles!' cries Nora joyfully, as the curtain descends. In Milwaukee, Wisconsin, in 1882 a version of the play was performed, in English, with the German ending. According to *Dagbladet*'s reporter, 'the actress who played Nora was unable to dance the tarantella, so this highly exciting and characteristic scene was omitted and the play suffered greatly on this account.'[17] This was the first of Ibsen's plays to be performed in English in America, under the title *The Child Wife*. Under a similarly misleading title, *Breaking a Butterfly* (for between Nora and Thorvald, who is really the butterfly?) it was performed in England at the Prince's theatre, London, in March 1884 in a version by Henry Arthur Jones and Henry Herman.

The fact is that Ibsen's respect for his wallet was as great as his respect for his art, and it was in both cases considerable. His pragmatism served his talent as a dramatist, pushing his instinct for the current of the times into the realisation that his public was ready for a play about a woman who leaves her husband and children. The same steady, sane pragmatism was at work in him as early as 1862, when he dismissed a hypothetical play on a sentimental, politically correct theme with an irrefutably realist argument:

> (A play in which) a lawyer who, in the capital city of the very heartland of the slave-owning states, is seen defending at the bar the human rights of a Negro, who extends his definition of freedom to include the Negro and describes slavery as a national shame – all this to general public acclaim – and who, using such a defence, persuades a jury to bring in a unanimous verdict of Not Guilty for the crime of having used force to free a child born in slavery – all of this, we repeat, stands in such contrast to what we know with certainty to be the prevailing state of affairs over there that we cannot possibly feel either moved or guilty.[18]

Such freaks as the 'German ending' and phantom fourth act did not prosper long, however. And on his own doorstep, at the Residenz theatre in Munich, Ibsen had the satisfaction of seeing his play performed in its original version. He attended every rehearsal, and was present at the première on 3 March 1880. John Paulsen was there too and left his account of the curious frustration Ibsen felt at the performance:

> The performance was overall a good one – Fru Marie Ramlo, who played Nora, was particularly good, and afterwards Ibsen thanked her and the other performers warmly. One would have assumed that in Ibsen's view it had been an ideal performance. But later, at home with Ibsen, when we discussed the performance, which I praised highly, he had innumerable complaints. Not only had a couple of the actors not fully understood their

roles, but he did not like the wallpaper in the living room – it didn't create the right mood – and he even complained about tiny matters, such as that Nora's hands weren't right (I can't remember whether it was because they were too big or too small).[19]

The Pillars of Society had aroused great interest among a self-confident, new bourgeois theatre audience who responded keenly to the mixture of flattery and rebuke implied in Ibsen's use of a contemporary setting. *A Doll's House* was a brilliant advance on this, narrowing the focus down, opening the curtains, peering right into the family living-room, and making the discovery Tolstoi made in *Anna Karenina*, that all happy families resemble one another, but each unhappy family is unhappy in its own way. One recalls the Lammers' movement in Skien which so attracted Ibsen's sister and brother; how it disapproved of literature as the devil's work, and the insistence of its most fervent supporters on living without curtains in their homes. For what, in a literal sense, could have been more horribly fascinating to Ibsen – and his Victorian audiences – than to open their own curtains to the scrutiny of strangers? This terrified prurience was as much a part of the attraction of *A Doll's House* for audiences as its exposition of a liberal humanist belief in moral progress. Henceforth Ibsen's plays would all to a greater or lesser degree make use of these two elements of appeal.

14

Ghosts

Two weeks after its première in Munich on 15 February 1880 Ibsen wrote to Hegel:

> It is with great joy I learn that a third edition of *A Doll's House* is needed already. From a financial point of view this looks like being a 'bumper' year for me. Today I had the pleasure of receiving the copy of the fourth edition of *The League of Youth* that was sent to me. At your convenience, might I ask you please to let me know the size of this edition, as also the size of the edition of *Emperor and Galilean,* so that I have a rough idea of how much I am in credit. The fact is that I shall unfortunately this year need a great deal more money than usual, because in the summer Sigurd is being sent to Kristiania to continue his studies there.

Ibsen's moral twists and turns were beginning to baffle his contemporaries. *Brand* and *Peer Gynt* both delivered what were ultimately quite conventional moral statements. *The League of Youth,* so unequivocally an attack on the radicals and their efforts to introduce parliamentary democracy into Norway, had become a firm favourite with the Norwegian right. *The Pillars of Society* also promoted a conventional morality, but in such a way as to cause unease among the establishment by directing its criticism and its warnings towards them. *A Doll's House* had probed yet more disturbingly into the fabric of the social structure. Now, as the financial success of the scandalous play became apparent, he wrote to Hegel suggesting that he make novel use of his reputation for baffling:

> I believe I am correct in my observation that the foreword to the new edition of *Catiline* has been read with considerable interest. What if I now wrote a complete, small book of about ten to twelve sheets containing similar details on the external and internal

conditions pertaining to the writing of each of my previous literary works? Regarding *Fru Inger* and *Vikings* I would for example give an account of my years in Bergen; and for *The Pretenders* and *Love's Comedy* a description of the subsequent period in Kristiania; after that my life in Rome, *Brand* and *Peer Gynt* etc etc. Naturally, I shall not engage in any interpretation of my books; best that the public and the critics be left to puzzle over these as much as they wish – for the time being at least. I would simply and straightforwardly describe the circumstances and conditions under which I have written, – all, naturally, with the utmost discretion, leaving a wide area open for all sorts of guesswork.

Is it your view that I should realise this plan or abandon it? Do you think it appropriate, and do you find the timing well-chosen, or would it perhaps be wise to wait a while? At your convenience, please give me the benefit of your experienced advice in this matter.[1]

Hegel replied on 6 June 1880, urging Ibsen on no account to proceed with his plan. The foreword to *Catiline*, he wrote, had an intrinsic interest as it involved the presentation of a revision of a work of his youth,

but apart from this it would, in my view, result in writing of a semi-private nature, which would hardly be of interest to the public were it not for the name Henrik Ibsen . . . Your works are, individually, clear and characteristic wholes, and their importance ought not to be related to small asides like this. These will unconsciously work their way into the reader's consciousness and gradually introduce a new and disturbing element into their reception, since the whole and these parts cannot be harmonised . . . If you divulge details of your private life to the public like this you will find that you alter the terms of your contract with them. They will form an exaggerated idea of their importance which may well change the terms on which they approach future works of yours in a way that will perhaps not work to your advantage.[2]

Hegel's response shows that he was not only a publisher of genius but an astute psychologist with a special insight into the field of public relations. He showed a clearer grasp than Ibsen himself of the extent to which Ibsen's mystique and status derived from the reading public's first encounter with him as the creator of Brand, the great punisher. Once before, in 1868, Hegel had acted to protect Ibsen's reputation as a man incapable of frivolity for its own sake. Ibsen had originally wanted to publish *The League of Youth* with an impudent and amusing subtitle, 'Or: Our Lord & Co'. Hegel replied:

> I urge you most emphatically to use only the first part of the title, *The League of Youth* alone, and that you do not use the phrase Our Lord & Co either in the title or in the text; for this will offend, not only here but more in Norway and most of all in Sweden, where the play may also be expected to have a future. I urge you very sincerely to take account of the advice I here take the liberty of offering you.[3]

Ibsen on that occasion deferred to the superior commercial instincts of his publisher, and he did so now. Perhaps it did not require too much to persuade him to abandon the idea, for the point at which the projected autobiography stops – with Ibsen aged about seven – is the point at which his father's financial ruin began, with its baleful effect on the atmosphere within the family, and on their status in the community. Yet one regrets that he did so, and turned his back on an undertaking that might have proved cathartic and increased his sum of happiness. As it is all that remains is this extended and tantalising fragment:

> I was born in a house by the market-place, Stockmann's house, as it was called then. It was right next to the church, with its steep staircase and the impressive steeple. To the right of the church were the stocks and to the left the town hall with prison cell and 'loony bin'. On the fourth side the place was bounded by the Latin school and the people's school. The church stood on its own in the middle.
>
> This then was the first view of itself which the world presented to me. Architecture everywhere, no grass, no landscape. But the air above this square space of trees and stones was filled the livelong day with the muted booming and soughing from Lange and Kloster falls and all the other waterfalls; and through the raging of the falls from morning to night cut a sharp sound that was alternately like the screeching and sighing of women – the sound of the hundreds of sawblades working out by the falls. Later, when I read about guillotines, I always thought of these

sawblades. The church was naturally the finest building in town. Owing to the carelessness of a servant girl one Christmas Eve towards the end of last century Skien was burnt down, and the old church with it. Understandably under the circumstances, the maid was executed. But the town was rebuilt with streets as broad as the old ones in the hills and broad valleys where it lies, and a new church was built, of which the inhabitants boasted with a certain pride that it was made with yellow Dutch stonework, that it was built by a master-builder from Copenhagen, as well as being exactly the same as the church at Konigsberg. In those days I had no proper appreciation of these fine points; but what did make a powerful impression on me was an enormous white angel with huge limbs which on weekdays hung high up under the arched roof with a bowl in its hands, but on Sundays slowly descended to join us when children were to be baptised.

But even more than the white angel I was fascinated by the black poodle which lived up at the top of the steeple, where the watchman made his calls in the night. It had glowing red eyes; but was rarely seen; in fact, to my knowledge, it only ever appeared once, one New Year's night, just as the watch called 'One' from the window opening at the front of the church. Then the black poodle came up the steps behind him and just stood there looking at him with those glowing eyes. That was all, but the watch went head-first through the opening and fell to the square, and that's where they found him, all the pious souls making their way to the early service in the morning. Ever since then the watch has never called 'One' from that particular window of Skien church.

This business of the poodle and the watchman took place long before my time, and later I've heard accounts of similar happenings in a number of Norwegian churches. But this particular window was always special to me as it was there that I had my first conscious, lasting impression of the world. My nanny carried me up there one day and let me sit in the open window, held firmly from behind, of course, in her trusty arms. I remember clearly how struck I was by the realisation that I was looking down at the crowns of people's hats. I saw down into our own rooms, saw the window-sills, saw the curtains, saw my mother standing down there in one of the windows. Why, I could even see over the top of the roof and down into the yard, where our brown horse stood tethered to the stable door swishing its tail. On the stable wall I remember there hung a shiny tin bucket. And then there was a great deal of running and waving and shouting to us from our front door, and my nanny hurriedly pulled me back and ran down the steps with me. The rest I don't recall, but I was often told later how my mother had caught sight of me up there and begun to wail, and that she fainted, as people did in those days, and that afterwards, when she had me back, she wept and kissed and petted me. As a boy after that I never crossed the square without looking up at that window. It seemed to me that it meant something special to me and to the poodle.

From these earliest years I preserve only one further memory. As a christening gift I had received among other things a large silver coin with a man's head on it. The man had a high forehead, a large, crooked nose and protruding lower lip. He was bare-necked too, which seemed odd to me. My nanny told me that the man on the coin was 'King Fredrik rex'. Once I began to spin it on the floor, with the unhappy result that it fell down a crack. I believe, since this was a christening gift, that my parents took it as an ill omen. The floorboard was taken up and a thorough search conducted, but King Fredrik rex was never seen again. For a long time after this there were times when I considered myself a wretched criminal, and whenever I saw the town constable Peter Tysker leave his office and make his way over towards our house I would run off into the children's bedroom and hide myself under the bed.

As it happens we did not live for very long in that house in the square. My father bought a larger house, to which we moved when I was about four years old. This new home of mine was on a corner, a little higher up the town, at the foot of 'Hundevad-bakken', called after an old German-speaking doctor whose elegant wife drove in a 'glass-carriage' which in winter was turned into a sledge. In this house were many large rooms both upstairs and downstairs, and soon an extremely lively social life developed. But we boys did not spend much time indoors. The square, where the two biggest schools were, was the natural gathering place and battleground for the young. The headmaster of the Latin school in those days was the distinguished and much-loved Herr Ørn. In charge of the people's school was, I think, the caretaker Flasrud, another worthy old gentleman, who also functioned as the town's hairdresser and barber. Many a fierce battle between the pupils of these two schools was fought down in the area around the church, but as I did not attend either school I was usually present only as an observer. I was in any case as a child not in the least inclined to fight. There was a much greater attraction in the stocks and in the town hall previously referred to, with all its dark, hidden secrets. The stocks consisted of a reddish-brown stake about as high as a man. At the top was a large round knob which had originally been painted black; now this knob looked like a friendly, inviting human face, a little inclined to one side. In front of the post hung an iron chain with an open collar on it. To me it looked as if it had two small open arms which would with the greatest of pleasure be willing to reach out and fasten themselves around my neck. It had not been used for many years, but I remember well that it was still there all the time I lived in Skien, although I don't know if it's still there now.

And then there was the town hall. Like the church it had a steep staircase. Underneath were the cells with barred windows facing out on to the square. Behind those bars I saw many a pale, nasty face. A room in the very basement of the building was known as the 'loony bin' and was apparently – though I can hardly credit it now – sometimes used as a place to lock up the insane. This room had iron bars like the others, but behind the bars the entire window space was filled with a massive iron plate, with small round holes bored in it so that it looked like a colander. This hovel is said once to have housed in its time the famous criminal Brendeis, who had been branded. And I believe it was also used for a prisoner serving life who had escaped and been recaptured and whipped in Li Square. Eyewitnesses related that he had danced on the way to where the punishment was to be carried out but that on his way back to the cell he had to be dragged on a trolley.

In my childhood Skien was a thoroughly happy and social town, quite the opposite of what it later became. Many highly cultivated, respectable and wealthy families lived in the town itself or on large estates nearby. These families were all connected with one another, and balls, dinner-parties, and musical evenings followed one another in quick succession both summer and winter. The town received many visitors, and as it had no proper hotels these visitors would stay with friends and relatives. In our large, roomy house we almost always had someone staying, and especially round Christmas and market days the house would be full. The market was in February, and it was an especially happy time for us boys. A good six months in advance we would begin to save up our shillings so that we could go and see the tightrope walkers and organ-grinders and trick-riders, and buy honey-cakes from the booths. I doubt whether this market played a significant role in the business life of the town, but to me it seemed like a huge street-party that lasted for almost a whole week.

National Day in Skien was a fairly quiet affair. Some of the young fired off rounds up on Blegebakken hill or 'burnt witches', but that was about it. I am inclined to think that this reserve in our usually so lively town may have been out of respect for the feelings of an extremely well-respected man who had his mansion on the outskirts of town and who for various reasons no-one wanted to upset.

All the more fun then, on Midsummer's Eve. There was no joint celebration. The town young would get together and five, six or more groups would each collect wood for their own fire. As early as Whitsun gangs of us would do the rounds of the shipyards and local stores to 'beg' for tar-barrels. One strange custom had persisted for as far back as anyone could remember. What was not given to us voluntarily would simply be stolen, and neither the owner nor the police would even think of reporting us for theft. After a while a group could amass quite a number of empty tar-barrels. We had the same time-honoured right to old rowing boats. If we came across one drawn up on land and managed to drag it off unseen and keep it hidden then it was ours by rights, or at least no one mentioned it afterwards. The boat would then, on the day before Midsummer, be carried in triumph through the streets to where the fire was to be, with a musician sitting in it. I have witnessed several such processions, and once even took part in one myself.[4]

Perhaps what emerges most clearly from this is the extent to which Ibsen's was always the bystander's perspective on life – 'as I did not attend either school I was usually present only as an observer'; 'I have witnessed several such processions, and once even took part in one myself' – the phrases sound through the prose with a touching directness. And there are aspects that shed light on his lifelong timidity and his ambivalent attitude towards authority: the adventure in the church steeple; the episode with the policeman from whom he hid beneath his bed; his fascination with the stocks and their invitation to ritual humiliation; the solipsistic removal of any references to brothers and sisters. There is even, in the schematic clarity of his description of the view from the Stockmann house, a hint that the world always seemed to him the creation of some cosmic set-designer, though this may be an anachronistic perspective. But though this brief attempt directly to address the past and perhaps jettison 'the corpse in the hold' failed, his next two plays, *Ghosts* and *An Enemy of the People*, would both contain echoes of and elliptical references to this aborted autobiography in incident, name, and theme.

At least Ibsen had roots, even if he choose to cut them. Sigurd had never had any. Now twenty-one years old, handsome, intelligent and elegant, he nevertheless struck those who met him as a strange young man. 'I wondered frequently about his son's personality,' wrote Ludvig Josephson. When dining with the family in Dresden he noticed how the young Ibsen would always enter at the last moment, bowing deeply to his parents as though to strangers, and taking his seat in silence. Throughout his presence in that habitually quiet house, Josephson recalled, he scarcely ever heard the father address his son. On the rare occasions when he did, Sigurd would answer briefly, slowly and formally. Josephson found it 'painful to observe and listen to' and speculated that Ibsen had deliberately trained his son to behave like this. Visiting them again several years later in Munich he found the formal nature of the intercourse between father and son unchanged.

The Pehrsen Family, John Paulsen's minimally disguised account of the Ibsen family's domestic life in Germany, concentrates on the relationship between father and son. Paulsen's standard defence, when attacked for having so openly depicted living people in his book, was that he had merely tried to show 'the dangers of silence' and in doing so had used models from real life, just as his mentor Henrik Ibsen did.

The novel is set in Rome, where Pehrsen, his wife Sophie and his son Sverre are regular visitors to the Circolo Scandinavo. In their well-appointed apartment, cold and soulless, 'the three members of the family, father, mother and son crept around each other like strangers'. The relationships are harsh in their formality, the marriage painfully like that 'ideal marriage' Ibsen outlined to Due in Grimstad in 1849, when Due thought he was joking. Sophie calls her husband by his second name and Pehrsen refers to her as *fruen* – 'madam'. In letters to Ibsen during their periods of separation Suzannah refers often to her debilitating headaches; Sophie Pehrsen is also a chronic sufferer from headaches, which she signals by wearing a red turban. 'Have you got a headache again?' is Pehren's brusque response.

Fredrik Pehrsen's background is much like Ibsen's: born into a small town to a wastrel of a father, he struggles his way upwards, goes bankrupt, takes briefly to drink but is rescued by the offer of a job from an old friend, and goes on to become a successful and wealthy businessman. He longs to be decorated with orders and has a habit of doodling medals and citations. Sverre Pehrsen complains pathetically about his father's tyranny, his habit of listening at doors, his meanness with money. What upsets him particularly is the fact that he has never met his grandfather, knows nothing about him, and for a long time assumed that he must be dead.

The young man longs for a recognition from his father, which is never forthcoming. He writes a paper on the Norwegian judicial system and is awarded the university's gold medal. He plucks up the courage to tell his father the good news and does so stammering, painfully embarrassed, rubbing his right hand up and down his side. 'Well, well!' is Father's response. Then, with a puff on his pipe, he leaves the room to take his afternoon nap. Sophie tries to comfort Sverre: 'How happy he was deep inside! It's just that he can't *say* it. That's the way he is. The only things he can express are his anger and bitterness, not his good feelings. You have just to take them for granted.' The portrait strikes one in general as a persuasive description of the cold, inhibited side of Ibsen's character. It is not hard to imagine him saying, with Pehrsen, 'Are you being sentimental now?' each time little Sigurd came to him seeking praise for some childish achievement.

A central scene in the book is the arrival of the telegram announcing of the news of the death of Pehrsen's reprobate old father at home in Norway:

He read it, closely watched by his wife and son, read it once more, folded it carefully and put it away calmly in his wallet. Yet his wife had noticed a slight down-turning at the corners of his mouth, and this aroused her curiosity.

Pehrsen put his pipe back in his mouth. But it had gone out, so he tamped it down and relit it – in his usual slow, methodical fashion – then paced up and down the floor, a touch more subdued, a little more hunched than usual.

His wife and son looked at him enquiringly. They guessed that something had happened, but dared not ask him what.

'Father is dead,' he said at last, and puffed out a long, curling billow of smoke.

His wife gestured, as though she wanted to say something, perhaps some conventional words of condolence; but when she saw the look in her husband's eyes she said nothing.

But Sverre stopped twisting his fingers. He looked almost angrily at his father, who continued his pacing up and down the floor and never said a word. Nothing more was said, by anybody, about the matter.

Finally the silence became oppressive. It was like a thick, choking fog that filled the room.

Sverre was breathing as though his throat was constricted.

Shortly afterwards Pehrsen yawned. This was the signal for them all to go to bed.[5]

The accuracy of this scene is evident from the angry letter Georg Brandes wrote to Paulsen after reading the novel. Paulsen responded to the accusation that he had abused the family's hospitality with his 'living models' excuse, to which Brandes replied that his art was not up to the task. As proof of this he reminded Paulsen that 'you have moreover yourself told me details about the death of his father and other matters that coincide exactly with what you describe in your book'.[6] No doubt Sophie Pehrsen's kind words to Sverre about Pehrsen's emotional inhibition were also something Paulsen had experienced at first hand and slipped straight into the novel.

If he could not openly express love for his son Ibsen had immense pride in the boy, and was growing ever more aware of the problem of Sigurd's lack of roots. He now made efforts on his behalf for him to complete his education in Kristiania. However, he felt that the standard of education Sigurd had already received was high enough, and that the Kristiania University requirement for all newly enrolled students to sit a common first-year examination, the *examen philosophicum*, need not apply to Sigurd. Shortly before leaving Munich, on 20 July he sent a letter to the King, outlining the problem and asking him to issue a Royal Decree giving his son a dispensation from the *examen philosophicum*. Quite how King Oskar responded to this package from one of his most admired writers, with its extensive details of Sigurd's curriculum and copies of his school reports, is hard to imagine. The requested dispensation was not forthcoming, however, and Ibsen had to consider his next step.

Ibsen, and Suzannah and Sigurd, went separate ways that summer, Suzannah and Sigurd to Norway, Ibsen again travelling alone to Berchtesgaden in the Tyrol. Here he had the company of John Paulsen, whose book had, of course, not yet been published, and of Jonas Lie and his young family. Ibsen regularly spent Saturday evenings with the Lies, talking to the boys about their day's fishing and to Lie's little daughter about her doll's house. She was much impressed by the news that Ibsen had created a doll's house of his own, which she believed he kept in Munich.

While in Berchesgaden, he worked sporadically on an idea for a play in five acts and, unusually for him, read some contemporary literature, including with great admiration the novel *Niels Lyhne* by the Danish writer J. P Jacobsen, whose eponymous hero may have struck a sympathetic chord in him. Jacobsen's novel is the story of a man in search of a viable philosophy of life in a world without God. It soon becomes mainly a record of his rejection and destruction of existing positions. The search for meaning takes him through romantic love, through the bourgeois dream of happy family life, and finally into the army, as a volunteer in the 1864 war with Prussia. Fatally wounded in the chest, he rejects the offer of a priest and meets his death on his own. Made aware of Ibsen's interest in his novel, the flattered author wrote to Edvard Brandes, Georg's brother, of how he had heard that Ibsen 'has spent four weeks reading it, talks about it every day and reads extracts from it to his guests and visitors in the evening'.[7]

From Kristiania Ibsen heard from Sigurd that his interview with Nils Hertzberg from the Department of Ecclesiastical Affairs to try to gain exemption from the *examen philosophicum* had not gone well, and he returned to Munich in the autumn in a bad mood, resigned to a move to Rome so that Sigurd could continue his studies there, and spraying threats in all directions that both of them would change their nationality. A letter to Hegel at the end of October 1880 contains a 'warning' similar to that issued in the wake of Clemens Petersen's review of *Peer Gynt* in 1867, when Ibsen threatened to become a photographer and to 'do' his enemies in the north. In more controlled vein he now announced his intention to take his revenge on the Department of Ecclesiastical Affairs:

> Allow me to express my thanks for all the friendship and courtesy shown to my wife and son during their stay in Copenhagen. As you must have heard, in typically Norwegian fashion difficulties have been placed in the way of my son's desire to continue his law studies in Kristiania. Two years ago he graduated with honours (*med præceteris*) from Munich University, thereafter studied for a year in Rome and the following year here. All of this has no validity up there. They want him to study for at least another year in Kristiania and submit himself to another examination before they will give him permission to enroll as a law student there. I do not wish him to waste his time like this, and neither does he. He could go to any foreign university, and we return now to Rome, where he will complete his legal studies and after that apply for naturalisation. When the right time comes I intend to pin some suitable literary memento on that black theological band that for the time being rules the Norwegian Department of Ecclesiastical Affairs.[8]

Hegel was not disposed to join Ibsen in his conspiracy theory and wrote back pointing out that 'it is probably circumstances which stand in the way rather than people, who are after all obliged to abide by the constituted laws'. Ibsen, with more than a touch of Nora in him, was never convinced that 'the constituted laws' should apply to him.

In November the Ibsens moved back to Rome, to their old apartment in Capo le Case 75. On 16 January 1881 he wrote to Hegel that they had spent a pleasant and enjoyable winter in the capital, 'the Scandinavian crowd consists of a number of delightful people and families, all of whom have formed a close association . . . The new Danish consul, J. H. Hegermann-Lindecrone, is already very popular with the northerners.'

But the harmony was deceptive and Ibsen as brittle and unapproachable as ever as he sat chewing over in his mind the themes that would give him *Ghosts*. Hegermann-Lindecrone's wife, a young American, met him several times at the studio of a painter, Christian Meyer Ross. During these afternoon social sessions, she wrote, at which music was played, 'Ibsen sits sullen and indifferent. He does not like music, and does not disguise his dislike. This is not, as you may imagine, inspiring to the performers. In fact, merely to look at him takes all the life out of you. He is a veritable wet blanket.'[9]

In June the family returned to Sorrento, where fourteen years earlier Ibsen had written *Peer Gynt*. This time he could afford the relative comforts of the Hotel Tramontano, built on the clifftop high above the sea. For a reminder of his own status he need look no further than the hotel's guest book to find the names of previous visitors like Byron, Goethe, Keats, Longfellow, de Musset, Scott and Shelley. Torquato Tasso, the author of *Gerusalemme Liberata*, was born in the hotel. Among his fellow guests that long summer were the German feminist novelist Fanny Ewald and Ernst Renan. There is no evidence that Ibsen and Renan took the opportunity to get to know one another, making this the second time, after the reception for Prince Louis Napoleon in Bergen in 1856, that they had failed to meet. Ibsen was in any case so absorbed in work on the first draft of *Ghosts* that he rarely took the time to see even those friends who were also spending the summer in cholera-free Sorrento – Lorentz Dietrichson and, briefly, Carl Snoilsky. He worked unaffected by the intense heat of the summer, which Suzannah was less able to tolerate. They bathed regularly in the sea.

On 23 September Ibsen finished the first, now lost, draft of *Ghosts*. On 25 September he began work on a second, starting the first act on that day and finishing on 4 October; the second act on 13 October and finishing on the twentieth; the third on 21 October and finishing on the twenty-fourth. On completion each act was sent off to Hegel. On 5 November the family returned to Rome and Hegel made sure *Ghosts* was in the bookshops on 12 December, in good time for the Christmas market.

As with Ibsen's two previous 'hits', a potent mix of considerations, vulgar, commercial, psychological and artistic, lay behind the creation of *Ghosts*. At its outermost level it reflected Ibsen's determination to be a contemporary writer who was seen to be dealing with contemporary problems, examining the sort of issues that were

debated regularly in the pages of the Norwegian and Danish newspapers he read so closely during his exile. The themes *Ghosts* overtly
discussed – syphilis, free love, prostitution, heredity, the survival of
the fittest, euthanasia – were the conversational concerns of the
Scandinavian intelligentsia in the 1870s and 1880s as they
responded to the appearance of translations (by the author of *Niels
Lyhne*) of epochal works like *On the Origin of Species* and *The Descent
of Man*; and to passing sensations, like George Drysdale's immensely
popular book on sexual health, published in Copenhagen in 1879
– the year of *A Doll's House*. Drysdale's book openly discussed the
reality of female sexual pleasure and summarised the secret of mental and sexual health for both men and women thus: 'each and
every individual organ, if it is to retain its health and power, must
engage in a sufficient measure of activity.' This included the sexual
organs, which must be kept in regular activity or they would degenerate. Drysdale also believed that 'there is in nature neither a moral
nor a physical law which decrees that people are obliged for the
duration of their lives to limit the address of their sexual desires to
one single object.' Bjørnson, Alexander Kielland and Brandes were
all influenced by the book.

Prostitution had been legalised in Kristiania in 1868. By 1880
the city had eight brothels housing forty-nine prostitutes, sixteen
prostitutes operating from their own homes, and 600 women working secretly.[10] By the end of the 1870s, however, liberal opinion had
swung away from the idea that brothels were useful safety valves for
bourgeois young men, and moved towards their abolition. Car-
penter Engstrand's plan to open a brothel was therefore a timely
reference.

Then there was the revenge motive to take care of, the threat to
expose the Church and the Church bureaucracy to ridicule for their
intransigence in obstructing his son's education, an aim he achieved
in *Ghosts* with his unflattering portrayal of Pastor Manders.

Ghosts is rare among Ibsen's dramas of contemporary life in not
offering any obvious germ of a story, situation or character to which
its subsequent growth can be traced. One overlooked candidate for
such an origin is Georg Brandes and his involvement with the Danish
David family, with whom Ibsen had a peripheral connection in Rome
in April 1866, when he described in such vivid detail for Georg
Brandes the suicide of Brandes' young artist friend Ludvig David.[11]
It was through his friendship with Ludvig David that Brandes came

into contact with Caroline David, a married woman with whom he had an affair. From her Brandes acquired his horror of the institution of marriage. Like Ibsen's Fru Alving, Caroline David hated her husband, and claimed that he was a philanderer with a sexual disease that made him repulsive to her. Though Caroline had been adopted as a child, Brandes was convinced that she was in fact the biological daughter of her adoptive father, and that in marrying her husband Harald she was marrying her half-brother. It was this conviction, whether justified or not, that led to Brandes's lifelong obsession with the subject of incest and which accounts, among other things, for the great amount of space he devoted in *Emigrant Literature* to the subject of Lord Byron's relationship with his half sister. (Paulsen refers on more than one occasion in his memoirs to Ibsen's interest in Byron.) It is possible that Ibsen's respect for Brandes' passions and interests, which the success of *A Doll's House* had undoubtedly strengthened, led him to regard Brandes' social instincts as a reliable barometer of what was likely to be pre-occupying the public in the near future; and equally possible that the forthcoming and open Brandes had told him the story of Caroline David's marriage, perhaps during their meeting in Munich in 1877, and that Ibsen decided to use some of the details as a starting point for *Ghosts*. Ibsen had moreover, from his own childhood, the example of the curiously near-incestuous marriage of his parents to ponder: Knud Ibsen's stepfather Ole Paus was also Marichen's uncle, and husband and wife had grown up together as cousins.

Finally the influences of his recently abandoned autobiography can be traced, in particular a pattern of relationships inside the Alving household that sounds a distorted echo of Ibsen's own relationship with Else Sophie Birkedalen and the birth of their illegitimate son Hans Jacob Henriksen. We learn that long before the play begins Captain Alving got the maid Johanne pregnant and arranged for her to be married off to the working-class 'dupe' Engstrand. Engstrand believes – or seems to believe – that Regine is his daughter. When she grows up Regine returns to the Alving household to work as a maid to Fru Alving and the young master Osvald. Osvald and Regine are sexually attracted to each other, until Regine discovers that she is Osvald's half-sister. She leaves, convinced that because her mother was – in terms of the perceptions offered within the play – a whore, she too will probably become a whore.

Technically *Ghosts* represented yet another advance on *A Doll's House.* Coupling incest with determinism enabled Ibsen to create a plot that was formally tight almost to the point of claustrophobia. This, plus its observation of the unities of action, time and space and its use of a theory of heredity in the place of Nemesis, has often led to comparisons between *Ghosts* and Greek tragedy, though there is no evidence that Ibsen ever read Greek tragedy. The Melpomene statue in the Vatican museums that he saw during his first year in Rome gave him as much, in his own eyes, as he felt he needed to know about it: 'that indescribably elevated, great and peaceful joy in the facial expression, the richly leaf-crowned head, with its unearthly quality of the luxuriant and the bacchantic.The eyes, that look within at the same time as they look through and far beyond what they are looking at – that is what Greek tragedy was like.' Minus the reference to 'peaceful joy' Fru Alving can certainly be played with the kind of enigmatic dignity suggested by the second half of Ibsen's description of the statue.

Ibsen's management of the permanently absent character – the dead Captain Alving – is also a striking new feature. Hedda's father General Gabler in *Hedda Gabler* has at least the physical presence of his painted portrait to underscore his role in the unfolding drama, but in *Ghosts* Alving manages without even this. He is present in Fru Alving's obsessive memories of him, in Pastor Manders' illusions of him, in Osvald's love of alcohol and pipe-smoking and in his disease, and in Regine. In a very real sense he is the villain of the piece, who has ruined the lives of all those around him. Ibsen's manipulation of his name is masterly. First there is the dishonest attempt by Fru Alving to have the Captain remembered as a great man by naming a children's home after him, compounding the lies she has told Osvald about his father. Then comes the burning down of this lying symbol by Engstrand, followed by Engstrand's mordant joke – if it *is* a joke – that he intends to name his seamen's home-cum-brothel 'the Captain Alving Home'.

What is generally underplayed in performances of *Ghosts* is the comedy. Engstrand is a character straight out of Holberg, one of his uneducated but cunning peasants, as surely as Manders is the kind of learned dupe whose innocence Holberg loved to expose. To concede this in the acting harms *Ghosts*'s status as a serious debate about the claims of duty versus happiness; but in presenting Manders as a dogmatic clown Ibsen denies him the honour of presenting seriously the argument that, under certain circumstances, a sense of selflessness and submission to duty can indeed be superior to the pursuit of personal happiness and self-realisation. Even Fru Alving sees Manders as 'a great big child' for his naive acceptance of Engstrand's ridiculous yarns on the subject of his own piety, including the absurd claim that he got his limp after being thrown downstairs by some drunken sailors to whom he had been trying to preach the gospel.

The truly dangerous thought in *Ghosts* is articulated by Fru Alving in the scene in which she defines the word *Gengangeragtigt*[12] (ghostlike) for Manders. She asks him, rhetorically, whether we obey the laws of society because we respect them, or fear them. The question itself she calls a 'ghost' *(genganger)*,* though what she really fears is the future, not the past. She fears the consequences of action. She asks herself, if I follow my instincts today, if I do today what I really want to do, what will tomorow make of my spontaneity? Will I be disgraced, exposed, ostracised, arrested? The question relates *Ghosts* to Ibsen's earlier plays on the unending 'conflict between will and ability'. Fru Alving's tragedy is that she wanted to leave the Captain, but lacked the ability and the courage to do so. The interesting difference between a Skule, a Julian and an Alving is that the male characters accept their inability to achieve their goals as a deeprooted failure of personality, whereas the female character in Ibsen is more likely to blame 'the system' for her failure. Fru Alving's question also shows Ibsen touching on the profound problem of *boredom* in Victorian society – its existence, and the longing for powerful emotional experiences to alleviate it. The grey aura of regret Fru Alving exudes throughout the play gives a foretaste of the bitter resignation with which Professor Rubek reviews his life of self-protecting dullness and stifled spontaneity in Ibsen's last play. John Paulsen's memoirs contain a haunting image of Ibsen as Paulsen saw him at his hotel window at about five o'clock one morning, smiling beatifically at the rising sun as it struck a distant snowy peak, a lonely, obsessed man writing about the need for 'the joy of life' in a play which only seemed to point to the utter impossibility of ever achieving it.

*   *   *

* The force of the word is not covered by the English 'ghosts'. The Norwegian means literally 'something that walks again', conveying the sense of something condemned to reappear over and over again.

In November Ibsen sent off copies of *Ghosts* to the theatres in Stock-holm, Copenhagen, Kristiania and Bergen, all of whom declined to accept it for performance. Schrøder at Kristiania theatre wrote in reply: 'I just do not believe that the Christiania theatre audiences are mature enough for a rational discussion of the profound social questions you confront them with in your play.'[13]

The theatre's script consultant Henrik Jæger, who five years later was to write the first full-length biography of Ibsen, had offered a mixture of literary and moral criticisms to support his rejection of the play: 'The play is lacking in dramatic effect and tries to hide this by the use of pathological and titillating material. The theatre can never accept that this should replace genuine dramatic effect.' If such were to be allowed, he wrote, they might as well close the theatres and start charging for admission to the hospitals.

Ibsen had been expecting his play to cause controversy, but the extent of the rejections took him by surprise. Hegel had published the book in a large edition of 10,000 copies and on 22 December Ibsen wrote to a German admirer, Ludvig Pasarge, that it would soon be sold out. Instead it turned out to be his biggest failure since his breakthrough proper with *Brand*. The book was the subject of debate almost daily in the Scandinavian press. Even Ibsen's most recent admirers, those radicals who had hailed *The Pillars of Society* and *A Doll's House* as socially progressive and edifying works, failed to respond to it. One reviewer wrote of 'a diverse collection of indecent, rascally and gossipy people living in the midst of degener-ating relationships and institutions'. It was also 'much less well writ-ten than the author's previous books'.[14]

The novelist Arne Garborg, then a young reviewer for the radical *Dagbladet*, found the book distressing to read: 'It is as though Ibsen has indulged himself in the pleasures of saying out loud all the bad things he can think of, and in as outrageous manner as possible', and complained that it was, once again, the institution of marriage, the pillar of their society, that Ibsen had attacked.

The variety of reactions to *Ghosts* illustrates one of the secrets of the appeal of Ibsen's plays about modern times: his judicial vision and multiple ambiguities meant that they could be all things to all men, functioning like Rorschach blots in which what stood out as a clear statement for one reader or member of the audience was wholly invisible to the next. Bjørnson was at this time in the throes of moving from a belief in free love to the condemnation of it, and towards the establishment of a single standard of sexual morality for both men and women. He responded with a public defence of Ibsen, calling *Ghosts* a plea for the making of real marriages, to which both parties must come in the same chaste state if they are to succeed. Ibsen, who had not seen Bjørnson for ten years, and for various reasons had little reason to expect any favours of him, was moved and surprised: 'He has in truth a great, kingly spirit, and I shall never forget him for it.' As well as printing Bjørnson's defence, an editorial in *Dagbladet* stated that in the writer's opinion the play should be accepted for performance at the Christiania theatre. The same paper also reprinted a review by Georg Brandes praising the book.

No theatre in Scandinavia would take the play, nor would any in Germany. Ibsen wrote to several correspondents that the passions aroused by *Ghosts* did not bother him, but his anxiety was evident in the fact that he wrote thank-you letters to the writers of any friendly reviews he came across, as well as long letters of thanks to Bjørnson and to Brandes – the first for six years. What was worrying him most was the sudden threat to his financial security. 'Has all the fuss harmed sales of the book?' he asked Hegel in a letter of 2 January.

The query elicited a response that illustrated perfectly why the co-operation between Ibsen and Hegel was so remarkably successful. In a tribute to Hegel written long after his death, Georg Brandes wrote that Hegel was, on the subject of writing about sex, 'quite exceptionally modest'. Questioning the claim of another writer that Hegel was 'as brave as a lion', he suggested that he was rather 'as brave as a first-class businessman, and at the same time as cautious as a Danish civil-servant'. Crucially, wrote Brandes, 'he knew exactly when it made sense to be bold and when not to'.[15]

Hegel's personal and professional senses both told him that here Ibsen had gone too far, and in his reply to Ibsen's letter he assured him that the outrage most certainly had harmed sales of the book, detailing the extent of the damage done with implacable severity. There was no word of support for Ibsen, no suggestion that Hegel was angry or disappointed on his behalf, simply the expression of a businessman's cold logic: this is what will happen if you continue to write books like this. He added pointedly that the scandal had even affected sales of Ibsen's other works. Very shortly afterwards, perhaps fearing that the scandal might cause Ibsen to bolt unwisely

A cartoon comment from *Vikingen*, 1882
on the appearance of *Ghosts*

into some overpersonal public statement, he repeated the warnings of his earlier letter on the need for his client to preserve his mystique: 'Even after your death – May it be a long way off! – I would prefer that there be no documents of this type remaining.' And to press home the point once and for all: 'Whatever you write, whether it be a drama or a letter, you are a public personality, to whom the quiet pleasures of a pleasant stroll through private life are wholly denied.'[16]

Ibsen vented his frustration at this turn of events on his fellow-countrymen: the old complaints were reiterated in angry letters, Norwegians were an ungrateful, morally spineless, peasant-like people, with no idea of what freedom was nor of how to achieve it, Norwegian liberals were a bunch of stagnant minds and Norway itself 'a free country inhabited by unfree people'.

Misunderstanding or criticism from a Dane or a Swede was another matter. A titled Swedish lady, Sophie Adlersparre, had defended *Ghosts* in lectures and writings, and in June Ibsen wrote to thank her:

Indeed, several of my Swedish friends and acquaintances have opposed me in the struggle over *Ghosts*; this will not harm our personal relationships. A literary attack by a Swede is never insulting to an author, for it is always aristocratically conceived and aristocratically executed. In Denmark they do it in bourgeois fashion, and in Norway like plebians. We three peoples have between us all the qualities needed to form a spiritually united single nation. Sweden provides the spiritual aristocracy, Denmark the spiritual bourgeoisie, and Norway the spiritual lower class.[17]

Ibsen became famous, as one Norwegian writer phrased it, partly by showing up (*å henge ut*) his own people. Yet they hardly deserved this kind of testimonial. Ibsen was fond of contrasting the atmosphere of freedom he had found in the large European countries to the repressive air of life at home in his own small country. Yet every country in which he had established access to the theatres rejected *Ghosts*, not just Norway. Moreover, it had been big, free Germany and not little, lower-class Norway that had problems with the ending of *A Doll's House* and asked him if he would change it. Democracy in Norway was much in advance of that in either Germany or Italy, as was the women's movement. The Germany Ibsen lived in was a police state and the *kulturkampf* of the 1870s and anti-socialist laws of 1878 that prohibited trades unions, the Social Democratic party and its newspapers were aspects of everyday political life. It disturbed his conscience no more than the fact that the Rome he lived in during his early years was the Rome of Pius IX, who published in 1864 his *Syllabus of Errors* which condemned eighty of them including 'naturalism', 'rationalism', 'moderate rationalism', 'indifferentism', secular education, the separation of Church and state, and at number eighty any suggestion that the Pope 'can and ought to reconcile himself and come to terms with progress, liberalism and modern civilisation'.[18] Yet when Garibaldi finally triumphed in 1870, to the jubilation of the common people of Rome, curbing the Pope's power and establishing the Italian state, Ibsen did not rejoice. To Brandes he complained, like any disappointed tourist, 'so now they've taken Rome from us people and given it to the politicians, 'and that it had once been 'the only free place in Europe, the only place that enjoyed real freedom, freedom from the tyranny of politics.'[19] It shows the extent to which Ibsen's enthusiasm for freedom was tempered by personal convenience.

Ghosts did not have to wait long for acceptance. Within eighteen months of publication a Swedish actress, Fru Hvasser, desperately keen to play Fru Alving, had translated the play into Swedish herself and mounted a single, symbolic performance in Stockholm. At about the same time the Swedish actor-manager August Lindberg, equally keen to perform the part of Osvald, had opened in Copenhagen with performances of *Hamlet* and *Ghosts* by his own troupe at the start of a European tour which took the play to Kristiania late in 1883, to Ibsen's own old theatre in Møllergaten. Hans Schrøder, who had declined to let Lindberg use the Christiania theatre's premises, was made the subject of virulent press attacks for his obstinacy and was the focus of three *pibekonserter*, including one outside his own home on Stortingsgade, which he observed from the comfort of a nearby club, smoking a cigar. He also made a point of attending one of Lindberg's performances and emerged with the same impression as the one with which he had entered, that the play was artistically impressive, but that no one would be the wiser or happier for time spent in the company of people such as those depicted in *Ghosts*. He was uneasy, too, about the play's open embrace of a biologically based determinism, fearing it might lead to an erosion of the sense of personal responsibility among young members of the audience who identified too closely with the 'romantic decadent' Osvald.

In the same season, 1883, the Royal theatres in both Copenhagen and Stockholm reversed their original decisions. Performances in Germany began at the Hoftheater in Saxe-Meiningen in December 1886 and shortly afterwards reached Berlin. The honour of staging the world première, however, belonged to a group of Scandinavian-Americans who performed a version of the play at the Aurora Turner Hall in Chicago on 20 May 1882.

These satisfactions were some years in the future for Ibsen in 1882, however. A curious effect of the scandal was, as Hegel pointed out to him, that it had done nothing to increase sales of the book, and sometime in the spring of 1882 it became alarmingly apparent to Ibsen that *Ghosts* was not going to provide him with an income for that year. With typical efficiency he at once set about the writing of a new play, *An Enemy of the People*, the fuel for which would be the anger he felt for his own countrymen, and the theme of which would be their utter stupidity.

15

The Anti-democrat
An Enemy of the People

Every great writer needs his true believers on the road to success. In Grimstad Ibsen had Christopher Due and Ole Schulerud. In Kristiania it was the turn of Paul Botten Hansen and the *Illustreret Nyhedsblad*. In Rome it was William Archer, the young Englishman who, building on the start made by Edmund Gosse, would turn Ibsen within ten years into the most talked-about dramatist on the London stage. Archer's credentials as a translator and promoter of Norwegian literature in England were impeccable. His grandfather, also called William, was an economic migrant from Perth, in Scotland, who had settled in Larvik on the Norwegian south coast and worked his way through a number of occupations based on the fishing industry there. His father, after an unsuccessful attempt to settle in Australia, had returned to Perth, where William Archer was born in 1856. A branch of the family still lived in Larvik, and on visits there William had become proficient in the language. He first discovered Ibsen's writing during a visit to Larvik in the summer of 1873, where he chanced to hear someone praising the brilliant wit of *Love's Comedy* and made it his business to read the play. He was hooked at once, and set about reading everything he could lay hands on. He was in Kristiania in 1876 for Ludvig Josephson's production of the Grieg/Ibsen *Peer Gynt*, where he perhaps entertained for the first time the idea of translating and producing Ibsen for a British public. After a heroic struggle he succeeded in mounting a performance of *The Pillars of Society* under the title *Quicksands*. The première, a single matinée, was at the Gaiety theatre in London on 15 December 1880, the first time Ibsen was performed in England and a modest overture to his eventually overwhelming success there.

Archer arrived in Rome in November 1881 to spend the winter

there, largely in the hope of making personal contact with Ibsen. Not long after his arrival, at a reception at the Circolo Scandinavo in Palazzo Corea, he saw him for the first time, 'the great sight of Rome'. He knew his face well from the portrait photographs he had seen, but was much surprised at how tiny Ibsen was. Archer asked to be introduced to him and they spoke together. He apologised for having produced *Quicksands* without seeking permission, and his apology was accepted. He quickly established that Ibsen was as reticent as legend suggested, that he was not much interested in French and Italian drama, indeed that, like so many revolutionary dramatists, he rarely went to the theatre. *Ghosts* was published a few days later. Archer read it through and found it 'a bombshell', 'a great achievement, with all its faults', although 'too ghastly and hasn't enough action'. But 'if it doesn't wake them up in the north I'm a Dutchman'.[1]

As the year turned and the debate over the play raged the two men met frequently and discussed the controversy. They talked in a café close to Ibsen's apartment, where Ibsen indulged Archer's curiosity about what might happen after the end of *Ghosts*, much as it had already become a sort of parlour game to discuss what might happen after the end of *A Doll's House*.* They agreed with one another that Fru Alving would most likely put off killing Osvald until his condition showed itself to be incurable, after which she would probably do so, and then take her own life.

Ibsen confided in Archer that he was especially annoyed at the way his fellow-Scandinavians insisted on regarding the statements made by characters in his plays as statements of his own personal opinion:

> I write a play with five characters and they insist on putting in a sixth – namely Ibsen. There never was a play with less utterance of personal opinion in it. . . . Then we chuckled over Ploug's remark that it was questionable whether Oswald could inherit disease through merely smoking his father's pipe. But here I noticed a little thing which seems to show that the criticisms rather gall him; for he accused Ploug of purposely misrepresenting him, so as to gain a temporary advantage over him, in

---

* Gosse confessed to Georg Brandes that he could not understand what happened *at* the end of *Ghosts*. Brandes replied that Osvald goes mad while suffering from syphilis and that 'a mental specialist declared recently that it was portrayed so accurately one might suppose Ibsen had studied this very case in hospitals'.

Max Beerbohm's view of the relationship between Ibsen and William Archer

the eyes of people who hadn't read the play. I suggested that it was probably a mere piece of carelessness, and he admitted it might be, but said, what was quite true, that a critic had no business to be careless in that way.[2]

The discussion about the pipe highlighted a new hazard facing Ibsen as the author of realistic plays with a contemporary setting – the heightened demand on the part of the audience for factual accuracy in the writing. As a writer of historical plays, whether set in the Saga Age, the Norwegian Middle Ages or Imperial Rome, the detail and dialogue he offered were accepted by the public as a matter for the author alone to decide on. *Brand* and *Peer Gynt* likewise benefited from the indulgence naturally afforded such obviously artificial representations of reality. But once the setting was contemporary Norway then every member of the audience became at a stroke a potential expert. The problem was not limited to matters of verifiable fact. Modern characters have modern psychologies, and it was open to anyone to question, for example, the speed of Bernick's conversion from bad to good in *The Pillars of Society*, or the credibility of Nora Helmer's personality change: might these be considered faults in Ibsen's psychological perception? Or did they merely show his recognition of the fact that audiences have homes to go to at night? Like the dispute over the pipe, the problems could be very specific: legal minds of the time questioned the assumption that Krogstad's blackmailing would have succeeded, and maintained that Helmer as a trained lawyer would have known that in the given circumstances no court in the land would have convicted Nora of forging her father's signature when he was himself too ill to sign.

But are these valid criticisms of the *plays*? Ibsen's sensitivity to Ploug's criticism suggests he accepted that, as a realistic dramatist, it was his business to get the facts right. It was one of the risks he took once he had decided to document his own times. Given his determination to make use of the latest scientific theories in his plays, the problem of the accuracy of his representations of reality was never quite solved. In time it became something he would make positive use of to densify the aura of ambiguity which invests all the later plays, showing that one of the secrets of being a great writer is to know how to make your weaknesses as well as your strengths work for you.

Archer left Rome after a stay of six months, on 13 May 1882, and Ibsen's social life resumed its exclusively Scandinavian character. His most frequent companions during this second period in Rome were the young Norwegian playwright Gunnar Heiberg, J. P. Jacobsen, the sculptor Stephan Sinding, and the archeology student Ingvald Undset, father of the novelist Sigrid Undset. In addition there were Suzannah's friends who met at the Ibsens' apartment in Capo le Case 75; Fanny Riis, Magdalene Thoresen who visited, Camilla Collett, the Norwegian author Marie Colban, who was among those who had sued Ibsen for unpaid rent in Kristiania in 1861, as well as a pair of titled ladies, a Polish Baroness Wittgenstein involved in the movement for a free Poland, and the Baroness Malvida von Meysenburg.

Another of the many young Scandinavian authors, painters and sculptors who knew Ibsen in those days was the Swede Georg Pauli. Like so many of them, he too wrote his memoirs in old age, where he recalled with an enduring mixture of amusement and respect Ibsen's enigmatic persona as he encountered it for the first time, walking down the street one day wearing his black coat and stovepipe hat, medals glinting in the sunlight, on his way to a favourite café. 'Look at the strange bloke on the other side of the street!' Pauli cried to his companion, the painter Julius Kronberg. 'He's like something out of Dickens!'[3]

Kronberg had painted Ibsen in his doctoral finery in Uppsala in 1877, so they stopped to chat and joined him for a drink. Pauli, swallowing his astonishment at Ibsen's appearance, ended up admiring him for his courage in sitting in the simple Roman drinking shop in his full Ibsen-outfit, an object of naked curiosity to Scandinavians and natives alike. Later, at the Circolo Scandinavo, Pauli noted with interest his willingness to make a matter of principle out of the most trivial thing, as when he protested that on three separate occasions he had come across someone at the society putting double the necessary amount of stamps on postal packages being sent back to Scandinavia. He also remarked Ibsen's grave manner of declining a request to put himself forward as their president of the club: 'I have to tell you, I must always belong to the opposition'.[4]

Ibsen's loyalty to his own appearance remained unshaken even at home, even in the Roman heat. When he and Suzannah invited people to afternoon tea at their apartment in Capo le Case he wore his black coat with orders and ribbons pinned in place, in striking contrast to the shirt-sleeved guests. His eccentricities tempted young men to play harmless tricks on him. John Paulsen, who was also in Rome that summer, recalled a time when he was taking painting lessons from a young female painter. Ibsen, recalling his own youthful efforts as a painter, followed Paulsen's with a severe and critical interest. For a joke one day Paulsen swapped pictures with his teacher and showed them both to Ibsen, and was delighted when Ibsen obligingly began praising his effort and criticising his teacher's for its beginner's faults. But Paulsen came unstuck one day in the winter of 1881 when he accidentally trod in a minefield. At afternoon tea the conversation turned to the subject of orders. Ibsen sat in unhappy silence as two of his guests began remarking on how the Danish royal house in particular was prodigal with them. Soon every other Dane would be entitled to wear one. Someone mentioned a professor from Copenhagen who could currently be seen sporting a whole row of them. At this young Paulsen innocently interjected, 'But Professor X is a painter By Royal Appointment.' Ibsen turned on him, beating the table in fury: 'What are you implying? Out with it! Are you implying that I am a writer By Royal Appointment?' Paulsen sat silent and humiliated. Ibsen continued that it was not the first time Paulsen had made reference to his orders, and that he could not understand why the matter interested him so much, since he was hardly likely to get any himself. Paulsen noted glumly that Ibsen had said nothing to the guests who had started the conversation, but then they were elderly men. It was perhaps the experience of being Ibsen's whipping-boy on such occasions that shortly afterwards led Paulsen to seek his revenge in *The Pehrsen Family*.

The fruits of his association with Archer and an English theatre public were still some way off in 1882, and the economic failure of *Ghosts* had to be dealt with immediately. Another failure, a revival of *Catiline*, added to his woes. Ludvig Josephson, who had been such a great friend to his work when in Kristiania, was now directing at the New theatre in Stockholm. Like so many of *Ghosts*'s opponents, including Henrik Jæger, he soon changed his mind about its being 'one of the most indecent things ever written for the stage'. But while his distaste endured he declined August Lindberg's request to use the New theatre for his performances, preferring to mount instead a production of Ibsen's first play. The Swedish public rejected it, and with great courtesy Ibsen found himself having to decline Josephson's request to him to waive payment of his royalty – 'I ask you to remember that I am to a large extent dependent on my theatre royalties for my living and travelling expenses. I fully expected the agreed sum to be paid out on time and have made all my plans accordingly.'

A greater disappointment was the Norwegian government's refusal to meet his request for an increase in the annual writer's grant. He had raised this issue for the first time in correspondence the previous year with Hagbard Berner, a former editor of *Dagbladet*, now a member of parliament and as a pioneer for the rights of women and the man primarily responsible for the establishment of the Norwegian Women's Union in 1884, temporararily at least a fellow-traveller. As the author of *A Doll's House* Ibsen knew he could count on Berner for a sympathetic assessment of his problem, which he summarised thus: the works of Norwegian dramatists (i.e. himself and Bjørnson) were not protected by reciprocal copyright laws in the many other countries in which they were now being performed; lack of such laws meant that in countries in which his reputation was just beginning to spread – Russia, England, Poland – he received no money at all for performances of his plays. In Germany, where he was already a famous dramatist, he had to share his earnings with translators. The value of the lack of reciprocal copyright laws to the literary public in Norway was evident, for as a small linguistic community the Norwegians needed free access to the works of writers from larger nations, who had correspondingly less need of the relatively few works emanating from Norway. But was the access really free, he asked? Were not he and Bjørnson subsidising the cultural diet of their own countrymen? Based on this argument, he asked Berner to put forward a proposal in the *Storting* for an increase in their grants proportional to their losses. Berner was indeed sympathetic, but did not manage to raise the matter until early in 1882, at a time when it had renewed urgency for Ibsen. Berner's suggestion to the house that both Ibsen and Bjørnson's grants be raised to 2,400 kroner annually was discussed on three separate occasions. Berner and his colleagues on the left argued that the money should be paid as a form of compensation, while their opponents in the conservative camp complained of both Ibsen and Bjørnson's attacks on Christian morality. They highlighted a legal flaw in Ibsen's description of his situation, that as long as writers chose to have their books printed and published in Denmark the responsibility for the protection of copyright rested with the Danes. On these legal grounds the *Storting* rejected Berner's proposals and the grant remained unchanged.

A minor defeat such as this only increased Ibsen's sense of hostility towards his own countrymen. It left him thoroughly disenchanted with Norway's accelerating progress towards a form of parliamentary democracy, one that would shortly make it the envy of reformers in both Denmark and Sweden. The ridicule of the party system essayed in *The League of Youth* in 1869 had done nothing to halt the development, and in the elections of 1874 the party labels *Venstre* (left) and *Høyre* (right) appeared for the first time, although the organisations themselves had no formal existence as political parties until 1884. One of the leading advocates of the party system, as well as of annual sessions of parliament, was Søren Jaabæk, and it will not have helped Ibsen's humour to recall that Jaabæk was the one who had vainly opposed the initial award of an annual grant to him in 1866. In a mood mixing his personal and public disappointment with developments at home he wrote to Brandes:

They do not really need works of literature at home. All they really need are *The Government News* and *The Lutheran Weekly*. And then of course one has the party political newspapers. I have no talent for being a good citizen, nor yet for orthodoxy, and what I feel I do not have the talent for I leave well enough alone. For me freedom is the highest and first condition of life. At home they do not really care about freedom but only freedoms, a few more or a few less, all according to the party's point of view. I find this immature and vulgar aspect of our public debate highly embarrassing. In the painfully well-intentioned attempts to turn our people into a democratic society what has happened is that we have accidently became a society of plebians. Spiritual nobility back home seems to be on the wane.[5]

The polarisation of opinion, very crudely put, between democratic rights and independence from Sweden (*Venstre*), and monarchism and acceptance of the colonial status (*Høyre*), created a huge interest in the political debate: in the 1879 elections only 49 per cent of the electorate voted; in 1882 the figure rose to 72 per cent. The movement towards independence entrained other changes in Norwegian society. In a conscious attempt to establish a distinct cultural identity Christopher Bruun, Ibsen's sometime hero from the Danish-Prussian war of 1864, campaigned for a reduction in the status of antiquarian studies, and particularly the study of Latin in the so-called 'Latin schools', which had for so long been the breeding grounds of government officials and sons of government officials. In place of this Bruun urged Old Norse studies and a concentration on the country's Germanic racial roots.

Ibsen's own nationalism, however, had long ago given way, under the twin impulses of life abroad and the acquisition of a theatre audience that transcended national boundaries, to a general sense of himself as a European citizen. At the same time, his sense of status and pride in his social progress from the son of a small-town bankrupt to a point where he kept the company of kings and Swedish aristocrats, recoiled from the socialist ideals implied in the call for democracy. He felt more protective towards the values of the establishment than did those who had merely been born into it. Increasingly he was inclined to view himself as an aristocrat. Though he often referred to a 'spiritual aristocracy', in practice he hardly distinguished between this and the aristocracy of the blood, as the self-abasing tone of his letters towards even the most minor of his titled admirers shows. *Forædle* (ennoble) is a word that recurs as a kind of life-aim in his correspondence and early writing. The goal of the theatre is to 'ennoble' the audience. Shortly after arriving in Rome he thanked Bjørnson for affording him this chance to 'be elevated and ennobled'. And in a letter of solace and encouragement to a beleaguered Brandes he once advised him that the best policy under such circustances was simply to 'remain still and be ennobled'. This process of self-ennoblement developed with his succcess into a contempt for ordinary people, the 'mass'. In January 1882 he wrote to Brandes that his views were the opposite of Bjørnson's; he believed that 'the minority is always right'.

Recent events had provided him with a rich source of the creative anger he needed to start work on a new play. There was the rejection of *Ghosts*; alarm at the spread of democracy at home; irritation with the *Storting* for failing to increase the annual grant; and anger over his failure to obtain a dispensation for Sigurd at Kristiania University. Into this he stirred some social Darwinism from Ernst Hækel and aspects of the 'criminal anthropology' proposed in Italy by Dr Cesare Lombroso, which associated the phsyiognomies of criminals with distinct groupings of lower animals. Together these elements formed a volatile brew for *An Enemy of the People*.

Ibsen had a first draft of the play ready by 21 June. His long term plans had been to visit Norway in the summer of 1882, but now the Ibsens had to remain in Rome while Sigurd took the third and final part of his law examination in June and in early July defended his doctoral thesis. Ibsen took great pride in the fact that, at the age of twenty-two, Sigurd was one of the youngest PhD's in Rome.

Leaving Rome on 9 July they returned once more to Gossensass, again staying at Gröbner's Hotel, where Ibsen worked on the fair copy of *An Enemy of the People*. The first four acts went off to Hegel on 28 August, slightly later than anticipated because 'I have written two fair copies in succession in order to perfect the dialogue'.[6] The fifth act followed on 9 September. A few days later he replied granting a request from America to authorise translations of *The Pillars of Society*, *A Doll's House* and *Ghosts*, on terms that he found thoroughly satisfactory. Hegel informed him of plans for a reprinting of his *Poems*. Things were looking up again.

Towards the end of September they began thinking about

returning to Rome. But it had been a rainy summer, with floods that put large stretches of the railway lines back into Italy out of commission. They eventually left on 9 October, making their way to Brixen, 'which is at a lower altitude and has a mild climate'.

The flooding continued to delay their return to Rome, but Sigurd was finished at the university and there was no urgency about their return. Ibsen loved the countryside and they remained, staying at the excellent Hotel Elefant, until late November and arriving in Rome after 'a difficult and at times really dangerous journey' on the twenty-fourth.

He awaited the publication of his new play, he told Hegel, with a nervous trepidation, not so much for its reception as for its potential to catch to the full the Christmas book market. He also asked Hegel to buy him 4,000 kroners' worth of shares in the Norwegian Hypotekbank, at 4 1/2 per cent. He had heard that, owing to the current political unrest in Norway, shares in government institutions were regarded with some scepticism by foreign investors, but 'I know those political loudmouths up there in Norway only too well, and they are incapable of decisive action'.[7]

'There never was a play with less utterance of personal opinion in it,' Ibsen had said on the subject of *Ghosts* to William Archer. In a letter to the Danish novelist Sophus Schandorph he was equally adamant:

> They try to make me responsible for the opinions expressed by certain characters in the drama. But in that whole book there is not a single opinion, not a single utterance which can be ascribed to the author. I was extremely careful on this score. The method, the technique employed of itself prevented the author from being present in the dialogue. My intention was to produce in the reader the impression that he was experiencing a slice of reality. But nothing would more successfully sabotage this aim than to allow the author's own opinions to be present in the dialogue. And do they really believe, back home, that I possess so little dramatic insight as not to realise this? But of course I realise it – and take the consequences. In no play of mine is the author so completely absent, so absolutely not present, as in this one.[8]

Clear talk. But *An Enemy of the People* was a different matter, and on a number of occasions Ibsen advertised his close identification with the views of his hero Dr Stockmann. He told Hegel in the covering letter accompanying the manuscript:

> Work on this play has been a pleasure, and now that I am done with it I feel a sense of loss and emptiness. Dr Stockmann and I got along famously together; there are so many things we agree upon; but the doctor is much more chaotic than I am. Moreover he has other qualities that allow him to say a number of things which would not be tolerated quite so well if they were to come from my lips.[9]

This was one of the rare occasions on which Ibsen hints at the pleasure he got from writing, though the enthusiasm is not at the level of that ecstatic outburst from the days when he was working on *Brand* and wrote to Bjørnson of the 'the indescribable good fortune of being able to write.'

His identification with Stockmann was deliberate and close. His stage directions even specify that at the climactic public meeting in Captain Horster's house in Act Four, the doctor is to make his entrance in an outfit familiar to Ibsen-watchers throughout Scandinavia, 'wearing a black coat, with a white cravat'. This was a necessary detail for Ibsen's private project of revenge, which gave the play beneath its overt plot a covert structure along these lines: a doctor (Ibsen used his title consistently after gaining it 1877) has produced an ugly but necessary piece of writing (Stockmann's newspaper article, Ibsen's *Ghosts*) on the subject of disease. The owners of the means of communication between the two doctors and their communities (the local newspaper, the Christiania theatre) refuse to comunicate it. After much abuse, bloody but unbowed, both doctors affirm their refusal under any circumstances to give up their struggles to communicate the truth.

Doctor Stockmann was Ibsen's first authentic hero since Brand. Like Brand, he comes down from the mountains (Nordland, in the far north of Norway) where he has been in practice for some years before returning to his home town. To reinforce for his audience the kind of environment he has in mind (southern, coastal, Norwegian) Ibsen introduces by reference or in person three characters from his previous plays with a contemporary, small-town setting, Stensgård and Aslaksen from *The League of Youth*, and Rørlund from *The Pillars of Society*. The device highlights the peculiar natural advantage it was to him as a dramatist to have grown up in Norwegian society,

a perfect miniature society in which the power structure was trans-
lucent, the seats of power easily identifiable and approachable, and
in which political and moral issues could be encompassed, symbolised and discussed in a way that was more difficult in larger countries
with more diffuse and mysterious power structures like England,
Germany or France.

Other evidence of the pleasure Ibsen took in the act of creating
emerges in his correspondence with Schrøder at the Christiania
theatre over the forthcoming production. His characters were real
people to him, with personal histories the public need never know
anything about but which were necessary to him in the creative act
and which would, he hoped, be equally useful to director and actors
working with them. Schrøder learnt that Hovstad, the editor who
at first supports Dr Stockmann and offers to print his article but
then changes his mind, 'comes from a poor farming background,
grew up undernourished in an unhealthy home, has been cold,
suffered all through his childhood ... Such an upbringing leaves
its marks on the outer as well as the inner man ... It is essential
that there be some sense of being burdened about him, something
shrivelled or stooped in his bearing, an uncertainty in his move-
ments.'[10] The note reveals the determinist nature of Ibsen's psychology, as the slight objection he raised to the news that Arnoldus
Reimers had been cast as the doctor revealed his belief in a correspondence between appearance and character – 'nor does Herr
Reimers' build correspond to a temperament like Dr Stockmann's;
hot-headed people are generally thinner ... he will have to make
himself as thin and little as possible.'

On 31 December he wrote to protest at the news that Stockmann's
two sons were going to be played by young women. This might do
in a vaudeville or a light romance where the suspension of disbelief
was hardly an aim, but in a play like *An Enemy of the People* 'each
member of the public must feel as though he were invisibly present
in Dr Stockmann's living room; everything here must be real; both
boys included'. But with a final message of good luck to the company
and the director Johannes Brun he left them to it.

The plot of *An Enemy of the People* is a simple fable of good and
evil. The town is known for its remedial baths to which visitors and
tourists flock in the season. Dr Stockmann has noticed a rise in
stomach disorders and typhoid among his patients. Suspecting that
the baths may be polluted by the effluent from a tannery he sends

a sample off for analysis. The results prove him right and he proposes that the baths be closed to remedy the problem. The bath authorities, led by his own brother, oppose him, fearing to lose their livelihood. He writes an article, but the newspaper refuses to publish it. He holds a public meeting at which he proposes to read the article to the people, but the meeting is hijacked by a conspiracy of his opponents. His landlord evicts him and his family. In a final twist his own father-in-law (the owner of the offending tannery) tries emotional blackmail, with the aim of getting him to announce that his analysis was mistaken. All is in vain. The doctor will not bow. As the curtain falls he gathers his wife, his daughter and his two boys around him and announces his discovery: 'the strongest man in the world, that's the man who stands most alone'.

Ibsen uses short cuts to establish at the outset Stockmann's heroic status, and secure our acceptance of the absolute rightness of his position on all matters. One is the doctor's repeatedly expressed but hopelessly improbable belief that the townspeople will actually be *happy* at his news that the baths are diseased. He even toys with the notion that in their gratitude they will offer him a rise, which he plans to refuse.

Another is the use of a device familar from *A Doll's House*, of giving his main character an opponent or opponents of inexplicable malevolence. Peter Stockmann is a character from the Ibsen gallery of anal-retentives that includes Rørlund, Torvald Helmer and Pastor Manders, who define themselves in delivering not dialogue but crude statements of impersonal, unlovely and unshakeable dogma. Any cool assessment of Peter's response to his brother's news will find him as evil a character as Bishop Nikolas in *The Pretenders*, but a far less convincing human being.

A third trick is Ibsen's way of deindividualising *all* the hero's opponents: Hovstad is not Hovstad, with Hovstad's opinions, prejudices and strengths but 'a journalist.' 'We journalists', he says by way of prefacing his opinions. Aslaksen is not Aslaksen but 'a homeowner'. 'We homeowners', he says. Whatever he says, it is because he is a homeowner. Thomas Stockmann also generalises, but in more subtly glamorous fashion, not as 'We doctors', but 'We frontier fighters' (i.e. in the battle for truth).

With battle lines drawn the issue then develops with great rapidity away from the matter of human life and actual human death that the diseased waters represent, and become an abstract struggle between the Truth (Stockmann) and the Lie (everybody else). This abstraction of the debate is accepted at once by all parties, creating a curious sensation of collusion among the characters, as though they came directly from a meeting with Ibsen at which the abstract approach had been agreed upon. And because Ibsen really wants to talk about truth and lies, Stockmann soon forgets about the disease, the typhoid, the potential real deaths of the real tourists. His aim is no longer to save lives but to 'wash clean society', 'to disinfect it'.

Having taken control of the audience's sympathies Ibsen can then allow Dr Stockmann to take the angry plunge towards the heart of the play. Some of the doctor's contempt for others has aleady emerged in a gratuitous remark about his patients in Nordland being such a low form of life that what they really needed up there was 'a vet and not someone like me'. Shortly afterwards he is turning the southern yokels into dogs:

> Imagine first of all a common, ordinary dog – that is, one of those disgusting, mangy, vulgar mongrels who does nothing but run about the streets peeing on walls. Then compare this mongrel with a poodle, from a strain who for several generations past has lived in a distinguished house, with excellent food to eat, where it has had the opportunity to hear harmonious voices and music. Is it not obvious that the cranium of the poodle develops quite differently from that of the mongrel? I can assure you it is!

He expands his example, explaining that it is actually a social philosophy:

> All right; but as soon as I extend the law to cover the two-legged, Herr Hovstad refuses to follow. He no longer dares think his own thoughts, no longer dares follow them to their logical conclusion. He turns the whole theory upside down and proclaims in *The People's Messenger* that the ordinary farm hen and the street cur – here are the finest examples our menagerie has to show. But that is the way things will always be, as long as one still harbours the plebeian inside, as long as one has not worked one's way up to spiritual distinction.

His audience cries out in protest, 'What? You mean you're turning us into dogs?' 'But we aren't dogs, Doctor!' The doctor assures them they are wrong, we are all animals, 'but there are not, of course, too many aristocratic animals among us. Yes indeed, there is an almost frightening gulf between the poodle-type and the mongrel-type.' The scene recalls the richly comic moment in Holberg's *Erasmus Montanus*, in which Rasmus uses sophistry to turn his terrified mother into a stone. But Ibsen's scene is not comic, because he forgets that Erasmus Montanus was Holberg's fool, not his hero.

Stockmann's status as a man of science is supposed to give authority to his eugenic theory and support his claim to be ethically prescient, a member of the minority, of the intellectual and moral *avant garde*. It is their ignorance of such theories, not their ability to tell right from wrong, that is the real sign of the crowd's contemptibility. As such it casts a doubtful light on the doctor's instincts for the coming ethics, since the 'scientific truths' of these eugenics are to form the basis of the creation and promotion of a society characterised by that 'spiritual distinction' which Ibsen consistently described as his great dream of the future. Its anti-democratic preaching, and a eugenic theory that the Nazis later rendered scandalous, mean that *An Enemy of the People* is now an embarrassment to many of Ibsen's admirers, as well as a disappointing betrayal of the motto expressed in the marvellous 'Letter in Rhyme': 'I prefer to ask; my call is not to answer'. What makes it rescuable and still performable is the accepted plasticity of the dramatic form, something Satyajit Ray's film version of 1989 demonstrates. By dropping the eugenics and with a touch of genius turning Norwegian spa waters into the holy waters of an Indian temple Ray was able to reveal the nobility latent in the play and the character.

Beyond calling them subjective and shifting, Ibsen's ethics are by this time hard to pin down. Sometimes, as in *A Doll's House*, he could appear almost divinely humanitarian. Yet *An Enemy of the People* bears a monstrous, misanthropic vision. Stockmann and Nora as heroes both illuminate a common characteristic of the Ibsen outsider: they must be righteous. An outsider by reason of human nature or uncontrollable personal failing was as repellent to him as it would be to any Pastor Manders. Clemens Petersen's sexual disgrace and subsequent flight to America made little difference to Bjørnson, who with nothing to gain from the admiration of a disgraced critic nevertheless kept in touch with him, encouraged him, did what he could to help him in his new life. Ibsen, who was at the time in the throes of breaking with Bjørnson, had nothing good to say about him. In a letter to a third party he noted, with obvious reference to the Clemens Petersen scandal, that Bjørnson consorted with 'the kind of people after whom I would have the floor swept if they set foot in my room.'[11]

Yet in a public-voice letter to Bjørnson some fifteen months after the publication of *An Enemy of the People* he could write something like this:

> If I had my way back home, then all the underprivileged would get together to form a strong, resolute and aggressive party whose programme would be directed exclusively towards practical and productive reforms, a wide-ranging expansion of the suffrage, a regularising of the position of women, the liberation of lower education from all taint of the medieval etc. Questions of a politi-cal-theoretical nature could be left alone for the time being; they do not noticeably achieve anything. If such a party were to appear then the current Venstre Party would soon show itself in its true colours, as a party of the centre, which in view of its constitution it cannot but be.

Marcus Thrane's Workers' Movement, with which Ibsen had been briefly associated in the early 1850s, had offered just such a revolu-tionary programme. And though Thrane's movement was broken by the state and its leaders sentenced to long terms in jail, the socialism he had introduced did not disappear. At the time of Ibsen's letter to Bjørnson the formation of the Norwegian Labour Party was just three years away. But Ibsen's personal timidity and his posture of professional dissidence could not allow him to admit that social-ism was working for the aims he outlined to Bjørnson. Nor would his image of himself as aristocratic allow it. Ultimately what lay behind the whole inglorious façade of Dr Stockmann was perhaps nothing more complex than the commonly felt bourgeois fear of the 'masses'. In *Tante Ulrikke (Aunt Ulrikke)*, a play written at this time by Ibsen's young friend and protégé, Gunnar Heiberg, a character articulates this fear, that the mob 'will unite, rise, march, fight. Rise and destroy. Just lay waste.' For Ibsen's bourgeois audiences there must have been deep satisfaction at the spectacle of a Stockmann defying the beasts on his own. Perhaps one explanation for the puzzle of Ibsen's ethics at this time is that he was writing with two distinct, alternating voices which had somehow got mixed up and were coming from the wrong places, one – a humane one – that came from his head, and the other – a hard one – that came from his heart.

The ambiguities of *An Enemy of the People* and the enigmas of Ibsen's radicalism did not go unnoticed at home: an editorial in the *Venstre* newspaper *Verdens Gang* hinted laconically that Dr Stockmann had been living in Nordland too long and was out of touch: 'Our party system does not require, as Dr Stockmann believes, individual independence; it requires the exact opposite.'[12] But there was no repetition of the failure to communicate between writer and public this time, perhaps not least because, whatever else it was, *An Enemy of the People* was also by implication a resounding defence of marriage. The surprise came too late for treatment in one of the first books on Ibsen's work to appear, Urban von Feilitzen's *Ibsen ock äktten-skapsfrågan* (*Ibsen and the Marriage Question*).

Hegel published the play in an edition of 10,000, taking a chance that the scandal over *Ghosts* might boost the sales of its successor; but sales were only modest and no second edition was required until 1897. It was accepted for performance at all of Ibsen's usual Scandinavian and German venues. The première was at the Christiania theatre on 13 January 1883, where it ran for a respectable twenty-seven performances. For their temerity in declining to perform *Ghosts* Ibsen demanded of the theatre – and received – 4,000 kroner, twice his usual fee. For similar reasons Bergen was also charged twice the normal amount. Danish and Swedish theatres were not similarly punished.

That Ibsen played safe with *An Enemy of the People* is not surprising. In his letter to Sophie Adlersparre he wrote, apropos the debate over *Ghosts*:

> I would like to add one thing, that I am in complete agreement with you when you say that I dare not go any further than *Ghosts*. It is my own view too that the general level of awareness in our countries would not tolerate it. Nor do I feel any compulsion to go further. A writer dare not distance himself so greatly from his own people that there is no longer any understanding between them.[13]

His pragmatic and anti-romantic approach to the job of writing had not changed since his 1852 encounter with J. L. Heiberg, who taught him that a writer without a public is as useless as a shoemaker without customers. To Paulsen he once confided that 'the creative spirit functions in precisely the same way as the stomach does. You take in certain materials from the outside world, digest it, and put it back out again – that's all there is to it!'

Ibsen summed up his intentions with the Stockmann character in a letter to Georg Brandes:

> In perhaps ten years' time the majority of people will stand where Dr Stockmann stood during the public meeting. But the doctor does not remain where he is during these ten years; he is yet another ten years further ahead of the crowd. The majority, the mass, the mob will never catch up with him. He can never tolerate being in the majority. In my own personal case at least I sense the inevitability of such progress. Where I stood when I wrote my various books there stands now a large, compact group of people; but I am no longer there myself, I'm somewhere else, further on, I hope.

But ten years is a long time to be ahead of everyone else. Ibsen's real talent was to be not ten years but ten months ahead, and in the case of *An Enemy of the People* not even that. It was all opinions and so much science under the bridge anyway. Two days before the première of *An Enemy of the People*, on 11 January 1883, he wrote to Hegel announcing plans for *The Wild Duck* – 'a new play of modern times. It will be in four acts and I hope within a month or two at the latest to begin work on the actual writing.'[14]

16

Old Haunts
The Wild Duck

The year 1883 began quietly with a minor revision of his Bergen play *The Feast at Solhaug*, which Hegel published in an edition of 4,000 along with a biographical-critical Introduction by Ibsen in which he was largely concerned to deny the influence of Henrik Hertz's *Svend Dyrings Hus* on the play and to promote a recently published book, *Henrik Ibsen, Portrait of a Skald* by a Finnish admirer, Valfrid Vasenius. This was an adapation of a doctoral thesis Vasenius had written in 1880, for which he had travelled to Munich to confer with Ibsen himself. Ibsen recommended Vasenius's 'correct and exhaustive' interpretation of *The Feast at Solhaug* on the very natural grounds that Vasenius had acquired it from the author in person.

In February and March he took the time to correspond with the owners of the steamship *Dronningen* (*The Queen*), in which he had five shares. He wanted to know why the shares were not bringing in any dividends. His first letter is worth quoting in full as an excellent example of the remorseless logic of his approach to practical life:

To the board of directors of the steamship *Dronningen*.
Rome, 23 February 1883

When, in the year of 1875, an invitation was extended to purchase shares in a new steamship which it was proposed should ply the route between Kristiansand and Kristiania, this was promoted by those making the offer as a particularly promising enterprise. Trusting the good name of those making the offer and their judgement I therefore purchased five shares in the ship in question.

The two first annual reports referred to various major accidents involving the ship, and for this reason no dividends were paid out to shareholders.

Since then I have received no further annual reports nor accounts. Yet from my newspapers I see that the vessel has in the intervening period trafficked its intended route without mishap.

In spite of this, I have still not received any dividend from my shareholdings.

I find it hard to believe that a consortium of practical businessmen would be willing to persist in an enterprise which over a period of several years reveals itself to be wholly unprofitable. And yet I have not heard of any intention to wind up the company or sell the ship.

It is therefore tempting to conclude that the enterprise is to be regarded if not directly then indirectly as a paying proposition for the shareholders, all of whom, I should suppose, apart from myself, live somewhere in a line between Kristiansand and Kristiania. It is reasonable to suppose that all of these gentlemen are in the freight business and that, by using the steamship *Dronningen* with its low freight rates they find the saving so great that they do not require any more direct profit from the capital they have invested.

No objection could be raised against such an arrangement if it were the case that all shareholders benefited equally in this way. But if this really is the arrangement, then I for one have no benefit of it, since I am not a businessman and in particular not in the business of despatching or receiving freight. When I bought my shares I did so in the belief that I would see some direct and real profit from my investment.

I imagine that the annual general meeting will shortly be held and I request that the meeting be made aware of this communication.

I then request that the meeting consider whether in the name of fairness and justice it would not be right for the company either to cash in my shares or at least arrange for me to receive an annual dividend corresponding to the amount of profit enjoyed by the other shareholders on their investment.

If, however, the almost inconceivable fact of the matter is that the steamship has indeed for all these years operated and continues to operate and shows neither a direct nor an indirect profit for any of the shareholders, then permit me to suggest that the vessel be sold as soon as possible and the company wind up its affairs.

In anticipation of news of the conclusions reached at the general meeting, and informing you in addition that my postal address is: Consolato di Svezia & Norvegia. Rome – I remain, respectfully yours

Dr Henrik Ibsen.

In reply the board was able to assure him that the *Dronningen* was indeed making a profit, and that the only reason he had neither heard from them nor received his dividends was because, with his frequent moves, they had lost track of his address.

In April Sigurd left his parents to live in Paris for a few weeks to learn something of French culture and language. He was twenty-four years old, and this was the first time he had been away from home on his own. Sigurd had been Suzannah's closest companion for the almost eighteen years the family had so far spent in exile, and with a husband wedded to his work her relationship with her son had acquired a curious intensity that made his departure, though temporary, hard to bear. Her reaction must have been striking to Ibsen, who stored it away until he was ready to use it some years later in *John Gabriel Borkman*. Ibsen had his writing to keep this first sign of the break-up of his little family unit in perspective; but *The Wild Duck* was still a long way from completion. Writing to Brandes in June he told him he was still 'struggling with the draft of a new drama in four acts.'

Sigurd was back by the end of June, and all three set off once more to spend the summer in Gossensass. The opposition to *Ghosts* was crumbling fast, and much of Ibsen's correspondence that summer was with directors wishing to produce the play. Writing to one of his German translators Emma Klingenfeld in July he was already able to refer to 'the violent protests aroused by *Ghosts* in its day'. Later in the summer he told Hegel how surprised he was at the ease with which the play had overcome the initial resistance.

The summer was spent in the usual quiet fashion, working, walking, fishing, beer- and wine-drinking for Ibsen; light mountain rambling for Sigurd and Suzannah. In the middle of October, when it turned cooler in Gossensass, they again travelled down the valley to Bozen, moving in the space of a two and a half hour train ride from deep snow to a community in the throes of grape-harvesting. Ibsen had actually intended to go straight back to Rome, 'but the weather, the temperature and indeed everything down here on the Italian border is so lovely that we cannot tear ourselves away'. After a fort-night they returned to Rome, a direct, twenty-hour train ride.

A sign that Ibsen's pleasant, relaxed mood persisted is that he did little work that winter. Apologising to a correspondent for a delay of several months in answering a letter he ascribed it to the onset of 'one of those periods when only with the greatest reluctance do I sit at my writing table'.[1] But the period of inactivity was already over even as he registered it, and in the same letter he wrote that he had been out and bought himself paper, ink and a new pen, and was about to start serious work on his new play.

Once again, however, he found himself distracted by the problem of his son's future. Sigurd had decided to try to use his cosmopolitan and linguistic talents – he spoke fluent Norwegian, German and Italian – in the Norwegian diplomatic service. The difficulty was that he had scarcely been to Norway, knew no one there, knew little of the culture and so in the normal course of events would have stood little chance of achieving his aims. This was the cue for some lively string-pulling from his father.

In 1859 Ibsen and Bjørnson had together founded *Det Norske Selskab* (the Norwegian Society), to encourage national art, literature and drama. The society was short-lived, and Ibsen's involvement minimal, but a high proportion of its members went on to become serving members of government, a fact which Ibsen now put to good use. While Sigurd was in Paris Ibsen arranged for him to meet Georg Sibbern, the Norwegian and Swedish ambassador to France. Sibbern, after formally rebuking Sigurd for attempting to bypass the entrance requirements for the university, then treated him to what Sigurd described as almost embarrassingly fulsome hospitality.

Later in the year, in November, Ibsen was in action again, writing about Sigurd to the Justice Minister, O. A. Bachke. Three years earlier he had also approached Bachke when contemplating a change of nationality in protest against Sigurd's exclusion from Kristiania University, asking Bachke whether such a step would require him to renounce the annual state grant he had been receiving since 1866. Bachke's reply had persuaded him to drop the planned protest, but now Ibsen revived the issue, this time on behalf of Sigurd alone. If only you, he wrote, in your official capacity, could extract a promise from the government that my son will be considered for the next diplomatic attaché post that falls vacant, then he will proceed no further with his plans to become a natural-ised Italian.[2]

Unfortunately Ibsen's letter came at the climax of the intense and decisive struggle for political power in Norway between the union king and his appointed officials on the one hand, and the elected representatives in the *Storting* on the other. The general election of 1882 had seen a landslide victory for *Venstre*, winning eighty-three seats to *Høyre's* thirty-one. *Venstre* used the mandate to impeach the cabinet for their consistent refusal to meet in the *Storting* and make themselves accountable to the country's elected representatives. As a result of the so-called *riksrett* (constitutional court) proceedings the government was found guilty of misuse of the royal veto and all of Oskar's ministers, including Bachke, lost their jobs.

Ibsen had to look elsewhere. He turned to Baron Hochschild, the Swedish foreign minister in Stockholm: 'I hereby humbly pre-sume to address to Your Excellency a tentative enquiry, on whether my son Sigurd Ibsen, *doktor juris* at the University of Rome, might entertain hopes of being considered when next the Norwegian attaché-posts are to be filled.'[3] He explained that his son was on the point of abandoning his Norwegian nationality to become an Italian: 'This is a painful decision, and it is in the hope of obviating its necessity that I presume to address this request to Your Excellency.' And to make himself quite clear: 'If it were possible for my son to entertain hopes of being appointed to one of the attaché posts, then this summer ... he will do himself the honour of presenting in person in Stockholm his university credentials'. The necessary hint seems to have been given, and later in the year Sigurd travelled to Kristiania to join the consular service.

The knowledge that his name was operational in this fashion, that his plays, so heavily critical of Norwegian society, had not after all rendered him an outcast among the powerful, must have contrib-uted to Ibsen's prevailing good humour. It must also have relieved him to see Sigurd starting out in a prestigious career, for over the years he had dropped here and there hints that he felt some guilt at the difficulties his insistence on living abroad had caused for his son.

At about the same time Ibsen received further proof that he was a much-admired and respected figure at home when he was once again invited, through Bjørnson, to return and take up the running of the Christiania theatre. The idea may have been resurrected by comments in a recently published book, *Acting Abroad* by Edvard Brandes, published in 1881, in which he had severely criticised the standard of acting at the theatre, referring particularly to their performance of *A Doll's House*, and concluding: 'But how absurd it is that Ibsen lives in Germany when his plays are being performed in Kristiania!'[4] But Ibsen was no more disposed now than on the previous occasion his name came up to return to active involvement in production. He took the opportunity of rejecting the offer to put the boot in, complaining that 'the company are demoralised, they will not accept discipline and unquestioning obedience', though how he could have known such a thing after an absence of almost twenty years is not clear. Perhaps he was harking back to that previous occasion, in 1870, when his name had come up as a compromise candidate after several of the company had gone on strike in protest against the leadership and finally left the theatre. Ibsen showed in no uncertain terms that he was on the side of the management and not the actors,[5] and his general position remained the same in 1884: no tradition of good ensemble acting could hope to establish itself in Norway because the 'anarchic tendencies' were altogether too strong there. Later in the year, in response to a rumour in *Dagbladet* that he was indeed going to take the job, he put forward another reason – the inadequate premises – as his grounds for not accepting the post.

The real reason was surely that given in his letter of 25 June to Georg Brandes, in a paragraph that is also a statement of his personal and professional strategy as an anarchist writer who didn't deliver his bombs personally but sent them home in the post. Commiserating with Brandes on the mixed reaction to Brandes's return to settle in Copenhagen, he offered two observations: one was that people were jealous of him for having acquired a European reputation; the other was that 'it is much easier to guide a party or steer a movement from a distance than at close quarters. A personal presence in several ways and for several reasons irritates. I have studied this phenomenon, and have made use of my observations "in quite a few wars".'[6] Expertly Ibsen had made a virtue out of temperamental necessity, for above all it was his temperament that made him so ill-suited to teamwork. In a friendly and encouraging letter of April that year to Gunnar Heiberg, who was about to take over his old job as director at the theatre in Bergen, personal experience sounds bleakly through his advice: 'On no account allow any member of the company to get too close to you in your personal life.'[7]

Even with the new pen and ink *The Wild Duck* did not come easily. The worry over Sigurd and the political unrest at home created an aura of peripheral chaos that made it hard for Ibsen to concentrate. 'I hope with all my heart that the country soon settles down again,' he wrote in March,[8] explaining why in a letter to another correspondent a few days later: 'events at home occupy more of my attention than is desirable'. He worried also that an intimate, personal play such as he was writing would drown in the political debate.

But by 21 April he was able to announce the surmounting of his little block and that he was 'writing at full stretch'. A factor in this liberation may have been the visit to Rome of a relative from his birthplace Skien. This was Christian Paus, in the complex field of Ibsen's relations the son of his half-cousin, from whom he was most anxious to hear news of Skien, and in particular of his family.[9] Paus did not recall the exact date of his visit but did remember the presence of Edvard and Nina Grieg and their giving a small concert of settings of poems by Ibsen, which dates it to late March 1884. Ibsen was no music lover, as Madame de Hegermann-Lindecrone's observations show; but Grieg told a friend of how he had reacted to performances of 'Jeg kalte deg mitt lykkebud' ('I called you my lucky charm') and 'Svanen' ('The Swan') – 'he came over to the piano with *tears* in his eyes, took our hands and could *hardly* speak. He mumbled something about "this being understanding" . . .'[10] Such public display of emotion was uncharacteristic. As, during the writing of *An Enemy of the People*, he had been observed by both Heiberg and Dietrichson trying out the Stockmann role for himself, insistently moving the conversation towards Darwinian theory-making, so he was perhaps here experimentally wearing in public the hat of his next and very different doctor, Relling, and in doing so drinking his alcohol for him too.

Suzannah and Sigurd went to Norway that summer as Sigurd pursued his plans for a career in the diplomatic service. Ibsen tried another channel of political influence through the new prime minister Christian Schweigaard, head of a coalition government that lasted a mere three months as King Oskar struggled to stave off the introduction of responsible government into Norway.

In his letter to Schweigaard Ibsen stressed the fact that his years away from home had been absolutely necessary for his work, and hinted at the injustice of a situation in which the burden of this necessity should fall on his son's shoulders: 'The Hr. Statsminister will I am sure easily understand how important it is to me that my petition be granted.'[11] He was able to tell Schweigaard that he had already received a personal assurance from Baron Hochschild that Sigurd would get the job the moment Hochschild received the Norwegian government's official recommendation. Schweigaard's government collapsed in June, however, and the matter became the concern of the new, *Venstre* prime minister Johan Sverdrup.

Sigurd had an audience with him in Kristiania in mid-July. He reported that Sverdrup had spoken generously of Ibsen's importance for Norway, and praised his independence of mind. They then talked about the future, and he promised Sigurd he would do what he could to help him get a job as attaché.

Ibsen, meanwhile, had travelled to Gossensass again, taking with him a draft of the five acts of *The Wild Duck* which he had completed on 13 June. What remained for the summer was 'a more detailed revision, a more thoroughgoing individualisation of the characters and their modes of expression'.[12] He told Suzannah that he felt in good shape for the work:

As for me, I am extremely well. The journey here was the same as usual. From Modena, at night, and all the way to Ala had to wear a topcoat; then off with it again. Excellent lovely weather and fresh air up through the valley here. The sandwiches were excellent; they were my only sustenance the entire way. I ate the last of them in Verona, for breakfast, with a cup of black coffee that was brought to me in my carriage. All I had in Florence was a half bottle of wine, and in Ala in the morning nothing. I always like to take sandwiches with me when travelling, since these can be eaten with pleasure at any time of the day.

This time he chose an isolated room in an annexe at Gröbner's. No verandah, and no neighbours, 'so there is no noise; I am delighted with it'. He found it strange to be alone, but had already established a work discipline:

So far I have been getting up at six thirty, get my breakfast brought up half an hour later, then go for a walk while the room is made up, and write from nine until one. After that a meal, with hearty appetite. I have also been able to write a little in the afternoon or at least make lines.* The second act will be ready in about five or six days. I am not drinking beer, and therefore feel well. On the other hand I am drinking milk and a little but not too much white wine with water added. A light supper at six-thirty. So far I have been in bed every evening before ten and am sleeping well.

He asked them to write to him, but not long letters – 'I won't be sending long letters myself, because of course I am busy with my play, and there isn't much of interest here to write about.'

That there was little of interest to write about in Gossensass was one of the essential conditions of the place; yet in his solitude, observing his fellow guests and their children, he found plenty to amuse him. Despite his earlier warning he wrote at gentle, gossipy length to Suzannah and Sigurd: 'Rose and Paula are here this year as well, so is Peter, who has been given a porter's hat with a broad gold band round it. He wears it down to the station to meet the incoming trains . . .' A group of eight ladies – 'dreadful old eagles, painters the lot of them' – sat nearby at meal times and conversed incessantly, 'but it all takes place in whispers, so it isn't possible to find out who it is they're gossiping about'. More relevant to his purpose there was also a German sculptor there, an acquaintance from Rome who had a thirteen-year-old daughter with him. She was 'the best model for Hedvig in my play I could wish for. She is pretty, has a serious face and demeanour and is slightly *gefrässig*.'

As always, he sent his love disguised as an eruption of anxiety. Warning Sigurd about the dangers of firearms he told him that in practically every Norwegian newspaper he read there were reports of accidents caused by careless handling of loaded firearms: 'It would displease me greatly were you not to maintain a great distance between yourself and people who carry loaded weapons. In the event of an accident I must be telegraphed at once.'

Finally he found his need to impress the degree of his fame upon himself and others well satisfied by a couple of observations: 'Several copies of Pasarge's book on me and Brandes's article in *Nord und Süd*', prefaced with my portrait in a superbly executed etching, are circulating among the guests here.' And visiting a nearby town later

---

* Presumably he meant ruling lines to write on.

in the summer he noticed the 'friendly, contented faces in shop doorways and in the windows round about, as there has been a great deal about me in the Innsbruck and Tyrolean newspapers this summer'.

The aura of contentment, of working well, eating well, reflected the mood of the play he was writing, *The Wild Duck*'s unusual air of tolerance, forgiveness, acceptance of human weakness. To a young Norwegian correspondent, the writer Theodor Caspari, he wrote that he had 'long ago ceased to make demands that are universally applicable, because I no longer believe that such demands can in good conscience be made.'[13]

The second act of *The Wild Duck* was finished on 12 July and the third started on the fourteenth, he wrote to Sigurd. He had made minor adjustments to his routine and remained in splendid spirits:

My daily routine remains as I have previously described it to you, the only difference being that I have had to give up drinking the local wine, which did not agree with me, and drink now instead an excellent Hungarian Carlowiz which, strange to relate, costs exactly the same. In the morning I drink tea at seven o'clock precisely. I am up at the latest by six, often earlier and feel extremely well on it, though I do not now go to bed until eleven. Everything I eat tastes extremely good to me. This year I am paying only sixty kreuzer a day for this pleasant, quiet room. My expenses, including tobacco and laundry, are around fifty francs a week. So every Sunday morning I change a fifty-lire note, which lasts me until the following Sunday. My provisions I pay for every day.[14]

The third act was finished by the end of July, the fourth and the fifth by the end of August. 'The range is wide,' he told Suzannah, 'broader than any of my recent plays. I have managed to include everything I wanted to, and I really do not think it could have been done better.'

He then read it through once again and on 2 September sent it off to Hegel, with a covering letter mentioning how much he had enjoyed the work. Declining to be specific he nevertheless revealed to Hegel that his working methods for *The Wild Duck* had differed in several respects from those used for earlier plays. He was also satisfied that it had its quota of debating points and enigmas: 'The critics will I hope discover what I mean; in any case, they will find plenty of scope for argument and interpretation.'[15]

Then, with his nineteenth full-length play out of the way, he boarded the train for the three-hour ride to Schwaz, where Bjørnson was staying with his family, to try to put an end to their mysterious feuding. As he told Bjørnson: 'It is now over twenty years since we last spoke together, and I had almost given up hope of our ever meeting again.'[16]

The history of their on-off feud goes back to the humiliating sense of obligation Ibsen felt for the financial support and encouragement Bjørnson afforded him in the difficult times before and just after his emigration to Italy. The first sign of Ibsen struggling to free himself from this was the furious letter he wrote Bjørnson in 1867 for failing to stop Clemens Petersen from writing a lukewarm review of *Peer Gynt*. Yet civilised letters continued to pass between them after this, and it was not until Ibsen used Bjørnson's mannerisms and figures of speech to flesh out the cheaply opportunist politician Stensgård in *The League of Youth* that the break became *de facto*. Even then Bjørnson, with his massive and inviolable self-confidence, scarcely took the proper kind of offence. He deeply regretted the attack on the nascent party-political system that was the main point of the play, but at a personal level he was more disappointed and puzzled than anything else. Writing to Hegel, Bjørnson referred to 'the offence which all these writers in the north are instantly prepared to take the moment my name is mentioned', adding that 'it has become comic to me'.[17]

About a year later, in March 1870, Bjørnson wrote to thank Hegel for a friendly greeting passed on to him from Ibsen, adding, 'I like him, in spite of all he says and does. The latest is apparently that I criticise him behind his back!' Ibsen's habitual reticence as a letter-writer led him to express his dramatically fluctuating ill-will towards Bjørnson without ever explaining the precise nature of his grievance. In March 1870 he wrote to Hegel that he would like to dedicate the new edition of *The Pretenders* to Bjørnson. Two days later he wrote withdrawing the suggestion.The motives he offered for his change of heart were bewildering. One minute it was because of 'something' contained in a letter just received from Kristiania. The next it was because Bjørnson's name was currently so controversial in Kristiania that such a dedication could only harm the sales of the book and Hegel's reputation as a publisher. Then in the next breath he insisted that there was nothing he would like more than reconciliation with Bjørnson.

But the feud only deepened with the outbreak of the so-called *signalfeid* (signals-feud) in 1872 and 'Signals from the North', Ibsen's poem in which he accused Bjørnson of professional self-interest in advocating better relations with Germany. By the mid-1870s the breech seemed irreparable. Georg Brandes, knowing both men, advised his correspondents who were about to meet either of them on no account to mention the other by name.

In 1877 Ibsen once more tried to re-establish good relations, sending a copy of *The Pillars of Society* to Bjørnson as a gift 'to your wife'.[18] A month earlier, in an ambivalent counter-gesture, he had sent a copy to King Oskar, recommending it as 'a timely piece of work'[19] and a passionate defence of the union monarchy: 'From another quarter a recent piece of writing has attacked those institutions which are an integral part of our national past, and on which all our human welfare and progress depend.' The 'other quarter' was Bjørnson, the piece of writing was *Kongen* (*The King*), published four months earlier, and the institution under attack was the monarchy. Bjørnson's theme was so controversial that no theatre would touch the play.

Two years later, in 1879, it was Bjørnson who attempted to heal the rift. Always much more the active politician than Ibsen, he had written asking for Ibsen's support in a campaign to get the Swedish insignia removed from the Norwegian flag, an obvious stage in the growing agitation for complete independence from the Swedish crown. Ibsen, without invoking his strongly monarchist sympathies, nevertheless declined to lend his name to the campaign. Unaware in his exile of the strength of feeling on the matter of Norwegian national independence, he complained that it was 'a crime against our people to make burning questions out of questions which are not burning'. He would much prefer, he said, a campaign to improve the general standard of education in Norway, one which would enlighten minds: 'Let the mark of the union stay where it is; remove instead the mark of the cloister from people's minds.'

Bjørnson was briefly in Munich that winter to attend rehearsals of his play *Leonarda*. Magdalene Thoresen, who retained a lifelong erotic fascination with Bjørnson, was staying with the Ibsens at the time and very much hoped he would visit. The Ibsens' reaction was more ambivalent. As the days slipped by John Paulsen noted an atmosphere of almost intolerable tension growing in the house over whether Bjørnson would call or not. When it finally became obvious that he would not Sigurd Ibsen went to the Café Probst to see Bjørnson for himself – Bjørnson was, after all, his godfather. Perhaps out of loyalty to his father he did not make his presence known but only sat and watched. Profoundly impressed, he later compared him to an emperor. Bjørnson left without visiting, and Paulsen later wrote a newspaper article on the nearly-event, eliciting a public letter from Bjørnson in which he said that his failure to visit was solely because Ibsen's letter had 'wounded my love of country'.

It was the appearance of *Ghosts,* Ibsen's attempt to remove 'the mark of the cloister' from people's minds, that finally brought this feuding to an end. At a time when his reputation in Norway suddenly seemed to be hovering in a peculiar way, Ibsen was surprised and deeply moved by Bjørnson's unequival public defence of the play. Someone called his relationship with Bjørnson 'an unhappy love-affair',[20] and nothing shows the aptness of the description better than the flood of pent-up emotion released in him by Bjørnson's generous gesture. Bjørnson had recently returned from a lecture tour of America, where he had praised Ibsen the dramatist to his Scandinavian immigrant audiences. Ibsen wrote thanking him for this, and for his defence of *Ghosts*:

> And let me also tell you that you, all the time you were away, were scarcely ever absent from my thoughts. I was unnaturally tense at that time, and a trip to America has always seemed to me a particularly unpleasant and hazardous undertaking – Then I heard that you were ill over there, and just as you were expected back home again I read that there were storms at sea. Then it suddenly dawned on me in all clarity how very very much you mean to me, as to all of us. I felt that if something should happen to you this would be a tragedy for our country, and all the joy of work would leave me.[21]

It was of a man with something like Bjørnson's public courage that Ibsen had been thinking when he created Dr Stockmann in 1882, making *An Enemy of the People* the third play, after *The Pretenders* and *The League of Youth,* to show the importance of Bjørnson's character for Ibsen. And to demonstrate his continuing good faith after Bjørnson's defence of *Ghosts*, when Bjørnson came to him in 1884 and asked him to sign a petition to the government to bring in individual property rights for married women, Ibsen joined Jonas Lie and Alexander Kielland in doing so in a show of solidarity from the 'four great ones'. He wrote that he did so 'with great pleasure', though honesty compelled him to add that he did not expect their petition to achieve anything, and that to ask a group of men to take action on such a matter was 'like asking wolves if they are in favour of more protection for sheep'.[22] Overcoming initial opposition, however, the proposal was indeed passed in the *Storting* four years later, in 1888, creating incidentally a situation in which a dilemma such as Nora Helmer's could not have arisen.

Waiting to receive him at Schwaz in September 1884, Bjørnson probably never quite knew what it was he had said or done that had offended Ibsen so bitterly. He was a spontaneous man who would get involved in physical brawling if necessary to defend his viewpoint, yet not a man to harbour a grievance, and his part in the conduct of the feud was, in the main, to respond to Ibsen's most recent twist on it. The difference between them as types was immense. An early example was their brief exchange of letters in 1867 on their contrasting attitudes to the question of whether or not writers should accept honours from the state. An even more striking illustration was in their respective modes of addressing Hegel. Ibsen stuck to *Kære herr Cancelliråd Hegel, Kære herr justisråd Hegel, Kære herr etatsråd Hegel* etc, (Dear Herr Minister Hegel, Dear Herr Justice Hegel, Dear Herr Secretary Hegel),* while Bjørnson experimented with a whole range of salutations such as *Nej, du søde forførende rådgiver*, (Oh come now, you sweet, seductive advisor), *Aller-slæmmeste mænneske* (Worst of all human beings), *Å, du kurrende due i skovgården* (Oh, you cooing dove in the woodlands) and so on.[23]

The best explanation for the feud is the one that involves this collision between Bjørnson's imperturbable self-assurance and Ibsen's all-too perturbable and fragile sense of self-worth that insistently turned itself inside out to appear as vanity.† Ibsen gave a near-explanation in a letter of 27 December 1869, to the Danish writer

* These are all honorary titles and difficult to give good equivalents for.
† Bjørnson would have none of the psychoanalytical explanation. On the subject of Ibsen's fondness for orders he wrote to Brandes in 1878: 'People excuse Ibsen by saying that he comes from a humble background, that he *needs* them for his own self-respect. Yes, yes.'

Rudolf Schmidt in which he referred to himself as 'one whom he (Bjørnson) has publicly and in the presence of numerous people insulted in the most shameful manner'. Paulsen had the details: in the course of a lecture in Denmark Bjørnson had occasion to tell his audience that 'In Norway we still have a chieftain class and a servant class. Ibsen is a member of the latter.'

For Ibsen, whose proudest claim was that his was an aristocratic nature, nothing could have been more hurtful, more wounding, nothing more calculated to arouse a cold, lasting rage sustainable through a decade and more. Social status meant everything to him. Writing to thank Brandes for an article on him in 1882 he was at pains to point out that Brandes' description of his family background as modest was inaccurate: 'On both sides we are descended from some of the most respected families in Skien.'[24]

By 1884 Ibsen had achieved so much that a great deal of this class complex had disappeared, leaving as its visible trace the row of medals and ribbons across his frock-coated chest. His letter to Bjørnson after *Ghosts* made what was obviously intentional use of words like *høvding* (chieftain) and *kongelig* (regal) in his thanks. He was gracefully signalling to Bjørnson the death of his 'Skule-complex', because it was now abundantly clear to him that though he might never be a great king he was a great writer, and that it was essentially the better thing to be. He paid Bjørnson the neatly enigmatic compliment of telling him that his – Bjørnson's – epitaph would be that 'his life was his best work'.

Ibsen approached the meeting at Schwaz cautiously, declining the room prepared for him by the Bjørnsons and lodging in a nearby hotel, where he ate breakfast alone. His other meals he ate with the Bjørnsons, whose hospitality towards him knew no bounds. Jonas Lie was expected to join them but absented himself due to pressure of work, giving Ibsen unrestricted access to Bjørnson during their three days together. They discussed literature, politics, and numerous other matters. 'I would not have missed the meeting for anything,' he told Suzannah. Bjørnson's respect for Ibsen's talent was unwavering, and Ibsen took an innocent pleasure in how struck Bjørnson was by some of his utterances, noting how he came back to them again and again in the course of their conversations. Ibsen felt, as he later told Jonas Lie, that 'I understand him now much better than before'.[25] Bjørnson sent a brief account of their meeting to Hegel:

My meeting with Ibsen (who has grown old!) was very warm; he is now a good, well-meaning old gentleman with whom I disagreed over many things in our attitude towards life and conduct. But it was extremely interesting to trade opinions with him. His intelligence is unusually rich in calculation, foresight and shrewdness; but it is not a versatile intelligence, nor is his learning versatile.[26]

The year ended well. In October Hegel wrote to tell him that he intended to publish *The Wild Duck* on 13 November in a healthily large edition of 8,000, and a few days later Ibsen was joined in the mountains by Sigurd and Suzannah. Their summer in the north had been rich in experiences, not all of them pleasant. The Hegels had invited them to dinner at their country house as they were passing through Copenhagen, and the arrival, presumably unexpectedly, of John Paulsen, now that his *The Pehrsen Family* was on the market, caused an air of deep embarrassment to settle over the proceedings. 'I spoke to him' wrote Suzannah, 'but he and Sigurd did not exchange a single word.'[27]

The best news was that the campaign to get Sigurd into the diplomatic service had worked, and neither he nor Ibsen were forced, after all, to become Italians. He travelled back to Kristiania at the end of October, leaving his parents to close the long summer together in Bozen. They returned to Rome on 13 November, in time for Ibsen to deal with correspondence relating to imminent productions of *The Wild Duck* in Bergen, Kristiania, Helsinki, Stockholm and Copenhagen. The book of the play sold out within a month and Hegel published a second edition in December. Ibsen's name was again mentioned in connection with the direction of the Christiania theatre, and he was again in the happy position of being able to refuse the job. Most importantly for him he knew, even before he left Gossensass, what he was going to write next. He told Hegel that he 'felt pretty nervous and overworked' by the time he had finished *The Wild Duck* and had decided to take a year off. But that was yesterday: 'I have, you see, already got the basic outline of a new play in four acts and I hope before long, once I have settled back in Rome, to take the necessary steps to complete it.'[28]

The plot of *The Wild Duck* uses the same basic situation as *Ghosts* but seen from the perspective of a different set of characters. Before the play begins Gina Ekdal worked as a maid at the Werles' mansion. When she became pregnant by the master she was married off to a dupe, Hjalmar Ekdal, who has raised Hedvig in the belief that she is his own daughter. An old friend of Hjalmar's youth, Werle's son Gregers, returns after an absence of many years. Realising what has happened he persuades Hjalmar that it will be better for all concerned if the truth comes out into the open. The truth proves too explosive, however, and the play ends in tragedy, with Hedvig taking her own life.

Even with its tragic end, *The Wild Duck* is the most human, charming, and humorous of all Ibsen's plays set in modern times, and the uneasy juxtaposition of comedy and tragedy in *Ghosts* functions here perfectly, as Ibsen lulls us into believing fate would not dare turn its hand against a gently pretentious buffoon like Hjalmar, only to present us with the death of Hedvig.

He again made extensive use of theories of genetic heritage to give him a tight plot, and involved an interesting biographical twist in his recipe with the creation of an off-stage dream-world, 'the dark loft', where the duck is kept and where Hedvig shoots herself. The image comes from the loft of the house at Venstøp, where little Henrik and his brothers slept, with the living room below them. The radiant of uncertainty at the heart of *The Wild Duck* is the truth about Hedvig's origins. In search for some basis in fact for Ibsen's own suspicion, related to Due and Schulerud, that his real father was not Knud Ibsen at all but Thormod Knudsen, it is not hard to imagine the young Henrik lying awake up there one night and hearing, through the floorboards, a quarrel between his father and mother, Knud drunk, looking for a way to hurt Marichen and pretending he couldn't even say for sure whether Henrik was his own son or the son of her old flame Knudsen. And Henrik upstairs burying this prickly, incredible possibility deep in some mental pit, where it stays for the next forty-five years, slowly edging its way up towards the surface to re-emerge in *The Wild Duck*. The uncertainty that surrounds factual issues in so many of his plays, pivotal uncertainties such as the doubt introduced into *Ghosts* about who really started the fire at the children's home, may have its origins in a first great experience of childhood uncertainty like this.

Ibsen expanded the number and range of his characters for *The Wild Duck*, and with the exception of scenes involving Gregers Werle, who makes over-explicit use of the duck-symbol, it contains the best and most natural dialogue he ever wrote. In Dr Relling, who has links with Brand's worldly opponent, the Sheriff, Ibsen introduced a character with a sufficient flexibility of imagination to change and humanise the stark 'good' and 'bad' oppositions of his recent dramatic worlds. If Stockmann and Relling are both closer to psychiatrists than medical doctors, then Relling is the better doctor, in his indulgent and understanding approach to human weakness closer to a modern psychotherapist than the harsh, 'pull-up-your-spiritual-socks' Stockmann. He treats people differently, each according to his or her needs, keenly aware of the dangers of uncontrolled spiritual pretentions. Don't try to become yourself, is his message, because you are yourself already. A complex man, he believes in the values of simple realities. He sees at once the threat posed to the Ekdal household by the arrival on the scene of Gregers Werle, a failed poet wielding with massive irresponsibility his duck symbolism until finally he kills Hedvig with it. Relling's humanitarian realism is salutory. *Ghosts* does not have a doctor among its characters, but had Relling wandered in out of the rain one night, as he might well have done, to pay a social call at Rosenvold, he would have told Fru Alving and Pastor Manders in no uncertain terms that the essential thing to remember about the orphanage was that it was a place to shelter orphans, and only secondarily a barometric symbol of the state of Captain Alving's reputation.

Hjalmar Ekdal has links with Peer Gynt, as Gina his wife has something of Solveig's tolerance of her man's pretentions. But Solveig is a fantasy figure. Gina is a working-class woman, a housemaid who has had to survive the experience of being seduced by her employer, and her life wisdom is deeper than Solveig's. It is also deeper than Nora's, though one imagines she and Fru Alving would feel an immediate sympathy with one another. Unlike Relling she neither could nor would give an intellectual justification for her way of being, she simply lives it out. John Paulsen, commenting once on Ibsen's knowledge of French literature, said that he believed it to be practically non-existent, apart from the fact that Ibsen knew and loved Madame de Staël's famous dictum, 'To understand all is to forgive all'. Ibsen told him that only a woman could have conceived such a thought.

As a fanatic Gregers Werle does not belong in the same class as Brand. Brand is magnificent in his Old Testament terribleness, Gregers is a cousin, rather, of Adjunkt Rørlund, Torvald Helmer and Pastor Manders, little men, impossible to admire, whose attachment to their ideas seems rooted in some deep psychological problem rather than personal conviction. Part of Ibsen himself may be reflected in these types: the craven, law-abiding Ibsen, terrified to transgress, abasing himself in letters to kings and minor aristocrats, deeply touched by self-hatred at his own cravenness, fervently drowning this self-hatred in a clamouring demand to be recognised as right and righteous. Letter-writing Ibsen in general – rigidly controlled, always public-voiced, terrified of self-revelation, utterly convinced of his rightness and goodness – is Rørlund-Manders-Gregers-Ibsen, jealous of other people's troubles, envious of the fruits of human weakness and of those who dare to taste them. The hidden cry of such people is always 'You shouldn't!' 'You'll get caught!' 'You'll get into trouble.' Their stilted dialogue is the stilted dialogue of the letter-writing style of Ibsen. Up against this tendency, giving these chamber plays their extraordinary intensity, Ibsen sets an opposing tendency – a Nora, a Fru Alving, a Dina Dorf, standing for freedom, for the right to be human, the right to do the wrong thing. Looked at in this light Ibsen's plays of this period dramatised an intensely personal psychological battle. In making Gregers so unequivocally his villain in *The Wild Duck* he signalled that the internal struggle at least was over, and that as the relative forbearance and tolerance of the years of *The Wild Duck*'s composition would suggest, he had achieved a kind of temporary personal harmony.

Ibsen's letter to Hegel referred to a new compositional approach to *The Wild Duck*. One aspect of this was the extensive use of interlocking dialogue, a development of that device of 'collusion' between author and characters that first appeared in *An Enemy of the People*. Here it is manifest as the willingness of two or more characters to adopt each others' metaphors and so achieve a sort of double level to the continued conversation, in which its prosaic and its 'secret' meanings co-exist. Gregers Werle's decision to treat the wild duck in the Ekdal family loft as a symbol rather than a duck is the most obvious example. Like all technical innovations, this attempt to float a metaphysical above a physical world had its pitfalls, and there is an artificiality about scenes that depend on the shared observation of the duck's dual role that can, if not played with great care, slip over into the obvious, creating a too-vivid awareness of Ibsen's creative presence on stage as the manipulator of his

22 Ibsen at a garden-party during his visit to Kristiania in 1874. Sigurd, aged fifteen, sits beside him. Suzannah is in profile on the far left of the picture. This is the only known photograph of all three Ibsens together

23 Georg Brandes, who replaced Clemens Petersen as the leading literary critic in Denmark. Brandes was an important intellectual support for Ibsen, enthusiastic but never obsequious in his encouragement for his revolutionary dramas

25 Sigurd Ibsen as a young man. Ibsen felt guilty because his life in voluntary exile had left his son without a homeland

24 Ibsen with medals in the early 1870s. After the success of *Brand* and *Peer Gynt* he changed his appearance, altering the cut of his beard and adopting a formal style of dress

William Archer.

John Paulsen

26 William Archer, whose enthusiasm for Ibsen in the 1880s laid the foundations of his enormous popularity in England

27 John Paulsen, the young Bergen writer who was briefly very close to the Ibsen family. The relationship ceased after the publication of his *roman à clef, The Pehrsen Family*

28 Gröbner's Hotel in Gossensass, where Ibsen several times spent the summer in the 1880s. Here he worked on *The Pillars of Society, A Doll's House, Ghosts, An Enemy of the People* and *The Wild Duck*

Hildur
_21 - 8 - 94._

29 Emilie Bardach, the first of several young women with whom Ibsen established intense but platonic relationships during the last years of his life

30 Hildur Andersen. After Ibsen's return to Norway in 1891 she became his regular companion during Suzannah's frequent convalescent trips to southern Europe

31 Eleanora Duse (_centre_) the Italian actress who played Nora Helmer in _A Doll's House_, Ellida Wangel in _The Lady from the Sea_, Rebecca West in _Rosmersholm_ and Helene Alving in _Ghosts_. According to Shaw, Duse 'knew Nora more intimately than Nora herself did'

32 The 'tarantella scene' from an early performance of *A Doll's House* at the Christiania Theatre, with Johanne Juell as Nora and her husband Arnoldus Reimers as Helmer

33 The first European performance of *Ghosts* in 1883, with August Lindberg as Osvald and Hedvig Charlotte Winter-Hjelm as Mrs Alving

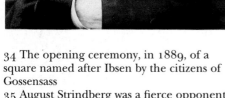

34 The opening ceremony, in 1889, of a
square named after Ibsen by the citizens of
Gossensass
35 August Strindberg was a fierce opponent
of the feminism of *A Doll's House*, yet he and
Ibsen were fascinated by one another. Ibsen
wrote his last plays with Strindberg's portrait
hanging on the wall behind him
36 Henrik Jæger (*left*) and Knut Hamsun.
Jæger was Ibsen's first biographer, and
Hamsun one of Ibsen's sharpest critics

37 Ibsen in his study in
Arbiensgate in 1898,
with a view from the
window to the royal
palace. The painting in
the middle is of Sigurd.
Here he wrote *John
Gabriel Borkman* and
When We Dead Awaken

38 A picture taken by
an American journalist
on 4 July 1905 in which
the effects of Ibsen's
several strokes can
clearly be seen

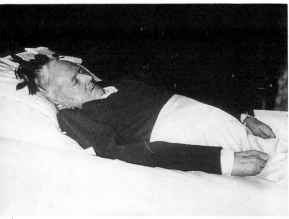

39 Ibsen in front of the statues of himself and Bjørnson outside the new National Theatre, which opened in 1899

40 Lying in state

41 Ibsen's grave in Our Saviour's, Oslo. The hammer motif was chosen by Sigurd Ibsen

characters, and a consequent sense of detachment on our part that can lessen our sense of involvement in the unfolding tragedy. The duck can sometimes be obtrusive. Twenty years earlier, in *The Pretenders*, he had used to greater effect a more subtly murmuring metaphor of crossing and burning bridges to hurry Skule on towards his fate.

In April 1885 Ibsen told Hegel that the family were not yet sure where they would be spending the summer but expected it to be the Tyrol again, where he hoped to get on with his new play. Less than six weeks later he and Suzannah arrived in Kristiania, where they stayed for almost four months. The sudden change of heart is untypical, and was perhaps the result of pressure from Suzannah, who did not share her husband's fearful dislike of his own country. No doubt he was also persuaded to change his mind by the prospect of a reunion with Sigurd, now working in Stockholm.

It was Ibsen's first visit home in ten years. On the previous occasion he had briefly thought about buying a house in Kristiania for investment purposes, and once again he found himself flirting with the idea of establishing a base there. He told Hegel that what he wanted was 'a small villa, or more accurately a country house in the vicinity of Kristiania, close to the fjord, where I could live completely apart and devote myself exclusively to my work. The sight of the sea is what I miss most out here, and this longing grows stronger by the year.'[29] He even contacted a builder and commissioned a set of drawings, but in the event his enduring ambivalence about living in Norway overcame him again and the villa was never built.

They arrived in the capital in time for Ibsen to be present on 10 June in the *Storting* for a debate on Bjørnson's proposal that the state should award an annual writer's stipend to the young novelist, Alexander Kielland. Kielland was known as a freethinker, and Ibsen was disappointed when, after heated debate, the proposal was voted down. The capital held few attractions for him, and the following day he and Suzannah boarded the train north to Trondheim, where they waited for Sigurd to join them.

While there, on 14 June, Ibsen addressed members of the *Trondhjems Arbeiderforening* (Trondheim Workers' Union) who had honoured him with a torchlight procession. His address was a typically enigmatic mixture of statements that must have puzzled and probably surprised his audience, such as the claim that the eight days he had so far spent in Norway had brought him more *livsglæde* (ordinary joy of living) than he had known in all of the years since his last visit. His speech was in essence a toned-down version of the one Dr Stockmann delivers to the gathering in the fourth act of *An Enemy of the People*. Announcing his disappointment at the failure of the new, party-based system of government to guarantee the inalienable rights of individuals in Norway, he expressed the view that democracy, such as it was, could never put right what was wrong. An aristocracy was needed, not the aristocracy of blood or money, but 'the aristocracy of character, of will, of the mind'. He placed all his hopes for the arising of such an aristocracy in two groups, the women and the workers, for these were the only two groups left in society which had not yet been hopelessly corrupted by the party political system. As a speech it was an example of his desire to run with the fox and hunt with the hounds, and it hinted in its abstraction at a final letting-go of any attempt to participate, in a practical, debating sense, in the real political issues of the day, pointing instead forward towards his own growing interest in the world of mysticism that would emerge as the new element in both of his next plays, *Rosmersholm* and *The Lady from the Sea.*

After Trondheim the Ibsens spent two pleasant months in Molde. The town met the most important demand referred to in Ibsen's letter to Hegel, it was by the fjord: 'There is a delightful fjord here, surrounded by an infinity of huge, snow-capped mountain peaks, and the vegetation is lush and almost southern.' They stayed at the Hotel Alexander, from where a local journalist reported that the couple kept to themselves, had no company, and seldom spoke to anyone. Ibsen was often seen standing on the quays outside the hotel and staring down into the water. Carl Snoilsky visited briefly, staying for four days. Another old friend, Lorentz Dietrichson, was also there that summer. Under the impression that Ibsen did not wish to be disturbed he kept his distance, a consideration Ibsen misinterpreted as insulting neglect. At the end of the summer this misunderstanding would provide Ibsen with the excuse he needed to let his brewing paranoia and unhappiness explode in a rage directed against his old friend.

Early in September the Ibsens headed south down the coast again, putting in briefly at Bergen, where Ibsen was greeted by many of his old acquaintances from the days of the first Norwegian theatre in the 1850s. He met Rikke Holst again. She visited him at his hotel, carrying a bunch of wild flowers. She was nervous. It was the first time they had seen each other for thirty years. Ibsen recognised her at once, greeted her and took both her hands warmly. He was now aged enough to address her by the informal personal pronoun *Du*. In the days when they walked out together it had always been the distancing, formal *De*. She thanked Ibsen for his plays, all of which she had read. Ibsen asked whether she had ever found traces of their former relationship in any of them and she answered no. She added with a laugh that she thought she might possibly have been in his mind when he created Pastor Strømand's wife in *Love's Comedy*, with her brood of eight children and her perpetual knitting needles. Rikke Tresselt, as she now was, was the happily married mother of fourteen children. How different, how social, how populated, how spontaneous her life had been compared to his. In his puzzlement and sadness Ibsen asked her, what had come between them, why had their relationship all those years ago come to nothing? Honest, extroverted Fru Tresselt at once reminded him of the day her father had squared up to him in the street and ordered him to stay away from her, and of how he had run away. 'Ah yes,' replied honest, introverted Ibsen, 'Face to face I have never been a courageous man.'

Continuing on to Kristiania his melancholy and paranoia increased, and on 26 September an opportunity arose to discharge it into his old friend Dietrichson. Dietrichson was then the elected president of the Kristiania Students' Union, whose members were at that particular time conservative rather than radical. They were keen to honour Ibsen on the occasion of his departure from Norway, and at a meeting a motion to request his permission to hold a torchlight procession in his honour was passed. Ibsen was staying at the Grand, the finest hotel in Kristiania, and the request was brought to him there in person by Dietrichson. Ibsen had recently declined a similar request from the Kristiania Workers' Society and in friendly fashion declined the students' offer too, observing that he did not enjoy such public appearances. Dietrichson said that the students would be very disappointed, to which Ibsen responded with the mildly paranoid joke that 'I'm sure you'll understand, I would rather not hear the students' cheers of joy at my departure.' Dietrichson reported back to the union on the failure of his mission, explaining Ibsen's dislike of public appearances, his refusal of a similar request from the workers, and extending the doctor's thanks to the students for their offer.

By the following week Ibsen was in Copenhagen, from where he astounded Dietrichson by informing him that he, Dietrichson, had misunderstood his reason for declining to receive the torchlight procession, that, in fact, he had done so because under no circumstances would he contemplate the acclaim of a students union under Dietrichson's leadership, which he considered neither radical nor freethinking enough.

Being Ibsen, of course, the absurd matter at once became public, a topic for newspaper articles, debates and public meetings from which the protagonist was, as ever, personally absent, though energetically present in the form of a seven-page public letter on the affair. The upshot of it all was that a small group of students loyal to Ibsen broke away to form the sort of union he said he was so keen to see, a circumstance which caused Ibsen to write to Hegel 'My war with the students' union has had the result I expected. Dietrichson has been swept away and a new freethinking union established.'[30] This new union was dedicated to the free and open discussion of all contemporary issues. Yet such pursuits were already old-fashioned among students, who were moving away from political and social involvement and towards the anarchic rejection of involvement preached by the bohemians. The breakaway movement soon disintegratrated and its last members voted to rejoin the main union.

The whole affair was the childish result of some personal grudge Ibsen nurtured against Dietrichson, no doubt for the imagined slights in Molde, or because Dietrichson had inadvertently been guilty of some other act of *lèse majesté*. 'Friends are an expensive luxury,' Ibsen once told Georg Brandes, and he acted as though he meant it. In 1873 he had broken with the actor Andreas Isachsen, whom he had known since his adolescence in Skien, with whom he had worked in Bergen, who had accompanied him on his walk in the mountains in 1862, because Isachsen had been giving readings from his plays without permission. That Ibsen wished to make his position on the matter very clear is understandable; what is less understandable, in what turned out to be his last letter to Isachsen, is the bullying, offensive, threatening tone in which he did it. There were other breaks, as casually manipulated. Only those prepared to see in his pettiness an ugly but necessary outcrop of his talent managed to swallow such outbursts and remain on fairly good terms with him. Bjørnson was one such, Dietrichson another. Dietrichson's private letter of farewell to Ibsen[31] over the students' union business contained no bitterness, only bewilderment and regret at the sight of a man so openly pursuing the public humiliation of an old friend. His tone left the door open for the reconciliation that took place when Ibsen returned home, for a third and last time, six years later.

By the time he finished off these dealings with Kristiania, Ibsen was back in Germany. He and Suzannah had moved to Munich, to an apartment at Maximilianstrasse 32, 'comfortable and spacious, in Munich's most exclusive and elegant street' where there was plenty of room for his collection of paintings.[32] 'We've settled in here and made it nice and cosy,' he wrote to Brandes, 'and now I start work on a new drama which I hope to finish in the course of the winter.'[33]

And still the haunted relationship continued: Ibsen had been home but not home, had not ventured the few miles from Kristiania round the coast to Skien, had avoided all contact with the members of his family. His younger brother Ole Paus Ibsen, learning from the newspapers that Henrik was in the country, wrote to him in August. Ole was only eight years old when Ibsen left home. 'I hardly knew him,' he told a journalist in 1915. 'I remember best his big mane of dark hair, and that he was quiet, just read and read all the time, or drew or painted.' Ole left home at an even earlier age than Henrik, to work as a seaman. 'There wasn't much room at home and we boys had to leave early. I went to sea even before I was confirmed.' After twenty years at sea he had moved to Brevik, where he ran a general store. Later he returned to Skien.

In his letter to Ibsen he described the last days of their mother and father, gave him news of his brothers and sister, and under the heading *Gamle Minder* (Old Memories) related the fates of their neighbours from the old days, told him who now owned the houses in which they had once lived, and reminded him of the puppet shows he used to give. He asked for a visit:

It would be so welcome, for both Jenny and me, if you, dear brother and wife, could pay us a *visit* when you come to Norway again, and maybe you will look in to Skien a bit more often. But

311

all things considered it does seem to me, in my opinion, that I miss a letter from you, dear Henrik – the first in my life. My letter is probably not worth much to you, dear brother, but you must be gentle and remember that I am no writer, but write this in simple brotherly confidence.[34]

But there was no visit and no letter. Not then, not ever.

Rasmus B. Anderson, a boastful and extroverted Norwegian-American professor who was at that time the most important cultural link between Norway and the New World, met Ibsen briefly in Copenhagen while he and Suzannah were on their way back to Germany. Two vignettes he left give a striking insight into the harried state of Ibsen's mind after sixteen tortuous weeks spent avoiding the enigmas of his past. In the first he meets him outside the Hotel d'Angleterre and is invited in. Ibsen orders two bottles of champagne, drinks most of them himself and talks non-stop about how his books are from now on going to be even more shocking, what he has written so far is only the beginning, society is rotten and needs a complete cleansing, he won't stop until he's turned society upside down – continuing in this vein until 3 a.m., at which point Suzannah entered in her nightgown and led him off to bed.

Anderson's second story describes a dinner-party at Hegel's at which Ibsen was present. Georg Brandes spoke in his honour and thanked him for exposing to his readers the ills from which society suffered. Ibsen, quiet and withdrawn throughout the evening, showed every sign of discomfort at this notion. When he was finally prevailed upon to reply he would only say that whatever he wrote was the product of his introversions. It was not society he had exposed to his readers but himself. According to Anderson, the claim baffled his fellow-guests.[35]

17

The Mystic

Rosmersholm · *The Lady from the Sea*

There were several reasons for the move to Munich. One was Suzannah's sciatica. Munich was not far from the baths at Bøhmen, where she could travel to take the waters. And Munich was cheap; their well-situated apartment cost Ibsen only half of what he had been paying in Rome. Sigurd was at last financially independent; for the past year in Stockholm Ibsen had been paying for his keep, but towards the end of 1885 Sigurd was granted a two-year stipend as attaché at the Norwegian-Swedish legation in Washington at 7,500 kroner a year, with a possibility of a third term to be added.

Ibsen had again pulled strings to obtain the posting for his son. A telegram sent to the government minister Ole Richter, on 26 September 1885, while Ibsen was still in Kristiania, urged him to 'postpone decision on the attaché stipend. My son sending his testimonials from the Foreign Ministry'[1] and Sigurd was eventually given the job, even though another young diplomat had already been accepted for the posting.[2]

Sigurd spent Christmas and New Year with his parents before leaving, via London and New York, to take up his posting in Washington in April. Not long afterwards, on 14 April, Ibsen saw *Ghosts* performed on stage for the first time, at the Stadttheater in Augsburg, where the local newspaper, in its review, inaugurated the tradition among non-Norwegians of describing Ibsen as 'the well-known Swedish dramatist'. Augsburg seems to have been the spur he needed to get down to serious work on *Rosmersholm,* the play with which he had been tinkering since his return from Norway.

He spent the summer in Munich in order finish it, abandoning his practice of recent years of heading for the Tyrol, and by 13 July had a first draft finished. The extensive rewriting process was not completed until 27 September. Then, after a final re-reading, it was sent off to Hegel.

Rosmersholm was published in good time for Christmas, on 23 November 1886, in an edition of 8,000. The first reviews were not encouraging. Hegel wrote to Alexander Kielland that the signs were that it would not sell as well as Ibsen's books usually did – 'I hear that the review in *Morgenbladet* has discouraged people from wanting to read the new play.'[3] Bjørnson, who had thought *The Wild Duck* 'repulsive' and psychologically incredible, shared a general feeling that *Rosmersholm* was thematically fascinating but not dramatic enough for the stage. Within six months it had been performed in Bergen, Kristiania, Gothenburg, Stockholm and Berlin. Its first performance in Germany was at Augsburg, on 6 April, at which Ibsen himself attended. A disappointment was the refusal of the Royal theatre in Copenhagen, under Fallesen, to stage *Rosmersholm*. This was not an artistic rejection but a matter of principle; Fallesen declined, for once, to accept Ibsen's standard demand that there be no productions of the play until it had been published in book form.

Ibsen also manufactured a few difficulties for himself in Norway, originally instructing Hegel not to offer the play to the Christiania theatre on the grounds that he did not believe the public there was mature enough for *Rosmersholm*, nor the company capable of performing it. In reply the manager, Schrøder, pointed out that 'Your plays have been performed far more times in little Kristiania than in Copenhagen or, to the best of my knowledge, in Stockholm', and quoted the figures to prove it. With Copenhagen suddenly out of the financial picture it was not hard for Ibsen to see the logic of this and he consented without further ado to their request to be allowed to put on a production, though he insisted on and got the right to cast the play himself.

The Kristiania première was on 12 April, and though artistically satisfying it managed only thirteen performances in 1887. Another three in 1889 gave it a grand total of sixteen in the life of this theatre, making it the least successful of Ibsen's plays ever to be staged there. Ibsen always liked his money in a lump sum, but on this occasion Schrøder had prevailed upon him to accept 10 per cent of the takings, pointing out that their productions of *A Doll's House* would have earned him upwards of 3,000 kroner had such an arrangment been in force. Ibsen allowed himself to be persuaded, but the box-office failure of *Rosmersholm* was a disaster for him and for later plays he insisted on reverting to the single payment.

Writing to Georg Brandes on the subject of *Rosmersholm* Ibsen told him that ' Impressions, experiences and observations from my trip to Norway last summer continued to disturb me for a long time afterwards. Only when what I had experienced became completely clear to me was I able to draw my conclusions, and put the profit of it all down in a play.' In the degree to which it is a personal, Norwegian play, *Rosmersholm* as the fruits of his experiences in Norway in 1885 marks the end of Ibsen's advocacy of the cultivation of a spiritual aristocracy, that impractical and imprecise ideal (*en halvferdig drøm* – 'a half-dreamed dream' Rosmer calls its) to which he referred so frequently in his semi-public correspondence, and in dramatic form most explicitly in *An Enemy of the People*. The trip to Norway gave him a cultural shock. Nothing in his newspapers had prepared him for the sheer violence of the passions aroused by the political revolution of 1884. The triumph of the party system and the inevitability of democracy were suddenly revealed to him as facts of life, and the sort of benevolent despotism he appeared to endorse (to judge by his letter to King Oskar accompanying *The Pillars of Society*) seemed at once an irrelevance. His reaction to these revelations was ambiguous, bringing his idea of himself as a radical artist into conflict with his innate conservativism.

Rosmersholm took shape in Ibsen's imagination as a meditation on his own position after the fact of this political revolution. The question he asked himself was: how does an apolitical idealist, an agnostic/atheist, defend his position at a time when the polarisation of opinion will tend to marginalise such a figure; at a time when influential friends urge him to make a clear statement of position for or against the democrats and reformers – especially when that man, like Rosmer, like Ibsen himself, has a name that both sides involved in the struggle are anxious to use? This last was an especially poignant issue, for Sigurd must have told his father how, the moment he had officially put on his attaché's uniform, King Oskar, in an extraordinary breach of protocol, had summoned this very junior member of the diplomatic corps and in confidence complained to him of the 'regrettable state of affairs' in Norway, sharply criticising the prime minister Sverdrup and Bjørnstjerne Bjørnson for their contribution to this. As one of Sigurd's colleagues, C. G. Fleetwood, noted in his journal, 'the King's intention was of course that his views would be communicated via the son to the father'.

On top of this Ibsen's string-pulling on behalf of his son must have made it increasingly hard for him to promote with his old self-confidence the gospel of universal self-ennoblement. Perhaps his feud with Dietrichson and his students at the end of the trip to Norway had been a sort of experiment in active political participation. If so then he can only have been, on reflection, dismayed by the banality of it. The result was a final rejection of involvement in the practical details of running society, and from about this time onwards he adopted the language and public profile of the mystical rather than the social visionary. There is a hint of the change-over in *Rosmersholm*: he explained to one critic that his reason for introducing the image of the white horses into the play was his observation that 'there is a developing fashion in literature at the moment for an element of mysticism'.[4]

Rosmersholm brings together two worlds previously kept apart in Ibsen's plays: the public, quasi-political world of *The League of Youth*, *The Pillars of Society* and *An Enemy of the People*; and the private, family world of *A Doll's House, Ghosts* and *The Wild Duck*. Though goings-on in the outside world impinge upon it so strongly, Rosmersholm – the estate – is the same kind of hermetically sealed environment as that inhabited by the Alving family. The past weighs down upon it as heavily, here in the form of portraits of Rosmer's ancestors, military men and church leaders, natural social chieftains who gaze down in perplexed wonder at the antics of the lost, gentle heir to their power.

In the continuing absence of God Ibsen had been cultivating Darwin, feeling a spiritual need for that sense of biological determinism that allowed him to replace original sin with an equally implacable genetic heritage. At least part of his project with *Rosmersholm* was to describe the fall of the blood aristocracy in the person of the indecisive and uncharismatic Johan Rosmer. Rebecca West, Rosmer's would-be lover, is also characterised in this deterministic way: her waywardness, her lack of scruple, her sensual nature are all satisfactorily explained for Rektor Kroll by the fact that she was in all probability the result of an adulterous liaison between her mother and Dr West, the man who adopted her as his own child after the death of her mother. As in the case of Thorvald Helmer's analysis of Nora's genetic heritage, and the housemaid Regine Engstrand's analysis of herself as a woman likely to end up as a whore because she is illegitimate, Ibsen appears to regard the Rektor's theory as self-evidently correct.

But as a social visionary Ibsen here accepts his defeat with a phlegmatic grace. In previous plays in which working-class characters had featured, notably in *An Enemy of the People* and lately in *Ghosts*, he chose to depict them as either weak and ultimately contemptible (Billing) or cunning and devilish (Engstrand). In neither case were they capable of understanding ideals. This viewpoint changes in *Rosmersholm*, where Mortensgård, editor of the radical local paper, is, if not a hero, at least not a villain. A new pragmatism, and perhaps also a resolution of Ibsen's long struggle to come to terms with the conflict between 'will and ability' shows through in the description of Mortensgård as a man 'without ideals' who 'never bites off more than he can chew'. For in spite of his non-aristocratic outlook, the future belongs to people like Mortensgård.

'In my view Rebecca's character is not difficult to get into and understand. But there are certain difficulties in acting and reproducing the character because it is so complex, ' Ibsen told Sofie Reimers, the actress engaged to play the part in Kristiania. Always encouraging in his address to actresses he added: 'But I do not doubt that you will overcome these difficulties if you go to life, and use life alone as the basis for your creation and interpretation of Rebecca's personality.'[5] Ibsen's fascination with Rebecca, his love almost, shows through his words, making her, with Fru Alving and Hedda Gabler, his best female creation. We hear that she is an evil woman, that she drove Beate Rosmer to suicide by lying to her that she was pregnant by Beate's husband; yet we find it hard to judge her as evil, and Ibsen makes it the easier for us to align ourselves with her by merely reporting and not showing her evil-doing. What we actually experience is an intelligent and normally sexed young woman in the process of having her sexuality and spontaneity destroyed by the lack of passion in the man she loves and desires. Rosmer's dream of greatest happiness is an 'undesiring' state, his deepest joy a state of 'silent, happy innocence'. Rebecca is a liberated woman, but as Kroll discovers, her freedom remains more abstract than real: still a spinster at twenty-nine, she is sensitive about her age; and the revelation that she may be illegitimate is a horrible prospect to her.

Rosmer is the puzzle, Rosmer and the psychology of the celibate man. There is not much doubt that for Ibsen the important factor in Rosmer's sexlessness was to offer contemporary audiences an alternative perspective on the morality of the apostate. Kroll's justification of his own ruthlessness towards Rosmer and Beate is that in renouncing their belief in Christian morality these two no longer had any morality at all. This perception of freethinking as synonymous with sexual licence was strengthened by the rise of a bohemian movement in the arts in Kristiania under the leadership of the writer Hans Jæger, who was jailed in the year of *Rosmersholm* for his 'obscene and blasphemous' novel *Fra Kristiania-Bohêmen* (*Life Among the Kristiania Bohemians*). Through the character of Rosmer Ibsen wanted to show that a freethinker could have as high a standard of conventional sexual morality as any churchgoing believer in God. Inevitably this aspect of the drama has become historical, and modern audiences are more liable to regard Rosmer's lack of sexual passion as a problem rooted in the details of his situation at Rosmersholm, with a psychological explanation to be found there. It shows clearly the way in which a combination of Ibsen's power to create tight dramatic structures harmonised perfectly with the essentially plastic nature of the form to allow the formulation of a thousand possible interpretations of his plays, none of which he need ever have intended, none of which is absolutely prohibited in terms of the text.

A slightly different example of the way Ibsen's plays encourage the reader into a creative response is the suggestion, made by Freud in an analysis of *Rosmersholm* in 1916,[6] that Rebecca has had an incestuous relationship with her father – if indeed Dr West *is* her father. The justification for the theory is the brief exchange between Rosmer and Rebecca, in which Rebecca tells Rosmer she has had an affair prior to meeting him. Freud adds this fact to her alarmed response to Kroll's suggestion that she is in fact the illegitimate child of Dr West and concludes that 'her agitation is so extreme that Kroll cannot attribute it to this information alone'. Freud, sharing Kroll's view that the response is unnaturally strong, finds in the assumption of an incestuous relationship between Rebecca and Dr West a convincing explanation for her reaction. But Kroll is the problem here, not Rebecca. Kroll has, on his own initiative, 'investigated' her background and uncovered the possibility of her illegitimacy which he now uses in his attempt to destroy her influence over Rosmer. In the course of a few seconds Rebecca's whole self-understanding has been up-ended by a cynical and cruel stranger.

Far from finding her reaction too extreme, as Freud and Kroll do, our wonder is rather that she does not attack the malevolent bully on the spot.

Freud was not sufficiently familiar with Ibsen's Kristiania to know that the contemporary reference, the one Ibsen intended by introducing Rebecca's affair, was to an ongoing *sedelighedsdebatt* (public discussion on sexual morality) in the city. By the mid-1880s the subject of the debate was the double standard, and Bjørnson's *A Glove* was the first play to suggest that a woman had as much right as a man to demand that her future partner in marriage come to her chaste. Ibsen's contribution was the complementary suggestion that to a freethinker like Rosmer the sexual past of the woman he loves is her own affair and will not affect his judgement of her as a person. The exchange also has the technical virtue of offering this argument and then ruling it out as an explanation of why Rosmer and Rebecca cannot marry.

Rektor Kroll is a straightforward character. The evil nature of his response to his old friend's apostasy, his attempt to disturb Rebecca's mind and Rosmer's peace, is justified for him by his perception that the revolution has almost triumphed when even the conservative ruling class, as represented by Rosmer, accept the analysis of themselves as oppressors. In this play, as in all Ibsen's plays of modern life, the brutal nature of competition in daily life is horrendously present, effortlessly impinging on the private sphere of the home. Every man is a Christ proclaiming that who is not with him is against him. Every man and woman is prepared to kill or destroy to achieve their ends. A psychological curiosity about Kroll is that while berating his former friend for his apostasy he himself makes smooth use of Darwinian theories of genetic heritage to explain and condemn Rebecca's behaviour.

A key figure in understanding Ibsen's changing attitudes at this time is the itinerant philosopher Ulrik Brendel, Rosmer's disgraceful, outrageous and delightful *alter ego*. He has affinities with Dr Relling, closer affinities with Daniel Hejre in *The League of Youth;* but there is more purpose in his florid verbal clowning than in that gossipy old magpie. His entry – effusively greeting Kroll in the belief that he is Rosmer – is a superb comic moment that shows Ibsen had forgotten none of the skills picked up in his years as a producer of vaudevilles and comedies in Bergen and Kristiania. Ibsen may have got the idea for Brendel from something that happened during his visit to Norway in 1885. For a joke, a Kristiania barber named Fredriksen carried out an impersonation of him in a series of restaurants and bars at a time when Ibsen was known to be in the capital. Fredriksen's resemblance to Ibsen was entirely physical. By nature he was a heavy-drinking, extroverted skirt-chaser who caused chaos throughout the course of his impersonation by telling smutty jokes and behaving with outrageous rudeness.[7] The story closely resembles events in *Rosmersholm*, where Brendel begs clothes and money from Rosmer, saying that he intends to hire a hall and deliver a philosophical lecture. The following morning comes news that Brendel has spent the night drinking in a local bar, and even pawned his jacket to pay for more drink when his money ran out. At his final reappearance he is gloriously unashamed and unabashed. Evidently the meaning of his philosophy lies in the fact that he preferred to spend the evening drinking rather than lecturing in Rosmer's old clothes in the vain attempt to improve people. Ibsen, with his religious cast of mind, always needed something to believe in, even when God was gone; yet when Brendel speaks of his feeling of 'homesickness for the great void' he hints at an existential vision of the sort Professor Rubek is still hinting at in Ibsen's final play, of a flat, entirely physical world, in which all you see is all there is. Brendel comes to Rosmer to parody his idealism and his desire to 'intervene in life with decisive effect'. He comes to teach him that the future of society is in the hands not of high-minded urgers but of tactically talented doers like Peder Mortensgård. And he points to the common decency in Mortensgård – it was Mortengsård, *plebeier* (the common man), who paid to get Rosmer/Brendel's coat out of hock again. Brendel's hilarious and melancholy disparagement of the way of the idealist is the first sign since *Emperor and Galilean* of the persistence of Ibsen's gnawing self-doubt about the rightness of his chosen course through life, and about its effect on his personal happiness, a self-doubt that he would confront most nearly in *When We Dead Awaken*.

A diversion that winter was an invitation from Duke Georg of Saxe-Meiningen to attend his company's private performance of *Ghosts* on 21 December. The duke's power in Saxe-Meiningen was subordinate to directives from Bismarck's government in Berlin, but his status was such that he was allowed to retain the right to decide on the moral value of works of art in his little state, and it was this anomaly that allowed him to stage the play. Ibsen spent four days with him, leaving on 19 December. In a letter to Suzannah he described his reception, how the duke sent his *hofmarschallen* with the *hofekvipage* to meet him at the station, personally showing him to his living quarters in the castle grounds, consisting of 'four colossal rooms with every conceivable comfort'. 'I have a lackey who is entirely at my personal disposal,' he wrote, adding that 'P. Lindau, R. Voss and Hans Hopfen are here as guests too, but they live underneath, and not nearly in the same style as me'. It was indeed a very long way from the dispensary-cum-bedroom which had been his home in the apothecary days in Grimstad.

There was heavy snow falling, he told her, but he hadn't been out, though a carriage had been placed at his disposal. The *hofmarschallen* had sent him his card, and Ibsen had sent his to the various courtiers, but 'visiting in person is not expected', he added with an almost audible sigh of relief. Suzannah appears to have been in the wars while Ibsen was away, and he concluded by asking her how her eye was, and hoped that a blow she had recently received to the mouth was healing.

He was home again on the twenty-third, with a decoration from the duke, who promoted him from a Knight to a Commander First Class of the duke's *Hertuglige Sachsiske Ernestiner Husorden*. He now had seven of these decorations. In the poignant, childlike letter of thanks he wrote to Duke Georg after his return home he reinvoked that old adolescent image of himself as the Icelandic skald, serving his prince with his pen in return for gifts and honour.

Shortly after returning to Munich he was off again, this time to Berlin to attend another private performance of *Ghosts* on 9 January at the Residenz theatre. He did not particularly want to go but felt under an obligation to support those trying to help the play. Besides the performances Ibsen had atttended at Augsburg the previous year and at Meiningen, *Ghosts* had also been played in Berlin on 2 January by the Berlin Dramatic Society. A plan for an open performance of the play was rejected by the Berlin police, but *Ghosts*'s notoriety saw the German edition of the book selling in such large quantities that a new edition of 5,000 copies had to be ordered from Leipzig. Ibsen's translator and his main advocate in Germany, the Dane Julius Hoffory, wrote afterwards that the audience took some time to get used to the tense, static nature of the drama, but that by the end 'not one of those present remained unmoved by the power of this great play, and when the curtain fell there was a salvo of applause unprecedented in the theatre, nor did it cease until the dramatist and players, time after time, had acknowledged the storm of applause.'[8] The performance marked the arrival of Ibsen as a superstar in Germany.

Apart from such outings Ibsen's life during these years was entirely dominated by routine and a self-discipline that was gradually becoming obsessional. Every afternoon he would leave his apartment in Maximilianstrasse and for ninety minutes or so walk the streets of Munich, always wearing a long Ulster, top-hat, gloves and carrying an umbrella, watching people, stopping wherever a crowd gathered to share in their curiosity, ending his walk at half past six with a drink in the Café Maximilian just down the road from his apartment, second or third table down from the entrance, with a dark ale or a little cognac and soda water to sip while he read his newspaper. Sometimes he seemed to be using the paper as a displacement object for what he was really reading – the people coming and going around him. He stayed an hour, never more, then called over the waitress, paid his bill, took up his umbrella and made his way home with short, silent strides. It was a life that suited him, a writer's life. There were few Scandinavians living in Munich anyway, although now and then he did get a visit. R. B. Anderson visited him that spring. He came unannounced and on being shown up (the Ibsens had a maid, Lina) found a round table in the middle of the room on which stood decanters of sherry and port. There were two chairs at the table, two glasses and a tray of cakes. Suzannah fetched a third glass and chair for him. They drank wine, ate cake, and Anderson smoked. It was eleven o'clock in the morning. 'Is this your daily custom to drink wine and eat cake at this time of day?' he asked. 'No, it is not our daily custom,' replied Suzannah; 'but it is my husband's birthday and we are celebrating it in this way. I am glad that you have come to join us in the celebration.' Afterwards Anderson reflected on what seemed to him the poignancy of the situation: Ibsen at fifty-nine, hugely famous and yet celebrating his birthday in this lonely fashion. The Victorian Anderson thought it would make an excellent subject for a large painting.

In the summer the Ibsens travelled north to Jutland. Ibsen had mentioned several times in correspondence to Hegel how much he missed the sight of the sea and the taste of sea air in his lungs and this seems to have dictated his choice of resort. What may have happened is that Suzannah, whose homesickness for Norway was now acute, wanted to spend the summer there, and Denmark was the compromise they agreed on. In a letter to Jonas Lie in January Ibsen mentioned their intention of staying in Skagen, a place much favoured by Scandinavian painters. 'The great open sea attracts us powerfully,' he wrote, 'but as for me I at least won't be going to Norway.'

The Skagen plan was abandoned and instead they began the summer in Frederikshavn. Ibsen enjoyed the maritime atmosphere of the place, wandering about among the ships and talking to the sailors. Perhaps it put him in mind of Grimstad. Suzannah was not so content. She found the sight of Norwegian steamers berthed there a perpetual temptation, and complained of the lack of decent walks in the area. As a second compromise they moved along the coast to nearby Sæby, where they stayed for some two months. 'It is a small, friendly town a few miles from Frederikshavn, by the open sea with gorgeous woodland all around,' he wrote to Nils Lund. 'The railway doesn't come here and in consequence there are few tourists, but all the more peace and quiet.'[9] It seemed to him a world away from 'that horrible summer we spent in Norway two years ago'.

William Archer and family were on holiday in Norway that summer, and hearing that Ibsen was in Jutland Archer took the boat over from Larvik to see him. He stayed the night at a Frederikshavn hotel and the next day drove over to Sæby in a trap belonging to a fellow-guest. It was

a perfect summer day, the corn ripe all round, the wild flowers brilliant, the Cattegat dancing in the sunlight . . . at last we rattled over a bridge, past a lovely old watermill, into the quaint old main street of Sæby – one-storey houses, with great high gables, all painted brightly or at the very least white-washed. The moment we were over the bridge, I saw a short, broad figure ahead in an enormously long surtout and a tall hat made of silk looking too small for his immense head. It was Ibsen, evidently on the lookout for me.'[10]

During Archer's short stay there they had pleasantly inconsequential conversations about Norwegian, Danish and Irish politics. Archer jotted down Ibsen's observations on the subject of symbolism, 'that life is full of it, and that, consequently, his plays are full of it', and several examples of Ibsen's amusement at the creative response of certain critics to his plays, quoting one who believed Manders was a 'symbol for mankind in general', and another who thought the character of Makrina a key to understanding *Emperor and Galilean*, when Ibsen had introduced her simply because she was the sister of Basilios.

In late August the Ibsens returned to Frederikshavn, and Suzannah took one of the steamers home to Norway for a short stay. Ibsen remained to greet his first official biographer, Henrik Jæger, who was writing a book about him for Hegel. The plan was to publish the book to coincide with his sixtieth birthday celebrations in 1888. The idea had been mooted earlier during a visit Jæger paid to Ibsen in Munich, when Ibsen 'expressed neither approval nor disapproval' since, as he explained to Hegel, 'I could not, of course, know what he intended to write about me'.[11] His basic feeling was that he didn't want it done. He explained to Hegel that he had only suggested delaying publication until 1888 as a way of buying time: 'The best thing I could wish for as regards the milestone in my life which I reach next year is that it pass quite unnoticed in the Nordic countries.'[12]

His disquiet at the prospect of Jæger's book was understandable. He had been written about biographically before, from Botten Hansen's portrait in 1867 in *Illustreret Nyhedsblad* onwards; but what Jæger was proposing was a full-length book. Moreover, Jæger was the literary consultant who had warned the Christiania theatre in such strong terms against *Ghosts*, and had even briefly toured with a lecture against the play. Though he changed his mind about it shortly aferwards and said so in public, his earlier condemnation cannot have been reassuring for Ibsen, with his horror of being misinterpreted.

Ibsen's main worry was where Jæger would get his information: 'Herr H. Jæger can only have obtained his biographical details at second, third or fourth hand. I doubt very much whether they are correct. The only entirely reliable source for such information is me, and so far he has not approached me.'[13]

Jæger remedied this now, travelling to Frederikshavn to meet Ibsen and living with him for three days, from 2 September to the fourth. In the course of these Ibsen provided him with a great deal of bibliographical information and observations on what were at that time considered his most important works – 'Terje Vigen', *The Pretenders, Brand* and *Peer Gynt* – such as who had been his models, and where and when these were writtten. Jæger raised the question of Kierkegaard's influence, to which Ibsen responded that he had read only some four or five pages from *Either-Or* and a few bits of *Øjeblikket* (*The Moment*). They discussed Ibsen's first encounters with great acting (Høedt, whom Ibsen saw in a play by Scribe during his trip abroad in 1852; Dawison, whom he saw play Hamlet in Dresden that same year); his reading habits when young (modest, chiefly Holberg and Oehlenschläger; though he singled out for special mention Hettner's *Das moderne Drama*); Ibsen's involvement with Thrane's workers movement in 1851 (Ibsen confirmed that what he had written would never have landed him in trouble even if he had been arrested after the police raided the newspaper office: 'his articles were of such a character that he would immediately have been released'.) Ibsen told him something about Skien and the view from his childhood home in the centre of town ('the stocks, prison and madhouse filled him with fear and horror'). He also confirmed his crusading for better protection for writers: 'In particular he has been disheartened by the way in which literary copyright has been treated.'

He passed on some of the secrets of the writer's room, referring to the long period of gestation before sitting down to write a play: how he thought on long walks, and during the long process of getting dressed in the morning; always stopping work with a few lines ready but unwritten so as to get off to a good start the next day, 'But even if he does get stuck, he does not give up, but carries on until the material starts flowing again.' He spoke of his second draft and the important third draft, the fair copy which went to the publisher, and said that he intended to hand his drafts on to Sigurd as a sort of investment: 'I don't like the idea of people seeing all the stupid mistakes I've made on the way to getting my work the way I want it.' There were details of Ibsen's monkish discipline when working:

Henrik Ibsen's daily life proceeds with great regularity. He rises at seven in the summer, a little later in winter; he dresses slowly and carefully, spends one hour on his ablutions; then he eats a light breakfast. At nine he sits at his writing desk, where he remains until one. Then he takes a walk before his midday meal, which in Munich is usually eaten at three. If someone wishes to visit him, he is informed that Ibsen is at home at one-thirty. In the afternoon he reads. He eats his supper early, at about seven, and at nine he drinks a toddy and goes early to bed. His appetite is excellent and he sleeps well. In the winter he spends much time thinking over his plans, in the summer he executes them. Summer is his best time for working; almost all his plays have been written in the summer; of the works published since he left Norway in '64 only two, *The League of Youth* and *Emperor and Galilean,* have been written in the winter. When he starts work on a new play he eats and drinks only what is absolutely necessary, so it doesn't get in the way of his work; a slice of bread and half a cup of black coffee are therefore all he allows himself before he sits down at his desk. He smokes a little tobacco while working, otherwise not at all. He cannot understand how people who are trying to work can use stimulants; the only thing he can imagine might achieve the desired effect would be a couple of drops of camphor on a piece of sugar. In this respect he is therefore like the larva that ceases to ingest nutrition when it is about to spin its cocoon.

Jæger noticed for himself how the habit of discipline dominated Ibsen's daily life:

He is generally speaking regimental to the point of pedantry: his day is divided by the clock. In the course of the three days I have now been living intimately with him, living within the same walls and eating at the same table, matters have been regulated by the clock from morning to evening to a degree that would soon become intolerable to me. One small detail: every day, after we have eaten our main meal and risen from the table, he walks over to the window and looks at the thermometer which hangs outside; it seems that to do this before he sits at table, or to ask the servant what the temperature is, never occurs to him.

Ibsen stressed the importance to him of a plentiful supply of fresh air, and throughout the three days of his visit Jæger noted that his host always had two windows open in the room, though it was September and extremely windy by the sea. He was in pantheistic, mystical mood, rhapsodising about the sea to Jæger: 'When one stands and stares down into the water it is as though one sees the same life as that on the surface, only in another form. There are connections and similarities everywhere. The sea will come into my next play.' He mentioned his fear of public speaking, saying that the only time he had been satisfied with his performance as a public speaker was during his visit to Berlin earlier in the year. He had spoken in German on that occasion, which no doubt enabled him to circumvent the otherwise muting self-consciousness he was referring to. Finally, he told Jæger that he took a cold shower every morning and every evening.

After Jæger left Ibsen headed for Sweden, staying in Gothenburg for a couple of weeks before moving on to Stockholm towards the end of September. A huge banquet was held in his honour on 25 September, at which Ibsen made his debut as a mystical visionary. After a few dissimulating preliminaries he described his idea of the future:

I believe, on the other hand, that our age might equally well be described as a conclusion, and that from it something new is in the process of being born.

What I believe is that the teachings of natural science on the subject of evolution are valid also in regard to the spiritual.

I believe that we are at the dawning of an age in which the political and social concepts will cease to exist in their present forms, and that from them both a new unity will grow which contains within it, for the time being, the conditions for human happiness.

I believe that poetry, philosophy and religion will fuse to make a new category and a new force in life, of which we who are now living can have no clear picture.

It has been said of me, on several occasions, that I am a pessimist.

And indeed I am, in the sense that I do not believe in the permanence of human ideals.

But I am also an optimist, in the sense that I have absolute and complete faith in the transplanting power of ideals and of their evolutionary capacity.

To be more specific, I believe that the ideals of our age, in their declining, are moving in the direction which I, in my play *Emperor and Galilean*, have hinted at in the phrase 'the third kingdom'.

Allow me then, to empty my glass to the nascent – the coming. It is Saturday afternoon as we sit gathered here.

After this comes the day of rest, the day of feasting, the holy day – whatever one will.

I for my part will be content with the profit of the work of my week of life (*min livs-uges arbejde*), if it aids in proper preparation for the morrow that is to come.

But above all I will be content if it helps to steel the soul for the working week that must inevitably follow.

With that, I thank you!

Two days later, when Ibsen arrived at his hotel to take a formal farewell, Ole Richter put him on the spot by asking what he actually meant by this. 'He then assured me,' Richter wrote to a correspondent, 'that he certainly had not intended his words as a challenge to Christianity alone, and to no other religion; and when I then quoted to him the words 'You triumph, Galilean', implying that nothing in what he had said ruled out the possibility that his development would lead him to make these words his own, he said that this was indeed quite correct.'[14] Having ceased to believe in God, Richter concluded, Ibsen now believed in anything at all. There were elements of Darwin in the credo, stronger elements of Ernst Hækel's 'biological Darwinism', and perhaps a touch of the theosophy of Madame Blavatsky and Colonel Olcott, which was one of Suzannah's growing interests as well as a fashionable belief of the period – Scandinavian contempories of the Ibsens who travelled to London seemed to make a point of 'meeting' Annie Besant, who became a leading figure in the movement at about this time.

Ibsen was never controversial in person, only in writing, and this must be one explanation for his surprisingly feeble response to Richter's probing. Another might be that he had personal reasons for not wishing to upset Richter. Fleetwood's journals for September 1887 reveal that it was generally believed in diplomatic circles that there was an ulterior purpose to Ibsen's visit to Stockholm. Meditating on his own chances of promotion to Washington he wrote: 'among his other reasons for being in Stockholm the 'big' Ibsen is here to ensure his son's appointment as Second Secretary; and if, as seems very likely, he gets his way, the job in Washington will be vacant.'[15] If Fleetwood and the rumours were correct then Richter was not a man to upset at that particular time. In the spring of 1888

Sigurd did indeed return from Washington to take up a post at the legation in Vienna.

On the way back to Germany Ibsen and Suzannah met in Copenhagen, where Hegel gave a dinner party for Ibsen. Then it was back to Munich in October. The summer had been successful and enjoyable for them both, Suzannah because she had been home to Norway, Ibsen because he had not. The whole idea that he had relatives remained scarcely tolerable to him, as is evident from his response to a second pathetic communication from his brother early in October. Referring to his 'very bad situation' Ole Paus Ibsen asked Ibsen to use his influence to help him get a job as a lighthouse keeper. He enclosed various testimonials. Ibsen duly passed these on to Johan Sverdrup, with a covering note suggesting he was largely indifferent to the matter:

> Your Excellency!
> My only surviving brother, Ole Paus Ibsen, resident in Tjøme, is applying for a job as lighthouse keeper and in connection with this has asked me to put his case to Your Excellency.
> May I therefore request that Your Excellency look with favour upon the enclosed letter and testimonials? Personally I have nothing to add.
>
> My profoundest respects
> Your Excellency,
>   Henrik Ibsen

Ole Paus got the job, and held it down for twenty years, dying childless in a home for retired seamen in 1917. But why so cold on such a modest errand? Was Ibsen signalling, even in such a trivial matter, the incorruptibility he believed he had achieved in his quest for 'perfection'? Was he ashamed of his working-class brother?

The year 1887 had been good, but it ended on a bad note for Ibsen. On 28 December he received news of the death, after a short illness, of Frederik Hegel, whose business and literary acumen had played such an important part in his success. Though they had never become close their relationship was entirely cordial, and apart from the brief stutter of mutual misunderstandings that surrounded the publication of *Brand* there is in the 300 or so letters Ibsen wrote to Hegel not an unfriendly or dissatisfied line. Ibsen needed somebody to work for, somebody to consider a hard but fair taskmaster, and in Hegel he found a publisher who understood this need, and who was not afraid to sound a warning when he thought Ibsen was about to take unnecessary risks with his reputation. 'The departed unforgettable and in numerous ways irreplaceable' he wrote in his telegram of condolence to Hegel's son Jacob, who took over the firm after his father. Ibsen, with his hypnotic reduction of the world outside his study to a state of unwavering sameness, was soon writing to the son exactly as though he were the father, and even soliciting his advice on what investments to make.

The milestone which he was dreading so, his sixtieth birthday in 1888, came and went relatively painlessly, and in great contrast to what was obviously a working birthday the year before, when Anderson had visited. On this occasion the day was given over to the many callers who looked in to offer their congratulations and pay their respects, bringing presents and flowers. There were telegrams from home, from Bjørnson, Gunnar Heiberg, Christian Hostrup; and *Aftenposten* contained a number of highly favourable articles on his life and achievement. The Norwegian *Storting* under their president sent a telegram with fifty-three signatures, eliciting a reply from Ibsen in which he thanked the parliament for its consistent financial support since first awarding him the annual grant in 1866: 'This support has over the years since then to an important degree eased my path through life and facilitated my work', adding that his respect for the *Storting*'s nobility of spirit allowed him to continue working free from any idea that he should censor his plays as a result of this national patronage.

He replied equally gracefully to a telegram from Kristiania Workers' Union, but the enthusiasm of the moment was running away with him when he claimed that 'of all the classes in our country it is the working class that stands closest to my heart.'[16] One visitor, the German M. G. Conrad, described how the aging couple were quite overcome by all the attention, with Ibsen repeatedly declaring himself speechless as he looked at all the presents, and Suzannah moving among the guests in happy astonishment. Jæger's biography duly appeared and Ibsen was delighted with Jæger's treatment of his life and works. His only complaint after the celebrations were all over was all the thank-you letters he had to write. 'I must keep this as brief as possible,' he told Gunnar Heiberg, 'because letter-writing is currently laying claim to so much of my time that I almost despair of it.'

A letter he wrote in the calm after these celebrations shows that he was further refining the attempt to form his own personal psycho-evolutionary theory which he had touched on at the gathering in Stockholm. Professor Ferdinand Lochmann, a dean at Kristiania University, had sent him a copy of his book *Den nyere Naturanskuelse* (*A Modern Theory of Nature*). Lochmann was a full-blown reactionary, an anti-Semite, an opponent of women's liberation, and among those who had burned his copy of Alexander Kielland's book *Arbeidsfolk* (*Working People*). Lochmann's book was essentially a defence of the Bible and the Christian view of life. Ibsen found some stimulation in it, 'all the more since I for some considerable time now have been preoccupied with the themes discussed therein', but not complete satisfaction:

> None of the conclusions science has reached so far satisfy me. I have therefore formulated my own personal, independent theory of nature. In my view both the theologians and the natural scientists are too deeply embedded in a one-sided view of things. 'Nature' is not something as material as many people seem to think. As for *what* lies behind it all – that is the great riddle, the temporary secret – temporary, in my view, because I live in the hope that the evolutionary process will little by little impart the great secret in a process involving complete and liberating recognition.[17]

This theory of his, self-consciously fostered by the summer spent gazing at the sea in Sæby, was in part based on a suggestion put forward by Hæckel in 1868 that human beings evolved from fish. The notion is fleetingly present in *Rosmersholm*, in which Rebecca is referred to as 'my attractive mermaid' by Ulrik Brendel. Something Ibsen told Jæger about *Rosmersholm* shows that he was trying hard to get to grips with this particular evolutionary theory. Jæger had asked him to explain the status or function of the white horses in the play, and noted down his reply:

> This afternoon Ibsen compared the people at home (i.e. in Norway) with tadpoles; in time they develop fully, but still have the black tail dangling behind them. They swim off wagging these black tails behind them, and what these tails are is obsolete ideas,

which they need a long time to be rid of. It was something like this he had in mind with the white horses in *Rosmersholm*.[18]

The Lady from the Sea, the play on which Ibsen now began work, was an attempt to take this idea a step further, to assume a coincidence of meaning between the simile and the thing compared and force a synthesis between symbol and reality. There is a synopsis dated 5 June, about three weeks after his letter to Lochmann, and this was immediately followed by a draft version of all five acts, with the fifth ready by 31 July. He remained in Munich for the summer, began rewriting in August and had the play ready for despatch to Jacob Hegel on 26 September. Hegel respected Ibsen's wishes that the book be allowed a clear run at the Christmas market before the play was staged, and published it on 28 November in an edition of 10,000 copies. There were simultaneous Norwegian and German premières on 12 February 1889, at the Christiania theatre, with Laura Gundersen, then fifty-seven years old, as Ellida; and at the Hoftheater in Weimar. Four days later it opened at the Royal in Copenhagen – a relief after the theatre's refusal to perform *Rosmersholm* – and within the year it had also been performed in Stockholm, Berlin and Helsinki.

The unusual ideas about the sea and evolution that lurk behind *The Lady from the Sea* show Ibsen trying, as always, to be be abreast of and even ahead of the times. Another current preoccupation of his bourgeois audience was hypnotism. He and Suzannah shared an interest in phenomena on the borderline between psychology and spiritualism. In 1884, when he was alone in Gossensass, he wrote to her of a personal encounter with a hypnotist: 'She has the power to make other individuals do what she wants by touching them. Here she has discovered a very effective medium in a Miss v. Pfeuffer, a highly-strung young lady, and has carried out a number of extra-ordinary experiments with her, later also with others.'[19]

These exciting and mysterious possibilities gave Ibsen the feeling of modernity he required for his play. For his characters, particularly for his female characters, he continued to need specific individuals to use as a basis for his psychological improvisations. The Lady herself, and her dilemma over whether to stay with her husband or leave with the former lover who arrives to claim her back, both derive from his mother-in-law Magdalene Thoresen. She fascinated

Ibsen with her courage to follow her instincts, take chances, take lovers, trusting life and being rewarded for her trust by survival. *The Lady from the Sea*'s basic situation derives from an episode in Thoresen's early life, which she later described in a letter to a friend:

> While studying in Copenhagen I met a young man, a wild, strange character, a pure child of nature. He studied with me, and I found myself bowing in the dust before the power of his monstrous, demonic will. He could have taken me over, bound me into a life of love with him – I still believe this. He let me go, perhaps he regretted it later ... I have never regretted that he let me go, for because of that I met a better person, and have lived a better life. But as I say, I have always known that he could have taken all the love that is inside me and made it flower and bear fruit. So my days are full of a sense of loss and longing, a reaching out here, a reaching there, always reaching for a shadow. And the power of this love did not vanish with the years but only grew.
>
> When my dear and noble husband called me to be his wife and the mother of those five poor children who ran around his heels, he was already aware of a most regrettable circumstance of my unruly life, for this was something that was my own responsibililty. But that which was gone, that which was lost, when I was so ignorant, without protection in the world, the thing I just couldn't handle, nor trust anyone else with – I asked him to look on this as a closed book, and to judge my character solely as a result of this struggle and – if he found me worthy of him – to regard all the rest as wiped out. And he did. Had he not, he would still have beaten his head against the wall; I would forever have remained silent as the grave.[20]

Put crudely, Magdalene is Ellida Wangel, Prost Thoresen is Dr Wangel, and Suzannah Thoresen and her sister Marie are Bolette and Hilde Wangel, the doctor's daughters by a previous marriage. Outside this nucleus of characters, but participating in sub-plots that cleverly echo and reflect goings-on within it, are Arnholm, Lyngstrand and Ballested, making this one of the most densely populated of the later plays. In another break with recent practice the action all takes place out of doors.

Suzannah, after a struggle similar to the one experienced by Hilde in the play, grew to love, admire and respect her stepmother. From her Ibsen would have heard the story of Magdalene's unruly early life, and details of the secret alluded to, an illegitimate child she had by this demonic lover of hers.* Given his own experience with Else Sophie Birkedalen, Ibsen's interest in the character and psychology of such a woman requires no further explanation, though it raises again the enigma of whether or not Ibsen ever told Suzannah about Else Sophie and his other son.

To the mystical and the biographical Ibsen added a third element – reason – to create the ethical conflict presented in the play. It is at this ethical level that *The Lady from the Sea* is most easily comprehensible and most successful. The Wangels learn in the course of events that a viable marriage can only be achieved if both parties feel free to leave without recriminations. It is an explicit statement of an idea that always seems to lurk under Ibsen's meditations on the nature of freedom: that, like a nuclear bomb, it can only be tolerated on condition that it never be used. When Dr Wangel, of his own free will, gives Ellida the freedom to leave him and go off with her mysterious visitor, he is showing her the kind of respect that Nora dreamt Thorvald would one day show her. It is respect demonstrative of a love so great that it wins him the victory over the stranger and saves the marriage. Ibsen, with his habit of mixing great complexity with great simplicity, rounds off the play with the kind of pedagogic flourish earlier employed to summarise his intentions in *The Pillars of Society, A Doll's House* and *An Enemy of the People.* Here the watchword, the message he wants his audience to remember, is the importance of *frihed under ansvar* (freedom with responsibility). Marriage, that seemed for idealistic reasons impossible to Falk and Svanhild in *Love's Comedy*, and for psychological reasons impossible to Rebecca West and Rosmer, is finally given this prescriptive chance of success.

With the possible exception of *When We Dead Awaken, The Lady from the Sea* is the most difficult of all the plays with modern settings to bring off. Ibsen takes his usual care to ensure that everything in the play has significance, but the experimental juxtaposition of dream-like, quasi-scientific elements involving the sea, the stranger and hypnotism with the recognisable realism of everyday life at the

---

* Magdalene Thoresen kept in touch with this child, and in time developed a good relationship with him.

Wangels' house in northern Norway does not succeed. The failure is due to the two characters most closely connected with these irrational elements, Ellida and the Stranger. The Stranger is an essentially unplayable role, perhaps the most notable aberration of Ibsen's judgement in all the years of his mastery. Demonic, mysterious, charismatic, exuding sexual power, his sudden arrival is to carry with it a threat to overturn the world of domestic contentment *chez* Wangel. But to convey this menace Ibsen gave him lines so spare, dull and 'pregnant' that in performance they compel a melodrama perilously close to the comic, particularly if the description of him as a red-headed man with a bushy beard and wearing a tartan bonnet is followed. The melodramatic effect is heightened by Ellida's fraught responses to him.

Yet Ibsen seemed, in correspondence, to encourage the melodrama. In a letter to Julius Hoffory about an impending German production he wrote: 'No one is to know what he is, any more than they are to know who he is or what his real name is. This uncertainty is precisely the main point of the method I have employed on this occasion.' And of a production he saw at Weimar he wrote 'I could not wish for or even imagine a better Stranger than this – a tall, thin figure with a high forehead, black, piercing eyes and a beautifully deep, muted voice.'[21] The explanation for the aberration must be that, for once, Ibsen was writing about a person he did not know, with a personality too remote from his own to be within reach of his imagination. A solid and real former lover would have permitted him to write a play presenting the same important and interesting ethical conflict as that which arises between the Wangels, without risking this descent into melodrama. Even productions that choose to treat it as a case-history and a kind of pre-Freudian essay in the psychosexual analysis of a certain kind of hysteria cannot overcome the problem. The net result was Ibsen's weakest play since *An Enemy of the People*. Writing to Delius about it Edvard Grieg called *The Lady from the Sea* 'an odd, genuinely Ibsenish thing ... its keynote is mystical, almost romantic, though of course it is influenced by hypnotism'.[22] Odd and genuinely Ibsenish it was, for even when he failed, Ibsen was always himself.

Despite the initial interest of European theatres in *The Lady from the Sea* it achieved only limited runs, and Ibsen could be glad he had resisted renewed pressure from both Christiania and Bergen to accept a 10 per cent royalty rather than his preferred lump-sum payment of 2,500 kroner. He was also canny enough to realise that the latter method put pressure on the theatres involved to earn back their money as soon as possible.

Critically the response to the play was largely one of good-natured puzzlement. At home Irgens Hansen, *Dagbladet's* reviewer, confessed openly that he did not understand the involvement of the sea in Ellida's character. Knut Hamsun in *Samtiden* referred to it as 'exalted lunacy'. For most of the new generation of younger Norwegian writers both Ibsen and Bjørnson were now seen as having reached their psychological limits. Bjørnson's conversion from free-lover to advocate of pre-marital chastity for young men was ascribed to the fact that he was getting too old to philander successfully any more; and Ibsen's ideas of freedom were already too safe, his notion of 'freedom with responsibility' an old man's notion too restrictive to be of use to writers and psychological explorers like Hamsun, Gabriel Finne, and Hans Jæger and his Kristiania bohemians. About all that old and young writers now had in common was a belief in the pan-Germanic ideal: in October that year Ibsen wrote to Brandes predicting that nationalism was moribund, 'it will be superseded by tribal consciousness ... I began by thinking of myself as a Norwegian, developed into a Scandinavian, and have ended up part of the great Germanic tribe.'[23]

The failure of the play notwithstanding, Ibsen's financial position was by now extremely solid. Towards the end of 1888 he was able to instruct Hegel to invest 8,000 kroner for him in some reliable undertaking; and on 20 January 1889 he wrote to him again asking him to buy a further 6,000 kroners' worth of shares.

18

Hedda Gabler

The apartment block at Maximilianstrasse 32 was the subject of building work that summer, and to keep out of the way of it Ibsen returned, after an absence of five years, to Gossensass. His fame was now at its height, and in recognition of the tourist business his patronage had brought to the town, the residents had decided, in 1886, to name a square after him. His trip there in the summer of 1889 was therefore also in response to an invitation to attend the official naming ceremony of the *Ibsenplatz*. This was the fifth time he had spent his summer in Gossensass, and it would be the last. Suzannah and Sigurd, now based in Vienna, went with him.

The square was up the hill, a popular look-out point for visitors. Ibsen headed the procession, and was carried the last part of the way on a litter borne by four local boys. There is a picture of him enjoying the occasion a little later from a bench, a dishevelled gnome looking older than his sixty-one years, resting his hands atop the rolled umbrella he always carried, rain or shine.

In the evening there was a party, with music and recitation. It was here, on 21 July, that Ibsen met Emilie Bardach, the first of a number of young women who played a significant role in the creation of the works of his final years as a dramatist. She was twenty-seven years old, born in Vienna on 5 August 1862, but with the face and manner of an eighteen-year-old. The daughter of an affluent Jewish family, she was visiting the Tyrol with her mother. In her diary she wrote: 'I got to know him after the concert, it was pleasant. But he is very shy and now that his wife and son have arrived we rarely manage a conversation.'

Ibsen's interest in young women requires no special explanation. T. E. Hulme said that philosophy is about people in clothes, by which definition the resolutely clothes-wearing Ibsen was the most philosophical of writers. The role of sensual, physical pleasure in his life seems to have been minimal. Yet one feels, not least from occasional references in his letters to the pleasures of bathing in the Mediterranean, that there was a repressed sensualist in him. Indeed, there is evidence that he was longing for a young woman even before this summer: two years earlier at Sæby, in 1887, he was much in the company of a fellow-guest at the Harmonien, Julie Jørgensen, a thirty-year-old Danish schoolteacher who, the following year, married the owner of the hotel. She and Ibsen often walked on the beach together, and they watched an eclipse of the sun together on 19 August. She was a pretty, lively young woman, and when she left without bidding him farewell he sent her a little note of comic rebuke in which he thanked her for 'that ray of sunshine with which you, in the freshness of your youth, have lit up an old man's journey towards death'.[1]

The flirtation with Emilie Bardach, though not serious, was more serious than this episode in Sæby. Their 'affair' remained dormant for some time after their encounter at the reception, partly through the chaperoning of Suzannah and Sigurd, partly because Emilie's brother Bob arrived and stayed for two weeks. There are no entries in her diary between 8 August and 17 August, when she writes about the sickness that struck her down – pains, sleeplessness, fever. Her mother informed her that Ibsen had been making sympathetic enquiries about her. A few days later, on 30 August, she notes that she is reading Ibsen's work, and that she has had frequent conversations with him. In a later note she described how intently he questioned her, wanting to know everything about her.

If she was flattered by the sudden attentions of this famous man she was also confused by his intentions. He told her how much joy it gave him to be with her, that he had never before been so enraptured, but insistently put their relationship on the asexual, idealistic Falk-Svanhild footing described in *Love's Comedy*. The profound level of his conversation sent shivers down her spine (*kalt über den Rücken*); he told her that he wanted her to be his *Mitarbeiter* (work-mate), but also admitted that he was studying her, and that he laid traps for her in his conversation in the hope of catching her out in a lie. She in turn encouraged his advances by telling him that she could not understand how any girl could fall in love with a young man.[2]

The flavour of their relationship is captured in her diary entries for September. Though this journal was probably rewritten some time after the events described, there is no real reason to doubt the authenticity of the picture it gives of them. The entry for the eighteenth is the longest for the whole summer:

I am lying down; Mama is going out, so I am mistress of the room, free, free at last to write about the feelings which I am experiencing these days, but now I see how little language is able to express what one feels. Only tears say more. One cannot escape one's fate. I always have to experience something out of the ordinary, for me there are no easy, calm pleasures, it always ends in a passion, which does not lead to anything positive and is always limited by circumstances. Always obstacles – either because of me or the circumstances themselves. But how can one compare the present with the past? How weak and petty everything seems compared to this. Things could never have progressed so far, and yet all the others were only ordinary people, and now it is one mind that dominates everything. I can compare only Baron Hellenbach's interest in me to this, yes, but that was so much quieter. But now, this terribly beautiful volcano. The day before yesterday in the afternoon, when we finally were sitting together alone, oh the words, if they only had been more deeply imprinted in me, clearer. Everything before was a lie.

Now it is true love. The ideal which he wrote about before the experience. Now he will be the poet of pain and denial. But happy to have found me, the most beautiful, most wonderful. Too late. How pathetic I feel myself, that I cannot throw myself into his arms – and then the obstacles once again – reality, the years of difference, his wife, his son – all this separates us. Did it have to be like this? Could I have guessed what would happen and prevented it? When he speaks to me it occurs to me now that I must get away, far away, and yet I feel pain at the idea of leaving him. I suffer because of his nervousness. I feel it even when we are sitting far away from one another in the dining room. It all seemed to happen so quickly. I saw the change from his former, predictable way of life. I was flattered by his interest in me, the special attention he paid me compared to the others. I have nothing to give him, not even a picture of myself, and yet he gives so much. His wife is pleasant to us; I spoke to his son for a long time yesterday. I think we both feel it would be better if we stay away from each other. Now for real life: the last few days have been very cold. It was icy on the Brenner. Yesterday we walked towards the Brenner in swirling snow; on the way back when you turn off to Gossensass, the weather seemed more 'southern', but near the hotel the wind was biting. It is very quiet here now; later this evening I will go downstairs; I am doing nothing now, just writing a few letters. Saturday I read the *Komödie der Liebe** until midnight, otherwise I am still busy with Beaconsfield's Edymon [*sic*]. Mornings we mostly took walks, then I dressed, went downstairs, and after lunch I always sat with Ibsen. Twice I played the piano in the evening. And so the days passed among these beautiful surroundings. The present occupies my mind so much I am not thinking of the future. We will be here just a few more days... Can I even think straight? We will write to each other; I will be Ibsen's collaborator; that is my life's goal. All the letters I have received are lying here unanswered. So many, but what should I write?[3]

20 September:

I wanted to write, but why? The things one buries in one's mind and heart but does not write down. I was with Ibsen the day before yesterday, in the evening between six until nearly half past seven and yesterday even longer, as we met at five o'clock. We dined at 'Zinner'. I am supposed to go to Sterzing, with the Raffs. She wants to sketch with me. Under different circumstances I would be very interested, but now I am looking for an excuse not to go. To lose a day? It is so hard. They have put it off because of me; it is difficult. The cold has let up. Yesterday it was spectacular, nature seems so beautiful in this peace and quiet and with what is happening to me at the moment.

23 September:

I have never been so undecided as I am now. I have just returned from a walk with Ibsen. Mama already wants to start packing and leave on Wednesday. Today I am calmer because he is. Yesterday evening he was terrible. Fräulein Raff, who unfortunately left today and who seemed to understand the whole thing, said it was as beautiful and terrifying as a thunder storm and she was amazed that I was still in control of my faculties.

In a sense they were ideal partners in their flirtation: on the one

* *Love's Comedy.*

side Ibsen, bored by his life, his wife and his self-discipline, and longing for the company of those most unlike his public self – the young, the spontaneous, the fresh; and on the other Bardach, who could bask in the admiring, if pedagogic, attentions of a hugely famous man and yet know that it was really all just a game. Her accounts of their conversations, and their correspondence that trailed briefly in the aftermath of the summer, show Ibsen reverting to the pierrot of the Grimstad days, whipping up a storm of words and ideals on the subject of the love between a man and a woman, which is always about 'working together', never about 'sleeping together'. It is good to reflect that this flood of romance burst from the heart and the lips of the scowling troll photographed at the naming ceremony for the *Ibsenplatz*, and Ibsen's successful conduct of the affair – for consummation of the relationship was never a realistic aim – must have confirmed for him the aphrodisiac powers of his fame.

Bardach fantasised that she believed him when he said he would divorce his wife and travel the world with her, 'but we both feel it best outwardly to remain as strangers'. It recalls Thorvald Helmer's explanation to Nora of why he avoided speaking to her when they are out at parties together, his fantasy that 'you are my secret lover, my secret young bride-to-be, and no one even guesses that there is anything between us'. The friendly attention she noted from Suzannah shows that Suzannah thought the flirtation harmless enough, at least as far as Ibsen was concerned. She was more worried about the effect of Ibsen's game-playing on Bardach: some years later she told a doctor friend that she had warned her husband 'that he must not drive that hysterical and disturbed woman completely mad'.[4] She was more inclined to react in later years, when the episode repeated itself with other young women in a manner that she found demeaned Ibsen as well as herself. She probably understood it as well, for ten years earlier she had derived a similar, though less intense, pleasure from the company of the charming young John Paulsen.

When Bardach left Gossensass in the small hours of 27 September on board the Verona-Vienna train Ibsen saw the family off at the platform. She left still believing that Ibsen was only biding his time to make an end of his marriage and begin a new life with her, but in her diary entry describing the parting honesty compels her to admit that it was 'easier than I had feared'.

After the summer was over they exchanged letters, intensively in the beginning, though Ibsen drafted at least some of his. Bardach's great adventure turned her head for a while, and she lived out the self-denying pangs of Svanhild, and imagined that her idealising lover was living out the pangs of Falk. She told her diary that she felt elevated above the common run of people by having known him and spoken to him. Now those around her seemed vulgar, shabby and trite in their feelings and her daily life a meaningless round of unpleasant obligations, visits, empty courtesies, parties. The entry for 25 October refers to 'this terrible and beautiful feeling of having been loved by him as he has never loved before'. Early in November a man paid court to her, 'and he says I hypnotise and fascinate him. But all my thoughts are in Munich.' The weeks pass. She paints, plays the piano, sings: 'My fate is remarkable; in fact, isn't it really tragic?'

But in his letter of 6 February 1890, bored, probably, and troubled by his conscience, Ibsen asked her to stop writing to him. He followed it up with a second injunction on 28 April: 'I feel as a matter of conscience that I must cease or at least limit this correspondence.' Meditating on this turn of events Bardach imagines that perhaps he will write again: 'What has happened is after all entirely typical of his nature. In spite of his goodness there is something gruesome about it.' And she concedes wanly: 'Prof. Maydol was right to say that this was an unnatural relationship.'

Ibsen did write to her twice more, on 18 September to console her on the death of her father; and at the end of December, to thank her for a painting she sent him. But again he asked her to stop writing to him, adding weight to his words by including a reference to Suzannah, whom he said also liked the picture, and to Bardach's mother, asking to be remembered to her. Later he asked Suzannah to burn a photograph Bardach had sent him, which she had inscribed with the words 'Prinzessen von Apfelsinia'.*

Bardach did as she was told. She broke her silence only once more, to telegraph her congratulations in 1898 on the occasion of Ibsen's seventieth birthday. The message revived all his memories of the summer of 1889 as he sent her his deeply pathetic response:

---

* According to Ibsen's doctor, Dr Edvard Bull, he had earlier thrown the photograph to the floor with the words, 'I don't know this young lady.'

My very dearest Fraulein!

My most sincere thanks for your letter. The summer in Gossensass was the happiest, loveliest time of my whole life.

Scarcely dare think of it. – And yet I must, always. Always!

Yours most faithfully.

Henrik Ibsen[5]

To Dr Julius Elias, one of his German translators and admirers, he
later spoke of Bardach as an unprincipled seductress – 'She never
got her claws into me, but I used her for my writing' – graceless
words, but in their crudity perhaps expressing the extent of Ibsen's
disappointment at her failure. For how often in the intervening
years he must have wished he had had the courage to cross Fru
Alving's margin and touch the woman, instead of teetering the
summer away on the border 'between will and ability'.

As for Bardach, she lived for the rest of her life on the story of
her nearly-relationship with Ibsen. She travelled much, living in
hotels, working as a piano teacher, for a while as a cinema pianist
in Bern. A pathetic, lonely figure, she became a sort of Ibsen bore,
carrying around with her a portable shrine consisting of flowers and
a photograph and launching into an account of their relationship
at the first sign of interest from strangers. The Viennese playwright
Arthur Schnitzler later came across her once or twice in his own
travelling. He described her as 'basically a literary Viennese Jewess
whom Ibsen, in his provincial eroticism, was unable to avoid'.[6]

With Emilie Bardach gone, Ibsen found two other young female
companions to play the game with him for the remainder of that
summer. One was a sixteen-year-old girl, Carlotta Spinn, daughter
of a German furniture manufacturer from Berlin. One day towards
the end of the summer, when her parents had gone out leaving her
alone, she joined Ibsen at his table in the dining room and they
began to converse. In the course of this her mother returned, and
finding her daughter alone in Ibsen's company gave her a slap
across the ear before dragging her off. The next day Carlotta wrote
a note to Ibsen asking him to forgive her parents who had shown
such little understanding of her enthusiasm for his works. Ibsen
replied:

My dear young lady!

I have just received your letter. Please accept my hearfelt
thanks! May our brief meeting never be forgotten. If only it were

possible for me to participate in your unfolding fate. Great good luck to you! May you always live well! And last of all – please give me a sign that you have received these lines.

    Farewell for ever
      Yours faithfully
    Henrik Ibsen[7]

The other was Helene Raff, daughter of the composer Joachim Raff. She was an aspiring artist, twenty-four years old, from Munich. There was a degree of competition between her and Bardach for Ibsen's attention while both of them were in Gossensass. That Bardach won the first round is probably due to the fact that she bore a striking physical resemblance to the young Suzannah Ibsen. Bardach would tell Helene Raff what Ibsen had said to her, and Raff would note down in her diary the fierce mood-swings induced in her friend by the unpredictable nature of Ibsen's approaches. The entry for 21 September reads 'The B. quite crazy about Ibsen.' The following day she wrote 'The B. crushed.' But once Bardach had left Raff had Ibsen more or less to herself.

All these close encounters with young women darkened still further his gloomy view of marriage. Among the company at Gröbner's that year were the German philosopher Wilhelm Dilthey and his wife Katharina. They met one day when Frau Dilthey fell on the hotel steps. Ibsen assisted her to her feet and the two families thereafter often sat together in the evenings after the meal. Ibsen and Dilthey were asked to be witnesses at the wedding of a young couple who had decided to get married locally. Frau Dilthey made the bridal head-dress and generally tried to create a festive atmosphere for the couple. Ibsen, however, was inconsolable. Staring morosely at her handiwork he abruptly asked her 'But why all this cheer?' And when she gave him the obvious reply he shook his head: 'On the contrary, in my view one should cry at weddings and rejoice at funerals.'[8]

On the day itself he did the couple proud, carrying out his functions in morning coat and top hat, with a full set of medals on display. Frau Dilthey expressed her surprise at his having these with him on holiday. Ibsen explained that he always packed them when travelling, 'since one never knew when one might need them'.

*   *   *

The Ibsens returned to Maximilianstrasse in October. Helene Raff made it her business to continue the relationship begun in Gossensass, loitering in the street outside Ibsen's apartment until one day she was successful in re-establishing contact. The pattern with Emilie Bardach was repeated. Ibsen began as though embarking on an erotic adventure, and at one of their early meetings, on parting, kissed her. He did this again, and shortly after that turned up at her studio one day with a present for her, a copy of Jæger's biography. But again he could not bring himself to take the matter any further, and presently he defused the situation by inviting her to visit him at home and say hello to Suzannah – 'My wife is very very fond of you – and so am I too' he wrote to her the day after her visit. Thereafter he kept the relationship on a firmly paternal footing, frequently telling her how he wished he had had a daughter like her.

But as her notes of their conversations show, he spoke seriously to her, and often quite personally. Of his inhibited personality he told her he could only speak freely through a character in a play, and that in any case he had an addiction to secrets, a secret was to him the most precious thing in life. He also offered what was either a rationalisation or a justification of his more usual silent way of being, speaking of it almost as though he were deliberately damming himself up, in the way Nietzsche sometimes refers to, as a way of building up his own resources of power, something like the explanation he gave to Brandes when he advised him to withdraw from the struggle against his enemies, go into internal exile and 'ennoble' himself in silence.

He speaks of a compulsion he suffered from as a schoolboy to perform acts of meaningless violence (not, so far as we know, indulged) such as hitting the teacher on the nose with a ruler, not out of dislike for the teacher, but out of inexplicable perversity. Who has not stood with a companion at the edge of some high place, he asks her rhetorically, and not felt the urge to push his companion off? Human perversity, irrationality, meaningless cruelty dominate his talk. He asks why it is we are compelled to do or say something cruel to someone we love, knowing full well that we will regret it later? He answers, again, that it is because people are like that, are attracted to the forbidden and the wilfully cruel. He does not use the word but is evidently meditating aloud on the subject of the sadistic instinct. Will-power fascinates him. Will-power is everything. Truly applied it is invincible. Most people don't even know what it is. In fact, most people die without ever having lived, and their greatest good fortune is that they never realise it.

Now he talks about hypnotism and will-power and mentions a couple who came to see him one day, he doesn't say why they chose him, but it seems almost as though they approached him as an alienist. They told him they wanted to get a divorce because the wife claimed her husband had been hypnotised by another woman. Does Frøken Raff believe in hypnosis? He tells her women have poorly developed will-power, that they spend their lives dreaming of something that will give their lives meaning. Their passivity makes them a prey to unhealthy emotional states and condemns them to lives of disappoinment.

The intensity of which Ibsen was capable in a face-to-face conversation comes through clearly in Raff's diary. She records his praise for Suzannah, 'a completely whole and free personality', and his admiration for her ability to believe in him whole-heartedly at the same time as she is fearless in disagreeing with him. He also restated the view central to his creation of a revolutionary drama, that the stage was as suitable a place as the church or the cathedral for the broadcast of important words, especially now that so many people had ceased to go to church. As for philosophers, if their learning had no practical application he had no time for them, just as he was deeply suspicious of scholars who lived exclusively for the subject of their study.

He was very interested to hear that Raff had been tutored privately and so avoided both the church and the school. He congratulated her, telling her she was a child of nature, and hers was the education of the future – no state, no school, no church. Yet Raff continued to feel uneasy about the exact nature of their relationship, and one day she asked him directly why it was that he liked her. Ibsen, who loved to ply his young women with personal questions, was obviously discomfited to get one back and reversed into his abstract mode, telling her that he enjoyed talking to her because she was 'youth personified'. Raff did not like his answer, and went on to tell him that some of the things he had said to her – presumably some of the more overtly romantic statements of how unique and important she was to him – were word for word what he had said to Emilie Bardach in Gossensass. She knew, she said, because Emilie had informed her. She told him not to speak to her as if she were

Emilie, but Ibsen shrugged her complaint aside with the sheepish explanation that 'that was in the country. One is much more serious in town.' By the time she made this entry, on 18 November 1890, Raff must have known, if she did not know it already, that their relationship was unlikely to develop into a physical one.

Many of these observations made to Raff were echoed in the play Ibsen was working on during the period of their intercourse, *Hedda Gabler*. He mentioned a new work in a letter to Emilie Bardach, written just after his return to Munich on 7 October, saying he hoped it would reflect something of the happy mood of his summer, 'but it will end in melancholy. I know it.'[9]

Progress was slow, and the summer of 1890 was spent in Munich labouring over the first draft. It was a wretched summer in his part of the world and on 24 August he told August Larsen at Gyldenal that 'It seems to me no sacrifice to remain in town and carry on working. It goes forward at an even pace and will hopefully be ready in reasonable time.'[10] His pace increased in September, when he started work on a new version of Act Two, and by 29 October he could write to his French translator Moritz Prozor: 'I am working all day every day now and must keep my correspondence to an absolute minimum.'[11]

On 16 November he finished his fair copy and sent it off to Copenhagen two days later. *Hedda Gabler* was published on 16 December in an edition of 10,000 copies. It was first performed at the Residenz theatre in Munich, on 31 January 1891. Ibsen was present and took a bow on the stage afterwards, but the reception was mixed, with boos and whistles among the cheers. After this he travelled to Berlin for the performance at the Lessing theatre on 10 February, which was again only a partial success. Even those critics usually sympathetic to Ibsen found the play incredible.

Of Ibsen's self-consciously modern plays, as opposed to the timeless *Brand* and *Peer Gynt*, *Hedda Gabler* is the one that has most effortlessly retained its modernity. It marks the first step in Ibsen's slow return to the more personal, introverted plays of the last years, exploring again areas he had not seriously explored since *Emperor and Galilean*. A strong hint of its personal relevance is the presence of an important writer – Eilert Løvborg – as one of the main characters, and the plot depends on an appreciation of the idea that the fate of a manuscript or book can be a matter of life or death for the writer. But the most potent autobiographical echo in the play lies in the character of Hedda herself.

Hedda Gabler marked the end of Ibsen's long involvement with determinism as a substitute for original sin, and the mystery of Hedda's passionate, inhibited, violent and repellent character is allowed to remain a mystery. The only clue – Ibsen's stroke of theatrical genius – is the portrait of her father, General Gabler, which hangs on the wall in 'her' sanctum and watches over events in brooding silence. The relation to the portraits on the walls of another aristocrat, Johan Rosmer, is obvious. The point of these 'ghosts' in *Rosmersholm* is to signal the decline into impotent intellectualism of this descendant of soldiers and bishops. No such point is intended here. Ibsen once wrote that he called her Hedda Gabler and not Hedda Tesman to indicate the degree to which she was her father's daughter rather than her husband's wife. Beyond this the portrait and the relationship between father and daughter remain enigmatic.

John Paulsen's novel of the Ibsens' family life contains a curious pre-echo of this dominating general. In one scene Sverre Pehrsen finds out, to his astonishment, that his paternal grandfather is alive and working as a cobbler in Norway. In an attempt to ease his surprise at this socially unsettling piece of information Fru Pehrsen adds, 'But *my* Grandfather was a general.' Suzannah Ibsen could point to military leaders and church leaders in her family background, and perhaps did it so frequently that Ibsen eventually borrowed a portrait of one of them to hang in Hedda's home.

There are familiar elements among the mysterious: as well as its many other concerns *Hedda Gabler* shows Ibsen's continuing interest in the plight of the talented woman unable to find a role for herself in the modern world. Here, in his cautiously revolutionary way, Ibsen contrasts Thea Elvstad and Hedda Gabler. Hedda rejects both of the roles open to her as a woman: as her husband's helpmeet in his life's work; and as a mother. Thea finds her role in life as the muse of a gifted man, Eilert Løvborg. After Løvborg's death she is able to continue her work in harness with Jørgen Tesman, as they sit together bent over Løvborg's working notes with the aim of recreating the manuscript burnt by Hedda. Thea's selfless devotion to Løvborg's talent seemed exemplary to Ibsen, and was surely inspired by his own experiences of the way Suzannah devoted her life to him. But his idea did not meet with the approval of contemporary feminists, for whom Thea was hardly an improvement on Solveig. At a party a couple of years later his neighbour at table, the painter Kitty Kielland, remarked that she couldn't bear types like Thea – 'those women who sacrifice themselves for the men'. 'I write to depict people,' replied Ibsen. 'It is a matter of complete indifference to me what feminist fanatics like or do not like.'[12]

But the theme of the woman influencing the world by harnessing the power of a sympathetic man was something Ibsen must often have thought about. His sympathy for the situation of women who lead lives of only partial self-realisation was not native to him but an understanding fostered by Suzannah, through her enthusiasm for her stepmother, through her interest in Camilla Collett's novel *The District Governor's Daughters* and her subsequent friendship with Collett. Ibsen was also interested in the idea of a marriage as an intellectual partnership, such as that between John Stuart Mill and Harriet Taylor, or closer to home the literary collaboration between Jonas Lie and his wife Thomasine on Lie's novels.

Something must have happened to Ibsen to enable him to write a play that did not rely on either God or genetic theory to give it a backbone of meaning. He had been operating, as a modern dramatist, in the philosophical space left by Darwin's discoveries, keenly filling the space – this vacuum – with determinist theories of behaviour and a character psychology derived from Taine. The major cultural influence that removed the need even for this replacement structure was the new psychology of younger writers like Strindberg and Nietzsche. Hedda has a marked resemblance to Furia in Ibsen's first play *Catiline*, and to the demonic Hjørdis in *The Vikings at Helgeland*. But these women have the excuse of a revenge motive to explain their behaviour. Hedda can offer no such justification. The psychologically new in Ibsen's play perhaps reflects his interest in August Strindberg's most recent dramas. He had read *The Father*, and *Hedda Gabler* suggests he had also read *Miss Julie*, published in 1889. Strindberg, not too unreasonably, imagined that Eilert Løvborg was based on him, though he ridiculed the frailty of Løvborg's psyche. And in correspondence with Bjørnson, Ibsen's comrade-in-arms in the matter of women's rights, Strindberg warned him 'Stop this old-fashioned romanticism! ... They're laughing at your proclamations in the magazines.' He also warned him that the feminist movement was 'a devilish tactic being used by the upper-classes against us', and accused Bjørnson of opportunism in adopting his *hanskestandpunktet* ('glove' attitude),* of courting the women only because everyone else had turned against him. Two years later, Ibsen would hear similar accusations of opportunism levelled at him for his own cultivation of the women's movement, by a fellow-Norwegian, the young novelist Knut Hamsun.

But the creator of *Hedda Gabler* could never be accused of currying favour with a female audience. Hedda *is* the play. She was his greatest creation since Brand, Peer Gynt, and Jarl Skule, and her play Ibsen's finest since the great works of his thirties. Mixing elements of Dostoevsky's Stavrogin and Melville's Bartleby her perverse, self-frustrating nature gave Ibsen access to a range that he had wilfully denied himself during the 1880s, when writing plays that self-consciously refused to end before they had provided some kind of explanation or justification for the goings-on, whether in the form of determinist theories of genetic heritage or of 'last-line' moral didacticism. Ibsen, who contained great, yet controlled, cruelty within himself, allowed cruelty to play uncensored across the full range of the character. Malice at the level described by Hedda does occur in earlier plays – one thinks of Dr Stockmann's opponents, of Rektor Kroll – but there is a subtlety to her cruelty that makes her an even greater exponent of it than Bishop Nikolas in *The Pretenders*.

The reason Hedda deserves mention in the same breath as Brand, Peer Gynt and Skule is that she contains, like them, so much of her creator. She lives out Ibsen's own punishing 'conflict between will and ability', and the experiences of the Gossensass summer, as well as the months afterwards in Munich, with Emilie Bardach and Helene Raff, realised the conflict at a personal level that must have pained him more than its manifestations at the abstract level of moral or professional ambition. He wanted to be Emilie's lover, as he wanted to be Helene's lover. Only his nature prevented him. A note for *Hedda Gabler* reads: 'Løvborg is by inclination a 'bohemian'. Hedda is also attracted towards this, but dare not make the decisive leap.'[13]

Hedda wanted to make love with Eilert Løvborg. In their scene towards the end of the second act, as Tesman and Brack sit chatting in the room behind them, she tells him that she broke off their relationship 'because reality was in imminent danger of entering

* From Bjørnson's play *A Glove*.

into it'. In her perverse anger she threatened to shoot Eilert with one of her pistols. He asks her why she didn't:

HEDDA: Because I am so afraid of scandal.
LØVBORG: Yes, Hedda, you really are a coward.
HEDDA: A terrrible coward.

A few lines later she confesses to him that not daring to shoot 'wasn't my worst cowardice that evening'. She doesn't say what her worst cowardice was, and Løvborg's assumption that she is talking about sex seems irrefutable. But refute it she does, for one part of her problem is that her basic instincts struggle against a perception of herself as someone too good, too pure, too civilised, too *social* to have sex. Ibsen is asking once again the tormenting question first asked by Fru Alving in *Ghosts*: do I obey the laws because I believe in them, or because I fear the consequences of breaking them? And the answer is unequivocal: it is fear that binds, not respect.

'The female imagination is not active and capable of independent creation like the male,' reads another of Ibsen's notes, 'It requires the assistance of a little touch of reality.'[14] But Hedda dare not even risk this little touch of reality. The price she pays for her timidity is that she is left with just the one talent – 'to bore myself to death'.

Ibsen also gave her a talent to destroy, and she uses it to ruin Eilert Løvborg's life and drive him to his death before her. It reminds us of the letter Ibsen wrote to Bjørnson about not sparing the child in the mother's womb after reading Clemens Petersen's review of *Peer Gynt*: 'If I cannot build, then I can certainly destroy everything around me'.

And destroy everything around her is just what Hedda does.

Echoes of Ibsen's summer in Gossensass permeate the play. Hedda's intense and penetrating cross-examination of Thea recalls Emilie Bardach's description of Ibsen's behaviour, how insistently and closely he questioned her about her life and feelings, frightening her at times as Hedda frightens Thea. Then the roles move around slightly, and it is Judge Brack who subjects Hedda to the same kind of intense, personal questioning. There is a literal echo in the references to the honeymoon in the Tyrol, and Hedda's mordant recall of an overnight stop in the Brenner Pass, where she and Tesman 'met all those lively summer visitors'.

The opening few minutes of *Hedda Gabler* show Ibsen in complete control of his art. Through the easy and natural intercourse between

Tante Julle, the maid Berte and, presently, Tesman we learn all we need to know about the background. Each of the main characters – Hedda herself, Brack, Eilert Løvborg and Thea Elvstad – is introduced to us in conversation before we actually see them. The first visual image we are given of Hedda is that recalled by Tante Julle, 'when she rode out with her father. In her long black dress. With a feather in her hat.' It is irresistibly, unforgettably specific. And when she finally enters, the little scene in which she pretends to believe that Tante Julle's new hat belongs to the servant speaks volumes about her character.

The weakest character is Jørgen Tesman. To an even greater extent than Rørlund, Thorvald Helmer and Pastor Manders he is a caricature, not a character. Ibsen wanted to parody the bookish man, the one-dimensional scholar, but Tesman's foolishness is too quickly announced and too insistently proclaimed. Ibsen wants us to feel how much he irritates Hedda, with his feeble verbal gimmick, 'Imagine that, Hedda!'; but it is repeated so often that it quickly reduces him to the level of a parrot. This is a shame, because along with Tante Julle and Thea Elvsted Tesman is of the meek and good in the play. Ibsen seemed able to appreciate the power of innocence, but unable to avoid mocking it. Foldal in *John Gabriel Borkman* is handled in similar fashion, as predominantly comic in his decency.

Judge Brack's last-line response to Hedda's suicide, to be delivered 'feebly, from his armchair', is another slight disappointment: *Men, gud seg forbarme – slik noe gjør man da ikke* ('But, Lord have mercy – one simply doesn't *do* that sort of thing!'). Even for an old cynic like Brack this is too feeble a response when a young woman has just blown her head off not two metres away from your armchair. It is as though Ibsen is trying to pre-empt the response of some hostile critic, or perhaps start the discussion going.

But of course there is a sense in which a 'surprise' last line like this can never work, for as audiences we are so familiar with the sequence of events in Ibsen's best-known plays that, as the curtain falls on shocking and sudden deaths (*The Wild Duck, Rosmersholm, Hedda Gabler*) the actors are the only ones in the theatre who are taken by surprise. Because Ibsen is now canon we judge the playing of these lines, but we cannot feel them. A similar problem exists with the climax to *A Doll's House*: there is nothing intrinsically unrealistic about the fact of Nora's leaving; but where is the despair? It is too obvious that an intellectual problem is being worked out, with a consequent failure to recognise the emotional enormity of what is happening to this particular family. The ending of *The Wild Duck*, where Ibsen makes time, after Hedvig's death, for a coda of responses from various characters, gains by not ignoring the ordinary 'realistic' responses to a violent death, the seconds and minutes in which a family is breaking into pieces. Old Ekdal, it is true, makes the symbolic and 'detached' observation that 'the forest takes its revenge'; but Hjalmar's inarticulate shouts of pain are close to the kind of real responses of grief and despair we instinctively demand of such a realistically depicted situation.

These examples in themselves relate to the subject matter of *Hedda Gabler*, for what Ibsen was documenting for his contemporary audience in this play was the boredom, the lack of higher meaning in bourgeois lives where the highest goal is security and the price paid for it the repudiation of all strong emotion, all open expression. Both Ellida Wangel in *The Lady from the Sea* and Hedda have fascinated psychoanalysts through the years, making it pertinent to recall that Emilie Bardach was a young, upper-middle-class Jewish woman from Vienna, just the sort of person on whom Sigmund Freud was at that time basing his psychoanalytic theories of personality and behaviour. In his personal conduct of the affair with Bardach, Ibsen was as implicated in the self-delusion and hysteria as she was. But afterwards, as an artist, he was able to show with penetrating, moving insight how quickly the disease of boredom can become fatal, not only for the sufferer (Hedda), but for all those who come into contact with her. In providing an ending that can be, if not carefully handled, melodramatic, Ibsen seemed almost to be trying to provide his audience with one of those sudden wild gusts of feeling he considered that they were all lacking in their personal lives.

By this time, 1891, Ibsen's career had acquired that aura of chronological chaos that is the sign of a snowballing reputation as admirers in recently conquered areas began catching up on his back list. Freie Bühne, a new Berlin theatre company dedicated to performing the work of new dramatists, chose to announce themselves with *Ghosts* on their opening night, 29 September 1889. In France André Antoine, whose Théâtre Libre was the inspiration for Freie Bühne, performed *Ghosts* for the first time on 29 May 1890, acting the part of Osvald himself and taking the play on a tour through France for over 200 performances. In April 1891 Théâtre Libre performed *The*

Wild Duck, and later that year *Hedda Gabler* was performed at the Versailles theatre. The first French books on Ibsen's revolutionary art began appearing, and August Erhard's *Henrik Ibsen et le Théâtre Contemporain* in 1892 was particularly influential. Prozor's translations of ten plays appeared in a six-volume edition between 1892 and 1893. A degree of resistance appeared to Ibsen's acceptance in France, and there were complaints from critics like Francisque Sarcey and Jules Lemaître that he was too serious and too remote from the French national spirit to do the country any good. But in the mid-1890s he found a staunch defender in Aurélien Lugné-Poë, who acquired sole rights to perform Ibsen's plays at his Théâtre de l'Oeuvre. *The Lady from the Sea* was performed there in 1892; *Rosmersholm* and *An Enemy of the People* in 1893, the dress-rehearsals of which attracted the attention of the Paris riot police; *The Master Builder* in 1894, *Little Eyolf* in 1895, and in 1896 *The Pillars of Society* and *Peer Gynt*. Ironically, in view of his love of the country, Ibsen never acquired the necessary championship in Italy that had been his fortune in Germany, France and England; but in Eleonora Duse he had an interpreter that made her name a legend in theatre history. George Bernard Shaw, who saw her playing Nora in *A Doll's House* in 1893, observed that she knew Nora more intimately than Nora knew herself. She also played Ellida Wangel, Rebecca West, and Fru Alving.

English interest, fostered first by Gosse and then later with enormous enthusiasm by Archer, had almost caught up with Ibsen's production by the time of *Hedda Gabler*. The British première of *A Doll's House* was at the Novelty theatre on 7 June 1889, with Janet Achurch as Nora, a performance marred only by the fact that Herbert Waring missed Helmer's line about no man sacrificing his honour, even for the woman he loves, so depriving Nora of her response, probably the most famous line in the play, 'Millions of women have done so.' The play was a great success and its original one-week season extended to three. Archer had already published a volume of translations, *The Pillars of Society and Other Plays*, in co-operation with Eleanor Marx and under the editorship of Havelock Ellis, and the success of this venture encouraged the publisher Walter Scott to bring out a five-volume edition of Ibsen's prose dramas, the fifth volume of which appeared in 1891.

In terms of performance 1891 was Ibsen's *annus mirabilis* in London. There was another performance of *A Doll's House* on 27

January at Terry's theatre, *Rosmersholm* on 23 February at the Vaudeville and *Ghosts* on 13 March at the Royalty theatre. Its scandalous reputation had preceded it, and over a thousand people applied for tickets to the opening night. Despite performances which remained too mannered for Archer's liking, and the hysterical hostility of certain critics, the play at once established itself, as it has done elsewhere in Europe, as the focus for a discussion about the claims of the theatre to be taken seriously as a forum for the debate of social issues. On 20 April *Hedda Gabler* opened at the Vaudeville, where Elizabeth Robins's performance in the title role was ecstatically received. Ibsen's unwaveringly bleak view of human nature continued to dismay critics like Clement Scott in the *Daily Telegraph*, who wrote of 'gazing on corruption. There they all were, false men, wicked women, deceitful friends, sensualist egoists, piled up in a heap. What a horrible story! What a hideous play!'

Audiences naturally rushed to see what all the fuss was about, and *Hedda Gabler* became the second of Ibsen's plays to achieve an evening run. May and June saw disappointing performances of *The Lady from the Sea* and another of *A Doll's House*, and the biggest single boost to Ibsen's career in the second half of the year came with the publication of Shaw's *The Quintessence of Ibsenism*. Stylish, opinionated, provocative and completely subjective, this was in many ways a model piece of literary criticism. Ibsen changed Shaw's life, rescuing him from his career as a failed novelist by opening his eyes to drama's possibilities as a new and effective way of artistic self-expression for the chaotic but passionate thinker. Shaw travelled to Germany in the summer of 1890 to see the Oberammergau Passion Play. On the way back he stayed briefly in Munich, but made no attempt to see Ibsen, explaining to Archer on his return to England that his ignorance of the Norwegian language 'prevented my calling upon him during my stay in Munich to explain his plays to him'.

Archer visited Ibsen shortly after this, on 23 August, and found him in an irritable mood. He complained for most of the day about the visit two weeks earlier of a reporter from the *Daily Chronicle*, who alarmed him with accounts of how his works were being commandeered as programmatic declarations by 'certain new moral philosophers' in England. This was a reference to Shaw, whose lecture on 'Socialism in Ibsen' in July of that year formed the basis for *The Quintessence of Ibsenism*. The journalist had found Ibsen 'very pleased to receive me, and glad to converse on the subject I called to see him about'.[15]

Ibsen seems to have spent most of the interview making it clear that he was not interested in political parties: 'He declared that he never at any time had belonged to the Social Democratic Party. He never had studied the Social Democratic question, nor does he intend to join the Social Democratic Party at a future date. In fact, he declared he never was nor ever would be a Social Democrat. He was surprised to find his name used as a means for the propagation of Social Democratic dogmas.' Shortly afterwards Ibsen wrote a letter to Hans Brækstad, a Norwegian associate of both Gosse and Archer in London, with a somewhat inconsequential account of how the journalist had misunderstood him. This duly appeared in the *Daily Chronicle*. That misunderstandings, real or of Ibsen's construction, could easily arise is evident from another interview earlier that year, published in the Scandinavian-American paper *The North* on 9 April. The journalist prefaced his article by saying that Ibsen was not an easy man to paraphrase: 'And yet I must confess', wrote the journalist, 'that it is almost impossible to reproduce his answers as concisely as he gave them; for I have never yet heard a man say so much in so few words.'[16]

As a curiosity, and a footnote to the upsurge of English interest in Ibsen's writing: Delius wrote to Ibsen about this time asking for permission to write music for a German version of *The Feast at Solhaug*.[17] Ibsen replied that not he but the translator, Emma Klingenfeld, owned the German rights to the work.

Ibsen travelled with his plays in the early part of 1891. After the performance of *Hedda Gabler* in Berlin in February he was in Vienna in April for a performance of *The Pretenders* at the Burg theatre, where he was called to take a bow after every act. At the reception afterwards he was celebrated until long into the night by young radicals and literary naturalists. One speaker, having praised Ibsen's revolutionary spirit, ended his speech by admitting how surprised he and the other young people at the gathering were to see Ibsen wearing orders on his jacket: why was this? Ibsen replied that it was to remind him to retain his self-control when he found himself in the company of bright young people who liked to party well into the small hours, a nice explanation under the circumstances. His habit of writing beneath Julius Kronberg's full-length portrait of him in academic gown, wearing an order and carrying a doctoral scroll in one hand, must have been for a similar reason, to remind him that he had a self-image to live up to.

A few days later, on 16 April, he attended a performance of *The Wild Duck* at the Deutsches Volkstheater, with a well-known actor, Friedrich Mittenwurzer, playing Hjalmar Ekdal. Again Ibsen was hailed and called to take a bow; but as the evening went on the booing and whistling grew louder. The play failed to attract an audience after the first night and was taken off after three perform-ances. Before leaving there was a farewell party given for him by the literary society Concordia. In a short speech he thanked the Viennese public for the warmth of their support as well as their 'honourable opposition'.[18]

On 19 April he travelled on to Budapest, where he had been invited as the guest of honour to a performance of *A Doll's House*. Both he and the play were rapturously received. The rapture and tumult continued outside the theatre until Ibsen, like some Vic-torian rock-star, had to be whisked away to safety in a waiting car-riage. Journalists clamoured to interview him during his stay, fascinated by his withdrawn personality.

The travelling, all the receptions, the huge media interest gave his procession the air of being 'Ibsen: The Last Tour', which is just what it turned out to be. He was beginning to feel his age. Originally he had declined the invitation to Vienna on the grounds that he was too old to make long journeys. And a few weeks after returning to Munich, on 18 May, he wrote declining an invitation to travel to London,* explaining that he was tired after his long journey through Austria and Hungary and was about to embark on a lengthy trip to the north. He made no secret of the fact that the prospect was as unwelcoming as ever. He was going, he wrote, 'because for various reasons it can be put off no longer'.[19] On 11 July he sent a note to the editor, Ole Thommessen, asking for his newspaper, *Verdens Gang*, to be delivered to Grand Hotel: 'Arriving Kristiania Thursday on the *Melchior*.'[20]

Had Ibsen been writing a play about his life, this return home after twenty-seven years in self-imposed exile would necessarily have been

---

* Øyvind Anker suggests his correspondent was the actor-manager George Cross, on the occasion of *Hedda Gabler's* run at the Vaudeville.

one of its dramatic climaxes. In real life, however, it passed off with a lack of moment that at times makes it seem no more than a whim. His huge ambivalence to the whole idea dominated him to such an extent that even when the trip was arranged he still preferred to think of return as only a possibility. On the two previous occasions on which he had gone home, in 1874 and 1885, he had reacted in the same fashion, conveying in his letters on the subject an impression of these trips being arranged at the last minute. And replying to a letter from his sister Hedvig in March 1891 his tone was in the same hesistant vein: 'And if I should once more, as I hope to, visit Norway, - yes, then I will see home again.'[21]

The unavoidable conclusion is that he did not really want to settle back in Norway in 1891, but that Suzannah, with Sigurd's support, had presented him with an ultimatum. In addition to the family trips of 1874 and 1885 she had been home with Sigurd in 1877, 1880, 1884, and 1887, and she had enjoyed her visits. All of her letters from Norway contained a gentle nudging to Ibsen on the beauties of his homeland. The view from the Grand Hotel along Karl Johan had changed out of all recognition, she told him, 'You can't possibly imagine how beautiful it is now.' In Trondheim she couldn't sleep for the light nights, and the trip to the North Cape with Sigurd in 1884 took her breath away: 'Come and see for yourself and you will never be able to forget the awesome beauty of it.'[22]

Sigurd, after his stateless upbringing, had shown himself in the course of his consular career to be a more patriotic Norwegian than his father. In the burning nationalist issue of the day, the debate which eventually led to the independence of Norway in 1905, Sigurd had alarmed some of his Swedish colleagues by the strength of his support for the view that Norway should have its own foreign minister, rather than file under a Swedish minister. Late in 1889 he was told that when his attaché stipend ran out at the end of the year he would be released from further duties, and his stance may have been a contributory factor. Formally it was because he lacked the necessary examination qualification to proceed.

Ibsen again tried to use his influence to keep his son in the job. His letter of 12 December 1889 to the newly elected Conservative prime minister Emil Stang shows the touch of guilt he felt that the way he had brought up his son had left this loophole for use against him:

It is conceivable that someone might suggest that it is my fault for failing to ensure that my son was educated at the university in Norway. But in reality this is not the case. I had no choice. My economic situation was in those days such that I was in no position to maintain him in his studies in Kristiania without moving there myself. But at that time it was impossible for me to contemplate such a thing. Had I done so my whole literary career would have suffered a catastrophic derailment.

Up there (i.e. in Norway) I would never have been able to achieve the position in world literature which is now mine. Up there it would never have been my happy fate as it is now to make the name of Norway known to a wider world than any other Norwegian before me in the field of literature – or indeed, in any other field at all.

Expressing a wish to avoid the embarassment of a publicly-heard appeal against the decision he urged the prime minister to intervene personally:

Thus do I earnestly and repeatedly beg you, Prime Minister, and through you the entire Norwegian government, to intervene on behalf of my son and me, and do what can be done to remove the obstacles which the Foreign Office is now placing in the way of his continued presence in and advancement through the diplomatic service.

Though he again threatened, on behalf of Sigurd as well as himself, to revoke his Norwegian citizenship, settle in Bavaria and become a naturalised German citizen if the promises made to him were not kept, he was not successful this time, and Sigurd left the diplomatic service on 31 December 1889. As Ibsen's son, and as an articulate and intelligent essayist, he soon acquired a name for himself through newspaper articles on the foreign ministry affair; but for the next ten years he was without regular employment.

Ibsen's nationalism, once such a clear element in his profile, had dwindled to nothing with the years of his success. His was now the outlook of a successful capitalist for whom all the world was a potential market for his product. In the newspaper interview with Skordalsvold in 1890 his idea of the way things would develop in Europe predict the formation of the EEC: 'In my opinion the various nations in Europe will one day form a league or union like the

United States, and if that happens then not only Scandinavians but other nations too will be 'swallowed up' by that union.'[23] He clearly viewed this prospect without alarm. Now that he was leaving Germany, and the position was no longer of any particular practical value to him, he even dropped his promotion of pan-Germanism, and in reply to a question about what he thought of those Norwegian emigrants to America who made such a point of retaining their cultural and ethnic roots, he said that 'they will, of course, end up as Americans anyway. Even a German who settles in a Scandinavian land will in time become a Scandinavian, as will his descendants.' Ibsen, though, had not become an Italian by living in Rome. More than most other members of the Circolo Scandinavo he had maintained a firm hold on his cultural roots in Norway. Sigurd, on the other hand, looked so Italian that, as Fleetwood noted on first meeting him, 'you would not have been able to guess that he had nordic blood in his veins, not to mention Norwegian blood.'[24]

Perhaps one final factor at work in Ibsen's decision to return home was the emergence of a degree of professional jealousy among some of his German literary colleagues. By 1891 he was far and away the most performed and influential dramatist in the country, and his success began to seem oppressive to some of the native dramatists. On 12 March 1891 the Munich Journalists' and Writers' Union threw a large party to celebrate the seventieth birthday of the Prince Regent. The poet and dramatist Martin Greif was one of the speakers, and he used the occasion to mount an attack on foreign dramatists, now and then adressing his remarks to Ibsen. Ibsen replied by praising the city that had been home to him for so many years, and expressing surprise at Greif's attack, claiming that Greif was a poet and not a playwright. He went on to say that he felt the criticism could not apply to him, since he had always felt so at home in Munich, where he was performed at least as often and with as much success as Greif, with whom he gladly shared his laurels.

The point was argued further into the night, and ended with Greif and Ibsen shaking hands. After the gathering Ibsen walked home with the peace-maker, M.G. Conrad, holding on to his arm and meditating aloud on events in a surreal ramble:

What does he actually want, this Martin Greif? I don't understand. What sort of plays does he write? Plays about people who died ages ago, whom he's never known. Can you write plays about people you've never known? What do the dead have to do with Martin Greif? He ought to leave them in peace and dramatise the living, as much as he likes. Now he disturbs the peace for the dead Bavarian princes in their graves. When he's done with them it'll be the turn of the Hohenzollerns. That's not difficult, there are enough dead princes, history is huge. But it is not the proper job of drama in our age.

Again he asked: 'What do these dead kings have to do with Martin Greif?'

Conrad reminded him that he had himself written a historical play, about Catiline: "Ha!" he shouted back at once. "In the first place Catiline wasn't a king but an anarchist. In the second place I wasn't a dramatist in those days, I was a chemist. *Catiline* was the chemist's first attempt to write drama. Has Martin Greif ever been a chemist? Eh?" '25

19

A Homecoming
The Master Builder

The pattern of the Ibsens' life together was established from the first days of what was originally referred to as their 'holiday' in Norway. Arriving on 16 July 1891 they parted at once. Ibsen sailed round the coast of Norway to see North Cape for himself, delighting the local press by tossing a bouquet of roses into the waters of the Arctic. This was another harbinger of things to come, an announcement that henceforth he intended to indulge the romantic side of his nature. The extreme gravity with which the Norwegian press treated his every word and gesture during these first weeks was a source of amusement to young writers like Knut Hamsun. In a letter to his friend O. L. Larsen he ridiculed press reports that Ibsen had 'declared himself satisfied with the North Cape. Satisfied with the North Cape! Imagine a little chap who nods his head and with a very serious look on his face declares himself 'satisfied with the Orion Nebula'. Pardon me while I collapse with laughter.'[1] Hamsun's one-man war against Ibsen, a perverse recognition of his greatness, would continue throughout most of the decade, and leave its mark in Ibsen's next play *Bygmester Solness* (*The Master Builder*).

Suzannah preferred to travel to Valdres in the Gudbrandsdal, where her sister Marie had spent some of the last months of her life eighteen years earlier. She stayed there until well into September, so that when Ibsen returned to the capital on 7 August, booking in at the Grand Hotel, he had the freedom to do as he pleased, see whom he pleased and go where he pleased.

Almost, at any rate: he still had to endure the dubious pleasure of being publicly fêted. Georg Brandes, who was also staying at the Grand, with great difficulty persuaded Ibsen to attend a party in his honour at the hotel. Michæl Birkeland's description of Ibsen's behaviour at Botten Hansen's wedding party, thirty years earlier, comes to mind: he 'was at his most incorrigible'.² Nothing was right. His lady at table was not some charming young delight but the painter Kitty Kielland, a radical feminist who bored him with her disapproval of Fru Elvsted in *Hedda Gabler*. She tried to flatter him by remarking that all the great deeds in Norway had been the work of westerners – 'because of course you're from the west too, aren't you?' Ibsen would have none of it. 'I am Norwegian,' he replied, and referring to her strong west-coast accent added, 'but I gather the lady is from Stavanger.'

Georg Brandes fared little better in his speech to the guest of honour, the main point of which was that the Scandinavians had understood Ibsen before the rest of Europe. There was every justification for this, bearing in mind the enthusiastic reception given to both *Brand* and *Peer Gynt* in Scandinavia and the tardy German response to *A Doll's House* and *Ghosts*; but Ibsen was on home ground again and determined to express his continued contempt for his own countrymen. He shook his head throughout Brandes's speech, scarcely rising to acknowledge the toast. Later on, hearing that Brandes intended to apply for a post as professor of literature, he remarked, 'Really? Well in that case he ought to steer clear of Norwegian literature because he doesn't understand it at all.' What he really wanted was the company of young women, and he did not cheer up until he had two of them, one on each arm, to stroll up and down the floor with him.

Ibsen's fondness for such companions became an enduring feature of his rebirth in Kristiania. The episodes with Bardach and Raff were dry runs, so to speak, for his more enduring relationship with the young pianist, Hildur Andersen, born in 1864. Ibsen had known her parents during his years as director and dramatist-in-residence in Bergen in the 1850s. He lodged with her mother's family, the Sontums, for one year, and after moving into the theatre annexe continued to eat his evening meals there throughout the six years of his stay. The Sontums were among the few whom it might be accurate to describe as intimates of Ibsen, though even there the term must be qualified. Hildur's uncle, Christian Sontum, was Ibsen's doctor after his return to Norway.

Hildur studied music in Dresden, later in Leipzig and was in Vienna in 1889 at the same time as Sigurd Ibsen worked at the embassy there. They met each other often, corresponded, and for a time it seemed as though they might make a couple. Suzannah's eyes and ears in Kristiania before 1891 was her distant relative and friend, Christiane Magelssen, and Magelssen mentions Hildur, her sister Valborg, and Sigurd several times in her letters. Meeting Hildur in 1887 she described her as 'bright and intelligent, while Valborg is the image of her father, very introverted and stiff, but an outstanding girl'.[3] She had to promise to send them a photograph of Sigurd. Writing in March 1889 she told Suzannah that Sigurd and Hildur were corresponding, and that when Hildur visited Vienna she was 'frequently in Sigurd's company out in the big wide world, she is very interested in him and pleased when he visits her.'[4] But a few months later she related to Suzannah that Hildur 'thinks he is too difficult, and so do I, but he has a right to be.'[5]

Ludvig Josephson, who gained such a curious impression of Sigurd Ibsen during his visits to Munich in the late 1870s, referred in his memoirs to a 'a strange rumour spread by his acquaintances and even more strongly rooted in Munich since Henrik Ibsen moved there, that Herr Sigurd suffered a deep-seated jealousy of his father.'[6] The very slight hint of a failed budding romance between Sigurd and Hildur Andersen, who was in the autumn of 1891 swept off her feet by the old man's offer of avuncular but intimate friendship might, in the light of Josephson's comments, explain the curiously strained relationship between father and son in the 1890s. It might also account for Sigurd Ibsen's desultory progress through later life, during which, among other things, long after his father's death, he tried his hand at writing plays.

By September Sigurd was out of the way in any case. In a pattern that would repeat itself throughout the decade, even after his marriage, he accompanied Suzannah on a winter journey south, to Saló by Lake Garda, for the sake of her rheumatism. Ibsen had decided to settle in Kristiania by this time and rented a large flat, Victoria Terrasse 7B, in the central Vika district of Kristiania, moving in on 21 October. Writing to Hegel in September he told him that the idea was 'naturally not to spend our whole year here but to go travelling as before. The only change is the point of departure.'[7]

But from now on Suzannah travelled alone or with Sigurd. Much to her disappointment Ibsen could never be persuaded to join her. He was too enamoured of the company of Hildur Andersen, whom he now paraded in Kristiania as his regular escort. Scattered across the periods of Suzannah's absence are Ibsen's written requests to the Christiania theatre for two tickets to the show tonight – on 18 October, on 30 October, to see *Carmen* on 2 December. He seemed to be experimenting with indiscretion, as though he wished people to believe they were having an affair. At Hildur's request he sent a photograph of himself to a Danish friend of hers, 'with fondest greetings from Hildur and Henrik Ibsen.'[8] Like Bardach and Raff before her, Hildur became his little *prinsesse*, to whom he was in turn 'the Princess's most loyal and devoted personal doctor'. Many of his letters, notes and dedications to her over the next ten years or so echo so closely things written or said to Bardach or Raff that it is clear that he considered all three of them to be more or less the same person, a tactic that simplified his life greatly.

One of their first public appearances together was at Knut Hamsun's three lectures on literature, at Brødrene Hals, on 7, 9 and 12 October. Hamsun, with *Hunger* already published, had been touring Norway with these lectures for some months, shocking the old and delighting the young with an impassioned attack on, *inter alia,* Ibsen, Bjørnson, Kielland and Lie, the four leading names in Norwegian literature of the day. The attack on Ibsen, numinous now among his own countrymen, was considered particularly scandalous. Citing *A Doll's House* as an example Hamsun accused the old master of writing *moteliteratur* (trendy literature). But what he criticised him for most was his psychology:

We have a third writer, who is not so openly pedagogic as Bjørnson, and not so openly a writer of entertainments as Kielland, but who, like them, has tirelessly written the literature of social concern, and in his descriptions of people perhaps more than any of the others has contented himself with a rigid and simple psychology of character, – I refer to Henrik Ibsen. *If there is anyone* among our writers who has created 'characters' in all their rigid simplicity, it is he; if there is anyone who insists on keeping such a tight 'hold' on his description that no so-called 'irrelevancies' appear in the character, it is he. And this is as much a consequence of the literary form this writer always uses as it is of the natural stiffness and lack of nuance in his own emotional life.[9] . . . What I really accuse Ibsen of is this, that he, who is of all of our writers the least pedagogic, the least democratic, still does not manage to exceed the others in the penetration of his psychology. . . He is himself too much of a caricature, he perceives and feels things in whole, typical, distinct numbers, instead of in fractions.[10]

Ibsen listened to this in silence, seated in the front row with Hildur Andersen, Edvard and Nina Grieg, and Ole Thommessen. Afterwards he observed to Thommessen that 'if we lived in a civilised country the students would have beaten that chap's brains out this evening',[11] and Thommessen loyally slaughtered the three lectures in the editorial column of *Verdens Gang*. Ibsen showed great courage in attending the lectures, but he was disturbed by Hamsun's attack. Herman Bang met him in the street at about this time and his first subject of conversation was the lectures. In the play that was then taking shape in his head the character of Ragnar Brovik, the young builder who challenges old master Solness to give him a chance or get out of his way, owed not a little to those two evenings Ibsen spent at Brødrene Hals*.

In February 1892 Hildur left Kristiania for a few months, to continue her musical studies in Vienna, and the flurry of excitement over the homecoming subsided as the dust settled over the Ibsens' lives again with Suzannah's return from the south. Occasionally they entertained friends from the old days. Suzannah had investigated the matter and decided that in his absurd dispute with Lorentz Dietrichson in 1885 her husband had been more to blame than her old friend, and relations with Dietrichson were accordingly restored. They also saw Ernst Sars, the historian and former 'auxiliary member' of the old Holland. But with the light temporarily gone from his life this dutiful social skirmishing was soon abandoned and Ibsen presently began real work on his next play. A short poem, dated 16 March, encapsulated the essence of the work in progress in the same way that 'Judas' had been a sort of microcosmic prediction of *Emperor and Galilean*. 'They sat there, those two', simple and devastatingly truthful, is one of his finest and most personal poems. He subtitled it 'a first note towards *The Master Builder*':

> They sat there, those two, in such a cosy house
> through the autumn and winter days.
> Then it burnt down. Everything turned to rubble.
> They had to rake through the embers.

* Ibsen had copies of four books by Hamsun in his library. *Mysteries*, which contained a further attack on Ibsen, has been cut up to page seventy-three.

For there's a jewel hidden there,
that can never burn.
If they keep on searching, it might easily happen,
that he finds it, or she does.

But even if they find it, that burnt-out couple
Find that fireproof, costly jewel -
she'll never find her burnt-out faith,
nor he his burnt-out happiness.

All that summer he was preoccupied with the work. By 20 September he had finished and at once set about the final rewrite. It was published in Copenhagen on 12 December in an edition of 10,000 copies. Its European première proper was in Berlin at the Lessing theatre, on 19 January 1893, where it managed only three performances. But generally speaking it did well, and within twelve months had been performed in Chicago, London (three different venues), Kristiania, Copenhagen, Gothenburg and Paris. Ibsen was still controversial, still good box-office.

The Master Builder was the first play Ibsen had written on home soil for twenty-eight years, since *The Pretenders*. In the intervening years Kristiania had changed out of all recognition. From the semi-rural town of 1864 it had become a busy little city. There was a large industrial workforce and widespread visible poverty. There were 2,000 telephone subscribers (including the Ibsens), the first typewriters had appeared in the offices, there was electricity in the homes and bicycles on the streets. Knut Hamsun's novel *Hunger*, published in 1890, was the document of this change and of the emergent phenomenon of urban alienation which became the staple of so much subsequent European literature.

Though he now lived in Kristiania, these things impinged hardly at all on Ibsen's world. Throughout the years of his exile Norway had always been a Norway of the mind. Like Joyce's Dublin or Nabokov's Russia it was a hybrid of memory, imagination, and newspaper reports. By 1892 his brief period as a social reformer was over anyway, and in *The Master Builder* he returned once again to the greatest subject of any great writer, the self. His first and natural literary thought was to take stock of the extraordinary changes that had occurred in his personal circumstances since his departure for Rome armed only with a spurious doctorate and his wife's unshakeable faith in his literary talent, and *The Master Builder* became the first of his three last meditations on the cost of fame.

Some of the play's 'furniture' came from the recent past. Hedvig's letter earlier in the year had set him thinking back to the early days in Skien, of the two great fires of 1854 and 1886 that razed the town, and of the significance of its rebirth and renewal after the restoration of 1886: 'The house where I was born and where I lived during the earliest years of my childhood, – the church, the old church with the christening angel up in the canopy has burnt down. Everything that connects me to my earliest memories, all burnt, all of it.'[12] From this he derived the fire that took everything of value from Aline Solness' life, not just the irreparable loss of her new-born twin sons, but of every trivial personal possession, the more trivial the more meaningful, such as those nine absurd, beautiful dolls she mourns:* 'You mustn't laugh at me', she tells Hilde Wangel.† The image of the burnt church might have set him thinking of the church tower and that local legend of the watchman who fell from it to his death; of his mother's terrified reaction at seeing him high up there in the arms of his nursemaid, explanation enough for that vertigo from which he suffered and to which Vilhelm Bergsøe testified in his account of their trip to the top of the *Punto Imperatore* on Ischia.

Towers and heights were anyway conspiring to bring themselves to his attention. In Kristiania in the 1890s there was an architectural craze for topping off larger houses with towers. Ibsen cannot fail to have noticed them on his walks around Victoria Terrasse; and an entry in Helene Raff's journal for 22 April 1890 records how she related to him one day the tale of the builder of St Michæl's church who threw himself from the top of it in his fear that it was badly constructed. Raff told him that similar tales were told of every church in Germany, and Ibsen said the same was true of Norway. He added, by way of explanation, that 'people sense one cannot build something that high without being punished'. This points clearly to one of the main themes in *The Master Builder*, *hubris*, which was itself just another version of Ibsen's eternal theme, 'the conflict between will and ability'.

---

* Ibsen referred with astonishment to a suggestion in a Swedish newspaper that these dolls symbolised the nine muses.
† In fact the line was cut from the Berlin performance precisely because of the fear that the audience would laugh.

The obsessional heart of *The Master Builder* is Solness himself and his troubled analysis of the price he has paid and demanded of others for his success in life. There is no point in quibbling over the obvious equation of Solness the builder with Ibsen the maker of plays. Solness says he titles himself 'master builder' because he is too humble to call himself 'architect'; yet he unhesitatingly claims the higher status of 'artist' in referring to 'The price my achievement as an artist has cost me – and others.' His analysis of this price is revealed in conversations with Hilde Wangel, the young woman who mysteriously arrives on his doorstep and moves into the house as a member of the family.

It is an occult analysis, developing the mysticism first essayed in the figure of Maximos in *Emperor and Galilean*, present to some extent in *Rosmersholm*, to a much greater extent in *The Lady from the Sea*, present again to a lesser extent in *Hedda Gabler*. The theme of hypnotism and the secret power one human being can acquire over another was presented via The Stranger in *The Lady from the Sea*; here in *The Master Builder* Ibsen suggests a much darker and more intimate experience of it by using it in the depiction of a life-situation and a personality closer to his own. It is entirely appropriate that his occult 'helper' in this analytic experiment should be Ellida Wangel's step-daughter Hilde. To this contemporary concern, mixing theosophy with the science of Charcot, Ibsen added everywhere touches of folklore and fairy tale. Hilde and Solness recognise the troll in each other – those ideas he spoke of to Helene Raff, about a voice inside that goads one on to do bad things, to harm a loved one, to break a trust, to be cruel and deceitful, for the sheer perverse pleasure of the moment. On to hypnotism and folklore he brought to bear a childlike belief in the terrifying power of a will which is truly focused on one end and one alone: success.

In *The Master Builder* Ibsen both exhibits and tries to analyse the unbalancing effect of great fame on the personality. Within the recent past he had re-read *Faust* in a new Danish translation by Peter Hansen, and in his letter of thanks and congratulations to Hansen he wrote that he was about to embark on Hansen's introduction next, 'and I hope it will help me to understand the second part of the poem, which till now has seemed to me to suffer from an altogether too obscure allegorising'.[13] Success and fame in *The Master Builder* have a Faustian dimension. Solness expresses several times the fear that he may be mad, and the play reflects this, juxtaposing levels of reality so disparate that only Ibsen's heroic technical control keep it from degenerating into incomprehensibility.

At its most accessible level – the level frequently chosen by directors – the play deals with the mid-life crisis of a highly successful professional man, an ageing master who finds himself challenged by a rising generation of young usurpers. Out of pure egoism he fiercely resists the rise of his talented young assistant Ragnar Brovik, relenting finally in a gesture of sentimental tenderness towards Brovik's dying father and giving written documentation of his approval of the plans Ragnar has drawn up for a new house for a young couple, their customers.

At a second, still predominantly realistic level, the play is about Solness' need for Hilde Wangel. He says he needs her in his struggle to resist Brovik's challenge, and uses her as a kind of homeopathic remedy to protect himself with youth against youth. An otherwise enigmatic pencil note on a draft for a letter dated July 1892 seems to refer to this aspect of their relationship: 'Sunrise, transfusion of the blood of the young animal. Airship that can be steered. Glimpse into the life of Martians.'[14]

His need for her is also the real, sexual need of an elderly man for a young woman. He longs to abandon his old, sick wife but is plagued by guilt at the prospect. Aline has given her life in order to serve him and his ambition: 'And now she's dead – for my sake. And I am chained alive to a dead woman.' Back home in Norway again Ibsen was reminded of the reading of his youth and lets Solness in his agonising invoke the Vikings of the old sagas, pre-Christian heroes who lived free of the burdens of conscience and guilt, who on their raiding carried off the women they wanted as spoils of war. Solness envies them their 'robust consciences' and is fascinated and tormented by the notion that women so taken often came to love their captors.

The Solness-Hilde situation, which so clearly reflects the Ibsen and Bardach-Raff-Andersen situation, is the least satisfactory from a dramatic point of view. It quickly becomes clear that neither one of them is able to navigate Fru Alving's margin and make a reality of their desires. And yet they will not give up. Instead they begin to indulge in a sort of surrogate sexual intercourse, rhythmically swopping metaphors, building and elaborating them all the time, imagining the kind of tower Solness will build for Hilde, how Princess Hilde will live in this tower, elaborating the fantasy until Hilde hits on the idea that it will be a 'castle in the air'. As neither of them is able or willing to admit that this is all just talk, they join each other in a *folie à deux*, in which the fantasy world they have created becomes more real than the actual world. Hilde's jubilation at the end of the play, when Solness falls to his death from the tower, is not an evil or heartless jubilation but a sign that she has not yet re-emerged from the fantasy world into which they have talked each other. His fall is a long, unreal moment for her, something like the experience of observers on the ground as they watched the Challenger spaceship, with its crew of astronauts on board, explode into magnificent flaming pieces fifteen seconds up from the launching pad.

The third level is that on which the whole play is Solness' dream. At several points Ibsen deliberately invites the possibility that Hilde is somehow not a real person at all. Solness is a demon and Hilde is one of his occult helpers, summoned to assist him by the power of his will which he believes to be demonic and capable of bending fate his way. He thinks he may have willed the fire that burnt their house down, for after the fire he parcelled off the land and sold it as building plots, and the profit from that dealing was the capital that set him on the road to wealth and success. The reference to the fire starting because there was a crack in the chimney, which he knew about but did not repair, is a borrowing from Norwegian folklore, where the devil often uses such cracks as a means of entering a house.

The reality of Hilde's version of what took place between the two of them on the first occasion they met, ten years earlier, and of Hilde's version of their agreement, that he would come to carry her off and make her a princess in a kingdom of her own; that he kissed her passionately 'many, many times' after the ceremony in Lysanger (one thinks of the *Ibsenplatz* ceremony and the celebrations afterwards at which Ibsen and Bardach met for the first time); that Solness was heard singing by Hilde while he was up the tower – all of these 'facts' are questioned by the master builder. His belief is that he has transferred such images into Hilde's head as thoughts and desires, but in reality done nothing.

The Master Builder is a strange and volatile brew. It shouldn't work but it does. Like the play it most resembles, *When We Dead Awaken*, there is something deeply touching about these naked, hopeless attempts to break free of conscience. As Solness well knows, they are doomed from the start, and he will always be 'chained alive to the dead woman'. The short scene between Solness and Hilde immediately preceding Solness' ascent of the tower provides a remarkable clarification of the paradox of Ibsen, whose anarchic dreams were in such stark contrast to his ultra-conservative exterior and his many ultra-conservative views:

SOLNESS: (standing still, staring intently at her) If I do try it, Hilde, when I'm standing up there I'll talk to him just the way I did last time.

HILDE: (in mounting excitement) What will you say to him!

SOLNESS: I'll say to him: listen to me, Almighty Lord, – you can judge me just as you think fit. But from now on I'm only going to build the sweetest thing in the world –

HILDE: (carried away) Yes-yes-yes!

SOLNESS: – build it with a princess, whom I'm so fond of -

HILDE: Yes, tell him that! Tell him that!

SOLNESS: Yes. And then I'll say to him: now I'm going to climb down, and put my arms around her, and kiss her –

HILDE: – lots of times! Say that!

SOLNESS: – lots and lots of times, I'll say.

HILDE: And then –?

SOLNESS: Then I'll swing my hat – and come down to earth again – and do what I told him.

HILDE: (with outstretched arms) Now I see you again the way you were when there was music in the air!

SOLNESS: (looks at her with head bowed) How did it happen, Hilde? How did you become the way you are?

HILDE: How did you make me the way I am?

SOLNESS: (curt and decisive) The Princess shall have her castle.

HILDE: (thrilled, she claps her hands) Oh master builder! My lovely lovely castle! Our castle in the air!

SOLNESS: With stone foundations.

Solness is referring to the first time he and Hilde met, ten years ago, at her home in Lysanger, when he climbed up to plant the wreath on the newly completed tower of the local church. He tells her that he spoke to God while he was up there. He liberated himself from God in proclaiming his equality with God:

SOLNESS: And when I stood right at the very top and hung the wreath over the weathervane I said to him: Now listen here, you all-powerful! From now on I'm going to be a free master-builder too. In my field. Just as you are in yours. I will never again build churches for you. Just homes for people.

But God does not want Solness to climb down the steeple, throw his arms around Hilde and kiss her. God's commandment to men like Solness is 'Thou shalt not', and to ensure that he does not break it God throws him off the tower. A more orthodox statement of Old Testament morality could hardly be imagined, nor a bleaker defence of marriage. Adultery, even in the mind, is a mortal sin, and the wages of sin is death. After forty years of trying Ibsen, who wrote so passionately to Bjørnson of his longing to remove *munkedomsmærket* (the mark of the cloister) from people's minds, still could not remove it from his own.

Ibsen's harem of chaste princesses, Bardach, Raff, Andersen, were all disposed to see their relationship with Ibsen reflected in *The Master Builder*, and Ibsen went out of his way to encourage them in this. The copy sent to Helene Raff was inscribed: 'Helene Raff! A voice inside me cries out for you. Please accept this book from your faithful and devoted Henrik Ibsen', clearly an invitation to her to identify with Hilde, the troll's helper, who says 'Tell me, Herr Solness *(bygmester)*, – are you sure you've never called out for me? I mean, sort-of . . . inwardly?'

And to flatter both Bardach and Andersen he included a private reference in the play, the dating of the occasion of that first crowning of the church spire to 19 September and the day Ibsen and Andersen celebrated as their 'anniversary'. Ibsen gave her a diamond ring with this date engraved on it, repeating the fascination with 'alternative' marriage ceremonies he had shown in his Bergen days with Rikke Holst, which occurs in *Rosmersholm* with Rosmer's and Rebecca's marriage-in-death, and in *The Lady from the Sea* with the 'marriage' between Ellida Wangel and the Stranger. Bardach's diary has no entry for 19 September, but her entries for 18 and 20 September also suggest that her relationship with Ibsen entered a new phase of intimacy and intensity over those two days.

But of the two of them it was Hildur Andersen who was the real muse for *The Master Builder*, as Ibsen mixed her real-life high spirits with the sadistic, mischievous personality of Hilde Wangel he had created four years earlier in *The Lady from the Sea*. The letter he wrote to her on 1 January 1893, with its direct and pathetic echo of Hilde's last words, that close the play, says all that really needs to be said about the nature of their relationship:

Saturday morning. 7.1.93

My wild woodland bird!

Where do you fly now? I just do not know. Are you still circling over Leipzig? Or have you set course again further north? Closer to home? I know nothing. Now I will go down to your mama and make my enquiries about you. And maybe there will be a letter there waiting for me.

Where and when you will read these lines is uncertain. Or at least, it is for me at the moment. I write them mostly for my own benefit, because I feel the need to send you something. To remain in contact with you, you know. – No newspapers today. Not so far this morning anyway. Later maybe – if I pick up your trail at your mama's.

If it would have been to your advantage to have visited Brahms earlier I really wouldn't know, for I know absolutely nothing of the musical scene there. But of course, one meeting does lead to another. And Brahms is at the centre of a large circle, that much I do know. As well as being a delightful personality.

I received the enclosed little New Year letter from Baroness Todesco. But its contents won't be of special interest to you.

Oh, how I long for the princess! Long to come down from the dreaming heights. Long to come down to earth again and do that thing I told you – so many, many times!

A thousand most heartfelt greetings, for now!

Your, your master builder[15]

Aline Solness, with her nine dolls and her air of tragic defeat, perhaps owed something to Ibsen's memories of his mother Marichen and her withdrawl from life after the fall of her husband Knud. Aline also contained elements of Suzannah, in her ill-health, in her mantric use of the word *plikt* (duty).[16] But if Hildur Andersen was his 'wild woodland bird' Suzannah was still his 'eagle'. Hildur scarcely worried her more than Bardach and Raff, towards both of whom she had extended a tolerant acceptance.

*   *   *

Ibsen had to contend with the reappearance of several personal ghosts after his return. One was another of his birds, 'the lark' Laura Kieler, whose marriage he had made use of in *A Doll's House*. She had achieved a degree of local notoriety, or fame, on the strength of this. Unlike Nora, she was not a radical; in fact she detested the Brandes brothers and all they stood for and in her 1888 play *Men of Honour* fiercely attacked the way modern artists were contributing to the erosion of fundamental social values. Brandes found her attack too personal, and was personal in his response, raising again the subject of her attempted forgery. Kieler, who suffered periodically from mental instability, seemed to think that a statement from Ibsen to the effect that she was *not* Nora would redeem her reputation on this score. Understandably Ibsen was not willing to make such a statement, for as he told a correspondent in 1890, he had never said she *was* Nora.[17]

The next year, shortly after Ibsen had settled in Victoria Terrasse, Kieler contacted him. Ibsen invited her up to the apartment for a meal and they discussed her problems. She told him 'how much damage *A Doll's House* had done to my life',[18] and said many years later in a newspaper interview that her story made him weep. This four-hour meeting was the last contact between them.

As a very famous man Ibsen attracted a great deal of this kind of attention from the unhappy, particularly if they believed he had made use of them in a play. Another was the Dane Julius Hoffory, one of Ibsen's most active promoters in Germany, whom many contemporaries believed to be the model for Ejlert Løvborg in *Hedda Gabler*. Hoffory had severe mental problems that either were caused by his alcoholism or caused it, and ended his days in an asylum in 1897. In 1892 Ibsen became the focus of his madness and was in regular receipt of Hoffory's old letters and hotel bills, all sent to him 'with no indication of what I am supposed to do with them', as he calmly protested.

On 5 June 1892 a woman died who had played a less glamorous but more lasting, significant role in his life and writing – Else Sophie Birkedalen, the mother of his illegitimate son Hans Jacob, who had given him the gifts of shame and guilt. Though in a good position to do so it seems she never caused him the slightest difficulty over their relationship in Grimstad. There is remarkably little folklore about her, even in the small community just outside Lillesand where she and Hans Jacob lived out their lives and where she worked as a housekeeper. They lived in poverty. In the 1875 census Hans Jacob's occupation was given as 'smith' while his mother was *almissen* (in receipt of poor relief). When they moved from their home in Birkedalen to Møglestu Hans Jacob is said to have scratched on a stone *Farvel til Sultefjæld* (Farewell to Hungry Hill). After he married he moved out of Møglestu, and Else Sophie was allowed to live in a tiny, red-painted wooden house at a place called Tyttebærmoen. Anna Folkvord, the wife of the local poor law commissioner Enok Folkvord, visited her regularly and tried to help her. One day she asked the old woman how the 'accident' had come about. Else Sophie replied, 'Well, you know, that Henrik, it wasn't easy to stop him.'

Hans Jacob had a difficult and disappointing life. He lost his first wife Mathilde at the age of thirty, with TB, and their only child Jens died in infancy. In 1882 he married for a second time, to Trine Marie Gunnersdatter. They had a child straightaway, but mother and child died in the smallpox epidemic that swept Lillesand in that year. Eighteen months later he married a third wife, Ida Gurine Olsdatter, who bore him five children. Three died young, and of the two who survived, both daughters, one was among the 800 who drowned when the emigrant ship the *Norge* sank off Rockall in 1904, and the other died of TB in 1922, at the age of twenty-seven, shortly before she was to be married. Hans Jacob himself was tormented by knowledge of his personal situation, and he and his wife Ida were often called Ibsen by Lillesand people. He struggled against alcoholism for much of his adult life, and a poem in nine verses survives, specially written 'For the Lillesand Temperance Society'. When he fell off the wagon he would go on a binge, taking with him his proudest possession, his birth certificate, by showing which he would hope to be treated to a drink. He was also a maker of fiddles which acquired a fine reputation locally.

Of the legend that he made his way to Kristiania and turned up on Ibsen's doorstep one day, and that Ibsen tossed him a handful of coins with the words, 'I gave this much to your mother, it ought to be enough for you', there is no reliable evidence. It may be a dramatisation of the story that Enok Folkvord wrote to Ibsen, after his return, on behalf of Hans Jacob and Ida and their children, asking if he would be willing to help them, and that Ibsen replied curtly that he considered he had long ago fulfilled his obligations to this son and his mother.[19]

There were more friendly ghosts, like Christopher Due from

Grimstad, like Rikke Holst, now Tresselt, from Bergen, Ibsen's princess for a few months in the spring of 1853, who visited him several times. And since Ibsen would never go to Skien, Skien came to Ibsen in the form of his sister Hedvig, who brought with her her only daughter Anna to see him. Though a grown woman, Anna referred to her distinguished uncle as her 'Sun God', a practice Ibsen did not discourage.[20]

But on the personal front the main event of the year was Sigurd's engagement in May to Bergljot, one of Bjørnson's daughters. Bjørnson, who had several children, was delighted at the match. The Ibsens were more cautious in their response, much more inclined to fear that they were losing a son. Relations between the two camps had been in one of their troughs since the Ibsens' return. Bjørnson complained that Ibsen had come back to Norway without sending him a greeting. His wife Karoline had spoken to her childhood friend Suzannah and found her exclusively concerned to let her know how famous 'they' had become. When the Bjørnsons visited the Ibsens in Kristiania to discuss the proposal Ibsen's sceptical reaction infuriated Bjørnson. He wrote to Bergljot:

Aulestad 1892. 21. Mars.

Dear Bergljot!

You are far too young to understand all the wicked things Ibsen has done to me.

I could say forget all about it. But he comes back here without a word to me. Sigurd got engaged, and he contacted neither my mother, my brother nor spoke to Bjørn other than casually.

He even denied there was any engagement. He did it lots of times, to lots of different people. At Ole Olsens he said to me that Sigurd had told his mother that *if* he ever got married, it would be to Bergljot.

I said hello to him, he said hello back. And apart from at parties and so on that has been it.

There is only one possible conclusion: he wants nothing to do with us. Fair enough! But in that case then I'll consider myself a free man too and say exactly what I think about his later writing and his manner. He has always had unpleasant friends who are bent on mischief making. Imagine tolerating someone like Hans Jæger! And others like him! Anyone prepared to receive 'that lot' – and anonymous letters – can never be trusted. So please spare me all the accusations. I have never complained about Ibsen, after all, either to you or to anyone else.

You can tell Sigurd exactly what I think. He is so honourable, so talented, that every hour spent in his company is a joy.

My fulsome greetings to the Sørensens! Your father and friend

B B[21]

The wedding was on 11 October, at Bjørnson's country mansion Aulestad. Ibsen had been invited, but Bjørnson's fear that he might not turn up was clearly reflected in the invitation:

Aulestad 1892. 3/9

Dear Friend!

The wedding has now been set for 11 October and it is our honour and pleasure to invite the two of you.

You should arrive at Lillehammer in the evening and can stay there or travel on and be here about nine or nine-thirty. In that case a carriage (ordered by telegraph at the Victoria) should be waiting to meet you at the quay.

If you are very busy you can travel back to Lillehammer on the day of the wedding (about ten miles) and be back in Kristiania the next day.

If you don't come, people will wonder why, and for the sake of the young couple, with every justification. This also: since neither I nor Karoline will be present at the church ceremony, since we both know it's a sham for them as it is for us, then you, who have requested it, ought to be there, so that the parents are not entirely unrepresented at a ceremony that means so much to you. I imagine for travelling companions you will have my brother and his family and the Thoresens, so that should be jolly.

No one else is coming but family and close relatives. We shall do our best to give you a warm welcome. If you like I could pick you up at the quay at Lillehammer; but that would be a nuisance for both of us, so beyond that we'll do our very best to make you comfortable. Karoline sends greetings to your wife, and I ask you to pass on also my respectful greetings.

All well and happy here.

Your friend

Bjørnst. Bjørnson[22]

And Ibsen did not turn up. Immediately before the wedding he announced that he was ill and could not travel, and Sigurd's side of the family was represented at the wedding by his mother and his uncle, Herman Thoresen. Ibsen was working to finish *The Master Builder* in time for the Christmas market and that was almost certainly the truth of his 'illness'. He was also an unforgiving man, and despite the reconciliation at Schwaz Bjørnsons's twenty-five-year-old insult to the effect that Ibsen was a 'servant-type' could never be entirely forgotten.

As Sigurd was still out of work Ibsen tried to compensate for his absence by giving his son a float of 3,000 kroner. He had been very much against Sigurd's decision to leave the diplomatic service in 1889 and continued to pull whatever strings he could to obtain preferential treatment and a high status job for him in politics. He wrote to him in early 1893:

Last Sunday we had a visit from O. Arvesen and his wife and I took the opportunity to speak with him, the gist of our conversation was as follows: he began by saying that he had recently met you and suggested to you that you should come to Kristiania so that you could be consulted on the foreign ministry business. I took the chance to tell him, quietly but very firmly indeed, what I really thought of the government's treatment of you. I said that for a considerable length of time now you had placed yourself at the disposal of the government; but that all the fine promises made to you remained unfulfilled. I told him that Steen had already, last year, on his own initiative, informed me that the decision to establish a political office under the Ministry of Home Affairs had already been taken, and that this would be implemented in the near future. But that on this score, so far, to the best of my knowledge, nothing had been done, and that I had now lost all faith in the government's promises and statements of intention. In conclusion, firmly, slowly and cold-bloodedly, I told him that I was now seriously considering giving up my Norwegian nationality, leaving the country in the autumn and having myself naturalised in Bavaria, and that I would suggest to you that you do the same.

Arvesen seemed quite astounded by my words, as did his wife. Both of them pleaded with me not to take such a step, at least not for the time being. He said that he would take the information

I had given him and use it in such a way that, hopefully, it would bring about a result that both you and I would find satisfactory.[23]

This was about the fourth time Ibsen had threatened to abandon his Norwegian nationality if he did not get his way, and though he did not get his way this time either he did not carry out the threat. In part one has to assume he enjoyed making the threat, and that the idea of being completely liberated from a nationality appealed to him in principle, though not enough for him to carry it out. There was, too, a slow trickle of orders to mollify him. In the King's birthday honours list of January 1892 he became the fourth Norwegian writer, after Welhaven, Andreas Munch and Jørgen Moe, to be created a Commander 1st Class of St Olaf 'For Services to Literature'; and at the end of 1893 he was awarded the Great Cross of St Olaf 'For his outstanding literary services to the greater honour of the fatherland', making him the first Norwegian writer to be awarded the Great Cross.

Apart from the decorations, 1893 was an uneventful year save for the birth on 11 July of a grandson, Tancred. Ibsen and Suzannah were present at the christening, carried out in church by Ibsen's old friend and sometime hero, the soldier-priest Christopher Bruun. As Suzannah walked forward to the font carrying the child Ibsen suddenly rose from his pew, crossed to Bergjlot, and taking her by the arm whispered, 'Do you think she'll drop him?' Love – as always – was worry.

Sigurd's marriage made superficially little difference to the routine the Ibsens had established since their return: Suzannah continued to travel south on convalescent trips and remain away for months on end; Sigurd went with her; and Ibsen stayed at home writing love-letters to Hildur Andersen and business letters to theatre managers at home and abroad. He had become, if anything, even more obsessional in his habits after his return. Each day at about 2 p.m. he left his apartment and walked with small, tripping steps on raised-heel shoes down Karl Johan to the Grand Hotel, always in his black coat and top-hat, with his rolled umbrella. Always he would stop and check his watch by the university clock. At the Grand he would take a seat in the reading room* on the ground floor, always the

* The separate reading room no longer exists since the extensions made to the hotel, though there is now an 'Ibsen Corner'.

After his return to Kristiania in 1891 Ibsen became a major tourist
attraction. The extreme regularity of his daily routine made him an easy
target for photographers with their Kodaks

same seat, immediately inside the entrance, to the left, where he
could sit, drink, read a paper and look out of the window at the
passers-by. He had his own chair, with his name on a metal plate
on the back. This was a gift of the management, well aware of his
value as a tourist attraction. 'There are an almost uncontrollable
number of tourists here this year, and these are a real plague to
me. And yet sometimes it can be quite amusing,'[24] he wrote to
Suzannah describing the experience of being hailed outside the
Grand one day by a party of forty or fifty who were led in a round
of applause for him by an Austrian field-marshal. Other foreigners
who observed Ibsen's public appearances, like the Englishman
Richard Le Gallienne, found the response to him as perplexing as
it was charming:

> The large café was crowded, but we found a good table on the
> aisle, not far from the door. We had not long to wait, for punctu-
> ally on the stroke of one, there, entering the doorway, was the
> dour and bristling presence known to all the world in caricature

– caricatures which were no exaggerations but as in the case of Swinburne, just the man himself. The great ruff of white whisker, ferociously standing out all round his sallow, bilious face as if dangerously charged with electricity, the immaculate silk hat, the white tie, the frock-coated martinet's figure dressed from top to toe in old-fashioned black broadcloth, at once funereal and professional, the trousers concertinaed, apparently with dandaical design, at the ankles, over his highly polished boots, the carefully folded umbrella – all was there, apparitionally before me; a forbidding, disgruntled, tight-lipped presence, starchily dignified, straight as a ramrod; there he was, as I hinted, with a touch of grim dandyism about him, but with no touch of human kindness about his parchment skin or fierce badger eyes. He might have been a Scotch elder entering the kirk.

As he entered and proceeded with precision tread to the table reserved in perpetuity for him, which no one else would have dreamed of occupying, a thing new and delightful – to me a mere Anglo-Saxon – suddenly happened. As one man, the whole café was on its feet in an attitude of salute, and a stranger standing near me who evidently spoke English and who recognised my nationality, said to me in a loud but reverent aside: 'That is our great poet, Henrik Ibsen.' All remained standing till he had taken his seat, as in the presence of a king, and I marvelled greatly at a people that thus did homage to their great men.

Ibsen's demeanour on these occasions was one of splendid isolation. In his journals Edvard Munch described how Ibsen declined to join him and his friends for a drink:

Ibsen had a regular seat in the early afternoons by the window in the reading room at the Grand, on the ground floor on Karl Johan. We got used to seeing him there – behind his spectacles and his newspaper. Because he came down Karl Johan regularly at around two. Then you could see him sailing down the street through the crowds of people like a trim little schooner . . .

He also used to eat his main meal regularly in the dining room at the Grand. One day Jappe Nilssen and I and a delightful little Kristiania lady were eating there. Opposite us, on the other side of the room, sat Ibsen behind his spectacles. A bottle in front of him and a little glass which he frequently emptied in one go.

We sit and look at him – the great master. Suddenly our charm-

ing lady friend with her pale, delicate little face says: Hey Jappe
– it would be fun to get Ibsen over here. Go and ask him if he'll
join us . . .

Jappe gets up as though it was an order he had to obey without
question and, with his hunched up back and decadent young old
man's look, goes over and sits opposite him.

Ibsen glares at him through his spectacles.

– Ibsen, why don't you come over and join us?

Ibsen answers curtly:

I am not used to be being disturbed by strangers in cafés.

Jappe obediently gets up at once and with the same easy, old
man's shuffle makes his way back to our table.

– Didn't work, he says.

Skål! – We carry on drinking and don't talk about it anymore.[25]

In October 1892 Munch held a one-man exhibition at Tostrup's
Gallery which aroused some domestic controversy; but when the
same exhibition was transferred to Berlin and closed down almost
immediately Munch became overnight a European celebrity. In recognition of his new status Ibsen did the unthinkable: while Munch
and friends were drinking in the crowded café section of the Grand
he approached, greeted Munch by name, and sat briefly with him.
'He said something – common courtesies – then left.'[26]

But beneath the continuing routines it was clear that Sigurd's
departure from the bosom of the family had opened up in both
Ibsens a realisation of how little they now had in common. Ibsen's
struggle for success had always been Suzannah's. With success the
formality of their daily intercourse, the habit of a lifetime, had grown
into a wall between them. He referred to her and often addressed
her as *fruen* ('the lady' or 'madam'). To her he was always 'Ibsen'
or 'the doctor'. Even by the standards of the Victorian age this was
remarkable. Magdalene Thoresen visited them in May 1894 and
was saddened by what she saw – 'They live in great comfort and
elegance, but in the most complete bourgeois silence; they are two
lonely people, living in their own worlds, absolutely in their own
worlds.'[27]

The public response to his return had exceeded all Ibsen's expectations and confounded his worst fears, and in 1892 he expressed
his pleasure in a jaunty rewriting of his best-known poem on the
subject of life in exile, 'Burnt Boats', the one with which he had

chosen to close the first edition of his *Poems* in 1872. He changed the last verse and added a new one:

> To snowbound huts
> from sun-rim's brushland,
> a rider comes riding
> each single night.
>
> Not long ago dismounting, -
> found every door open.
> Could homeless guest
> not have come home before?[28]

Acceptance, adulation, wealth, the opportunity to flirt – the benefits for Ibsen were obvious enough. For Suzannah they were less so. Her dearest friend Christiane Magelssen, who had for so long been urging her to come home, died within a year of her doing so. The winters she spent abroad increased her invisibility within the marriage, something that moved Magdalene Thoresen to compose her own letter of tribute to her on the occasion of her thirty-fourth wedding anniversary, assuring her that 'you have been more important to your husband than perhaps even he realises, and the world that lays its praises at his feet perhaps owes you just as much as him. Perhaps, without you, he would have gone under – one can never know – but with you such a thing was impossible.'[29] In his next two plays, *Little Eyolf* and *John Gabriel Borkman*, Ibsen would meditate with increasing bleakness on the fate of marriages in which respect and responsibility, rather than the kind of complete love which includes both, are the only binding factors.

20

The Demons of Achievement
Little Eyolf · John Gabriel Borkman

Anecdotes of behaviour inevitably become more numerous with Ibsen's return to home soil and Kristiania. It was like berthing the *Queen Mary* in a fishpond. His behaviour was minutely observed and reported upon, and the fact that he kept it to a minimum hardly discouraged the curious.

Every Saturday morning it was his habit to give small change to the poor boys in the street outside his apartment. His cleaning lady rebuked him, saying that the boys only spent the money on toffee. 'Why shouldn't little boys buy toffees?' replied Ibsen. She must have been surprised, for she was presumably only trying to say something she thought he would agree with. Ibsen had this effect on certain people, of making them pretend to be more moral than they really were. John Paulsen tells a story against himself of a time in Munich when he and Ibsen were discussing a painter they both knew, a delightful but frivolous man whose studio parties often gave rise to gossip:

> It occurred to me to play the moralist. Was it in some vague hope of pleasing the severe Ibsen? Who knows. Whatever, I spoke disapprovingly of the young painter. I shall never forget Ibsen's expression at that moment. He looked at me half in wonder, half in compassion and said almost pityingly:
> 'And *you* say that?'
> I felt very small . . . I gathered that Ibsen found me intolerant, that he thought that I of all people should have understood the young painter.[1]

Such misunderstandings arose because of the frequency with which Ibsen did indeed appear harsh in his treatment of casual acquaint-

385

ances. On one occasion a maid who worked in the same apartment block as the Ibsens had gone out on her half-day off and forgotten her key. Returning home, she rang Ibsen's bell in error. Ibsen came down the stairs, opened the door, lectured her on her thoughtlessness and then closed the door again, leaving her on the doorstep to ponder the wages of carelessness. Even members of his wife's family could feel intimidated by him. In one of his letters to Suzannah, Ibsen told her that her half-sister Dorothea Falsen had approached him in the street one day, requesting a conversation with the words, 'Might the scabby sheep have a word with Dr Ibsen?'

His greatest dislike, and a constant hazard of being home again, was to be accosted in public by admirers. His brusque way with such people was legendary. On a business trip to Kristiania the Frenchman Paul Clemenceau recognised Ibsen walking along Drammensveien. He doffed his hat: *'Cher maître! Permettez-moi de vous exprimer ma profonde admiration.' 'Je ne parle pas Français,'* replied Ibsen, and walked off. He was by all accounts particularly unwilling to meet people who had known him as a child in Skien. To one lady who greeted him at his table in the Grand he responded that he could not remember her, and turned demonstratively away. When a man from Skien tried his luck in similar fashion Ibsen beat on the table to summon the waiter, pointed to the intruder and said: 'Waiter, get rid of this man!'[2]

This combination of arrogance, shyness and fear of the past could not disguise the fact that Ibsen remained deeply interested in news of his birthplace. The letter from his sister early in the year of his return to Norway, and subsequent meetings with her and with her daughter Anna, must have set him thinking about his family again, and some of the factual points of departure of his next play, *Little Eyolf*, come from Skien. Eyolf himself seems to owe something to Ibsen's younger brother Nicolai, who was dropped by his nanny as an infant in an accident that left him with a twisted spine. Nicolai died childless in 1888, in Estherville, where he had lived for some years and run a small farm with forty sheep. Sigurd Ibsen had apparently acquired details of his death and burial for his father while working in Washington.[3] The Rat Wife, though her functional origin is obviously the Pied Piper of Hamelin, owed her physical form to Faster Ploug, the demented old lady who shared the house at Venstøp with the Ibsens when Henrik was a boy.

On 19 April Ibsen wrote to Hegel that his preparations for the new work were advancing steadily and that he hoped to be ready at the usual time – 'I dare not risk a summer holiday this year.' On 15 June he apologised to his daughter-in-law Bergljot for not visiting on her birthday, excusing himself with a clear account of the hold his work had over him: 'You see, yesterday I began serious work on the actual dialogue of my new play. That means I am chained to my desk and to my thoughts, and cannot allow myself time for anything else, and am not fit for anything else either – only this one thing – to get the work finished. I am always like that. Sigurd knows.'[4]

On 14 October *Little Eyolf* was despatched to Hegel in Copenhagen. Towards the end of November, while it was going through the printers, some of the material was leaked to the press. The incident gave rise to a series of articles in *Aftenposten* and *Politiken* from Ibsen and others that was excellent publicity for the official publication on 11 December, in an edition of 10,000. For copyright reasons, Heinemann arranged a reading of the play in English at the Haymarket Theatre on 7 December, four days before publication. The translation was by Archer. On 3 December Archer had read the play privately to Bernard Shaw and H. W. Massingham at his apartment in Queen's Square. Shaw called his reading 'clear, intelligent, cold, without a trace of emotion and rather wooden in the more moving passages.' Near the end Archer stopped, handed the manuscript to Shaw and asked him to carry on, explaining that 'my feelings will not allow me to proceed.'[5] Archer found it arguably Ibsen's greatest play, and was 'only doubtful whether its soul-searching be not too terrible for human endurance in the theatre'.

It had its world première at the Deutsches theatre in Berlin on 12 January, where it was not well received. Its Norwegian première was at the Christiania theatre on 15 January, where it ran for thirty-six performances. The London première was at the Avenue theatre on 23 November, with the three female parts taken by the three outstanding British actresses of the day, Janet Achurch, Elizabeth Robins, and Mrs Patrick Campbell. Critics noted the high proportion of women in the audience, something which was rapidly becoming a feature of performances of Ibsen's plays. Aesthetically there was the by now familiar mixture of puzzlement, doubt and derision from the critics. Ibsen's name was already big enough to outweigh critical disapproval, however, and *Little Eyolf* played to full houses for four weeks.

*   *   *

There was still a widespread critical assumption that Ibsen's plays were always didactic moralities, and to some of its first readers it seemed obvious that *Little Eyolf* was a criticism of parental selfishness and an admonition to parents to mend their ways. Ibsen firmly scotched this suggestion, telling Henrik Jæger in 1897: 'I had absolutely no pedagogic intentions in this play. I do not consider that kind of thing to be my job at all. My purpose is always purely artistic.'[6] His personal concern in the play was, after *The Master Builder*, a re-examination of the possibilities remaining in a dead marriage if that marriage is somehow to survive its death. The four last plays all deal with such a situation, and all feature the same hint at a solution that none of those involved have the courage to live out – a *ménage à trois*.

The important trio in *Little Eyolf* are the writer Alfred Allmers, his wife Rita, and Asta Allmers, whom he believes for much of the play to be his half-sister, only to discover that there is no blood relationship between them at all. The use of the brother-sister relationship is unique in Ibsen's work, and in terms of its inspiration must owe something to the reappearance in his life, shortly after his return, of his sister Hedvig, after an absence of over forty years. Hedvig was the only member of the family to whom he felt close, and with whom he remained in any kind of contact. It was to her, on that last visit home in 1850 before leaving for Kristiania and the university, that he had confided his goal in life, to achieve 'the greatest and most perfect possible forms of greatness and perfection'. She was the first woman in his life, and in her sisterly and undemanding adoration of him in some ways his ideal woman. 'I think we two have been close to each other. And that our closeness will continue', he wrote on a portrait of himself he sent to her. Ibsen liked to plant small secrets in his plays, like the hidden 'September' greeting to Hildur Andersen in *The Master Builder*, and in *Little Eyolf* Allmers makes play of the fact that he and Asta have the same initials, as Henrik and Hedvig Ibsen have. They may once, as children, have speculated on the hidden importance of this as a quasi-mystical coincidence.

It must have been a strange experience for Suzannah Ibsen, after a lifetime as her husband's closest confidante, suddenly to be confronted with another woman who enjoyed similar intimacy with him. She may have been jealous, much as Rita in *Little Eyolf* is jealous of the intimate relationship between her husband and his half-sister –

in earlier drafts of the play Asta and Alfred were full siblings – and the terrible possessiveness Rita expresses might hint at Suzannah's reactions.

Little Eyolf is, even more than *Rosmersholm*, a play of conversations. The fateful event, the death by drowning of the Allmers' crippled young son Eyolf, closes the first act, and the remaining two acts explicate what this death discloses about the three main characters, exposing what Eyolf's presence in the marriage has kept hidden. Ibsen may have gained insight into such a situation with Sigurd's marriage to Bergljot Bjørnson, although Suzannah in particular continued to exert a strong hold over her son, treating him as a surrogate husband/travelling companion long after the marriage.

Allmers resembles Dr Stockmann in his arrogance, Rosmer in his sexual timidity. He fears Rita's natural sexuality, as Rosmer feared both Beate's and Rebecca West's. He shares with the narrator of Ibsen's great poem 'On the Heights' a longing to escape from the tortures of the lower, physical world into the abstract 'high' world of mountains; to be alone, not to have to worry about other people any more. Tortures, because a sexual trauma is one of the problems gnawing away in the house to which the Rat Wife refers on her brief, symbolic visit to the Allmers' house. The two major events from the past that create the agonised present of the play are both associated with a single sexual encounter: Allmers and Rita were making love when the infant Eyolf, unattended, fell from the table and received the injuries that crippled him; and on that same occasion, at the moment of orgasm or ejaculation, Allmers told Rita that he used to call his half-sister Asta 'Little Eyolf' when they were children, so introducing the idea of incestuous desire for her, if not actual incest. If Allmers had ever known sexual joy, henceforth it was associated in his mind with guilt. As the play opens he is resting after his return from a long thinking-and-walking trip in the mountains. Later Rita reveals how much she had been looking forward to love-making on his return; but that he ignored her desires, preferring instead to talk about his plans for Eyolf, using such good and moral intentions to protect himself from her, much as he had formerly protected himself from her by intense involvement with his current work, the unfinishable 'Human Responsibility'.

The sister love of Asta, adoring but sexually undemanding, seems a better bet to him. As the play approaches its conclusion – climax is too strong a word – and after Allmers has been told that there is no blood impediment to the development of a full, sexual relationship with Asta, he proposes, with Rita's support, that Asta move in with them, filling the hole in their lives left by the death of their son, the one Little Eyolf replacing the other. Asta realises that there is no future for her in such a situation, and that Allmers, like all Ibsen's would-be male lovers, is a mathematician whose tortuous emotional calculations will never arrive at a workable solution. She ships out instead with the robust roadbuilder Borgheim, a pre-echo of the no-nonsense hunter and wild man Ulfheim who walks off with Rubek's young wife Maja at the end of *When We Dead Awaken*.

Little Eyolf's strength is in the conversations, not the plot. The Allmers mount to a symbolic height, with a long view over the fjord, the mountains, and the slums below them, and after an outburst of blind contempt from Allmers that recalls Dr Stockmann's address to the 'mob' in *An Enemy of the People*, a solution to the problem of the dead marriage occurs to them: Rita will open their home to the local poor boys, each of whom will take a turn at being Little Eyolf. Thus the demands of both philanthropy and therapy are satisfied. Yet there is nothing in what we have seen of the behaviour of either Allmers or Rita to suggest that there is any substance to their assumption of moral superiority over these urchin boys and their parents, whose fates they intend to *forædle* (ennoble). Ibsen slipped into an old mode here.

Allmers's unexpected outburst against the slum-dwellers glimpsed far below, whom he damns as drunks and child-beaters, whose homes he charges Rita to see burned to the ground as a punishment for not having saved Eyolf (the possibility that they could have done so has not been aired earlier), might also echo the mood of personal vengeance in which Ibsen wrote *An Enemy of the People*, with his grievance this time being the failure of Norwegian society to give his son Sigurd the job to which he thought he was entitled. Ibsen was never averse to using his plays to pursue a personal vendetta or seek personal revenge if the opportunity arose to do so discreetly, and if it could be done without jolting the play into the private domain. The possibility of a local, personal and Norwegian reference is strengthened by Allmers's last act: when his rage has subsided and he has decided to join Rita in her philanthropy he raises the Norwegian flag to the top of the flagpole, a patriotic conclusion to events which met with the warm approval of Bjørnson. The final moments of the play, in which Allmers says that 'the spirits' of the dead and the departed will return to comfort them in the work of their daily lives, and that they will glimpse them wandering among the stars, provides one of the very few moments of pure lyricism in all of Ibsen's later works.

For ten months, almost the whole of 1895, the Ibsens lived apart. Suzannah travelled south to Meran in the southern Tyrol, with Sigurd as her chaperon. Presumably she travelled under her real name, for Ibsen was much offended when she suggested once that she might call herself Mrs Nesbi in order to avoid being plagued by the curious.

The parting, the longest since Ibsen left for Rome alone in 1864, suited him well. Hildur Andersen was back in Kristiania and once again available as his consort, and the visits to the theatre began anew. He presented her with original manuscripts, *The Master Builder* in November, *Hedda Gabler* and *Rosmersholm* later. They were together so often that in Suzannah's absence they became the subject of gossip. It seems they may even have had a fantasy child together: a bystander outside the apartment one day saw Ibsen at the window as Hildur approached with a friend. Hildur and her friend waved. Ibsen 'lifted his arms to his breast and rocked them back and forth, as though he were holding a little child in his embrace.'[7]

His pleasure in the relationship, and the status he gave it as a factor in his life and reputation, emerge clearly in a letter he wrote to Georg Brandes on 11 February 1895, thanking him for a copy of Brandes's little book on the relationship between Goethe and Marianne von Willemer:

> The episode you describe was unknown to me. I may have read about it long, long ago in Lewes [G. H. Lewes' biography of Goethe], but if so then I had forgotten it because I had no personal interest in the relationship. Now the situation is quite different. When I think of the quality of Goethe's work in the relevant years, the rebirth into youth, then it seems to me I might have known that he had been blessed with an event like this, this meeting Marianne v. Willemer. Fate, luck, happenstance can still, once in a while, seem like a benevolent, lovely power.[8]

Ibsen wrote regularly to Suzannah during this long absence, letters in which he seemed suspiciously well-content. He mentioned particularly the care and the cooking of the young maid Lina Jacobsen, who had been with them since the beginning of October 1892. On 11 December 1894:

> Frøken Blehr's* food is very tasty, and there is always plenty of it, and enough left over for supper if I want it. But I prefer to eat herring with the delicious potatoes Lina cooks in the new machine. She sees to my needs with the greatest solicitude. Bergljot ate dinner with me last Sunday, apart from that no-one has been here. The evenings are lonely, of course, so I sit and read at the dining table. In the morning I drink coffee, brought to me in my bedroom at eight o'clock sharp. Everything runs like clockwork, just as if you were here. Every morning Augusta brings me a little saucer of bread for the birds. Lina is kind to her and lets her have the leftovers, there is always a lot.

On December 20: 'Lina is impeccable in every respect. She seems to exist only to do everything just as she knows you would have done it. She makes the most delicious suppers out of the leftovers from the evening meal.'

Christmas in Suzannah's absence was a success, and Lina's food was again praised. Ibsen did not tell Suzannah that he had given the maid a dress as a Christmas present, but continued to sing her praises. On 15 February: 'Apart from that I sit quite alone and read my newspapers and feel happy enough. Lina looks after me very well. She gives me warm soup and other meat dishes or fish left over from the main meal, so we hardly ever need to send out for anything.'

What was happening, quite apart from what was happening with Hildur Andersen, was that Ibsen and Lina were becoming, in their enforced intimacy, a sort of couple. Unlike the austere Suzannah, Lina was sentimental and indulgent towards her employer. He disliked the food Dr Sontum recommended for his digestion, the meat balls, the vegetable stew and the macaroni; Lina gave him what he did like – veal in cream sauce, woodcock in cream sauce, mutton and parsley, beef fried in mountain-butter. She gave him meat broth with cooked potatoes, and he wept as he ate it, because it was the food his mother had given him as a child in Skien. With his dinner he drank red wine and water, and with his supper a bottle of Schous

---

* Frøken Blehr ran a school for housewifery in the basement of the Victoria Terrasse block. The Ibsens often bought food ready-cooked there.

beer. In April he told Suzannah: 'Sigurd and Bergljot came here for supper yesterday and Lina provided an excellent table with hot and cold dishes'.*

Hildur his consort out, Lina his hostess at home – it was too good to be true. Suzannah got wind of his contentment, from Dorothea Falsen and Magdalene Thoresen. He seemed to suspect he was being watched. In the letter of 6 February he says: 'It is good that the situation between you and your mother is better now. I hear that Sigurd visited her in Copenhagen. But I have not as yet heard what it is they were discussing.'

A not unreasonable assumption is that they were discussing the problem with Father, for sometime in May Suzannah's worries about her marriage surfaced in a letter from the hot springs at Monsummano. The letter is lost, probably destroyed by Suzannah in the *auto da fé* she held after Ibsen's death. Ibsen's reply survives:

Kristiania, 7 May 1895

Dear Suzannah!

It was painful to read your latest letter, dated 1 May. And I hope that you now, on reflection, regret having sent it to me. So it is your stepmother,† that wretched old sinner, who has been at it again, trying to cause trouble by setting us against each other. But it's easy enough to see who's been getting at the poor confused thing. It is of course her precious daughter‡ who is still wandering the streets here and is no doubt furious with me because whenever I catch sight of her I duck down a sidestreet. I've actually done that a couple of times. Now she's trying in her own way to get revenge. And you allow yourself to be taken in by all this!

I cannot understand your stepmother's overexcitable manner of speaking and her spurious profundities. Have never understood them. But when she writes something about my 'wanting my freedom at any cost' – then with hand on heart I can assure you that I have never seriously had any such thought or intention. Anything I may have blurted out to you when in one of your

---

* Sigurd Ibsen came home in February for a few weeks but rejoined his mother later in the spring.
† A provocative use of the word. Suzannah insisted that Magdalene Thoresen always be referred to as 'mother'.
‡ Dorothea Falsen

moods you drove me temporarily to despair is just a passing thing and not something to attach any importance to. But my heartfelt advice to you is that if you wish to retain the peace of mind necessary for your cure then you will break off all correspondence with your confused stepmother. It may well be that she thinks she is doing it for your own good; but that woman's attempts to interfere in a relationship have always had disastrous results. If you don't want to tell her this yourself then I will do it. But first of all, of course, I would need your permission. – With that I am done with the subject for today.

Now for the other main point in your letter. You insist that I rent another apartment. Naturally, since it means so much to you, I will do so. But in your letter you complain that I rented the one we live in now without consulting you. (You were anyway in Valdres at the time and in the mood you were in there was no way I would have approached you for advice.) When you come home this time and find the new apartment rented and furnished, remember that I have acted entirely in accordance with your specific instructions and that once again you were not available for consulation. Remember how Sigurd and Bergljot had to search and search before at the last minute they found somewhere acceptable. Here the difficulties will be even greater. You refuse to live on the ground floor because of the cold coming up through the floor, and you won't or can't live higher up because of the stairs. But, as I say, your demand will be met and a new apartment will be rented.

I neither can nor want to write about other things today. I have nothing else to write about anyway. Werenskiold is here every afternoon and paints for an hour, apart from that everything ticks along as usual here in the house. Presumably you are kept abreast of the political news by Sigurd and the newspapers.

So send me soon a calmer and calming letter. And, above all, keep the damned witches at bay! That's the best advice I can give you. Warmest greetings!

Your devoted H.I.[9]

Presumably the reason Suzannah did not burn this letter is because she could not know what construction literary historians of the future might put on her husband's relationship with Hildur Andersen, particularly if she was aware of the fact that the two of them

394

corresponded, and more particularly if she suspected, as was the case, that Ibsen wanted his correspondence with Hildur to be published one day.[10]

On 21 June Ibsen wrote to Suzannah again to tell her that he had found a new apartment:

I have now handed in notice on the apartment at Victoria Terrasse and rented the second floor in a new block the Hoff Brothers have just built on the corner of Arbinsgate and Drammensveien – It was Sigurd and Bergljot who suggested it and I think you will find that you will be pleased with it. I have a large study with entrance directly from the hallway, so that people who want to see me do not need to go through any of the other rooms. That means you have at your complete and free disposal a large corner salon with balcony and next to it a living room that is nearly as big with a door into the dining-room, where there is room at table for up to twenty-two people and with an alcove for a buffet, which I shall be getting. From the dining-room you can go directly into the spacious library and from there straight into your bedroom, which is considerably bigger than the room I have here. My bedroom is next to it and has a balcony. You won't need to use the corridor except when you go to the bathroom. Large, well-lit kitchen, with naturally a dining alcove and pantry and of course lots of fitted cupboards. As I say, I think you will be pleased with it.[11]

This was a clear victory for Suzannah, but she was not quite finished yet. All the references to Lina Jacobsen's consideration for him and his well-being had aroused her suspicions. She believed, and rightly so, that an intimacy had developed between them. She knew all about Ibsen's Hildurs, but Lina was a different kind of threat. Lina ministered to the almost lost sensualist in him, and Ibsen's pleasure in her ministering was a threat to the hold Suzannah's high-mindedness had over him. For all her cultivation of an exaggerated anonymity in the context of Ibsen's worldwide fame and the huge, almost worshipping esteem in which he was held, Suzannah was very conscious of her role in the creation of his public figure. She took the figure very seriously, and was concerned that he must never step down from the pedestal on to which the two of them had laboured so long and so hard to raise him. In the circumstances, what could she make of a housemaid who said to visitors, as Lina said – twice – to the writer Anna Munch, 'the Doctor is just a big child'?[12] How could she tolerate a maid before whom Ibsen was not ashamed to weep, even if such weeping were partly the result of drinking, and perhaps especially if this were so? She could not, and her next demand was that Ibsen sack Lina. He tried to make a fight of it. Replying to a letter from Suzannah he wrote: 'To dismiss the maid while I am still alone and in the middle of moving is quite impossible. It'll do when you come back. Don't think about such things, just concentrate on the cure and let me know how it is progressing.'[13]

Suzannah was obviously still not happy, and Ibsen resorted to a tactic that both of them had used before: he replied to her through Sigurd, who had rejoined his mother in Monsummano and was working on his book. Ibsen's irritation at these sudden attempts to exercise long-distance control over his life alone resurfaced:

> Tell your mother that she must not under any circumstances return before I have told her that the new apartment is ready. If she arrives in the middle of the moving and gets involved in all the worries and bother the beneficial effects of the cure could easily go to waste. And I am able to manage extremely well on my own. If she, when she does come home, really insists on dismissing the maid, then of course she can do so. I will pay her a quarter of her annual salary and that will be that. But any attempt to impose a guardianship on me, in the form of Mrs Lie or anyone else, will not be tolerated. I hope that you will give me your complete support in these matters.[14]

Isaac Bashevis Singer once said that he sometimes dreamt of killing his wife but never of leaving her, and Ibsen's feeling towards Suzannah was probably something very similar. She was still away when he duly moved into the new apartment on the corner of Drammensveien and Arbinsgate. Bergljot and Sigurd helped him with the choice of furniture and decoration, but it was Hildur Andersen who acted as his main aesthetic consultant. As for Lina, Ibsen bowed to the inevitable and fired her, but showed his appreciation by personally drafting a testimonial in which he praised her without reservation.

Ibsen's view of women had become progressively less straightforward since the days of A Doll's House and Nora's abandonment of her family. Though one may sympathise with their torments as human beings, Rebecca West and Hedda Gabler could on no account be described as sympathetic portraits of women *as women*. Ibsen took a keen and open-minded interest in the rise, in the 1890s, of an independent, personal art that tended to depict women as sexual rather than social beings, mysterious, compelling, frightening figures. Hamsun and Strindberg were the main literary exponents of this anti-feminism, and Edvard Munch its outstanding painter.

At about the same time as Ibsen was moving into Arbinsgate, a major exhibition of Munch's paintings opened at Blomkvist's Gallery on Karl Johan. The Kristiania art critics received it in much the same way as London critics continued to receive Ibsen, with derision and incredulity. A psychiatrist, Johan Scharffenberg, delivered a long speech to the Students' Union on the subject of Munch, explaining that he was mentally ill and that this accounted for the abnormality of his art. Munch was understandably dispirited by such responses; but the tide of public opinion on him turned with Ibsen's appearance at the exhibition one day. He asked Munch to show him round. Munch described his reactions in his journal:

I had to walk round with him and he had to study every picture. Much of the Frieze of Life was exhibited. The melancholy young man on the beach – Madonna – The Scream – Anxiety – Jealousy – The three women (or Woman in three stages) on a bright night. He was particularly interested in Woman in three stages. I had to explain it to him.
– There is the dreaming woman – the woman who loves life – and the woman as nun – the one standing pale behind the trees.–
– He was amused by my portraits – the way I had accentuated the features – so they were almost caricatures.

Munch believed that these paintings exerted an influence over Ibsen which came to fruition four years later, in *When We Dead Awaken*:

I discovered several motives which resembled my paintings in the Frieze of Life – the man who sits between the rocks with his head bowed in melancholy. Jealousy – the Pole with a bullet in his head. – The three women – Irene the white-clad dreaming of life – Maja the lover of life – the naked one. – The women in grief – with staring pale face between the treetrunks – Irene's fate, the nurse. – These three women appear in Ibsen's play – as they do in many places in my picture. – On a bright summer night the dark-clad woman was seen walking in the garden with Irene, who was naked or in some kind of bathing suit – the bright white figure against the black of grief – all in the mystical light of the summer night. – The light summer night where life and death, day and night go hand in hand. In Ibsen's play he also mentions the sculptor's portraits – that they were caricatures – animal heads that the person who commissioned got into the bargain. – As in Ibsen's *The Dead Awaken* [*sic*] the sculptor's piece on resurrection was split up and never completed – just as happened with my work.

Munch and Ibsen were too different as individuals to become friends, and not long after this the fragile relationship between them collapsed as a result of an incident at the Grand one evening. Munch's alcholism was in the process of establishing itself at this time. Walking down Karl Johan he was suddenly overcome by a feeling of sickness and at once booked into a room at the Grand. In the evening he drank in the reading room with two friends. Ibsen sat alone in another corner of the room. Munch's party broke up and the waiter presented them with the bill. Munch had already drunk a lot 'in order to subdue his bronchitis' and had no money left. He explained to the waiter that he was a guest and asked for the bill to be added to his hotel bill. The waiter refused to accept this. Munch went over to Ibsen, told him what was happening and asked for a loan. 'You should be like me,' said Ibsen, 'I always pay.' He then gave Munch some money, but something about the transaction offended Munch, and he left him with the words 'Well, Ibsen, we won't be seeing each other again.'

Later in life he regretted his words: 'Since then I have wondered if I didn't perhaps hurt Ibsen on that occasion. Perhaps he felt as shy and lonely as I did, and didn't care to talk to a drunk man and just wanted to be rid of me.'

Munch's admiration for Ibsen's work remained undiminished. For many years he treasured a remark Ibsen made to him at the Blomkvist exhibition, 'Believe me, it will be the same for you as it was for me – the more enemies, the more friends'. He was only slightly disappointed to discover later that Ibsen, always the economist, had said exactly the same thing to John Paulsen many years earlier.

The attraction of the wilder type of artist, with a lifestyle diametrically opposed to Ibsen's cautious, disciplined ways, is an interesting phenomenon. Munch admired Ibsen principally for those works in which he was at his most demonic, in which he was most the artist – *Peer Gynt* and *Ghosts*, where he felt a special affinity with the painter Osvald; *Hedda Gabler* with its dissolute artist-figure Løvborg; and the last two autobiographical plays, *John Gabriel Borkman* and *When We Dead Awaken*. While Ibsen's mass audience still insisted on seeing him as always and ever the social reformer, Munch saw the artist-mind in him. Munch's friend Ravensberg wrote that he 'believes that he (i.e. Ibsen) like so many neurotic, brooding people, had the ability to split himself in two, carry out a self-interrogation'.[15]

It was Munch who designed the poster used by the Théâtre de l'Oeuvre for their production in Paris in 1896 of *Peer Gynt*. Alfred Jarry, another of Ibsen's wilder type of admirer, was responsible for adapting the play for the stage. Lugné-Poë had asked him to become *secrétaire-régisseur* to the company in 1896 and Jarry brought with him his two pet projects of the time, *Peer Gynt* and his own *Ubu Roi*. Jarry may even have acted in the second night performance of *Peer Gynt* on 12 December, when the part of the Mountain King was played by the pseudonymous 'J. Hemgé.'* Certainly his close knowledge of Ibsen's play influenced the development of *Ubu Roi*, which appeared the following year in 1897. The Mountain King, physically grotesque ruler of a world of inverted moral and aesthetic values, is a clear precursor of Ubu, and Jarry's 'Ubu' as a nonsense name is close to Ibsen's 'Huhu', the speaker of nonsense in *Peer Gynt*.† Jarry's *Docteur Faustroll* is another borrowing, marrying Ibsen's trolls with Goethe's Faust. Not unexpectedly, the production was not a success. It was not the Ibsen the Parisians had been led to expect, not the pedagogic visionary.

The most illuminating example of a mutual fascination that cuts surreally across the perceived image of two artists involves Ibsen with Strindberg. Strindberg, like Hamsun after him, saw Ibsen as an artist in decline since attaining the heights of *Brand* and *Peer Gynt*. Ibsen's feminism in *A Doll's House* seemed to him treacherous,

* In Noël Arnaud's *Alfred Jarry: d'Ubu Roi au Docteur Faustroll*. (p 187. Paris, 1974) Arnaud suggests that the name 'Hemgé' was shared on an *ad hoc* basis by members of the company, so Jarry's appearance in the role is not certain.
† Ubu is also known 'Père Ubu', sounding an echo of how Jarry's French ears might have heard the Norwegian title *Peer Gynt* as *Père Gynt*.

and when Bjørnson too began to agitate for the improvement of women's role in society, it served to confirm for Strindberg that they had been more or less bewitched by women. In the 1890s he always spoke disparagingly of Ibsen; yet paid him the compliment of following his work closely.

Ibsen returned the compliment, and in a very strange way: in March 1895 he purchased a large oil painting of Strindberg by the Norwegian artist Christian Krohg. This painting hung in his work room in the new apartment in Arbinsgate. Ibsen gave it a title of his own, 'Madness incipient'. He referred to it in a humorous, half-joking way, saying that Strindberg 'hangs there and keeps watch, because he is my archenemy.'[16] Every scene he wrote had to be held up to the scrutiny of Strindberg's image and to survive his imagined criticism. And true though the description of him as 'archenemy' may have been, who could doubt that in importing the image of this wild and spontaneous man into his work-room, to hang opposite Kronberg's 1877 portrait of himself from Uppsala, with his doctor's scroll and his good-conduct order for services to literature pinned to his gown, Ibsen also discovered that a certain deeply truthful, perhaps even restful psychological balance was struck in his room?

In 1893 Ibsen received an invitation to attend the World Fair in Chicago, and it seems that for a moment at least he thought of accepting. On hearing of this Hedvig wrote to rebuke him for contemplating a trip to America when he would not even visit Skien.[17] 'It would be easier for me to go to Chicago than to Skien' he replied.

Two years later, on 16 May 1895, he attended the golden wedding anniversary celebration of his father's half-brother, his uncle Christopher Paus, and his wife. It was Paus who had helped Ibsen with the money that enabled him to enroll at Heltberg's crammer in 1850, so Ibsen had reason to feel grateful to him. But as with the financial help he received from Bjørnson during his first years in Rome, the role of debtor made him uncomfortable. During the course of the afternoon he had a conversation with Squire Løvenskiold, of the manor at Fossum, near Venstøp. Løvenskiold invited him to visit the manor, and Ibsen appeared both flattered and pleased at the invitation. Later in the evening, however, he returned to the matter. His mood was changed, he seemed troubled and depressed, and told Løvenskiold that he would not be coming after all. He explained that such a visit would inevitably involve him in a

visit to Skien itself, and this was a prospect he could not contemplate.[18]

This was the last realistic opportunity Ibsen had to revisit his
home-town, and he did not avail himself of it. Why not? Perhaps
this is the place to try to unravel the unhappy mystery of Ibsen's
lack of a relationship with his own family. He advanced two reasons
for it himself. The first was mentioned in that feverish letter to
Bjørnson in 1867, after Clemens Petersen's review of *Peer Gynt*, when
he swore that in pursuit of his revenge he would not spare 'the child
in the mother's womb'. A few lines later, as though to underline for
Bjørnson the extent of his capacity for ruthlessness in the name of
principle, he wrote: 'did you know that I have broken with my
own parents, my own family, for life, because I could not bear a
relationship in which there was only partial understanding?' Many
see in this a reference to the adolescent enthusiasm of Hedvig and
Ole Ibsen for the Lammers movement. Hedvig was in no doubt that
religion was what lay behind the break. She told a journalist 'When
I was young I was a great enthusiast for the Lammers movement
and left the state church, and he didn't like that at all. That's
probably why he never came here again.'[19] Yet as Hedvig later told
Ibsen's biographer Halvdan Koht, neither Knud nor Marichen Ibsen
were followers of Adolf Lammers. Moreover Ibsen once wrote half-
approvingly of the movement to her: 'The last time I was home in
Skien was back in 1850. Not long after that a spiritual storm broke
over the town and spread further afield. I've always liked stormy
weather. And though absent, I was part of that storm too. My writing
is a witness to the fact that I was part of it.'[20]

So the revivalist atmosphere in his home town cannot have been
the main reason for the break. Did the 'relationship in which there
was only partial understanding (*halvt Forstaaelsesforhold*)' refer to
something more personal? Was Ibsen perhaps punishing someone
– Marichen, for example – for some unsatisfactory response to his
escapade with Else Sophie Birkedalen? But he is said always to have
spoken of his mother with warmth. Perhaps it was Knud Ibsen, for
depriving him of his social and financial birthright, for disapproving
of his abandoning a career as an apothecary? That is more likely.
Bergljot Ibsen wrote that 'He recalled even the least injustice he
suffered at the hands of his father', citing the story about the money
promised for planting potatoes and never forthcoming. But in the
letter Ibsen sent to his uncle Christian on the death of his father

in 1877 Ibsen wrote that the reason he had never contacted his parents was because he had never felt able to offer them any financial assistance.

Even when taken together, these reasons scarcely seem to justify the drastic response of a complete break from the age of twenty-two onwards. A possible solution to the riddle is that the break was not directed at any one person or event at all, that it had no element of revenge in it but was essentially an exercise in spiritual power – Ibsen's, over himself. As he hinted in *The Master Builder*, Ibsen had discovered a frightening, religious dimension to his own will to succeed as an artist. Hedvig said that the Bible was among his earliest reading matter, and though the events of his adolescence made Christianity an impossibility for him, perhaps a childhood sense of the awesome power of Christ's personality remained with him, dictating his personal response, in the name of art, to Christ's strange and repellent words to the Pharisees 'If any man come to me, and hate not his father, and mother, and wife, and children, and brethren, and sisters, yea, and his own life also, he cannot be my disciple.' To put it another way: the climactic scene in *The Wild Duck* is that in which the fanatic Gregers Werle persuades Hedvig Ekdal that she must sacrifice the thing she loves best in the world, which he knows to be the duck, in order to restore purity to the corrupted Ekdal household. This is an abstract challenge. Hedvig cannot possibly understand it intellectually or emotionally; for what has the duck ever done except let her love it? Yet she knows she is being asked to kill the duck. She takes the gun, goes into the loft and shoots herself instead. Ibsen had a great deal of Gregers Werle in him at the age of twenty-two, and a great deal of Faust. Perhaps on his last trip home in 1850, meditating one night on his sins and his huge ambition, he heard Gregers telling him that to achieve it he must sacrifice the thing he loved best in the world. He took the gun, went into the loft, and shot the duck.

On 1 May 1896 Ibsen wrote to William Archer that he had 'already begun a long time ago to busy myself with the preparations for a new drama.'[21] Perhaps it was as long ago as the Paus' anniversary celebrations in May 1895, for it was to Skien that Ibsen returned for the basic situation of his next play, *John Gabriel Borkman*, where the complex structure of relationships between Borkman, his wife Gunhild and his true love, Gunhild's sister Ella, depends on the fact that Ella has a financial hold over the Borkman family. It echoes the hold Knud Ibsen's half-brothers had over the Ibsen family after the ruin of 1834–5, and a scene early on in the play conveys the bitter sense of helplessness Gunhild Borkman feels about the situation. Ella Rentheim suddenly announces her intention of moving into the house with the three Borkmans: John, Gunhild and their son Erhart:

MRS BORKMAN: (stares at her) Here in this house?

ELLA RENTHEIM: Yes, here.

MRS BORKMAN: Here, in our house? All night?

ELLA RENTHEIM: I will stay out here for the rest of my days if needs be.

MRS BORKMAN: (controls herself) Well yes, Ella, the house is yours after all.

ELLA RENTHEIM: Oh – what!

MRS BORKMAN: Well it's all yours. The chair I sit in is yours. The bed where I toss and turn the sleepless nights away belongs to you. The food we eat, is by your grace.

ELLA RENTHEIM: As regards that there's no choice. Borkman can't own anything. If he did someone would immediately come and take it off him.

MRS BORKMAN: I'm well aware of that. We just have to put up with living at your mercy and on your charity.

ELLA RENTHEIM: (coldly) I can't stop you looking at it like that, Gunhild.

There is perhaps a hint of Ibsen's confused unease at meeting even the respectable members of his family, the affluent Paus, in the two brief letters he wrote in connection with the wedding anniversary celebrations. In the first he thanks his uncle and aunt for the invitation and concludes with a salutation that curiously mixes his usual business style with the personal: 'With, for the moment, many greetings to uncle and to aunt I remain, Your devoted and obedient Henrik Ibsen.'[22] And in the greeting of 16 May announcing his attendance later in the day he signs himself 'Your devoted nephew, Henrik Ibsen', an unfamiliar self-image, Ibsen as someone's sixty-seven-year-old nephew.

The summer of 1896 was spent in writing *John Gabriel Borkman*. By the end of August he had finished and was engaged in rewriting throughout September and October, despatching the play to Hegel on 20 October, as usual in good time for Gyldendal to capture the Christmas market. Pre-publication interest was so great that a second printing of 3,000 copies was added to the first print run of 12,000 before publication day on 12 December. The world première was at the Swedish Theatre in Helsinki on 10 January 1897, and before the year was out there were performances in Stockholm, Copenhagen, Frankfurt, Berlin, Munich, Bergen and Kristiania, where it ran for nineteen performances. Théâtre de l'Oeuvre, who had visited Norway in the winter of 1894 with performances of *Rosmersholm* and *The Master Builder*, added *Borkman* to their repertoire in Paris in November 1897. Munch again provided them with a striking poster, using Ibsen himself as his model for Borkman. The London première was on 3 May 1897 at the Strand theatre, in a performance co-directed by William Archer and W. H. Vernon, who played Borkman. Though the play itself was praised, with one critic comparing it to *King Lear*, the actors were miscast and the production closed after just five matinées.

The pre-history of *John Gabriel Borkman* describes a complex situation going back twenty-one years before the action of the play begins. At that time Borkman was an ambitious but poor young financier. Among his associates in the banking world was a wealthy friend, Hinkel. Both men were in love with the same woman, Ella Rentheim. She loved Borkman. Hinkel was in a position to secure a job as bank-manager for his ambitious friend, but made it his price that Borkman should not marry Ella. Borkman agreed, and married instead her twin sister Gunhild. For eight years they lived in flamboyant style. Borkman became famous. But still Ella Rentheim refused to marry Hinkel. Hinkel believed that Borkman was responsible for this, and aware that Borkman was engaged in a large-scale act of speculation that involved him, however briefly, in illegally investing money placed in the bank by depositors Hinkel betrayed his friend to the law. He achieved his aim: Borkman spent three years on remand, was tried and jailed for five years. Returning home from his imprisonment he found Gunhild embittered and unable to forgive him for having brought ruin on the family, above all for having besmirched the family name. For eight years the couple have lived entirely separate lives in the same house. Gunhild keeps to the ground floor, obsessively comforting herself with the notion that their only child, their son Erhart, will one day achieve something that will wipe out the stigma attached to the name Borkman. On the floor above, Borkman paces endlessly back and forth, as though he had never left jail. He broods endlessly on the faithlessness of his old friend Hinkel and on the perfidy of a world that, with its banal insistence on applying the law to him, prevented him from becoming the Napoleon of world trade that he remains convinced he could have become had he been allowed just eight more days to complete his last great deal. The play of these twenty-one years across a single winter's evening in the old house outside Kristiania is described in four acts that end with Borkman's death.

The kind of *ménage à trois* that shapes events in both *The Master Builder* and *Little Eyolf* is moved down a generation in *John Gabriel Borkman* to involve Erhart Borkman, Fru Wilton, and Frida Foldal, while the three older characters return to Ibsen's theme of the two women, sometimes sisters, who fight over one man. Borkman is the passive object of this struggle, left alone to meditate on his past, to judge himself, as fairly as he finds practical, in the series of duologues which comprise the heart of the play, with his young friend Frida, with his oldest and most loyal friend Foldal, and with his wife Gunhild and her sister Ella.

Beyond the simple association of 'indoors' and 'outdoors' with 'death' and 'life' there is here no obtrusive verbal symbolism like *Rosmersholm's* white horses, no ponderously self-conscious repetition of concept-words like 'transformation' (*forvandling*), no hybrid characters, part-human and part-symbol, like 'the Stranger' and 'the Rat Wife', no lines like *Little Eyolf's* 'The crutch is floating!' for disrespectful young members of the audience to laugh at. The stagecraft is flawless: the sleigh-bells that are heard at the beginning and end of the play, the one-act delay before John appears, the pacing footsteps and music from the floor above while we wait to meet him, the syncopated double introduction of Fru Wilton and Erhart in Act One, Foldal's off-stage accident in the last act which leaves him with a limp and no glasses, John's ascent with Ella, hidden from the audience by bushes, to the lookout point high over the Kristiania fjord – in the face of such superb detail directors can afford to let the staging take care of itself and concentrate entirely on the acting.

Borkman is Ibsen's first main male character since Julian whom it is possible to like, and this is largely because Ibsen allows him to be complex. The few 'decent' and likeable types of the modern plays, such as Dr Wangel and Jørgen Tesman, are minor figures compared to their wives, and their chief dramatic purpose is to assist in the depiction of the women as strong and interesting characters. The 'villainous males' – Torvald Helmer, Pastor Manders, Rektor Kroll – are too closely identified with ideas of which their creator disapproves to interest us as characters. Rosmer is too indecisive to excite our pity, Stockmann too arrogant. Halvard Solness and Alfred Allmers both approach the condition of honesty; but Solness remains too ragingly involved in his egotistical struggle to survive to get there, and Allmers veers off at the end into pious and senti-mental self-delusion. Borkman completes the journey. The criticism that surrounding characters offer of him is allowed to stand, whereas Ibsen seems to struggle to defend Allmers and Solness from what others say about them. The fact that all the male characters in the four last plays are forms of self-portraiture does not need to be argued; if it did, nothing would argue it better than Ibsen's inability to let criticism of them stand uncorrected or undefended: they *have* to be his heroes.

It is not wrong to see in *Borkman* a final dropping of Ibsen's guard, a final abandonment of the fear of letting personal criticism stand. Ibsen reintroduces the theme of self-doubt, the great theme that made *The Pretenders, Brand, Peer Gynt* such extraordinary plays. Borkman tells Frida never to reveal self-doubt. Its destructive power is so great, he tells her, that she must not even admit to it in the privacy of her own mind. How much the advice tells us about Ibsen's own conduct, the terrible nature of his own battle to achieve self-belief and the eternal vigilance demanded once it had been achieved. It tells us why he pinned those orders to his chest on the most trivial of occasions, to remind himself not who he *was*, but who he had *become*, and to warn himself never to slip back again. Solness climbed up his tower and fell to his death because he could not admit the validity of self-doubt. Borkman is a bigger man; or maybe it would be truer to say that Borkman fell, but survived the fall to reflect on its meaning. In the midst of his Napoleonic dreams of commercial empire – and we believe him when he says that with eight days' grace he would have completed the great deal and had the depositors' money back in place – he entertained self-doubt; and in his self-doubt he thought to protect against failure the dearest thing in the world to him – Ella Rentheim. He kept her money out of the speculation, so that when the crash came she was not harmed by it.

Borkman offers us the notion of the major artist as criminal, an important, fascinating, possibly fraudulent figure, someone who believes his calling places him beyond the law. Ibsen would explore the theme once again in his final play, explicitly making its hero Rubek an artist. The exemptions both Borkman and Rubek argue are at a frighteningly fundamental level. Even the crime of love betrayed is defended in the name of the 'higher goal' to which Borkman and Ibsen both claim their lives were dedicated, the greater good of the many. Gunhild Borkman accuses Borkman of failing to care about her happiness. 'When the ship goes down, someone usually has to go down with it,' Borkman replies. But the acting direction that accompanies it reads *uden at sé på hende* (without looking at her). It is typical of the larger and smaller honesties and freedoms that invest the whole play. Ibsen was now so old, so sure of the value and power of what he had achieved, that he was able to reject even the Victorian version of political correctness that defined him in the public mind, rightly or wrongly, as a moralist, a philanthropist, a humanist on the basis of the morality of *The Pillars of Society* and the radicalism of *A Doll's House*. Borkman makes observations about women in *John Gabriel Borkman* that might have been dictated to Ibsen by Strindberg from his place on the wall.*
One occurs in a conversation between Borkman and Foldal:

BORKMAN: Ah those women! They corrupt and distort our lives! Twist and pervert our fate, – our whole victory parade.
FOLDAL: Oh but, not all of them!
BORKMAN: No? Name me a single one that's even halfway good.
FOLDAL: No, you've got me there. The few I know, they're not up to much.
BORKMAN: Then what's the use? Of such women existing? If you don't know them?
FOLDAL: Oh but yes, John Gabriel, there *is* a point. It's such a happy thought, such a blessed thought, that out there, somewhere, far away – really is an ideal woman.
BORKMAN: (shifts uncomfortably on the sofa) Oh don't give me all that drippy literary stuff! (*digtersnak*).

Later there is a scene with Ella Rentheim in which Borkman tells

* The portrait actually hung behind him. It was the portrait of himself by Julius Kronberg that hung above him as he worked. The arrangement can be seen in Ibsen's study in the Arbinsgate Ibsen Museum.

her 'But you must remember I am a man. As a woman there was nothing in the world more precious to me than you. But if the situation demands it, then one woman can always be replaced by another.' Whether or not this accurately reflected Ibsen's own attitude is not the point. He simply wished to claim the freedom to say it.

Ibsen was now, by local standards, a very wealthy man. On 5 January 1897 he could afford to place his 14,000 kroner advance from *John Gabriel Borkman* for investment with Hegel. A few days later, on the tenth, he was able to send another 8,000 kroner, money that included royalties from Heinemann in England, for investment, requesting as ever 'good, safe, profitable holdings'. His financial situation was further guaranteed when Norway was accorded the copyright protection of the Bern Convention after the Paris conference of 1896. He was at once able to use this to rebuke his German publisher Fischer, whose habit of asking him to pay the translator's fee had long been an irritant. With the acid comment that he was 'unfortunately not wealthy enough to continue using Herr Fischer as my publisher, which is more or less the same as saying giving my books to him for nothing',[23] he gave *John Gabriel Borkman* to a newly established German publisher, Albert Langen, who was married to one of Bergljot Ibsen's sisters, and who had made Norwegian writers like Knut Hamsun and Bjørnson his first speciality. Langen had offered him five times what Fischer had paid for *Little Eyolf*, as well as paying for the translation, this in turn meaning that Ibsen was no longer required to share his income from German performances with his translator as had hitherto been the case. He was also delighted with his arrangement with Heinemann, who paid him at the same rate as Langen, and had promised to pay even more now that Ibsen was protected by the Bern Convention.

Fischer retained the rights to publish a first German edition of Ibsen's collected works, however, and work and correspondence in connection with this occupied much of his time in 1897. Dr Julius Elias, who was probably Ibsen's model for Jørgen Tesman, the dull but diligent scholar of *Hedda Gabler*, was in charge of the project. This inevitably involved the locating of some of his earliest work, and Ibsen was pleasantly surprised by the quality of *The Warrior's Barrow*, his first play to be staged, as long ago as 1850. He was less keen on Elias's attempts to include *St John's Night* among the collected works – 'the play is a wretched thing, not even really my own work. It is based on a cheap, sketchy outline which was given to me by a fellow-student and which I adapted and signed my name to. But I cannot possibly recognise it now'.[24] In forbidding its inclusion among his life's work he used a phrase that perhaps showed how it was possible for him to have lived so many years without revealing a flicker of interest in the existence of his illegitimate son, Hans Jacob Henriksen: the work in question, he wrote, 'far from illuminating any aspect of my earlier production, has absolutely no connection with it at all; therefore I have for many years now regarded it as unwritten and non-existent.'

Coincidentally two other early works were revived by the Christiania theatre at about this time. *The Feast at Solhaug* had not been performed since 1866 when Schrøder revived it in December 1897. Ibsen expressed little interest in the production and did not even take up the offer of free tickets; yet it proved popular and ran for a remarkable thirty-five performances, extending perhaps a nostalgic, pastoral appeal to urban audiences still only a generation away from Norway's rural past. Clearly, however, it was without real personal meaning for Ibsen. *Love's Comedy* was a different matter. Its revival in the spring of 1898 may have influenced the mood of brooding retrospection in which Ibsen was approaching what was to be his last play, *When We Dead Awaken.* After *The League of Youth, Love's Comedy* was much the most frequently performed of Ibsen's plays during the lifetime of the main Christiania theatre until its closure in 1899. Of his 'problem' plays with modern settings only *A Doll's House* could equal it in popularity.

In his personal life the fate of his son Sigurd continued to exercise him. Since 1894 Sigurd had been preoccupied with the idea of establishing a chair in sociology at the University of Kristiania, with himself as its first occupant. The discipline had already become established as a valuable tool for the understanding of modern times in the universities in Rome and Germany where he had studied. While Sigurd looked after Suzannah in Italy and worked on his book Ibsen did what he could to promote Sigurd's ambition among his influential political and journalistic acquaintances. An obvious difficulty was that the new 'science' was regarded as a piece of dubious radicalism by the Norwegian right in the *Storting,* and Ibsen warned Sigurd not to be over-optimistic in the first instance. His lobbying did, however, result in the government's granting a one-year stipend to cover the cost of a trial series of lectures on sociology during 1896–7. These were well-attended, but something about the atmosphere was not right. In her memoir *The Three Ibsens* Bergljot Ibsen writes 'I always accompanied Sigurd; but no-one spoke to us when we arrived, nor when we left either. We felt very isolated.'[25]

So it was perhaps not too surprising when the committee considering the new chair reached its conclusions at the end of Sigurd's series of lectures: 'Dr Ibsen has not in the course of these lectures displayed qualities which would warrant his employment as a teacher of sociology at the university.' Norway is a small country, Kristiania a small city with no hiding place for a victim of public opinion, especially when the victim's name was Ibsen. Sigurd left at once for the anonymity of Italy. In a sense it was his own fault, and his father's fault, for they had refused to countenance the idea that a new chair in sociology should be open to competition. Sigurd, like his father, was both very shy and very arrogant, and there was a good deal of ill-will towards Ibsen's attempts to re-establish a quasi-aristocracy in the country, which would give the holder of a famous name some kind of hereditary right to preferential treatment.

Ibsen once again threatened to give up his Norwegian nationality. He wrote to Bjørnson on 15 June 1897 that 'if all roads are blocked for Sigurd here in Norway then I cannot see any point in remaining. I have other places I can flee to.'[26]

What lay behind the repeated threat was that life in self-imposed and wandering exile had finally destroyed his need for a home and a nationality. As long as he had peace and quiet in which to work he hardly cared where he lived; and since he could work anywhere he found it oppressive to remain in the same place year after year. On 3 June 1897 he wrote to Brandes: 'Oh, my dear Brandes, one does not live for twenty-seven years in the free and liberating air of the great cultures without its having an effect. In here, or more correctly, up here, by the fjords, is the land where I was born. But – but – but, where is the land that is my home? What attracts me most of all is the *sea*.'

Suzannah was away again, with Sigurd, in Italy. Ibsen wrote to her. The hortensia are budding again, as many buds as last year. He has had to order a dozen new dress shirts, the shirts from Munich are completely worn out. Eating raw smoked ham, scrambled egg, lots of salmon. There is no Lina to bother her anymore, somebody called Mina is looking after him now. Occasionally he eats in the library. He's had the whole apartment spring-cleaned and his work-room completely redecorated. In his letter of 7 July he told her: 'I feel so extremely well, and it seems to me there is no better place to be in the summertime'. The unsurprising reason for his exhilaration follows in the next line: 'And I have begun thinking about a new play! For this reason I have extended my walks, every day first to Skillebæk and back, – then down to town; excellent.'[27] As yet the details of his play were not clear to him. But his brief description of what he had so far seems almost like a hint to Suzannah that he was coming back to her in his mind after the restless mental philandering of recent years: 'I sense the basic mood of it already; but as regards the characters, so far I see only one.'[28]

He still, however, had to face the imminent celebrations of his seventieth birthday. The very thought made him feel old. In June he had bought himself one of Reiersen's new patented electro-magnetic belts to stimulate the circulation of the blood; but by December the good mood of the summer had vanished without trace. In an unusually expressive letter to his French translator Moritz Prozor he wrote: 'Physically I am in excellent shape, but in my mind I often feel oppressed and depressed'. Hegel, who was also planning to publish an edition of his collected works, wrote to ask where he intended to spend his birthday. 'If it were up to me, ' replied Ibsen, so securely the prisoner of his own fame, 'I would run off and hide in the mountains, some place or other that was nice and lonely.' But he did no such thing, of course.

21

The Artist and His Model
When We Dead Awaken

Flags flew all over town in celebration of his seventieth birthday on 20 March 1898. Even the ships in the harbour were flagged. The Ibsens held open house to receive the tide of gifts and floral tributes that poured in. There were personal greetings from the King and the Crown Prince; from Norwegian national heroes like Bjørnson and Fridtjof Nansen; from Stockholm, Bergen, Berlin, Vienna, Leipzig, Frankfurt; and from Skien, where the council had decided to name the local park after him and opened a subscription list for contributions towards a statue. A special issue of the magazine *Samtiden* carried tributes from, among others, King Oskar II, Carl Snoilsky, Jonas Lie and Georg Brandes. At the theatres there were performances of scenes from *Peer Gynt*, *The Feast at Solhaug* and *The Master Builder*.

Newspapers at home and abroad carried extensive appreciations of the most influential dramatist of his age, and, with the possible exception of Leo Tolstoi, the most famous of living writers. From England Archer and Gosse sent a public greeting and an inscribed cup from forty 'English Friends and Admirers' including Herbert Asquith, J.M.Barrie, Thomas Hardy, Henry James, Gilbert Murray, Arthur Wing Pinero, George Bernard Shaw and Herbert Beerbohm Tree. *Morgenbladet's* London correspondent indicated the role of the camera in the creation of Ibsen's vast celebrity, claiming in his report that 'Ibsen's physiognomy is more familiar here than that of any of England's own outstanding contemporary writers'. The polarised nature of Ibsen's reputation in England, so swiftly the literary and cultural phenomenon of London in the 1890s, was reflected in newspaper reactions to the anniversary: *The Times,* the *Standard* and the *Daily Telegraph* wrote nothing, while the *Daily Chronicle, Daily News, Pall Mall & St James' Gazette* all carried fulsome tributes.

The official banquet was on 23 March. Ibsen replied to the speeches with his usual brevity and solemnity, striking the same confessional note as he had when addressing the students on his visit home in September 1874. He spoke of his plans to write a prose work, 'a book that will bring my life and my writing together in an explanatory whole',[1] and of how, after a lifetime spent writing drama, such a task would seem almost like a holiday – 'And as a matter of fact I have never had a holiday since I left Norway thirty-four years ago. It seems to me I might be in need of one now.' He spoke with some ambivalence of the effect of the years in exile, referring to:

> a misunderstanding which has in many ways caused problems for me, to the effect that the unusual, fairytale fate I have experienced – to have made my name in so many different lands – has been a source of undiluted happiness. And I have won warm, under-standing hearts out there. This above all. But real, inner happiness – that does not come by chance. It is not a gift. It has to be earned, and there is a price to pay which often feels like a burden. Because he who has won himself a home in many different coun-tries, deep down inside himself feels at home nowhere, - scarcely even in the country of his own birth.[2]

After he had sat down, Lorentz Dietrichson, Suzannah's faithful champion, rose and briefly paid tribute to the great part she had played in her husband's success.

At the end of the month Ibsen travelled to Copenhagen for a similar series of theatre performances and festivities. He was met at the station by Pietro Krohn, director of the Museum of Applied Arts, and Jacob Hegel, who took him to his hotel, the hotel d'Angleterre. Up in his room a surprise awaited him: a package containing the Great Cross of the Dannebrog Order. Ibsen unpacked the beautiful object and passed the presentation box around for the appreciation of his companions. But great was his consternation when he removed the medal from its box and discovered that it was made of papier-mâché. Neither Krohn nor Hegel could offer any explanation for this. Both were deeply embarrassed. None of them knew that the protocol of such awards was that the recipient himself should pay for the actual medal. It was agreed that Hegel would buy the order for Ibsen the following day. Accordingly he went to the royal jewellers, obtained the medal and took it to the hotel d'Angleterre, where he found Ibsen already admiring a Great Cross which the old king Christian IX had sent with his chamberlain as a personal gift. Hegel's cross was returned to the jeweller.

There was a performance of *The Wild Duck* in his honour at the Royal theatre, at which the part of Hedvig was played by a woman of forty-eight. Afterwards Ibsen walked the short way back to his hotel. Or attempted to – he got caught up in a riot of enthusiastic revellers from the artist's Café à Porta. The crowd swelled as passers-by joined the mob out of curiosity. Ibsen's silk top-hat received a bad dent, one of his trouser bottoms came loose from its boot, his shiny boots were scuffed and trampled on as he fought his way forward, hair and beard in disarray, the Great Cross dangling around his neck, crying repeatedly 'No no, oooh, no no'. Finally he was rescued by two students who pushed their way forward through the crowd and shepherded him the rest of the way to the hotel. The mob followed, and remained outside chanting 'We want Ibsen! We want Ibsen!' Peter Nansen, representing Gyldendal, had just heard that the main speaker at the evening's banquet was ill and that he would have to improvise something himself. Pacing up and down in the hotel foyer trying to think of what to say, and distracted by all the noise, he told Ibsen he must show himself. Ibsen flatly refused. The clamour increased. Nansen repeated his request. Ibsen again refused. Finally the hotel manager took command. He led Ibsen up the stairs to the royal suite and up to the double doors to a balcony facing out on to the square below: 'Now just stand still, Doctor. I'm going to count to three, the doors will be opened, you take three steps forward and bow. That's all there is to it.' Ibsen, safe on high, did as he was bidden. The crowd, satisfied, dispersed.

Later he had a brief audience with King Christian, and attended dinners in his honour given by the students and by a women's group. On 3 April he saw, for the first time in his life, a performance of *Brand* at the Dagmar theatre.

Three days later he travelled on to Stockholm, where he had an audience with King Oskar at which Oskar presented him with the Great Cross of the North Star. Ibsen's monarchism was as resolute as ever. The year before, Oskar had sent him the third of fifty signed copies of his own book *Verse and Prose*. In thanking him Ibsen described the book as 'my favourite reading' and praised 'the captivatingly spiritual articulation of its thought and the artistic and poetic perfection of its execution'. The volume also included the speeches Oskar had given in Norway, among which Ibsen noted particularly those on the occasion of the opening of new railway lines, which he took to be 'a symbolic harbinger of the fact that one day Your Majesty will know the happiness and joy of opening up the great spiritual railway lines between lands – and between people's hearts'.[3] His adolescent view of himself as the King's personal skald persisted, and in a speech at the main banquet on 13 April he called the award of the Great Cross 'the greatest honour I could imagine'. He added that he valued it primarily as a sign of the state's recognition of the power of literature,[4] and a brief altercation that evening shows that he meant it. King Oskar scolded him for having written *Ghosts*, telling him that it was not a good play – 'no, *Lady Inger of Østråt*, now that's a good play.'[5] Ibsen was visibly desolate and Queen Sophie tried to change the subject. For a few moments he said nothing, then suddenly he blurted out, 'But Your Majesty – I *had* to write *Ghosts*.' For a man so painfuly aware of the gulf between what we want to say and what we do say, it was a most courageous response.

The last night of his stay in Stockholm was more relaxing. On 16 April he was the guest of a Women's Union. There were speeches, and then the guests were entertained by a folk-dancing troupe.

By the time he returned to Kristiania on 17 April the celebrations had been going on for about thirty days and he must have been exhausted. But five weeks later, on 26 May, he responded to an invitation from the Norwegian Women's Union to attend a dinner in his honour. Suzannah had also promised to attend, but shortly before the event her health declined and she was unable to go. During the meal a procession of costumed women entered the room, all dressed as characters from Ibsen's plays. As they filed past him they identified themselves with a whisper in his ear and presented him with a rose. The main speech was given by Gina Krog, who along with H. E. Berner was responsible for the creation in 1884 of the influential pressure group for women's rights that this union had become. Ibsen's reply to her speech made it seem almost as though he had attended the dinner with the express purpose of clearing up certain misconceptions that he felt were growing up about his work as a dramatist:

I am not a member of the Women's Union. Whatever I have written, I have not written in the service of any particular viewpoint. I have been more a writer and less a social philosopher than people in general seem willing to admit. I thank you for your toast, but must decline the honour of deliberately having worked in the interests of the women-question. I am not even really sure what the women-question is.[6]

He then expressed a view on the subject of the role of women in society which was considerably less radical than might have been expected from the creator of Nora:

For me, the task has always been to elevate the country, give the people a higher platform. In the pursuit of this, two factors are of account: it is the responsibility of the mothers, by dint of hard, steady application, to awaken the consciousness of culture and discipline. This must be present in a people, before one can raise them yet higher. It is the women who must resolve the human problem. And it is as mothers, and only as mothers, that they can do so. Herein lies a great responsibility for women. Thank you, and good health to the Women's Union!

Ibsen feared, and not without reason, that his work was going to be appropriated by feminists for their own doctrinal ends. Yet in writing *A Doll's House* he had made himself a hostage to fortune, for as a play it was and remains a superb piece of sexual, political propaganda. Nothing he could say would ever change the fact that *A Doll's House* was written by a feminist. But like the burning nationalism of his youth, the pan-Scandinavianism of his middle years, the pan-Germanism of his later years, and probably even the mysticism of his last years, feminism was only a phase he passed through, passionately but swiftly. If this return of his last years to the belief that women should surrender to their biologically determined fate and live it out indicated a disillusionment with the way the social role of women was developing, it was a disillusionment he shared with Suzannah. In a letter to Bergljot Ibsen she wrote:

Honourable women are a rarity nowadays, and often it seems as though the morally bankrupt will triumph and walk off with the victor's prize. The liberation of the modern woman has been to little avail, and nowhere is this more true than in regard to married women, for whom the words *duty* – and gratitude – do not exist. So a woman must all the more firmly demand of herself a pure, spotless life. This is her only sure support.[7]

The letter was written when Bergljot and Sigurd were expecting their first child, and perhaps Suzannah's love for Sigurd was showing through here, for what loving mother would want a Nora as daughter-in-law and mother to her son's children? Ibsen was similarly affirming the importance of motherhood in *John Gabriel Borkman*, when he wrote with such moving insight into the predicament of the childless Ella Rentheim, and the fear among the childless of the complete personal annihilation that will come with death.

This was the first time Ibsen had been out of the country since his return in 1891, and it proved to be the last. Travel had once been his anodyne. Now he sought relief in his company of young women. Rosa Fittinghoff, a Swede in her mid-twenties, was the latest addition. She was one of the troupe of folk-dancers who had entertained Ibsen when he was a guest of the Women's Union in Stockholm. They corresponded for about three years after the event, and met briefly in the summer of 1899 when she visited Kristiania with her mother. Ibsen's letters to her were in the familiar, wanly flirtatious style. In one he told her that when he wanted to look deep into her eyes all he had to do was take out the group photograph she had given him of herself in the dancing troupe and gaze at her. He told her that he kept all her letters in 'a special little place in my writing desk, and when I go to my work each morning I always look into that little place and say hello to Rosa.'[8] She bought a touch of chaste sensuality into his austere life. One of his favourite Christmas presents was a large sponge given to him by Bergljot in 1894 – 'which I wash and rub myself with morning and evening', and Rosa's Christmas present to him in 1899 was similarly unpretentious and welcome: a small pillow: 'Each day I bury my head in it and pretend that it is my little pixie who has come to me,'[9] he told her. Emilie Bardach had also recently been in his thoughts, breaking the silence imposed on her by Ibsen to send him a greeting on his seventieth birthday. His reply to her was that impassioned telegram about the unforgettable summer of 1889.

Hildur Andersen remained an essential presence in his life. Of Ibsen's numerous 'princesses' she was probably the only one who meant something to him as an individual in her own right and not merely as a 'personification of youth'. In his way he loved her, and he expressed his love in the same awkward, elliptical fashion as he expressed his love for Sigurd, attempting to smooth her way through life. When she was engaged to play a concert in March 1899 at the Odd-Fellow-Paleet in Bredegade, Copenhagen, he sent near-identical letters of greeting to Edvard Brandes and Otto Borschenius, editor of the Danish *Morgenbladet*, in both of which he solicited good reviews for her work.[10]

At about the same time as this – in the spring of 1899 – he resumed work on the play he had mentioned to Suzannah in early 1898, which had been so seriously interrupted by the seventieth birthday celebrations. On 7 July he was 'very busy on a new play at the moment'.[11] On 25 August, he declined an invitation to dinner at the Thommessens: 'I am in the middle of a new literary work at the moment and dare not interrupt the train of thought'.[12] In a note to Georg Brandes's daughter Edith of 10 October: 'Sitting here alone as usual and brooding over a new work which I hope will be finished soon'.[13] Finally, on 20 November, he sent a telegram to Copenhagen to inform Hegel that *When We Dead Awaken* was finished and would be in the post to him tomorrow. The play was published on 19 December in an edition of 12,000 copies.

An aging sculptor, Professor Arnold Rubek, returns to Norway after a lifetime spent abroad. Wealthy and fêted, he brings one of his trophies home with him, his young wife Maja. They visit a mountain sanatorium, where Rubek once again meets the first great love of his life, his muse and his first model Irene, now mentally unbalanced and in the care of a mysterious minder. Overwhelmed by guilt at having betrayed both her and the artistic ideals of his own youth he rejects his young wife and returns to Irene. As the play reaches its climax they begin the symbolic ascent of the mountain together, but are prevented from reaching the summit by an avalanche. As they tumble past her, Irene's minder, in a self-conscious echo of the end of *Brand*, cries out '*Pax vobiscum*,' and the play ends.

The sanatorium in which the first act takes place is only one of several factors that associate Suzannah with Irene and suggest that she was Ibsen's model. The setting carries strong echoes of letters she wrote to him during her convalescent absences from Norway in Italy. Perhaps the idea came to him as he sat alone one afternoon reading through old letters, thinking about her, about all her summers spent in sanatoria and spa towns. A letter from their parting in 1877 contains one of the play's most important ideas, the association of Irene with mountain heights and with the beauty in harshness and austerity:

> We left with a reliable guide at three in the morning from Odde. First we crossed a lake, and the weather seemed good then, and we hoped for the best; but after two hours' stiff climbing the whole heavens darkened and were hung with heavy black cloud. What should we do? We comforted ourselves with the thought that it was perhaps just a shower, but within an hour we were as wet as could be, and onwards and upwards we went. After four hours we were up on the snow-line, and what kept us going and kept us warm was rum. Then we were up on Fonden and the endless snowfields, and there we wandered in a snowstorm for two hours. Imagine, my hair was quite stiff with ice and snow, and the guide's beard had icicles dangling from it. Sigurd said: 'What would Papa say if he could see us now?' We really were like two snowed-in ptarmigans, and then in the middle of the storm and the sea of snow came a dense mist, rolling along, a terrible, beautiful sight I will never forget. If you have not experienced it, you cannot possibly imagine it. Thank God we had such a good guide with us, but that endless sea of snow, where all life seemed to have died out, was almost too much. The descent, which took us seven hours in a driving rainstorm, - not a single farm where we could get something warm – was, as you might imagine, difficult.[14]

Another creative trigger may have been an undated letter from the hot springs of the Monsummano 'grotto'. Suzannah's description of the underground chamber where she takes her cure suggests the underground chamber of Irene's insane fears, as the white, surplice-like gown she mentions is also a feature of Irene's apparel. Among her fellow-guests she sketches out the two 'strange ladies' of Ibsen's play, one of them Russian, as well as the two statues these 'strange ladies' suggest in their manner of walking.* There is a passing reference to a sculptor:

> The clinic is in a park with lovely big trees, so the view from my window is just a waving sea of cypresses, chestnut trees and all the other lush growths of the south. At the entrance to the grotto

---

* Irene's stiff, 'statuesque' way of walking probably echoes the gait and upright carriage that Suzannah's severe rheumatism obliged her to adopt.

are two marble statues of the discoverer of it and his son, the Tuscan writer Giusti. It's all very impressive, stylish as you would expect from Italians.

You can't imagine what a strange life it is in the grotto. The first day I was due to go down there Sigurd had to see me in my white cape; actually I think he's very afraid of the grotto, so it's a good job he has no need of it. I spend two hours down there, and I breathe easily and freely in the heat. You can't imagine how strange it is. When we next meet I could tell you about what I have seen here for months on end. Men and women everywhere; a painter or sculptor could learn a lot about plasticity here. . . When we arrived here there were two very important ladies, both writers: Fru Boy Ed, German, and Princess Altieri, Russian, but married to Prince Altieri, who lives a couple of hours from here. Both of them them were very kind to me, unforgettably so. They have left now, but both have written to me and sent me several of their books.

The specific type of mental disturbance Irene experiences in the play, with her references to 'they' and the way 'they' seem to control her by means of some kind of electric current, may also owe something to Ibsen's fascination during these last years of his life with August Strindberg's personality and writing. He had read 'with *great* interest' the *Inferno*, Strindberg's description of his paranoid and mystical breakdown in Paris between 1894 and 1896 from which he emerged a follower of Emanuel Swedenborg, and called Strindberg 'a very great talent'.[15] He had also read *To Damascus*, Strindberg's dramatisation of the Inferno-crisis published in 1898, in which the main character, on his road to a new self-understanding, meets again those against whom he has sinned along the way in much the same way as Rubek re-encounters Irene. *To Damascus*'s most striking effect is what Gustaf af Geijerstam called, in a letter to Strindberg, its 'terrifying half-reality', which would also serve as an apt description of the mood of Ibsen's play.

As an epilogue to the life and works, *John Gabriel Borkman* needed no artistic addition, no artistic correction. But Ibsen had personal reasons for wanting to write one last play which would be to and for Suzannah. As an apology, as a pained tribute, and as a final confirmation of his absolute need for her. Apology, because of the way he had betrayed her in his mind with Emilie Bardach, Helene

Raff, Hildur Andersen, telling each of them in turn that she had been his true inspiration, that only after meeting her did his writing become real. According to her journal, he told Bardach that he had found 'true love. The ideal which he wrote about before the experience. Now he will be the poet of pain and denial. And yet happy to have found me, the most beautiful, the most wonderful.' He took his betrayal furthest with Hildur Andersen, presenting her with original manuscripts of both *The Master Builder* and *Rosmersholm*, and dedicating an edition of his collected works to her with an inscription, dated 19 September: 'These twenty-five twins are all ours. Before I found you, I wrote in searching, in longing. I knew you were out there somewhere in the world, and once I found you I wrote only about the princess in all her shifting shapes.'[16]

This creative betrayal was real to Ibsen, for he knew quite well that these young women, for obvious reasons, had had little or no real influence on his lifetime of writing. Certainly they had sacrificed nothing for him. Suzannah had sacrificed her life, her self, her identity for his art. Irene's words to Rubek leave no doubt on this score. For this reason *When We Dead Awaken* has to be read as an allegory of the Ibsens' life, with Ibsen as Rubek the sculptor, Suzannah as Irene his constant model, and Rubek's new wife Maja as the young Bardarch/Raff/Andersen figure who enters the relationship disruptively towards the end of Rubek's life. Rubek's works are Ibsen's plays. These begin as a joint enterprise in a mood of highest idealism that involves both artist and model. Later in life Rubek loses his idealism, or finds it badly sullied, and begins to produce those portrait busts he refers to. These are lifelike human representations which can be identified with Ibsen's later 'realist' plays with modern settings. Rubek's cynical, misanthropic nature led him to sculpt not only the superficial likeness of his subject but also the brute that lurked beneath, the dog beneath the skin, as Ibsen the modern dramatist portrayed people who were ugly and self-centred beneath their superficial respectability.

Irene calls this realism a betrayal, of himself as artist, of herself as his model, and of her self-sacrifice. Much of the dialogue in their scenes together involves Rubek in agonised attempts to justify his apparently cold and cynical behaviour towards her. Over and over again he returns to the excuse that it is because he is *en kunstner* (an artist). Irene will not permit this. She finds it too self-exculpatory, too dishonest in its claim that there is, in spite of all, a kind of heroic magnificence beneath the shabbiness. She prefers the word *digter*, (writer, inventor of tales). Perhaps it was an Ibsen family insult – once, when Sigurd Ibsen was a child, his father caned him for disobedience. On his way out Sigurd turned at the door and howled at him 'Writer! Writer! All you know about is writing lies and nonsense!'[17]

Besides apologising to Suzannah for betraying her with another muse Ibsen had another 'artistic' sin on his conscience. In the plays that had resulted from this experiment in betrayal, *The Master Builder* and *John Gabriel Borkman*, the self-portrait figures of Solness and Borkman were both married to women whom the Kristiania theatre public readily identified as Suzannah, since it was widely assumed that Ibsen was depicting his own marriage in these plays – Magdalene Thoresen's observation about them being two lonely people leading entirely separate lives shows with what justification. Solness and Borkman do not hide their distaste and dislike of their old wives. Solness goes furthest, with his comment about 'being chained alive to a dead woman'. Suzannah cannot have enjoyed being the subject of this kind of portrayal, and on reflection Ibsen must have had difficulties in reconciling his humanity with what he had done. The creator has dehumanised his model: 'I have stood on the revolving wheel in the variety halls,' Irene says. 'Been the naked 'living statue' in *tableaux vivants*. . . . I have stood on the revolving wheel – naked – and shown myself off to hundreds and hundreds of men – after you.' Just so might Suzannah have complained of her exposure by Ibsen.

By the time of *When We Dead Awaken* the mystical element present in varying degrees in *Rosmersholm*, *The Lady from the the Sea*, *The Master Builder* and *Little Eyolf* had become a dominant feature. According to the family doctor, Edvard Bull, Suzannah Ibsen was in her later years a confirmed theosophist, and this trend in Ibsen's later plays probably reflects the way her interest increasingly became a feature of their conversation. Ibsen always affirmed his independence of any fixed system of belief. In an 1898 interview he protested 'People in this country talk about my philosophy. I *have* no philosophy.'[18] Yet Dr Bull's cautious statement in his memoirs, 'I could not say whether he completely accepted the theosophical viewpoint' (*Om han helt ut hyllede teosofiske Anskuelser, ved jeg ikke*), suggests Ibsen was at the very least familiar with theosophy's background and ideas. As a personal greeting of the order of the '19 September' greeting to

Hildur Andersen in *The Master Builder* he introduced an association between Irene and the founder of theosophy, Madame Blavatsky, giving Irene a Russian background and a name, von Satow, that is a compression of Saratow, where Blavatsky grew up.

There are other esoteric images, notably the pairing of white-clad Irene and the dark-clad nun which relates to the Victorians' vivid interest in the phenomenon of 'spirit photography'. Edvard Munch was fascinated by its possibilities and used it in his art, and long before Munch, Blavatsky or Freud, Ibsen himself, in *Peer Gynt*, had played with the symbolic possibilities of photographs and their negatives. Rubek's words to Irene close to the end of the play, 'All the powers of light may look upon us. And of darkness too', are likewise probably echoes from Suzannah's conversation. 'Maja' was a fairly common name in nineteenth-century Norway; but in the light of the influence of esoteric Buddhism on early theosophy it acquires a second, special meaning in the play by opposing the young, wordly and sensual woman to the austere, ethereal Irene. The name 'Rubek' itself is an anagram of the Norwegian *kerub* (angel). As a curiosity one can add that Suzannah's collection of esoteric literature included a recent Danish translation of Allan Kardec's *Le Livre des Esprits*. Kardec was the so-called father of spiritism in France, and his book was said to have been dictated to him via the mediumship of a 'professional sleepwalker'. The main tenet of Kardec's spiritism was the belief that spiritual progress in humans is effected by a series of compulsory reincarnations, and some students of the play believe that it does contain ideas about the need for reincarnation.

In these autobiographical terms the pattern of relationships and their development in *When We Dead Awaken* is simple. Ibsen/Rubek announces to his lifetime wife Suzannah/Irene that he has finished dabbling with Bardach/Maja figures and is returning to her, to the font of standards and supreme goals which she represents to him. Their purpose as they head on into the mysterious cloud-drenched mountain heights is to get married once more in one of those 'private' marriage ceremonies that Ibsen returned to again and again in his writing. In *Brand* the hero dies alone in his avalanche. For Ibsen personally perhaps one of the most important aspects of *When We Dead Awaken* was that Rubek and his old love are allowed to die together.

Attempts have been made to impart a deeper, logical meaning to *When We Dead Awaken*, to make it somehow more worthy of its status as Ibsen's last play. For the play has faults, lesser and greater. Ulfheim's servant Lars is missing from the list of characters; Irene is referred to both as de Satow and von Satow. And because Ibsen was not Strindberg, the uncertain status of her reality is a distracting matter. Ibsen himself was not sure whether she should be played as a young or an old woman. Ulfheim the hunter, who takes up with Maja as Rubek returns to Irene, is another of that small band, including the Stranger and Ellida Wangel in *The Lady from the Sea* and the Rat Wife, that tax the actor's art to its limits. It is tempting to suggest that the play would have benefited in clarity had Ibsen presented us with Irene as a straightforward character, an old lover from the past reappearing by chance in the life of an egocentric artist who had once made use of her, then thrown her on the scrap-heap when he had no further need of her. The same areas of self-doubt and self-justification could have been explored.

And yet one feels that Ibsen wilfully reserved to himself the right of emotional self-indulgence in the plays of his late middle-age and old-age; in *When We Dead Awaken* the result is that the drama is too private. Its religious structure is an unconvinced and unconvincing syncretism that mixes an Old Testament God with Jesus Christ and Madame Blavatsky. The dialogue is often overblown and prone to hobble along on the crutch of a pun, as in the 'engagement scene' between Ulfheim and Maja:

ULFHEIM: (looks at her a moment) Listen here, my fine hunting companion –
FRU MAJA: Well? What is it now?
ULFHEIM: Shouldn't we two put our rags and tatters together?[2]*
FRU MAJA: Does Squire Ulfheim want to be a tailor?
ULFHEIM: Yes by jove, he certainly does. Couldn't the two of us try to stitch our rags together here and there, - and make a sort of human life out of it?
FRU MAJA: And when those poor rags wear out too, what then?
ULFHEIM: (gestures with his hand) Then there we will stand, bold and free, as who we really are!

In the more measured scenes, like the dialogue early on between Rubek and Maja, there are fascinating glimpses of a play that might have been, a startlingly modern exposition of controlled existential

* *slå vore stakkers pjalter sammen*, meaning figuratively 'to join forces' or 'get married'. The subsequent dialogue is based on the literal meaning of the phrase, as indicated by Ulfheim.

despair suggested in their exchange about travelling on the night train through Norway:

> PROFESSOR RUBEK: Then I realised that we must have crossed the border. That now we were really home. Because the train stopped at every tiny station, even though there was no one there.
>
> MAJA: Why did the train stop like that, when there was no-one there?
>
> PROFESSOR RUBEK: Don't know. Nobody got off, nobody got on. And at every station we came to I heard two workers walking along the platform – one of them carried a lamp – and they talked to each other, quietly, dully, saying nothing into the night.
>
> MAJA: Yes, you're right. Always two men walking along and talking together –
>
> PROFESSOR RUBEK: – About nothing.

In spite of the play's faults, indeed because of them, *When We Dead Awaken* remains an extraordinarily touching and affecting play, if viewed as a personal testament and afforded the indulgence a great artist deserves at the end of a lifetime of work. Reviewing *Little Eyolf* in *Verdens Gang* in 1894 Georg Brandes wrote that 'We who have followed Ibsen ever since the days of *The Pretenders* really cannot criticise him any more. Our gratitude and respect have grown from play to play. It is no fun for us to advance criticisms, and he has no need of our praise,'[19] and the same might be said of *When We Dead Awaken*. The play is suffused with a sense of loneliness and regret. Rubek, misanthropy and all, is desperately honest in his attempts to rationalise his life, character and work to Irene, moving and sympathetic in his admission that it really won't do anyway. Some prefer the spiritualist-theosophical-Christian interpretation of the lines that contain the play's title as referring to rebirth, second chance, reincarnation; but to do so dishonours the bleak courage of the dramatist's realisation that now, too late, when it is almost all over, he has failed to live his life:

> PROFESSOR RUBEK: (*Repeats dreamily*) A summer's night on the mountain heath. With you. With you ... (*His eyes meet hers*) Oh Irene, – that could have been our life. – And we wasted our chance, – we two.

IRENE: What is past redemption, that's what we never see until
– (she breaks off abruptly)
PROFESSOR RUBEK: (looks questioningly at her) Until –?
IRENE: Until we dead awaken.
PROFESSOR RUBEK: (Shakes his head wearily) Yes. And what is
it we see after all?
IRENE: We see that we have never lived.

In *The Master Builder* God did not permit Solness to climb down
from his tower and kiss little Hilde 'many many times', and by the
end of *When We Dead Awaken* it is clear that while spiritual love has
been rekindled, as regards the sensual life nothing much has
changed in the artist's universe. Rubek's fantasy of finally making
love with Irene on the sunlit mountain heights ends in a similar
cosmic act of rejection. Request denied. 'Thou shalt not.' Well might
he say, with Julian, 'You have won, Galilean.'

When We Dead Awaken had its première at Kristiania's new, purpose-
built National theatre on 15 January 1900, just four months after
the gala opening on 1 September 1899. For Norway and, dare one
say it, for Ibsen personally, it was a gratifying end to a fifty-year
struggle to establish an independent cultural identity, and one in
which Ibsen had played an important part. *When We Dead Awaken*
was performed later in the year in Stuttgart, Copenhagen, Helsinki,
Stockholm, Munich and Berlin.

It was also performed at the Moscow Art theatre, which was
opened in 1898 by Nemirovich-Danchenko and Konstantin Stanislavsky. This was another of those semi-private enterprises, like Freie
Bühne in Berlin and Théâtre Libre in Paris, which did so much to
further the spread of Ibsen's reputation in Europe towards the close
of the century. William Archer duly translated the play into English,
but his heart was not in it. He found the play 'a sad fiasco', 'utterly
without dramatic fibre', [20] and made no attempt to stage it. Ibsen
perhaps suspected that it had caused him trouble. In a letter
thanking Archer for his copy of the English translation he wrote 'it
was quite easy for me to read and I understood most of it; but I can
well believe it was difficult to translate'.[21]

It was in this same letter that he referred to the nineteen-year-old
James Joyce's long and appreciative review of the play printed in
the *Fortnightly Review*. Joyce already considered Ibsen the greatest

writer he knew of; but his enthusiasm for the master's new play surely owed more to adolescent loyalty than to the play's innate qualities. Perhaps its real importance for the young Joyce was its underlying message that art, for the artist who would be great, is literally a matter of life and death. That is Rubek's belief, as it is Irene's belief; and that the needs of a great artist override every other consideration was also Ibsen's belief. He once listened to a tirade from John Paulsen against Goethe for his 'servile attitude'[22] towards Napoleon. Paulsen claimed that Goethe probably did not even care whether Napoleon swallowed up the whole of Germany, as long as he was allowed to carry on working on his theories of colour and writing *Faust*. When he had finished Ibsen smiled and replied that the only thing that mattered was that *Faust* got written. 'Germany could disappear if necessary from the ranks of the free nations, just so long as a great work like *Faust* saw the light of day.'

In the middle of March 1900 Ibsen suffered a slight stroke that affected his right side and put him out of commission for a while. In the summer Suzannah again left for Italy, while Ibsen travelled to a sanatorium at Sandefjord, where his condition improved with daily massaging. From the earliest days of his return to Kristiania it seems as though Ibsen may, with the greatest discretion, have indulged a mild form of alcoholism. One thinks of Laura Kieler's otherwise unlikely tale that he wept during their meeting in 1891; of Lina Jacobsen's references to his tears whenever she cooked him the food his mother used to feed him as a boy; and even of his daily visits to the Grand Hotel on Karl Johan. And according to Bolette Sontum, the daughter of the head doctor at Sandefjord, when she and her little sister used to visit him sometimes during his summer there, more or less to play with him, he would give them claret and champagne to sip.

By mid-August he was almost well again, and on 31 August he dedicated a photograph of himself to one of the Sandefjord doctors, Justus Anderssen (facing the camera, black coat, white cravat, right hand resting on a small armchair, left hand on the handle of a supporting umbrella) 'With sincere thanks for a good heart and strong arms in my wretchedness'.[23] On 4 November he sent another dedicated photograph to 'my friend and rescuer Superintendant Sontum, as a small memento of the summer 1900 in Sandefjord', and by December he was well enough to engage briefly in a debate on the subject of the Boer War. He had been publicly rebuked in an open letter by a patriotic Dutch newspaper editor, C. K. Elout, for certain remarks of a casual nature he had made in a newspaper interview, to the effect that the English in South Africa were merely doing to the Boers what the Boers had done to the aboriginal population, and that, moreover, the Boers had never attempted to civilise the country they had stolen. Elout demanded that he substantiate his remarks or withdraw them. Ibsen, whose approach to the fretful old problem of the divide 'between will and ability', saying and doing, wishing and acting, remained perfectly unresolved, responded by mocking the claims of the Dutch to be the natural defenders of the Boers in Europe. He implied that their support would be the more effective if they travelled out to South Africa with it, and concluded sarcastically: 'And then, to defend one's relations with books and brochures and open letters! Are there not, my dear editor, more effective weapons?'

Ibsen's attitude towards such matters had not changed since Archer heard him address the Circolo Scandinavo in Rome in December 1881, when he said that 'he did not believe that peace was the most desirable condition; on the contrary, he held warfare to be more wholesome for human nature'.[24] In an interview in 1898 he expressed the view that war was a biological necessity: 'If we are to dispense with war, then we shall need to find some other method of culling the human population ... In my view mankind, at least in its present situation, needs some such thing. Otherwise the blood would get too thick. .... If military service were to be abolished now, the probable result would be to retard human development.' At about the same time he also expressed public support for capital punishment, though it was over twenty-five years since it had last been used in Norway, and was within five years of being abolished by law in January 1905.[25]

This was Ibsen's last public 'appearance'. In the summer of 1901 he had a second stroke, after which he was no longer able to write. A third stroke followed in 1903. Hildur Andersen disappeared from his daily life after this, presumably on Suzannah's orders. Sigurd had been briefly called in from the cold in 1899 to head the newly established Norwegian Foreign Ministry in Kristiania. In 1903 he went to Stockholm to be the Norwegian Government Minister, a circumstance which led Ibsen to refer to him always in conversation as 'His Excellency'. Two years later, as the issue of Norwegian independence from Sweden came to a climax, Sigurd's support for a policy of dialogue and discussion rather than a unilateral declaration of independence obliged him to resign the post and return to Norway. This marked the end of his political career, a disappointment for him but a blessing, if a mixed one, for his father, who doted on him and was pleased to be able to see him once again on a regular basis. 'Shouldn't Grimbart be here by now?'* he would say to Suzannah, sitting with his watch open on the table in front of him as the appointed minute ticked by.

But Suzannah and Bergljot were his main companions during these last five years of his life, together with those joined to him by reason of his incapacity – his doctor, his nurse, his masseur, his barber. These 'auxiliaries' were for the most part undemanding, sympathetic company whose memories of him show that, despite the slow ebbing away of his faculties, Ibsen was rarely less than Ibsen.

Dr Sontum, who had been his doctor since his return to Norway, died unexpectedly, late in 1901, and after a brief and unsatisfactory interlude with a replacement, Dr Edvard Bull was recommended to him. Bull visited him for the first time just after his third stroke, and remained his doctor until the end of Ibsen's life. He often called more than twice daily, and estimated that in the three years he served as Ibsen's doctor he visited him more than a thousand times. To begin with the relationship was extremely uncomfortable. Ibsen revolted against the authority of a new and unknown person in his life, and often during his first visits Bull heard his patient cursing him under his breath. A six-page memoir Bull wrote not long after Ibsen's death provides an interesting record of their relationship during these last years, discreetly confirming matters such as Ibsen's extreme shyness about exposing his own body and a coyness in referring to his bodily parts and functions – the penis and the anus were respectively 'the small arrangement' and 'the big arrangement' – and solidly precluding the possibility of adultery: 'there was no eroticism in him. It is my firm conviction that he has never "had relationships" with women.'

Bull stuck to his task and gradually won Ibsen's confidence. A strong point in his favour was that he was the doctor at the new National theatre. Each day he brought with him news of the repertoire, gossip about the actors, and when the set designer Jens Wang

---

* Grimbart was his affectionate nickname for Sigurd.

produced designs for productions of his plays Bull would bring photographs and sketches for Ibsen to inspect. In this way his interest was kept alive.

During these last five years Ibsen also developed a close relationship with Arnt Dehli, nominally his masseur, who visited him every day and spent two hours with him. When Ibsen was well enough they would walk arm in arm in the park opposite the Arbinsgate apartment. This was Queen's Park, a private section of the palace gardens to which King Oskar had give Ibsen his own key. In a striking and pathetic observation Dr Bull noted how Ibsen, in obedience to an obsessional pedantry, always had to have this key, his watch, his red handkerchief, and two small golden boxes, one containing his daily ration of snuff, the other his chewing tobacco, arrayed on the table before him in a straight line. He would fiddle with these objects ceaselessly to achieve this effect, exercising in this sad fashion the remnants of a power to order the world that had, in the course of his long prime, enabled him to produce twenty-five full-length plays.

Deprived of the focus of work other neuroses flared up uncontrollably, like the obsession with punctuality. If his medicine were not brought to him at exactly the right time he would become utterly confused. His barber observed him in the same helpless thrall to the clock. Carl Larsen would call to shave him every Tuesday and Friday, at ten thirty precisely. When he arrived Ibsen would be sitting with his old silver watch open on the table in front of him. If Larsen were more than two minutes late Ibsen would simply say 'Come back tomorrow.' It took Larsen a long time to persuade Ibsen to allow him to shave him. 'Yes, but, but do you really think you can do it?' Ibsen kept asking. All of his casual contacts at this time had to be to some extent philosophers. Once, when Larsen and Ibsen were looking out of the window together, they saw some birds feeding on horse-droppings in the street below. A discussion arose about what kind of birds they were. The barber knew perfectly well they were sparrows and said so. Ibsen thought they were magpies, and when Larsen repeated that they were sparrows Ibsen rounded on him in fury: 'When I have said they are magpies, then that is what they are.' And so, of course, they were magpies.

Like Larsen the barber, Dehli had to allow autocracy its way. When Ibsen was too weak to walk he and Dehli would ride down Drammensveien in a carriage.One day they were greeted by a tall man on foot. Ibsen asked who it was and was told it was Professor Nansen.* He said that he did not know any Professor Hansen. Dehli told him that the name was *Nansen*. In deep exasperation Ibsen retorted that '*Når jeg har sagt, at jeg ikke kjenner noen professor Hansen så gjør jeg det ikke*' (When I say I do not know any Professor Hansen then it means I do not know any Professor Hansen).

One of Dehli's jobs was to announce the arrival of visitors to the apartment. One day Dr Bull happened to arrive in the room just in time to hear Dehli say: 'Here comes Dr Bull.' 'Are you sure about that?' replied Ibsen. Dr Bull went over to his patient and asked him how he was. Dehli, who functioned as Ibsen's interpreter when his speech became too difficult for strangers to understand, replied 'Dr Ibsen is quite well today thank you'. Ibsen countered with an answer of his own: 'Hm, well, God knows.' 'Oh yes,' said Dr Bull, 'if Dehli thinks so then it's probably right.' 'Maybe!' muttered Ibsen, using a favourite phrase which was, according to Bull, 'absolutely the greatest degree of concession he was prepared to make.'

Those closest to Ibsen, who loved him, in particular Suzannah, knew that such peculiarities were simply part of his personality, and no more sinister than that. He permitted himself the liberty of swearing and cursing at her when the mood took him, and she, fruit to his scorpion, greeted the ejaculations with a tolerant smile, realising that he could scarcely help himself. Dr Bull wrote that when Ibsen grew too weak even to indulge in cursing it was 'as if something were missing in the house, and one longed again for the thundering of the days of his prime'.

A regular stopping place on the rides down Drammensveien with Dehli was the National theatre, with Stefan Sinding's statues of Ibsen and Bjørnson, twice life-size, guarding the main entrance. Ibsen had become a much-sculpted man during these last years. After Sinding, Vigeland made busts of him in 1901 and 1902, and returned to Arbinsgate in 1903 to make a third. Sitting, or more accurately standing, for Sinding in the mid-1890s presumably had its influence on his choice of sculpture as the art form practised by Professor Rubek. His very approach to the work of creation was like that of the sculptor who sees form latent in an uncarved block and whose art consists in chipping away what is extraneous until it stands revealed.

In any general discussion about aesthetics, even in the early days

* The explorer, Fridtjof Nansen.

as a reviewer of plays in Kristiania, Ibsen's examples would character-istically be drawn from the world of sculpture. Enthusing once on the talents of an admired actor, Anton Wiehe, he remarked that when he recalled Wiehe's art 'it is as though I am walking down a row of statues from antiquity'. Fredrik Hegel even wrote to him that his own works 'stand like a row of statues in a gallery', adding that they 'should, like real statues, observe a certain distance from the public.'[26]

Ibsen was attracted to sculpture not only as form but as fate, and his feelings as he and Dehli drove by the massive statues outside the National Theatre must have been complex. He enjoyed the idea of the statue as a stone photograph, as a passport to something close to the kind of eternity which the Greeks and Romans enjoyed. And yet for most of his adult life he lived in fear of petrification. He expressed it most clearly in his most courageous poem, 'On the Heights':

> No, now I can manage alone
> but thanks for your offer;
> no river floods through my veins anymore,
> in the vault of my chest I seem to feel,
> signs of my turning to stone.

The sensation never left him. Borkman's heart attack is 'an icy hand gripping my heart'. Then it is 'a hand of stone'. A mere handful of surviving letters – to Carl Anker, to Bjørnstjerne Bjørnson, to Magdalene Thoresen – articulate the pain this process of slow inner dying caused him. The most simple and moving statement of it came in a letter to Bjørnson's wife Karoline:

Whatever you do, you must not attach any importance to the fact that this letter is a little incoherent and desultory. Because letter-writing really isn't my strongest point. I am almost afraid that I have struggled so long and so hard with the form of the drama, in which to a certain extent it is necessary for the author to kill and drown his own personality, or at any rate hide it, that I may have lost a great deal of that which I myself prize most highly in a letter-writer. But be assured, it lies no deeper than in the form.[27]

Throughout the years of his decline Ibsen continued to eat and sleep well, and he experienced little pain. On 23 November 1905 he suffered a collapse, brought on by agitation at an unscheduled visit from Sigurd. Dr Bull was called and revived him, and within forty-eight hours he was up again. But from that time onwards, Dr Bull noted, his terminal decline began. He ceased to go out, ceased to wander through the apartment, and spent most of his time in bed. His condition deteriorated further through the winter and the spring of 1906, and after 16 May he ceased to get up at all and was most of the time in a semi-conscious state. On 22 May, shortly after Dr Bull had made what turned out to be his last visit, those remaining in the room with Ibsen stood at the window discussing his condition. The nurse said she thought he seemed a little better, and from behind them Ibsen suddenly said, quite clearly, 'On the contrary.'* This was his last word. In Dr Bull's opinion it was 'almost certainly by mere chance that it resembled a thought'. The following day, 23 May, as the family were gathered to eat, at two-thirty in the afternoon the nurse sitting with him suddenly noticed that he had stopped breathing. She hurried to the bed, and he was dead.

It had been five years since Ibsen had been able to write, but in his dreams and his dying he never stopped work. On the night of 30 January 1905 he was heard to cry out in his sleep: 'I'm writing, it's going wonderfully.' Was the dream-play as good as *Peer Gynt?* Possibly – as Jatgeir the skald told his master Skule, unwritten verses are always the best. But as an artist Ibsen was never able to repeat the achievements of *Brand* and *Peer Gynt* from those incredible first three years in Rome. It was inevitable, for in *Peer Gynt* he took a well-established art form to the summit of its development, while in the run of plays that began with *The Pillars of Society* he laid the foundations of a new one. His achievement scarcely needs repeating, but for the sake of form: he created the modern theatre. He tried to show contemporary audiences that even without God it was still worth trying to live at a moral level, and in pursuit of this vision lived out the truth of the professional writer's life: a lonely, hard, pot-bellied life, its pathos all but obscured by the blinding glare of fame. He was given a state funeral on 1 June and lies buried in Our Saviour's churchyard in Oslo. Sigurd chose his gravestone, a black obelisk marked by a hammer. Suzannah survived him by eight years. Convinced in her theosophy that he lived on invisibly with her in

---

* One word in Norwegian: *Tvertimot.*

Arbinsgate, and knowing how particular he was about such things, she preserved the rooms and the position of the objects within them scrupulously unchanged until the day of her own death.

Chronology

Ibsen's Life	International Events	Social & Scientific Events
1828: 20 March: Born in Skien	1810–44: Karl XIV King of Swedish-Norwegian Union 1828: Tolstoy born. 1831: Goethe: *Faust*, part II Pushkin: *Eugene Onegin* 1832: Bjørnson born. Goethe dies.	1827: J. N. Niepce makes photographs on metal place.
1834–36: Father's financial losses. Family moves to Venstøp, Skien.	1837-1901: Queen Victoria on the throne. 1839: Stendhal: *The Charterhouse of Parma*. 1840: Zola born. 1842–48: Paludan-Müller: *Adam Homo*.	1838: Daguerre produces photographs using silver salts (Daguerrotypes). 1839: W. Fox Talbot invents photographic paper.
1843: Family moves to Snipetorp, Skien.	1843: Kierkegaard *Either-Or*.	1843: Great Britain lifts its ban on the export of machinery.
1844–50: Apothecary's apprentice in Grimstad. 1846: Else Sophie Birkedalen has his son, Hans Jacob Henriksen. Ibsen ordered to pay alimony for fourteen years. 1849: Writes *Catiline*. 1850–51: Student in Kristiania. First play performed. *The Warrior's Barrow* premiered at the Christiania Theatre, 26 September.	1844: Nietzsche born. 1844–59: Oskar I King of Swedish–Union. 1848: Marx and Engels: *The Communist Manifesto*. 1848: Year of revolutions around Europe. 1849: Strindberg born. 1850: Death of Oehlenschläger.	1845: D. O. Hill developed artistic photographic portraits. 1848: Establishment of first commercial bank in Kristiania. 1848–51: Marcus Thrane's revolutionary socialist movement. 1850: About 12,000 employed in factories in Norway.
1851–57: Assistant director at Det Norske Theater in Bergen. 1852: Trip to Denmark and Germany to learn practical stagecraft. 1853: *St John's Night*. 1854: *The Warrior's Barrow*, revised edition.	1851: Melville: *Moby Dick*.	1854: Opening of the Kristiana-Eidsvoll railway.

435

Ibsen's Life	International Events	Social & Scientific Events
1855: *Lady Inger of Østråt.* **1856**: *The Feast At Solhaug.* **1857**: *Olaf Liljekrans.* **1857–63**: Moves back to Kristiania as Artistic Director at Kristiania Norske Theater **1858**: Marries Suzannah Thoresen. *The Vikings at Helgeland.* **1859**: Son Sigurd is born. *On the Heights* (poem): *In the Picture Gallery* (cycle of poems). **1861**: *Terje Vigen* (poem). **1862**: Kristiania Norske Theater closes. Ibsen collects folk tales during a mountain walking trip. Deep in debt. *Love's Comedy.* **1863**: *The Pretenders.* **1864–8**: Lives in Rome. **1864**: Summer in Genzano. **1865**: Summer in Ariccia. **1866**: *Brand.* Awarded lifetime government grant to write. **1867**: Summer in Ischia and Sorrento. *Peer Gynt.* **1868**: Summer in Berchtesgaden in the Bavarian Alps. **1868–75**: Lives in Dresden. **1869**: Summer in Stockholm, autumn in Egypt for the opening of the Suez Canal. *The League of Youth.* **1871**: Published *Poems.* **1872**: Summer in Berchtesgaden. **1873**: *Emperor and Galilean.* Summer in Vienna. **1874**: Summer in Norway. **1875–8**: Lives in Munich. **1875–85**: Lives mainly in Rome. **1877**: *The Pillars of Society.*	**1855**: Whitman: *Leaves of Grass* **1856**: Freud and George Bernard Shaw born. **1857**: Flaubert: *Madame Bovary.* **1859**: Hamsun born. Darwin: *On the Origin of Species.* **1859–72**: Karl XV King of Swedish-Norwegian Union. **1860**: Chekhov born. **1861**: Death of E. Scribe. **1861–5**: Civil War in USA. **1863**: Renan: *Life of Jesus.* **1864**: Dano-Prussian war over Schleswig Holstein. **1864–9**: Tolstoy: *War and Peace.* **1866**: Dostoevsky: *Crime and Punishment.* **1867**: Marx: *Das Kapital.* **1869**: John Stuart Mill: *On the Subjection of Women.* **1870**: French troops withdraw from Rome. Italian unification with Rome as capital. Death of Dickens. **1870–71**: Franco Prussian war. **1871**: Darwin: *The Descent of Man.* **1872–90**: Brandes: *Main Currents in 19th Century Literature.* **1872–1905**: Oskar II King of Swedish-Norwegian Union.	**1855–70**: The state is responsible for the development of telegraphic network in the country. **1869**: Annual meeting of the Storting (Parliament) introduced. **1871**: Maddox introduces the dry photographic plate. **1875**: About 45,000 employed in factories in Norway. About 50,000 working at sea. **1875–83**: Major programme of railway-building carried out. **1876**: Bell invents the telephone.

Ibsen's Life	International Events	Social & Scientific Events
1879: Summer in Amalfi. *A Doll's House.* 1880: Summer in Berchtesgaden. 1881: Summer and autumn in Sorrento. *Ghosts.* 1882: *An Enemy of the People.* Spends the summer in the Tyrol. 1883: Summer in Gossensass. 1884: Summer in Gossensass. *The Wild Duck.* 1885: Summer in Kristiana. 1885–91: Lives in Munich. 1886: *Rosmersholm.* 1887: Summer in Saeby, Jutland. 1888: *The Lady from the Sea.* 1889: Summer in Gossensass. Meets Emilie Bardach and Helene Raff. 1890: *Hedda Gabler.* 1891: Returns to Norway. Victoria Terrasse, Kristiana. 1892: *The Masterbuilder.* 1893: Grandson Tancred is born. 1894: *Little Eyolf.* 1895: Moves to apartment in Arbinsgate. 1896: *John Gabriel Borkman.* 1898: 70th birthday celebrations. 1899: *When We Dead Awaken.* 1900: First stroke. 1906: Ibsen dies.	1882: Death of Darwin. 1900: Death of Nietzsche. 1902: Death of Zola. 1904: Death of Chekhov.	1879: Edison produces carbon-filament incandescent electric light. 1883–4: Constitutional Court trials. Responsible government introduced. Establishment of political parties *Venstre* (Left) and *Høyre* (Right). 1887: Establishment of Norwegian Labour Party. 1888: George Eastman made film-rolls of photographic paper. 1889: Eastman's Kodak Camera mass-produced. 1891: Increased pressure towards Norwegian independence from Sweden. Demand is voiced for Norway to have its own Foreign Minister. 1894: Louis Lumière invents the cinemotograph. 1895: Military tension grows. Re-armament and fortification along the Swedish-Norwegian border. 1898: Extension of the franchise to include all male citizens. 1905: Peaceful dissolution of the union with Sweden. King Haakon VII ascends the Norwegian throne.

Notes

Abbreviations used in the references:

BVCHT   *Henrik Ibsens brevveksling med Christiania Theater 1878–1899*, ed. Ø. Anker

H 1, 5, 20   volume number of the *Hundreårsutgave (Centenary Edition)*

IÅ 1952   *Ibsen Årbok 1952 (Ibsen Year Book)*

NS Br 123   the number of the letter in *Henrik Ibsen: Brev 1845–1905, Ny Samling*, ed. Ø. Anker

K   *Henrik Ibsen: Brev 1845–1905. Ny Samling. II: Kommentarene. Registre*, ed Ø. Anker

UBO Brevs   the call number of the letter or ms in the University of Oslo manuscript collection

U123/456   Book number/page number of the newspaper clippings books in UB Oslo

Chapter 1

1 *Nordisk Tidsskrift för vetenskap, konst och industri* 4, 1940, article by Albert Boeck
2 Jæger, p. 5
3 *Nationen* 1920, nr 197
4 H 16, p. 318
5 Mosfjeld, p. 154
6 H 10, p. 97
7 *Norden.* 16.10.1920
8 Mosfjeld, p. 106
9 H 15, p. 421

Chapter 2

1 Faaland, p. 68
2 H 16, p. 23
3 *Aftenposten* 24.3.1996. Article by P. K. Heggelund Dahl

4 Due, p. 18
5 *Ibid.*, p. 19
6 *Ibid.*, p. 28
7 *Ibid.*, p. 31
8 Paulsen, *Samliv* 1 p. 134
9 H 15, p. 250
10 H 1, p. 119
11 Due, p. 42
12 H 16, p. 27

Chapter 3

1 H 20, p. 9
2 H 15, p. 61
3 *Ibid.*, p. 81
4 *Aftenposten* 24.3.1996. Article by P. K. Heggelund Dahl

Chapter 4

1 Ross, p. 44
2 *Arbeiderbladet* V: Lørdagskvelden 1, 22 December 1923 nr. 51.
3 H 20 p. 10
4 Blytt, p. 11
5 Wolf, p. 200–2
6 IÅ 1977 p. 63. Article by Rudler
7 H 1, p. 250
8 IÅ 1977 p. 63. Rudler
9 *The Collected Works of Henrik Ibsen* 1, p. xxxiv. ed. Archer and Herford
10 *Arbeiderbladet* V: Lørdagskvelden I, 22 December 1923. nr 51
11 H 20, p. 12
12 *Tidens Tegn* 1914, nr. 93
13 *IÅ 1977*, p. 74. Article by Rudler
14 H 16, p. 74

Chapter 5

1 Lund, p. 22
2 Bull, *Vildanden*, p. 44
3 *Samtidens Festskrift*, ed. Gran, p. 14
4 Bjørnson, *Gro Tid II*, p. 194
5 Ording, p. 217
6 Birkeland, p. 97
7 H 18, p. 188
8 Interviewed by Hans Eitrem 27.4.1908. See Eitrem's papers, UBO Ms Octavo 1797
9 Lund, p. 19
10 *Ibid.*, p. 44
11 *Ibid.*, p. 57
12 H 15, p. 226
13 H 16, p. 203

Chapter 6

1 Bjørnson, *Gro Tid* 1, p. 76
2 H 16, p. 317
3 Østvedt, *Høyfjellet*, p. 50
4 *Aftenposten*, 26 January 1983. Article by P. K. Heggelund Dahl
5 H 16, p. 317
6 NS Br.77

7 IÅ 1985–86, p. 206
8 *Byminner* 1989, 1 p. 20–5. Article by P. K. Heggelund Dahl

Chapter 7

1 H 15, p. 414
2 Nordhagen, p. 90
3 Sletten, p. 61
4 *Ibid.*, p. 155
5 *Ibid.*, p. 163
6 H 16, p. 102
7 *Ibid.*, p. 119
8 H 19, p. 132
9 Dietrichson I, p. 342
10 H 16, p. 365
11 *Ibid.*, p. 104
12 Bergljot Ibsen, p. 28
13 H 16, p. 122
14 *Ibid.*, p. 112
15 *Ibid.*, p. 133
16 H 5, p. 170
17 Nordhagen, p. 166
18 Benestad and Schjelderup-Ebbe, p. 101
19 Østvedt, *Italia*, p. 62
20 IÅ 1984, p. 202
21 H 16, p. 169
22 Bjørnson, *Gro Tid* 1, p. 208

Chapter 8

1 H 16, p. 121
2 Bergljot Ibsen, p. 29–30
3 Nordhagen, p. 120
4 H 16, p. 194
5 *Ibid.*, p. 185
6 Holberg, p. 69. Transl. P. M. Mitchell
7 H 16, p. 318
8 *Ibid.*, p. 138
9 *Ibid.*, p. 144
10 *Ibid.*, p. 197
11 *Ibid.*, p. 234
12 Knudtzon, p. 215–218
13 H 16, p. 208 and p. 213
14 *Ibid.*, p. 211

15 H 16, p. 213
16 Nielsen I, p. 297
17 NS Br. 159
18 Nielsen 2, p. 42
19 H 20, p. 63
20 H 16, p. 259

Chapter 9

1 H 16, p. 274
2 H 17, p. 140
3 H 19, p. 191
4 H 15, p. 345
5 NS Br. 151
6 H 16, p. 261
7 Marum, p. 105
8 Edholm, p. 259
9 H 16, p. 323
10 NS Br. 185
11 H 16, p. 311
12 Mosfjeld, p. 95
13 H 16, p. 202
14 Koht 2, p. 54
15 H 16, p. 283
16 Brandes, *Letters*, Transl. Jones, p. 62
17 *Ibid.*, p. 29–30
18 H 16, p. 366
19 *Ibid.*, p. 367
20 H 17, p. 94
21 NS Br. 166
22 Midbøe, *Streiflys* p. 162
23 IÅ 1977, p. 20. Article by Geir Kjetsaa
24 NS Br. 164
25 H 16, p. 383
26 *Ibid.*, p. 380
27 H 17, p. 120
28 H 16, p. 362
29 H 17, p. 77
30 Gran 2, p. 7

Chapter 10

1 Nielsen 1, p. 254
2 H 16, p. 351
3 H 7, p. 350
4 Svendsen, p. 377

5 Brandes, *Letters*, transl. Jones, p. 30
6 H 17, p. 67
7 *Ibid.*, p. 73
8 Faaland, p. 178
9 *Ibid.*, p. 174
10 Bull, *Kunstnerliv i Rom*, p. 204
11 H 17, p. 96
12 Nielsen 2, p. 314
13 H 17, p. 129
14 H 18, p. 154
15 *Brev fra Henrik Ibsen* 1, p. 266
16 H 17, p. 78
17 *Ibid.*, p. 63

Chapter 11

1 NS Br. 159
2 *Ibid.*, 163
3 *Jonas Lie og hans samtidige.* Breve i udvalg, ed. C. Nærup. Kria 1915. p. 94
4 U738/102
5 H 15, p. 394
6 H 17, p. 139
7 H 18, p. 41
8 H 16, p. 364
9 UBO Brevs. 200. 31.10.1874
10 H 19, p. 320
11 UBO Brevs 200. 12.11.1874
12 UBO Brevs 200. 1869
13 Nielsen 1, p. 220
14 H 17, p. 173
15 Bergjlot Ibsen, p. 73
16 *Aftenposten* 1.10.1992, where the letter is quoted.
17 H 17, p. 161

Chapter 12

1 Thoresen, p. 60
2 Berggreen, p. 129
3 H 17, p. 136
4 *Ibid.*, p. 122
5 *Ibid.*, p. 236
6 Paulsen, *Samliv* 2, p. 25
7 *Bokvennen*, nr 3. 1994 Article by Atle Næss

8   H 17, p. 236
9   H 16, p. 374
10   H 17, p. 159
11   Josephson, p. 33
12   Benestad and Schjelderup-Ebbe, p. 179
13   Blanc, p. 294
14   H 17, p. 289
15   *Ibid.*, p. 265
16   *Ibid.*, p. 273
17   H 8, p. 154
18   NS Br. 345
19   H 8, p. 21–2
20   H 15, p. 162
21   Reznicek, *Ibsen in Deutschland*, p. 29

Chapter 13

1   BVCHT p. 13
2   *Ibid.*, p. 14
3   *Ibid.*, p. 17
4   H 19, p. 255
5   H 17, p. 16
6   H 16, p. 170
7   Agerholt, p. 3
8   *Ibid.*, p. 29
9   H 17, p. 85
10   H 18, p. 212
11   Østvedt, *Et dukkehjem* p. 113
12   H 17, p. 303
13   *Ibid.*, p. 362
14   Paulsen, *Paa Vandring*, p. 88–108
15   NS Br. 422
16   Østvedt, *Et dukkehjem*, p. 181
17   Bryan, p. 60
18   H 15, p. 328
19   Østvedt, *Et dukkehjem*, p. 183

Chapter 14

1   H 17, p. 400
2   Nielsen 2, p. 347
3   *Ibid.*, p. 303
4   H 15, p. 365
5   *Familien Pehrsen*, p. 229–30
6   IÅ 1960–2, p. 234. Article by Reinart Torgeirson

7   *Brev fra Henrik Ibsen* 2, p. 233
8   H 17, p. 411
9   Zucker, p. 185
10   Kronen, p. 162, quoting Bredsdorff
11   H 16, p. 138–46
12   H 9, p. 92
13   BVCHT, p. 23
14   Koht 2, p. 126
15   Nielsen 1, p. 450
16   Nielsen 2, p. 356.
17   H 19, p. 309–310
18   Hobsbawm, p. 106
19   H 16, p. 326

Chapter 15

1   Whitebrook, p. 41
2   H 19, p. 162
3   Pauli, p. 108
4   *Ibid.*, p. 113
5   H 17, p. 447
6   *Ibid.*, p. 478
7   *Ibid.*, p. 491
8   *Ibid.*, p. 450
9   *Ibid.*, p. 480
10   BVCHT, p. 25
11   H 16, p. 265
12   *Verdens Gang* 1882, nr 143
13   H 19, p. 309
14   H 17, p. 496

Chapter 16

1   H 18, p. 12
2   H 17, p. 532
3   H 18, p. 21
4   BVCHT, p. 28
5   H 16, p. 292
6   H 18, p. 27
7   NS Br. 499
8   H 18, p. 18
9   Mosfjeld, p. 182
10   Benestad and Schjelderup-Ebbe, p. 199
11   NS Br. 502
12   H 18, p. 29
13   *Ibid.*, p. 29

14 H 19, p. 334
15 H 18, p. 32
16 *Ibid.*, p. 31
17 Nielsen 2, p. 34
18 H 17, p. 284
19 NS Br. 360
20 H 9, p. 192
21 H 17, p. 465
22 H 18, p. 16
23 IÅ 1952, p. 40. Article by Halvdan Wexelsen Freihow
24 H 17, p. 284
25 H 18, p. 49
26 Nielsen 2, p. 135
27 UBO 200. 7.7.1884
28 H 18, p. 44
29 *Ibid.*, p. 63
30 *Ibid.*, p. 80
31 UBO Brevs 143 (12.10.1885)
32 H 18, p. 77
33 *Ibid.*, p. 79
34 UBO Brevs 200 (12.8.1885)
35 Anderson, p. 486

Chapter 17

1 NS Br. 519, 5
2 Fleetwood, Vol 1, p. 712
3 Nielsen 2, p. 483
4 Midbøe, *Streiflys* p. 152
5 H 18, p. 131.
6 MacFarlane, *A Critical Anthology*, p. 392
7 U 1544/90: from *Morgenbladet* 4.4.1964
8 Reznicek, *Ibsen in Deutschland*, p. 56–7
9 NS Br. 571
10 Whitebrook, p. 71
11 H 18, p. 92
12 *Ibid.*, p. 139
13 *Ibid.*, p. 92
14 Fuglum, p. 220
15 Fleetwood, p. 738
16 H 18, p. 160
17 NS Br. 604
18 Midbøe, *Streiflys* p. 152

19 H 19, p. 349
20 Thoresen, *Breve*, p. 98
21 H 18, p. 204
22 Benestad and Schjelderup-Ebbe, p. 201
23 H 18, p. 182

Chapter 18

1 H 18, p. 143
2 UBO MS Quarto 3159
3 UB MS Fol 3648
4 UBO MS Quarto 3159
5 H 18, p. 408
6 *Die Presse* 11.6.1994. Letter to C. K. Pollaczek of 18 January 1925. Article by P. M. Braunworth
7 NS Addenda 2, Br. 663, 5
8 U244/24
9 H 11, p. 273
10 NS Br. 699
11 NS Br. 701
12 U438/1
13 H 11, p. 501
14 *Ibid.*, p. 501
15 H 19, p. 186
16 H 19, p. 182
17 NS Br. 674
18 H 19, p. 153
19 NS Addenda, Br. 752, 5
20 NS Br 755
21 H 18, p. 290
22 UBO Brevs 200 25.7.1884
23 H 19, p. 183
24 Fleetwood, p. 631
25 H 19, p. 187

Chapter 19

1 *Knut Hamsuns brev 1879–95* ed. Harald S. Næss, p. 231, Oslo, 1994
2 Birkeland, p. 97
3 UBO Brevs 200, 20.5.1887
4 *Ibid.*, prob. March 1889
5 *Ibid.*, 20.8.1889
6 Josephson, p. 93
7 H 18, p. 301

8   *Ibid.*, p. 306
9   Hamsun, *Paa Turné*, p. 30–1
10   *Ibid.*, p. 34
11   Bull, *Vildanden*, p. 41
12   H 18, p. 290
13   *Ibid.*, p. 233
14   H 19, p. 60
15   NS Br. 820
16   Bergljot Ibsen, p. 140
17   H 18, p. 249
18   U 228/41
19   *Fædrelandsvennen*, 20.5.1985. Article by Kjell Rosenberg
20   H 18, p. 452
21   Bergljot Ibsen, p. 130
22   *Ibid.*, p. 134
23   H 19, p. 358
24   *Ibid.*, p. 388
25   Langslet, p. 16
26   *Ibid.*, p. 19
27   Thoresen, *Breve*, p. 240
28   NS Br. 783
29   UBO Brevs.200

Chapter 20

1   Paulsen, *Samliv* 2 p. 218
2   Mosfjeld, p. 183
3   K Br 610 (Addenda 2)
4   H 18, 349
5   Whitebrook, p. 176
6   H 12, p. 191
7   U303/31
8   H 18, p. 367
9   H 19, p. 376
10   K Br. 762
11   H 19, p. 381
12   U257/115
13   H 19, p. 383
14   *Ibid.*, p. 385
15   Langslet, p. 22
16   H 19, p. 218

17   Rosenkrantz Johnsen, p. 13
18   Bull, *Tradisjoner og Minner*, p. 195
19   Mosfjeld, p. 159
20   H 18, p. 289
21   NS Br. 945
22   NS Br. 916
23   H 18, p. 387
24   *Ibid.*, p. 400
25   Bergljot Ibsen, p. 161
26   H 18, p. 398
27   H 19, p. 394
28   *Ibid.*, p. 392

Chapter 21

1   H 15, p. 412
2   *Ibid.*, p. 414
3   NS Br. 1007
4   H 15, p. 432
5   H 9, p. 13
6   H 15, p. 417
7   Bergljot Ibsen, p. 140
8   H 18, p. 428
9   *Ibid.*, p. 441
10   *Ibid.*, p. 427 and NS Br. 1084
11   *Ibid.*, p. 431
12   *Ibid.*, p. 433
13   *Ibid.*, p. 433
14   UBO Brevs 200
15   H 15, p. 430
16   Bull, *Vildanden*, p. 39
17   Paulsen, *Samliv* 2, p. 99
18   H 19, p. 216
19   *Verdens Gang* 1894, nr 297
20   Whitebrook, p. 209
21   NS Br. 1125
22   Paulsen, *Samliv* 1, p. 79
23   NS Br. 1135
24   H 19, p. 458
25   H 15, p. 441
26   Nielsen 2, p. 357
27   H 18, p. 36

Bibliography

The cornerstone of any study of Ibsen's life and works is the *Hundreårsut-gave (Centenary Edition)* of his collected works, in twenty-one volumes, edited by Halvdan Koht, Francis Bull, and D. A. Seip and published in Oslo between 1928 and 1958. This contains the published versions of all of Ibsen's plays; revised versions; drafts, with textual corrections and emendations; Ibsens's poems; his journalism and prose; interviews with Ibsen; and all the correspondence available at the time of publication of the letter volumes XVI, XVII, XVIII in 1940, 1947, and 1949; plus a supplement of family letters and correspondence in volume XIX, published in 1952. In 1979 this material was supplemented by a further collection of over 1,200 letters, published as the *Ibsenårbok (Ibsen Year Book)* in 1979, with an invaluable *Kommentar (Commentary)* volume, under the editorship of Øyvind Anker.

Agerholt, Anna Caspari, *Den norske kvinnebevegelses Historie*, Oslo, 1937

Almquist, Olaf, *Johannes Brun. En skildring af hans liv og hans samtidige*, Kristiana, 1898

Andersen, M. M., *Ibsen håndboken*, Oslo, 1995

Anderson, R. B., *His Life Story*, Madison, 1915

Anker, Øyvind, (ed.), *Henrik Ibsens brev. Kronologisk registrant*, Oslo, 1978

Anker, Øyvind, (ed.), *Ibsenårbok 1979, Brev 1845–1905, Ny Samling*, I and II, Oslo, 1979

Anker, Øyvind, (ed.), *Henrik Ibsens brevveksling med Christiania Theater 1878–1899*, Oslo, 1964

Anker, Øyvind, (ed.), *Christiania Theater's Repertoire 1827–1899*, Oslo, 1956

Anker, Øyvind, *Kristiania Norske Theaters Repertoire 1852–1863*, Oslo, 1956

Arvesen, O. *Oplevelser og erindringer*, Kristiana, 1921

Benestad, F., & Schjelderup-Ebbe, D., *Edvard Grieg, Mennesket og kunstneren*, Oslo, 1990

Berggrav, E. og Bull, F., *Ibsens sjelelige krise*, Oslo, 1937

445

Bergsøe, Vilhelm, *Henrik Ibsen på Ischia og 'Fra Piazza del Populo'*, Copenhagen and Kristiana, 1907

Bergwitz, Joh. K., *Henrik Ibsen I Sin Avstamning Norsk eller Fremmed?*, Oslo, 1916

Birkeland, Michael, *Breve 1848–1879*, ed. Ording, Kristiana, 1920

Bjørnson, Bjørnstjerne, *Brevveksling med Danske II, 1854–1874*, eds. Anker, Bull, Neilsen, Copenhagen & Oslo, 1972

———————— *Brevveksling med svenske 1858–1909*, eds. Anker, Bull, Lindberger. I–III, Oslo, 1960

———————— *Brytnings-aar (brev fra årene 1871–1878)* ed. Koht I–II Kristiana, 1921

———————— *Gro Tid (brev fra årene 1857–1870)*, ed. Koht I–II, Kristiana, 1912

Blanc, T., *Christiania Theaters historie, 1827–1877*, Kristiana, 1899

Blytt, Peter, *Minder fra den første norske scene i Bergen*, Bergen, 1894

Bradbrook, M. C., *Ibsen The Norwegian*, London, 1946

Brandes, Georg, *Selected Letters*, ed. & transl. W. Glyn Jones, Norwich, 1990

Bryan, G. B., *An Ibsen Companion, A dictionary guide to the life, works and critical reception of Henrik Ibsen*, Westport. Conn., 1984

Bull, Edvard, *Ibsens tre sidste leveaar*, ed. Nevdal B. Nytt Nordisk Tidskrift, 1994 nr.2

Bull, Francis, *Land og Lynne*, Oslo, 1969

———————— *Nordisk kunstnerliv i Rom.*, Oslo, 1960

———————— *Tradisjoner og Minner*, Oslo, 1946

———————— *Vildanden og Andre Essays*, Oslo, 1966

Daae, Ludvig, Article on Paul Botten Hansen in *Vidar*, Copenhagen, 1888

Dahl, Herleiv, *Bergmannen og Byggmesteren. Henrik Ibsen som lyriker*, Oslo, 1958

Dahl, P. K. Heggelund, *Fra Ibsens Christiania-år 1857–1864*. In *Ibsen-årbok 1985–6*

Dahl, P. K. Heggelund, *Ibsen-data fra Skien og Grimstad*. In *Ibsen-årbok 1985–6*

Dahl, P. K., Heggelund, *Enkeltheter omkring Ibsens utreise 1864*. In *Byminner 1 1988*

Dietrichson, Lorentz, *Svundne Tider* I–IV, Kristiana, 1894–1917

Dresdner, A., *Henrik Ibsen som Nordmand og Europæer*, Copenhagen, 1918

Due, Christopher, *Erindringer fra Henrik Ibsen's Ungdomsaar*, Copenhagen, 1909

Dunker, B., *Breve til A. F. Krieger*, Oslo, 1957

Duve, Arne, *Henrik Ibsen's hemmeligheter?*, Oslo, 1977

Ebbell, Clara, *I ungdomsbyen med Henrik Ibsen*, Grimstad, 1966

Edholm, Erik af, *På Carl XVs tid*, Stockholm, 1945

Eide, Elizabeth, *China's Ibsen – From Ibsen to Ibsenism*, London and Copenhagen, 1987

Bibliography

Eitrem, Hans, *Ibsen og Grimstad*, Oslo, 1940

Faaland, Joseph, *Henrik Ibsen og Antikken*, Oslo, 1943

Fenger, Henning, *Den unge Brandes*, Copenhagen, 1957

Fleetwood, C. G., *Från studieår och diplomattjänst*. I–II, Stockholm, 1968

Fosli, Halvor, *Kristianiabohemen*, Oslo, 1994

Freihow, H. W., *Bjørnstjerne Bjørnson i Henrik Ibsen liv. Ei skisse* in *Ibsenårbok*, 1952

Fuglum, Per, *Ole Richter B2 Statsministeren*, Oslo, 1957–64

Gran, Gerhard, (ed.), *Henrik Ibsen, Til han 70de.fødselsdag*, Samtiden, Bergen, 1898

Gran, Gerhard, *Henrik Ibsen Liv og Verker*, 2 vols, Oslo, 1918

Gray, Ronald, *Ibsen – A Dissenting View*, Cambridge, 1977

Grønvold, Marcus, *Fra Ulrikken til Alperne*, Oslo, 1925

Haakonsen, Daniel, *Henrik Ibsen Mennesket og kunstneren*, Oslo, 1981

Hamsun, Knut, *Mysteries*. tr. Bothmer, New York, 1971

Hamsun, Knut, *Paa turné*, Oslo, 1960

Heiberg, Hans, *født til kunstner. Et Ibsen–portrett*, Oslo, 1976

Hobsbawm, E. J., *The Age of Capital 1848–1875*, London, 1976

Holberg, Ludvig, *Moral Reflections and Epistles*, ed. & transl. P. M. Mitchell, Norwich, 1991

Ibsen, Bergljot, *De Tre. Erindringer om Henrik Ibsen. Suzannah Ibsen. Sigurd Ibsen*, Oslo, 1949

Ibsen, Henrik, *Brev fra Henrik Ibsen*, eds. Koht and Elias, I–II, Kristiana and Copenhagen, 1904

Ibsen, Henrik, *Samlede Verker, hundreårsutgave*. eds. Koht, Bull, Seip I–XXI, Oslo, 1925–58

Ibsen-bilder, ed. Mentz Schulerud, Oslo, 1978

Ibseniana, Skien Public Library, 1952

Iversen, Ragnvald, *Alliterasjonen i Henrik Ibsens 'Digte' (1875)*, Trondheim, 1941

Jæger, Henrik, *Henrik Ibsen 1828–1888*, Copenhagen, 1888

Josephson, Ludvig, *Ett och Anat om Henrik Ibsen och Kristiania Teater*, Stockholm, 1898

Just, Carl, *Schrøder og Christiania Theater*, Oslo, 1948

Katalog – Minneustilling Henrik Ibsen 23mai 1956, Oslo, 1956

Kjetsaa, Geir, *Henrik Ibsen og Oscar von Knorring*. In *Ibsen-årbok* 1977

Knorring, Oscar von, *Två månader i Egypten*, Stockholm, 1873

Knudtzon, F. G., *Ungdomsdage*, Copenhagen, 1927

Koht, Halvdan, *Amerikabrev fra Henrik Ibsen eldste bror* and *Henrik Ibsen og søskena hans –* In *Ibsen-årbok*, 1963–4

———— *Henrik Ibsen: eit diktarliv*, I–II, Oslo, 1954

———— *Henrik Ibsen i 'Manden'*, Oslo, 1928

Kommandantvold, K. M., *Ibsen og Sverige*, Oslo, 1956

Kronen, Torleiv, *De store Årene. 1860–1900*, Oslo, 1982

Lampl, H. E., *Nova über Henrik Ibsen und sein Alterwerk*, Oslo, 1977

Langslet, Lars Roar, *Henrik Ibsen–Edvard Munch To genier møtes*, Oslo, 1994

Lie, Erik, *Erindringer fra et dikterhjem*, Oslo, 1928

Löwenthal, Leo, *Om Hamsun og Ibsen*, Oslo, 1980

Lugné-Poë, *Ibsen i Frankrike*, Oslo, 1938

Lund, Audhild, *Henrik Ibsen og Det Norske Teater 1857–1863*, Oslo, 1925

Lyche, Lise, *Norges Teater Historie*, Asker, 1991

Mæhle, Leif, (ed.), *Bibliografi over Norsk Litteraturforsking 1965–1989*, Oslo, 1993

Marum, Reidar A., *Teaterslag og Pipekonserter. u.å.*

McFarlane, James, (ed.), *Henrik Ibsen – A Critical Anthology*, Penguin, London, 1970

———— *Ibsen & Meaning*, Norwich, 1989

Meyer, Michael, *Henrik Ibsen A Biography*, London, 1974

Midbøe, Hans, *Streiflys over Ibsen*, Oslo, 1960

Møller, Sophie, *Henrik Ibsens Haandskrift. En studie. u.å.*

Mosfjeld, Oskar, *Henrik Ibsen og Skien*, Oslo, 1949

Næss, Atle, *Ibsen, Gossensass og Emilie Bardach*. In *Bokvennen* nr. 3., 1994

Næss, Atle, *Sensommer – a novel*, Oslo, 1987

Neiiendam, Robert, *Gjennem mange Aar*, Copenhagen, 1933

Nielsen, L. C., *Frederik V. Hegel. Et mindeskrift* I–II, Copenhagen, 1909

Nilsen & Reznicek, *Ibsen in Italy*, Oslo, 1989

———— *Ibsen in Meiningen*, Kiel, 1992

Nordhagen, P. J. *Henrik Ibsen i Roma 1864–1868*, Oslo, 1981

Nordisk Kulturell Identitet, Fiksjon – faktum – fremtid? 1988

Noreng, Harald, *Terje Vigen med Bakgrunn i dikt og virkelighet*, Grimstad, 1990

Noreng, Hofland, Natvig (eds.), *Henrik Ibsens Ordskatt*, Oslo, 1987

Northam, John, *Ibsen's Poems* in translation, Oslo, 1986

Øksnevad, Reidar, *Dagbladet og Norsk Litteratur, 1869–1910*, Oslo, 1952

———— *Social-Demokraten og Norsk Litteratur, 1886–1923*, Oslo, 1955

———— *Verdens Gang og Norsk Litteratur 1868–1910*, Oslo, 1954

Ording, Frederik, *Henrik Ibsens vennekreds. Det Lærde Holland*, Oslo, 1927

Østerberg, Dag, *Ibsen og ibsenism i lys av datidens sosio-kulturelle bevegelser –* in *Forfatternes Litteraturhistorie I*, Oslo, 1980

Østvedt, Einar, *Et dukkehjem: Forspillet, Skuespillet, Etterspillet*, Skien, 1976

———— *Høyfjellet i Ibsens liv og diktning*, Skien, 1972

———— *Henrik Ibsen og hans venner Heiberg, Vinje, Snoilsky*, Skien, 1974

———— *Henrik Ibsen og la bella Italia*, Skien, 1965

———— *Gustav Lammers som modell til Ibsens Brand*. In *Ibsen-Årbok* 1952

———— *Henrik Ibsen som student og blant studenter*, Skien, 1971

———— *Med Henrik Ibsen i fjellheimen*, Skien, 1967

Østvedt, Einar, *Henrik Ibsen og hans barndomsmilø*, Skien, 1977

Paludan–Müller, F., *Vejledning for Danske i Læsningen af Peer Gynt*, Copenhagen, 1928

Pauli, Georg, *Mina romerska år*, Stockholm, 1924

Paulsen, John, *Mine Erindringer*, Copenhagen, 1900

——— *Familien Pehrsen*, Copenhagen, 1882

——— *Samliv med Ibsen I–II*, Copenhagen & Kristiana, 1906 and 1913

——— *Erindringer. Siste samling*, Copenhagen, 1903

Paulsen, John, *Nye Erindringer*, Copenhagen, 1901

Paulson, Andreas, *De baktalte Åtti-År. Særtrykk nr 57 of Bergens Arbeiderbladet. u.å.*

Pharo, Øyvind, (ed.), *Fin de Siècle. Tidsskriftet Samtiden i 1890-årene*, Oslo, 1990

Reznicek, L. *Ibsen in Italia*, Oslo, 1980

Rønneberg, A., *National Theatret gjennom femti år*, Oslo, 1949

Rosenkrantz Johnsen, P., *Om og omkring Henrik Ibsen og Susanna Ibsen*, Oslo, 1928

Ross, Immanuel, *I Norge 1845. Historisk Essay*, Kristiana, 1899

Rudler, Roderick, *Ibsens første teateropplevelser and Ibsens debut som sceneinstruktør* – In *Ibsen-årbok*, 1960–2

Rudler, Roderick, *Uroppførelse av Gildet paa Solhoug og Fru Inger til Østeraad.* In *Ibsen-årbok* 1977

Rudler, Roderick, *Ibsen i Bergen*. In *Ibsenårbok*, 1981–82

Schack, A., *En efterskrift om Henrik Ibsens Digtning*, Copenhagen, 1897

Skard, Eiliv, *Kjeldone til Ibsens Catilina. Særtryk av Edda. u.å.*

Sletten, Klaus, *Christopher Bruun: Folkelæreren – Stridsmannen*, Oslo, 1949

Sontum, Bolette, *Personal recollections of Henrik Ibsen, The Bookman* nr. 37, New York, 1913

Svendsen, Paulus, *Gullalderdrøm og utviklingstro*, Oslo, 1979

Testa, Martha, *Johan Bravo. En skandinav i Rom*, Lynge, 1993

Thoresen, Magdalene, *Breve 1855–1901*, eds. Clausen & Rist, Copenhagen, 1919

Tjønneland, Eivind, *Selvmordene i Ibsens Rosmersholm*, Profil nr. 2, 1992

Tjønneland, Eivind, *Ibsen og moderniteten*, Oslo, 1993

Törnkvist, Arne, *Henrik Ibsen*, 1992

Vidal, Gore, *Julian. A Historical Novel*, London, 1964

Waage, P. N., *Det oversette mesterverk – Henrik Ibsen og keiser Julian*, Oslo, 1989

Whitebrook, Peter, *William Archer – A Biography*, London, 1993

Wiers-Jenssen, and Joh. Nordahl-Olsen, *Den Nationale Scene, De første 25 aar.* Bergen, 1926

Wiesener, A. M., *Henrik Ibsen og Det norske theater i Bergen 1851–1857*, Bergen, 1928

Wolf, Lucei, *Skuespillerinden Fru Lucie Wolf's Livserindringer*, Kristiana, 1897

Young, Robin, *Time's Disinherited Children*, Norwich, 1989
Zachariassen, Aksel, *Fra Marcus Thrane til Martin Tranmæl*, Oslo, 1962
Zucker, A. E., *Ibsen the Master Builder*, London, 1930

Index

Index

Index

Index

Index